Reading in Chinese as an Additional Language

Reading in Chinese as an Additional Language focuses on Chinese literacy acquisition, which has been considered most difficult by both learners and teachers of Chinese as an additional language (CAL).

Three major areas are covered: (1) acquisition of Chinese characters; (2) reading comprehension subskills and reader's identity; (3) reading instruction and assessment. The first part delves into the foundation of Chinese literacy development—how to learn and teach Chinese characters. The second part examines various learners' reading comprehension subskills, as well as the evolution of learners' literacy identity. The third part explores effective instructional methods and assessment practices for CAL reading development. Theoretically, this book provides frameworks and evidence from both cognitive and sociocultural perspectives on the nature of CAL reading development. Pedagogically, the book showcases how to teach and assess CAL reading skills. Methodologically, this book includes empirical studies using both qualitative and quantitative methods. In terms of scope, the book covers a much broader spectrum of issues about CAL reading research and classroom teaching than has previously been available. Writing is also discussed in several chapters. In terms of technology, the book includes discussion on how the use of computers, the Internet, and social media impacts students' Chinese literacy acquisition.

This book will help CAL researchers and educators better understand the nature of CAL reading development and become well informed about CAL classroom teaching and assessment, including the application of interactive approaches to teaching and assessing diverse reading skills.

Liu Li is Associate Professor of Chinese at the Department of Modern Languages and Classics at Ball State University, U.S.A. She received her PhD in Second Language Acquisition from Carnegie Mellon University. Her research interests include Chinese literacy acquisition, computer-assisted language learning, language learning context, and heritage language learners.

Dongbo Zhang is Professor of Language Education in the Graduate School of Education at the University of Exeter, U.K. His research interests include second language reading and vocabulary knowledge, bilingualism and literacy, and language teacher education. He previously held appointments in the Department of Teacher Education, Michigan State University, where he directed the Chinese Teacher Certification Program and also coordinated the Doctoral Certificate in English Language Learner Education.

Routledge Studies in Chinese as a Foreign Language
Series Editor: Chris Shei
Swansea University, UK
Der-lin Chao
New York University, USA

The series will strive to produce not only scholarly books investigating aspects of Chinese language learning such as pedagogy, policy, materials and curriculum, assessment, psychology and cognition, aptitude and motivation, culture and society, media and technology and so on, but also textbooks drawing from results of this research and compiled following the pedagogical models suggested by these studies and taking into consideration the individual and social factors related to Chinese language learning uncovered by this series of research. The two strands of books published within this series complement and strengthen each other in their academic achievement and practical implication.

Teaching and Researching Chinese Second Language Listening
Wei Cai

Teaching Chinese by Culture and TV Drama
Lingfen Zhang

Reading in Chinese as an Additional Language
Learners' Development, Instruction, and Assessment
Edited by Liu Li and Dongbo Zhang

For more information about this series, please visit: www.routledge.com/Routledge-Studies-in-Chinese-as-a-Foreign-Language/book-series/RSCFL

Reading in Chinese as an Additional Language

Learners' Development, Instruction, and Assessment

Edited by Liu Li and Dongbo Zhang

LONDON AND NEW YORK

Designed cover image: michaeljung via Getty Images

First published 2023
by Routledge
4 Park Square, Milton Park, Abingdon, Oxon OX14 4RN

and by Routledge
605 Third Avenue, New York, NY 10158

Routledge is an imprint of the Taylor & Francis Group, an informa business

© 2023 selection and editorial matter, Liu Li and Dongbo Zhang; individual chapters, the contributors

The right of Liu Li and Dongbo Zhang to be identified as the authors of the editorial material, and of the authors for their individual chapters, has been asserted in accordance with sections 77 and 78 of the Copyright, Designs and Patents Act 1988.

All rights reserved. No part of this book may be reprinted or reproduced or utilised in any form or by any electronic, mechanical, or other means, now known or hereafter invented, including photocopying and recording, or in any information storage or retrieval system, without permission in writing from the publishers.

Trademark notice: Product or corporate names may be trademarks or registered trademarks, and are used only for identification and explanation without intent to infringe.

British Library Cataloguing-in-Publication Data
A catalogue record for this book is available from the British Library

Library of Congress Cataloging-in-Publication Data
Names: Li, Liu (Professor of Chinese), editor. | Zhang, Dongbo, 1978– editor.
Title: Reading in Chinese as an additional language : learners' development, instruction, and assessment / edited by Liu Li and Dongbo Zhang.
Description: Abingdon, Oxon ; New York, NY : Routledge, 2023. | Series: Routledge studies in Chinese as a foreign language | Includes bibliographical references and index.
Identifiers: LCCN 2022029242 (print) | LCCN 2022029243 (ebook) | ISBN 9780367464868 (hardback) | ISBN 9780367464875 (paperback) | ISBN 9781003029038 (ebook)
Subjects: LCSH: Chinese language—Study and teaching—Foreign speakers. | Chinese characters—Study and teaching. | Reading. | Reading—Ability testing. | LCGFT: Essays.
Classification: LCC PL1065 .R43 2023 (print) | LCC PL1065 (ebook) | DDC 495.180071—dc23/eng/20220920
LC record available at https://lccn.loc.gov/2022029242
LC ebook record available at https://lccn.loc.gov/2022029243

ISBN: 978-0-367-46486-8 (hbk)
ISBN: 978-0-367-46487-5 (pbk)
ISBN: 978-1-003-02903-8 (ebk)

DOI: 10.4324/9781003029038

Typeset in Times New Roman
by Apex CoVantage, LLC

Contents

List of figures	vii
List of tables	viii
List of contributors	x
Acknowledgements	xiv

Introduction   1
LIU LI AND DONGBO ZHANG

PART I
Acquisition of Chinese characters   11

1 **The effects of stroke-order accuracy on L2 Chinese character writing**   13
TIANXU CHEN, BING FENG, MENGYUE WANG AND KHANH-NGAN DOAN

2 **The more the merrier? A synthesis study of single-coded and dual-coded word learning in theory-driven L2 Chinese instruction**   28
SIHUI KE AND CHIN-HSI LIN

3 **Impact of typing vs handwriting on CFL students' character learning**   43
LIU LI

4 **Effects of timed dictation on Chinese character writing: A preliminary study in beginning-level CFL learners**   61
SIYAN HOU AND ATSUSHI FUKADA

PART II
Reading comprehension subskills and readers' identity — 87

5 The role of character-recognition skills in shallow and deep reading comprehension — 89
   WEI-LI HSU

6 Development of morphological awareness and its impact on reading among young learners of Chinese as a heritage language — 111
   YANHUI ZHANG, KEIKO KODA, CHIN-LUNG YANG AND CHAN LÜ

7 Developmental interdependence between word decoding, vocabulary knowledge, and reading comprehension in young L2 readers of Chinese — 132
   DONGBO ZHANG AND XIAOXI SUN

8 A tale of two less successful CSL readers: A qualitative study of reading difficulties and strategies used — 156
   SHA HUANG

9 Literacy environment and heritage language learner's literacy identity — 179
   LIU LI

PART III
Reading instruction and assessment — 197

10 Beyond the pages of a book: A Chinese language teacher's discursive behaviors of conducting guided book reading — 199
    ZHENG GU

11 Teaching modern Chinese literature to second-language Chinese students through the use of drama — 217
    ZIV W.N. KAN AND ELIZABETH K.Y. LOH

12 Reading assessment in Chinese as a foreign language — 246
    KEIKO KODA AND XIAOMENG LI

13 Validation of a Chinese online placement test — 264
    LIU LI

Index — 281

Figures

1.1	An example on how to write "天" stroke by stroke	15
1.2	Development of learners' stroke-order accuracy	19
1.3	Development of learners' character-writing efficiency	19
1.4	An example on how to write the first three strokes of '休'	22
4.1	Example list of key sentences	68
4.2	Example of creating TD activity on Timed Dictation Player	69
4.3	Student portal of Timed Dictation Player	69
4.4	Pause duration options	70
5.1	Example of the PS subtest	98
5.2	Example of the RS subtest	98
6.1	Means and standard deviations of the morphological awareness subtest scores (% correct) for CHL learners	121
6.2	Comparison of means and standard deviations of the morphological awareness subtest scores (% correct) for native Chinese (Li et al., 2002) and CHL learners	121
6.3	Means and standard deviations of the reading comprehension subtest scores (% correct)	124
7.1	The DVC reading skill triangle (based on Perfetti, 2010, p. 293)	133
7.2	Cross-lagged panel analysis with three-wave data	142
7.3	Cross-lagged path analysis on developmental interdependence between word decoding, vocabulary knowledge, and reading comprehension	142
11.1	Students analyzed and described details of the graduation ceremony upon completion of the in-role speech activity	232
11.2	Pictures of Group A's still images	242
11.3	Pictures of Group B's still images	243
11.4	Pictures of Group C's still images	244
11.5	Pictures of Group D's still images	245

Tables

1.1	Summary of Participants' Results (N = 62)	18
3.1	Number of Students in Each Class	50
3.2	Mean Scores for the Tests in the Previous Semester	51
3.3	Statistical Description of the Character Recognition Task for Beginning-Level Students	52
3.4	Statistical Description of the Character Recognition Task for Intermediate-Level Students	52
3.5	Statistical Description of the Character Production Task for Beginning-Level Students	52
3.6	Statistical Description of the Character Production Task for Intermediate-Level Students	53
3.7	Average Time Spent on Homework	54
3.8	Average Time Spent on Practice	54
4.1	Characteristics of Three Groups	67
4.2	Descriptive Statistics of the First Chapter Test Scores	72
4.3	Descriptive Statistics of the Timed Hanzi Test Scores	73
4.4	Participants' Self-report on Time Spent on Learning and Practicing Hanzi	73
4.5	Descriptive Statistics on Participants' Perceptions on TD/Copying	73
5.1	Average Performances	96
5.2	Intercorrelation Matrix	100
5.3	Hierarchical Regression of the Cloze Subtest	101
5.4	Hierarchical Regressions of the Passage-Comprehension Subtest	102
6.1	Background Information of the Participating Students	117
6.2	Examples of the Graphic-Morphological Tasks	118
6.3	Means and Standard Deviations (in Parentheses) of the Character Knowledge Subtest Scores (% correct)	123
6.4	Means and Standard Deviations (in Parentheses) of the Reading Comprehension Test Scores (% correct) for Overlapping Passages	125
6.5	Correlations among Character Knowledge, Morphological Awareness, Oral Language Skills, and Reading Comprehension	126

7.1	Descriptive Statistics, Normality Estimates, and Reliability	141
7.2	Bivariate Correlations Between Literary Measures at Three Different Times	143
7.3	Goodness-of-Fit Indexes of Path Models Comparing Effects Across Predictors and Times	144
7.4	Parameter Estimates of Cross-Lagged Panel Analysis Testing Developmental Interdependence Between Measures from Time 1 to Time 2	145
7.5	Parameter Estimates of Cross-Lagged Panel Analysis Testing Developmental Interdependence Between Measures from Time 2 to Time 3	145
8.1	Causes of Comprehension Breakdown and Their Frequencies	163
8.2	Linda's Reading Strategies	165
8.3	Teresa's Reading Strategies	171
10.1	Examples of Wang Laoshi's Discursive Behavior in Shared Book Reading	205
10.2	Episodes of Discursive Behaviors When Reading Different Book Genres	208
11.1	Participants' Background Information	224
11.2	Summary of the Lesson Designs	227
11.3	Summary of Students' Still Image Captions	230
12.1	Features of Five Widely Used Chinese Textbooks	255
13.1	Pearson Product-moment Correlations Between Scores on the Placement Test and Scores on the Midterm Exams	273
13.2	Discrimination Index of 8 Randomly Selected Items	274
13.3	Facility Value of Some Items	274
13.4	Descriptive Statistics for the Placement Test	275

Contributors

Tianxu Chen, a Ph.D. from Carnegie Mellon University, is Associate Professor at Minzu University of China. His research interest is L2 reading, vocabulary learning, and teaching Chinese as a second language. His recent publications have appeared in *Reading and Writing*, *Foreign Language Annals*, *Language Awareness*, *Journal of Psycholinguistic Research*, and so on.

Khanh-Ngan Doan is a graduate student working with Dr. Tianxu Chen on Learning and Teaching Chinese as an Additional Language.

Bing Feng is a graduate student working with Dr. Tianxu Chen on Learning and Teaching Chinese as an Additional Language.

Atsushi Fukada received his Ph.D. from the University of Illinois at Urbana-Champaign. He is a Professor of Japanese and Linguistics at Purdue University. His research interests include all areas of Japanese linguistics, pragmatics, technology, and language pedagogy.

Zheng Gu is Visiting Assistant Professor of Chinese Language at Oxford College of Emory University. Her research interests include academic language learning in Chinese as a second language classes, and transnational Chinese teacher education. Now she teaches Chinese language courses, and undergraduate-level Applied Linguistics courses.

Siyan Hou is currently a PhD candidate at Purdue University. Her research interests include pragmatics, technology, and language pedagogy in Chinese as a second/foreign language.

Wei-Li Hsu received her PhD in Second Language Studies at the University of Hawai'i at Mānoa, specializing in Chinese and English as a learning Chinese as an L2, L2 reading, and L2 assessment. Her research interests include L2 Chinese reading strategies, and validating tests with a communicative framework.

Sha Huang received her PhD in ESL and Foreign Language Education at the University of Iowa. She is Associate Professor in the Department of World Languages and Cultures and Interdisciplinary Studies Department, Kennesaw State University. Her research interests include second language pedagogy, teaching and learning Chinese as a second language, literacy development, and instructional materials.

Ziv W.N. Kan has over 14 years of experience in teaching Chinese as a second language. He is familiar with education systems such as GCSE, IGCSE, GCE AS/A Level and IB. He obtained his doctoral degree at the University of Hong Kong. His research centered on using music in acquiring Chinese grammar.

Sihui (Echo) Ke is Assistant Professor of Second Language Acquisition at the Department of Modern and Classical Languages, Literatures & Cultures, University of Kentucky, and the principal investigator of the Bilingual and Biliteracy Research Lab. Her primary research interest is in second language reading and biliteracy development.

Keiko Koda (she, her) is Professor and Director of the Doctoral Program in Second Language Acquisition and Japanese in the Department of Modern Languages at Carnegie Mellon University. Her research interests include second language reading, biliteracy development, psycholinguistics, and foreign language pedagogy. Her work has been published in a wide range of journals. She has authored, edited, and co-edited nine books, edited and co-edited special issues of journals, and contributed chapters to books on reading and second language acquisition. She has served on the editorial boards of many highly regarded journals, including *Reading Research Quarterly, Reading and Writing, Research in Second Language Learning, TESOL Quarterly*, and *Modern Language Journal*. She has also served as a member of many national and international panels on reading and literacy development in additional languages. She has delivered talks and lectures as an invited speaker at universities and conferences in East Asia, Southeast Asia, Europe, and South America. Her recent projects have focused on the development of higher-order reading subskills in adult foreign language learners, the contributions of metalinguistic awareness to biliteracy development, and integrative approaches to foreign language reading instruction and assessment.

Liu Li is Associate Professor of Chinese at the Department of Modern Languages and Classics at Ball State University. She received her PhD in Second Language Acquisition from Carnegie Mellon University. Her research interests include Chinese literacy acquisition, computer-assisted language learning, language learning context, and heritage language learners.

Xiaomeng Li is a doctoral student of Second Language Acquisition in the Department of Modern Languages, Carnegie Mellon University. She earned her master's degree in Applied Linguistics and Second Language Acquisition (ALSLA) in the Department of Education, University of Oxford. Her research interests are primarily in second language reading, especially in second language visual word recognition and cross-linguistic comparison of writing systems. Her research was published in *Language Teaching* and presented in worldwide conferences.

Chin-Hsi Lin is Associate Professor in the Faculty of Education at the University of Hong Kong. His research interests revolve around learning processes and outcomes in online language learning, with special attention to self-regulation, interaction, course design, and teacher effects in fully online courses.

Elizabeth K.Y. Loh is Assistant Professor, Assistant Dean (Knowledge Exchange) and Director of Double Degree Programs at the University of Hong Kong's Faculty of Education. Her research, granted over US$12.8M, focuses on CSL curriculum development and pedagogy (preschool to secondary), with over 70 publications, apps and a social enterprise promoting IT-assisted CSL education.

Chan Lü is Associate Professor at the University of Washington. She received her PhD in Second Language Acquisition from Carnegie Mellon University. Her fields of research include bilingualism and biliteracy, immersion education, second language reading, and Chinese as second language acquisition.

Xiaoxi Sun holds a PhD in applied linguistics from Shanghai Jiao Tong University. She is a lecturer in Chinese in the Department of Modern Languages and Cultures at the University of Exeter, the United Kingdom. She teaches in the BA Modern Languages and MA Translation Studies programs. Her research interests include second language pragmatics, speaking fluency, and Chinese language assessment.

Mengyue Wang is a graduate student working with Dr. Tianxu Chen on Learning and Teaching Chinese as an Additional Language at Minzu University of China.

Chin-Lung Yang is an experimental psycholinguist and Senior Scientific Researcher in the Department of Linguistics and Modern Languages at the Chinese University of Hong Kong. His research program aims to understand the cognitive/neurocognitive bases, universal and language-specific, of high-order language comprehension (i.e., sentence/text) in reading and language learning, and he applies multi-disciplinary paradigms to study the relationship between language processes and language experience. His articles have appeared in a broad range of journals and books covering topics on the cognitive/neurocognitive basis of sentence and text comprehension.

Dongbo Zhang is Professor of Language Education in the Graduate School of Education at the University of Exeter, the United Kingdom. His research interests include second language reading and vocabulary knowledge, bilingualism and literacy, and language teacher education. He previously held appointments in the Department of Teacher Education, Michigan State University where he directed the Chinese Teacher Certification Program and also coordinated the Doctoral Certificate in English Language Learner Education. His publications, including those on reading in Chinese as an additional language, have appeared in top-tier applied linguistics and literacy journals, such as *Applied Linguistics*, *Language Learning*, *Modern Language Journal*, and *Reading Research*

Quarterly. He is a co-editor of *Preparing Foreign Language Teachers for Next-Generation Education* (IGI Global) and *Chinese as a Second Language Assessment* (Springer).

Yanhui Zhang received her PhD in Second Language Acquisition and M.Sc. in Computer-Assisted Language Learning from Carnegie Mellon University. Her research interests lie in computer-assisted language learning, corpus linguistics, and bilingual literacy development. Her research aims to transfer the synergy of interdisciplinary discoveries to promote robust language learning.

Acknowledgements

Editing a book during the Covid pandemic was harder than I expected. Yet it was more rewarding than I could have ever imagined. None of this would have been possible without my co-editor, Dr. Dongbo Zhang. As an outstanding researcher and excellent educator in the field of foreign language education, he has vision, dynamism, sincerity, and motivation, all of which have deeply inspired me. His dedication to this book project has made the entire process smoother and more efficient, despite all the problems we were faced with in the pandemic. His support and friendship are invaluable to me.

I am extremely grateful to the authors who contributed to this book. They had to work on their manuscripts while facing tremendous teaching tasks in the pandemic, including the unexpected switch from in-person instruction to online teaching. Yet all of them completed their manuscripts with flying colors, despite the problems and uncertainties caused by the pandemic.

I am also thankful to my parents, who taught me discipline, hard work, love, respect, and so much more that has helped me succeed in life. Ever since I was a small child, they encouraged me to go out to explore the world and help others explore the world. I am still walking toward these goals in the journey of my life. It is because of their love and encouragement that I have a legacy to pass on to my daughter.

A special thanks to my mother-in-law, Margaret Zimmerman, who has been helping me in various ways these years. As an excellent copyeditor, she proofread and copyedited all the manuscripts in this book. Her love and support mean a lot to me.

To my husband, Dan: for always being the person I could turn to no matter what. A lifelong partner like you makes both the journey and destination worthwhile. To my daughter, Angela: for being so lovely and loving. You made me better understand what unconditional love is, and you are one more motivation for me to work hard.

Finally, my thanks go to all the people who have supported me to complete this book, directly or indirectly.

Liu Li

Introduction

Liu Li and Dongbo Zhang

The number of students learning Chinese as an Additional Language (CAL) has been increasing rapidly in the past three decades. For example, between 1998–2002, there was a 20% increase of enrollment in university-level Chinese classes in the United States (Welles, 2004). From 2002 to 2009, enrollment at the American colleges increased from 34,153 to 60,976 (Furman et al., 2010). The rapid growth of Chinese education calls for a better understanding of CAL learning and teaching.

One of the biggest challenges of CAL learning and teaching is learners' literacy development (Everson, 2011; Lee-Thompson, 2008). This formidable task is mainly ascribed to the linguistic features of the Chinese language, including its unique character-based writing system; its distinct grammatical structures at the word, sentence, and discourse level; and the linguistic distance between Chinese and the learners' first language(s). Because of the rapid growth of Chinese language programs in the world, both educators and learners are urgently in need of information and knowledge based on research about how learners develop Chinese literacy abilities and how teachers teach Chinese literacy skills effectively.

To meet such demands, this book first delves into the foundation of Chinese literacy development: the acquisition of Chinese characters. Then, it examines various learners' reading comprehension subskills, as well as the evolution of learners' literacy identity. Finally, it explores effective instructional methods and assessment practices for CAL reading development. Accordingly, the content of this book can be divided into three parts:

(1) Acquisition of Chinese characters. Chapters 1–4 discuss various aspects of learning or teaching Chinese characters effectively.
(2) Reading comprehension subskills and reader's identity. Chapters 5–8 fall into this category.
(3) Reading instruction and assessment. This part explores pedagogical approaches of teaching reading inside and outside the classroom and discusses the implications for CAL curriculum design. It also includes effective ways to assess CAL reading skills. Chapters 9–13 are in this category.

Part One of this book looks at several less-explored factors and their impact on learners' character acquisition: stroke-order awareness, use of technology, typing with pinyin, and timed dictation. In the field of Chinese reading, it is not surprising that numerous studies have been concerned with character/word recognition (e.g., Perfetti & Tan, 1998; Shen, 2017), due to the unique orthographic system used in Chinese and the challenges it presents to the learners. Most of these studies, however, examined the role of phonological awareness (e.g., Song et al., 2016) and morphological awareness (e.g., Liu & McBride-Chang, 2010). Since other aspects of character acquisition have been unduly overlooked, these four chapters in this part of the book intend to draw attention to some of these long-neglected aspects. The review of how to use technology to teach Chinese characters (Chapter 2), typing Chinese characters with pinyin during online education (Chapter 3), and using timed diction to improve students' character learning for both face-to-face teaching and distance education (Chapter 4) are particularly relevant during the Covid and post-Covid period, in which online learning/teaching and the use of technology have been significantly more important than before.

Specifically, Chapter 1 examines the effects of stroke-order accuracy on L2 Chinese character writing. Participants at three different Chinese-proficiency levels completed a stroke-order task and a character-writing task. Elementary-level Chinese learners additionally completed a vocabulary knowledge task and a general literacy task. The findings showed that learners with higher stroke-order accuracy performed better on character writing than those with lower stroke-order accuracy. Language proficiency did not change the relationship between stroke-order accuracy and character writing. In addition, this study found that elementary-level learners' stroke-order accuracy, when vocabulary knowledge was controlled for, marginally contributed to general literacy. This study helps us further understand how stroke-order accuracy affects L2 learners' character learning, particularly among elementary-level Chinese learners.

Chapter 2 is a comprehensive review of research between 1996 and 2019 on technology-enhanced L2 Chinese character learning. There are two tracks of studies: one track focused on the multimedia presentation of characters and its effect on L2 Chinese character learning effectiveness; the other track investigated the effectiveness of using a technological tool to facilitate L2 Chinese character acquisition. The authors first reviewed evidence and found that dual coding through visual and audio presentation is more beneficial than a single form of presentation by approaches using only visual or only audio. Yet, the effectiveness of multimedia presentation is subject to the influence of the character-learning outcome measurement characteristics, the delivery mode, and the L2 learners' profiles. Based on these findings, the authors evaluated whether the design and implementation of the technological tools in the primary studies conform to evidence-based best practices.

Chapter 3 compares the effect of typing and handwriting on CAL students' character learning. To find out the impact of typing characters through pinyin on CAL students' literacy development, this study used the results of characters quizzes to compare how the two different character-production modes—handwriting with a pen versus typing with pinyin through a keyboard—impact beginning-level and intermediate-level CAL learners' character learning. The participants include two classes at the beginning level and two classes at the intermediate level. At each level, one class was the typing group, using the pinyin input system through a keyboard to produce Chinese characters. The other class was the handwriting group, using a pen to write Chinese characters. Parallel classes at each level were taught by the same instructor, using the same textbook and teaching materials. Paired *t*-test results of participants' character quizzes indicate that the typing group read Chinese characters as well as the handwriting group at both levels. The results also indicate that the pinyin input system helped participants produce significantly more correct characters at both levels. Surveys were conducted to find out how much time the learners spent learning Chinese each week and their attitudes toward typing and handwriting. The survey data revealed that typing Chinese with pinyin would increase the efficiency of doing homework at the beginning level. Also, the majority of the participants at both proficiency levels preferred typing or a combination of typing and handwriting in their study of Chinese.

Chapter 4 examines the effects of Timed Dictation (TD) on enhancing beginning-level Chinese as a foreign language (CFL) learners' accuracy and fluency in writing Chinese characters. TD is a character writing activity that encourages a high level of learner autonomy and helps instructors to achieve character-training effect with the help of technology. The participants in this study, which comprised 42 first-year CFL learners, were divided into two groups. One group went through TD training; the other group served as the control group. Both groups were post-tested, which revealed that TD was more effective in enhancing both face-to-face and distance learners' writing accuracy and fluency compared to the traditional copying activity. Furthermore, results from a perception survey showed learners' positive feedback and preferences for the TD activity compared to the copying activity. Most participants in the TD group considered the TD activities beneficial and enjoyable, whereas the control group did not show a similar perception toward the copying activity. This study sheds light on how to help beginning-level students acquire characters effectively. The results also provide a potential solution for distance Chinese instruction in terms of maintaining character training effects while reducing instructors' workload.

Part Two of this book consists of studies on reading comprehension and related subskills at different levels. This part includes theoretical discussions and empirical studies on the development of reading and related sub-skills, such as metalinguistic awareness development at various levels and sociocultural factors affecting reading development and comprehension. Less attention has been paid to the nature of the Chinese L2 reading process as a whole, particularly regarding the aspects other than character recognition. The studies in this part may well help both the learners and teachers understand the nature of literacy development among CAL learners, identify the critical cognitive and sociocultural factors affecting the development of reading skills in Chinese, and consider ways to facilitate the advancement of reading skills for Chinese learners with various backgrounds.

Chapter 5 discusses the roles of character-recognition skills in differentiating shallow and deep reading comprehension. Five instruments were administered to measure the participants' character-recognition and reading-comprehension skills. Three character-recognition skills were differentiated and assessed, including morphological skill (MS), ortho-semantic (radical) skill (RS), and ortho-phonetic skill (PS). Shallow comprehension was assessed with a fill-in-a-gap cloze test. Deep comprehension was assessed with a multiple-choice comprehension test. Two regression models were separately conducted with the scores of the cloze test or those of the multiple-choice test as the dependent variable. The two models suggest the importance of MS in both levels of comprehension. Yet, when shallow comprehension was the reading purpose, ortho-phonetic skill may be sufficient, and readers may not detect contradicting details in their comprehension; only when readers were required to construct deep (and coherent) comprehension did the importance of radical skill emerge and precede ortho-phonetic knowledge. Pedagogically, the finding that radical skill is a distinguishing feature of deep comprehension suggests that it should deserve special instructional attention and be taught early in L2 Chinese classes.

Chapter 6 delves into the development of morphological awareness (MA) among Chinese heritage language learners. The study explores morphological awareness and its impact on character knowledge acquisition and reading subskills development among school-age Chinese heritage language (CHL) learners. Based on a systematic analysis of the print input that was available to the focal group of grades 3, 4, and 5 CHL learners at the time of data collection, it was predicted that the specific features of MA shaped through the input, and tested the predictions using a variety of MA tasks. The data demonstrated that CHL learners performed better on the tasks assessing sensitivity to the structural properties of characters than on those measuring the constraints imposed on character meanings. It also showed that little difference existed in MA and character knowledge across the three grade levels. It was found that grade 5 students scored considerably higher on the reading comprehension test than the younger cohorts; and that MA was not systematically related to either character knowledge or reading comprehension. These findings seem to indicate that the print input available to CHL learners provided an adequate foundation for forming sensitivity to the structural constraints on character formation, but was far from sufficient for gaining a good grasp of the functional properties of characters. Lacking the finely tuned functional insights, their MA does not appear to promote morpheme-based constructive approaches to character learning and processing during reading.

Chapter 7 explores the developmental interdependence between lexical competence and reading comprehension in young L1 and L2 readers of Chinese. This chapter reports on a study that examined the reciprocal or developmentally interdependent relationship between lexical competence and reading comprehension in L2 readers compared to their L1 peers. The data were drawn from a large project that examined bilingual reading development in Singaporean children. For this study, two groups of ethnic Chinese children were identified based on their parents' report on home language use patterns. Those whose dominant home language was English or Chinese were identified to be L2 (N = 89) or L1 readers of Chinese (N = 124), respectively. Word decoding, oral vocabulary knowledge, and reading comprehension were measured three times: at the end of grade 3 (Time 1), in the middle of grade 4 (Time 2), and at the end of grade 4 (Time 3). The three waves of data were fitted to a cross-lagged panel model in which, besides its earlier performance predicting the later performance (i.e., a lagged or autoregressive effect), each of the three literacy variables also predicts the two others at an immediately later time (i.e., a lagged effect). There were two notable findings about the relationships between the variables. First, in the L1 group, earlier decoding and vocabulary knowledge consistently predicted later reading comprehension after controlling for earlier reading comprehension. In the L2 group, however, only decoding surfaced as a unique longitudinal lexical predictor of reading comprehension; this was the case from Time 1 to Time 2 and from Time 2 to Time 3. This finding occurred possibly because of the involvement of meaning activation during the word decoding process and a possibly greater "disassociation" of oral and written word knowledge in L1 readers of Chinese. Second, reading comprehension was not found to be a significant longitudinal predictor of both lexical measures after accounting for their respective autoregressive effect. This was true for both groups. This finding is not interpreted to mean that reading is unimportant in word knowledge development in Chinese, but rather is discussed considering the short duration of this study and the unique situation of Chinese language learning in Singapore, where children generally lack interest in reading in Chinese.

Chapter 8 is a qualitative study of less successful CAL readers. Endeavoring to find out the causes for comprehension breakdown and strategy use, this qualitative case study analyzes how two less successful CAL learners read a Chinese text. Through think-aloud and recall protocols, close observations, and interviews, this study answered three groups of research questions: (1) What were the causes of the comprehension breakdown experienced by the two readers? Do these causes differ from one reader to another? (2) What strategies did they use? How did they use these strategies to cope with comprehension difficulties? How effective were these strategies in enhancing comprehension? (3) Are there similarities and differences in their patterns of strategy use? Findings revealed that although there were some common causes for comprehension breakdown, the type and frequencies of difficulties occurring in the process of reading varied from one reader to another. As for strategy use, both readers heavily relied on bottom-up strategies, and lacked confidence and were therefore reluctant to infer unknown words. Despite these similarities, the two readers differed in patterns and effectiveness of their strategy use. While one reader focused on decoding every character and struggled in parsing sentences and in comprehending the text globally, another reader had a high tolerance of ambiguity and better knowledge of syntax and text structure, which helped her compensate for some comprehension gaps. These findings suggest differences in reading difficulties and strategy use among less successful readers and point to the importance of analyzing each case when providing instructional suggestions. The data also reveals the interaction between sentence parsing and word recognition and suggest the important role of syntax knowledge in word decoding and inference. The findings appear to suggest that effective use of top-down strategies may help with some difficulties in lower-level processing. This study provides pedagogical suggestions to improve L2 Chinese reading instruction.

Chapter 9 examines the relationship between the literacy environment and heritage language learner's literacy identity. From a social-cultural perspective, this case study examines some aspects of an 11-year-old Chinese American boy's Chinese literacy development: whether his home environment and community environment would affect his identity, and whether his identity would in turn affect his biliteracy learning. Through analyzing data collected from observation, questionnaires, and interviews, it was found that both the home and community environments played important roles in the boy's evolving identity, which in turn affected his Chinese literacy development. Specifically, a Chinese weekend school in the community clashed with the boy's literacy learning identity. His home literacy environment, literacy practice, and the attitude of the parents and grandparents also had impacts on the boy's development of Chinese literacy identity.

Part Three of the book focuses on hands-on instructional methods and reading assessment in Chinese. Even though scholars (Everson, 1986; Walker, 1984) long ago pointed out the importance of reading instruction in the CAL curriculum, research on CAL reading instruction (especially beyond the character level) and reading assessment has been sparse (Everson, 2002; Everson & Ke, 1997). Therefore, this part of the book attempts to provide some insight into CAL reading instruction and assessment.

Chapter 10 investigates shared book reading in a Chinese language immersion classroom. From a sociocultural theoretical (SCT) perspective, the case study in this chapter focused on a grade 3 Chinese language immersion classroom in a public school in the United States, with the goal of exploring the teacher's instructional strategies during shared book reading. The study aimed to answer two research questions: (1) What instructional strategies does the Chinese immersion teacher use when conducting shared reading of books of different genres? (2) Does the teacher adopt separate strategies for each different book genre? The participants were a native-speaking Chinese language teacher and her class of about 30 third graders. The teacher's strategies of reading a story book and a math book were observed and compared. One of the many interesting findings was that the teacher seemed to change her strategies in alignment with her pedagogical purposes designed for each book genre. Specifically, while reading the math book, the teacher focused on scaffolding students' learning of mathematical concepts through in-depth, whole-class discussions. But while reading the story book with the class, she focused more on teaching reading strategies. These findings shed light on shared book reading strategies and teachers' choices of books in Chinese immersion classrooms in the United States and beyond.

Chapter 11 demonstrates how to improve CAL students' reading comprehension skills through drama performance based on students' reading of modern Chinese literature. This chapter first explains the theoretical underpinnings of using drama to teach reading comprehension of modern literature, and then presents the procedures of using this method. The students were from a school in Hong Kong with an international background and had an intermediate level of Chinese. Over a period of three months, various drama conventions were conducted in class. These included, for example, still image, reader's theater, in-role writing, and teacher-in-role, to teach *Memories of Peking: South Side Stories*, a classic piece of Modern Chinese literature. Findings of the study indicated that the students were engaged with the story and gained a deeper understanding of the characters. Moreover, the drama conventions motivated the students to take part in various classroom activities and writing tasks, to concentrate on reading the text, and to memorize the details they were not interested in originally.

Chapter 12 talks about the CAL reading assessment. Reading is a complex process that entails multiple operations for constructing and analyzing meanings at all levels of text units. As such, reading ability has been conceptualized from diverse perspectives in several related disciplines, including psychology, education, and linguistics. To date, research has shown that text-meaning construction heavily relies on knowledge of the language in which reading is learned. It is known that meaning construction operations vary systematically across languages; and that second language reading involves two languages. Researchers generally agree that reading ability in a second language is more complex than that in the first. However, a consensus has yet to emerge as to what constitutes reading ability in a second language, how it differs from first language reading ability, and how best progress in reading acquisition can be tracked in language classrooms. This chapter addresses these questions in an attempt to clarify the unique nature of Chinese literacy and its implications for reading assessment in Chinese as a foreign language.

Chapter 13 reports a case of study on test development and validation using the method of action research. Situated at the intersection of theories of second language (L2) reading, cognition, and assessment, the study in this chapter explores how to develop and validate a Chinese online placement test. This chapter first presents the process of developing the placement test. Three levels of proficiency needed to be separated through the placement test: Beginning, Intermediate, and Advanced. The language skills and knowledge assessed in the placement test included vocabulary, grammar, and reading comprehension. Listening and speaking abilities were excluded in this placement test because some test takers may speak Chinese at home, but have never studied Chinese literacy. Then, this chapter discusses the procedure of administering the test and validating its authenticity. Various data were included in the analysis. The validation examined the validity and reliability of the test, and was carried out both quantitatively and qualitatively. Two analyses of validity were conducted. The first examined test content in relation to curriculum content. The results indicate that their rating was highly consistent. The second analysis compared the placement test scores with the students' midterm exams. The correlation coefficients reveal that there was a moderate relationship between the placement test and students' midterm examination scores. The coefficients also demonstrate that the placement test had a strong relationship with the grammar and text comprehension sections in the students' midterm examinations. Reliability coefficients were examined. The results showed the reliability of the placement test was high, indicating that the test was fairly reliable. Qualitative data was obtained through a post-test survey using questionnaires and semi-structured interviews. Through the questionnaire, it was found that most of the students considered that it was a fair test of their literacy ability. Follow-up semi-structured interviews were conducted with some test takers, covering their concerns about the test. Overall, the results show that the placement test was valid and could successfully assess the learners' literacy abilities at the different proficiency levels. This study strengthens validity arguments and enhances understanding of the complexity of Chinese placement test construction.

The variety of topics discussed in the book will help readers better understand the nature of CAL reading development and become well informed about CAL classroom teaching and assessment, including the application of interactive approaches to teaching and assessing diverse reading skills. It is expected that teachers and educators interested in CAL reading would particularly benefit from this book. Readers with pedagogical interests in Chinese literacy education or second language education in general may also find the book a useful resource.

In terms of scope, the book includes comprehensive coverage of key issues of CAL reading. It covers a much broader spectrum of issues about CAL reading research and classroom teaching than has previously been available. Previous studies in the field have focused primarily on character recognition and lexical processing. This book goes further, to include studies on development and processing at the sentence and discourse levels as well. In the book, learners of diverse backgrounds are examined. In addition to delving into key questions on topics, such as how students learn Chinese from the learner's perspective, the book also explores better ways for educators to implement new approaches that will improve teaching and curriculum design. Moreover, rarely touched-upon topics dealing with reading assessment have been included in the book as well. Through this book, readers can achieve a better understanding of reading development from both cognitive/psycholinguistic and sociocultural perspectives, learn methodologies that are used to measure CAL learners' reading development, acquire the competence to improve diverse learners' reading ability, and be introduced to new technologies used to teach reading inside and outside the CAL classroom.

The scope of the book transcends the borders of countries and the barriers of ages. Geographically, this book brings together cutting-edge research on reading Chinese as an additional language by authors from North America, Asia, and Europe. These scholars represent a wide range of contexts of teaching Chinese as an additional language in the world. The research subjects in the books also come from a diverse range of backgrounds, including heritage learners, K-12 and college students, and teachers of Chinese.

The book is innovative in several ways. Theoretically, this book provides empirical evidence from both cognitive and sociocultural perspectives on the nature of CAL reading development. For example, the first chapter explores which character-recognition skills best differentiate surface and deep levels of comprehension, a subject that has received little attention in previous studies. Another chapter investigates the effects of stroke-order accuracy on learners' character writing ability and general literacy, which has rarely been examined.

Methodologically, this book includes empirical studies using both qualitative and quantitative methods. Readers, teachers, and researchers interested in how to measure CAL reading development, pedagogy, and assessment will obtain useful information about innovative methodologies from these studies.

Pedagogically, how to teach and assess CAL reading skills is another important focus of the book. There are many chapters that discuss practical implications and offer hands-on suggestions for CAL instruction as well as evaluation. For example, several chapters specifically focus on various ways to teach Chinese characters, including how to use technology in character-teaching. The book also contains studies on classroom instruction and assessment. From these studies, teachers and learners will gain new insights into CAL pedagogy and assessment.

References

Everson, M. E. (1986). *The effect of word-unit spacing upon the reading strategies of native and non-native readers of Chinese: An eye-tracking study* (Unpublished doctoral dissertation). The Ohio State University.

Everson, M. E. (2002). Theoretical developments in reading Chinese and Japanese as foreign languages. In J. H. Sullivan (Ed.), *Literacy and the second language learner* (pp. 1–16). Information Age Publishing.

Everson, M. E. (2011). Best practices in teaching logographic and non-Roman writing systems to L2 learners. *Annual Review of Applied Linguistics, 31,* 249–274.

Everson, M. E., & Ke, C. (1997). An inquiry into the reading strategies of intermediate and advanced learners of Chinese as a foreign language. *Journal of the Chinese Language Teachers Association, 32*(1), 1–20.

Furman, N., Goldberg, D., & Lusin, N. (2010). *Enrollments in languages other than English in United States institutions of higher education, Fall 2009*. Modern Language Association. www.mla.org/content/download/2872/79842/2009_enrollment_survey.pdf

Lee-Thompson, L. (2008). An investigation of reading strategies applied by American learners of Chinese as a foreign language. *Foreign Language Annals, 41,* 702–721.

Liu, P. D., & McBride-Chang, C. (2010). What is morphological awareness? Tapping lexical compounding awareness in Chinese third graders. *Journal of Educational Psychology, 102*(1), 62.

Perfetti, C. A., & Tan, L. H. (1998). The time course of graphic, phonological, and semantic activation in Chinese character identification. *Journal of Experimental Psychology: Learning, Memory, and Cognition, 24*(1), 101–118.

Shen, H. (2017). Lexical accessing for ambiguous words among advanced Chinese L2 learners. *Chinese as a Second Language, 52*(3), 209–231.

Song, S., Georgiou, G. K., Su, M., & Hua, S. (2016). How well do phonological awareness and rapid automatized naming correlate with Chinese reading accuracy and fluency? A meta-analysis. *Scientific Studies of Reading, 20*(2), 99–123.

Walker, G. (1984). 'Literacy' and 'reading' in a Chinese language program. *Journal of Chinese Language Teachers Association, 19*(1), 67–84.

Welles, E. B. (2004). Foreign language enrollments in United States institutions of higher education, Fall 2002. *ADFL Bulletin, 35,* 7–26. https://apps.mla.org/pdf/enrollments.pdf

Part I
Acquisition of Chinese characters

1 The effects of stroke-order accuracy on L2 Chinese character writing[1]

Tianxu Chen, Bing Feng, Mengyue Wang and Khanh-Ngan Doan

Introduction

Recently, researchers have paid much attention to how orthographic knowledge affects word reading and writing, particularly in alphabetic writing systems. Some studies have shown positive correlations between the ability of spelling and reading. For instance, skilled spellers have faster word activation in reading (Holmes & Castles, 2001; Martin-Chang et al., 2014). In contrast, others have indicated that reading processes may be unaffected by incomplete or inaccurate orthographic representations. For example, Holmes and Carruthers (1998) indicated that a person could read words that he/she could not spell just as quickly as words that they were able to spell accurately. Burt and Tate (2002) also found incomplete orthographic representations may suffice for reading accuracy.

Interestingly, the contradictory findings seem not to exist in Chinese, which is a morphosyllabic language (DeFrancis, 1984). Traditionally, L1 Chinese learners are advised to practice writing Chinese characters following strict stroke orders to develop appropriate automatic character-writing skills. It is widely acknowledged that a stroke is the basic graphic unit in a character, and a character is a morphemic unit in the Chinese writing system (e.g., Chen, 2019; Taft & Zhu, 1997). According to the State Language Commission of China's (1997) report, there are 31 strokes in the Chinese character system, which are divided into two types: basic and composite. Basic strokes include a horizontal stroke'一', a vertical stroke'丨', a left-falling stroke'丿', a dot'丶', and an angled stroke'㇗'. Also, 16 stroke orders exist in the Chinese writing system, among which seven basic stroke orders are the following: (1) horizontal stroke before vertical stroke, as in '十'; (2) left-falling stroke before right-falling stroke, as in '八'; (3) from top to bottom, as in '亏'; (4) from left to right, as in '孔';(5) from outside to inside, as in '月'; (6) from outside to inside before the sealing stroke, as in '日'; and (7) from center to both sides, as in '小'.

A question has always been centered on pedagogical practices of stroke order: do Chinese learners necessarily follow correct stroke orders when they write Chinese characters? L2 Chinese instructors may respond to this question positively (Dang, 2013) because strokes are viewed as a foundational component of the Chinese writing system, and errors in stroke order may imply learners' misconception of characters' internal structures. However, few previous studies have provided empirical evidence. Thus, the present study investigated how learners' stroke-order accuracy develops as their language proficiency increases, as well as whether language proficiency changes the relationship between learners' stroke-order accuracy and character writing among 62 adult L2 Chinese learners in a Chinese university.

Literature review

Although many Chinese language instructors traditionally believe that strokes and their writing orders play an important role in character reading and writing, a handful of empirical studies have investigated the stroke-order issue of Chinese learners (e.g., Li et al., 2007). No agreement has been reached yet regarding how stroke-order accuracy impacts character recognition and production for L1 Chinese learners. The controversy lies in the following aspects:

First, with respect to the effects of stroke order on reading characters, some studies support a positive relationship between stroke order and character recognition (e.g., Giovanni, 1994; Yim-Ng et al., 2000). For example, Giovanni (1994) claimed that L1 learners' stroke order has been coded in memory as an essential component of the orthographic knowledge of a character. Yim-Ng et al. (2000) found a similar result that specific stroke order would affect character naming by finger tracing. Despite these studies, other researchers provided different evidence to emphasize the effects of stroke configuration as a whole, which implies that individual stroke order is not essential in reading characters (e.g., Chen et al., 1996).

Second, as for the relationship between stroke order and character production, some provided positive evidence (e.g., Lo et al., 2015). For example, Lo et al.'s (2015) findings indicated that stroke-order knowledge contributes both concurrently and longitudinally to children's character-spelling performance. On the contrary, other studies had different findings (e.g., Li et al., 2007; Naka, 1998; Tamaoka & Yamada, 2000). For instance, Li et al. (2007) indicated that Chinese learners tend to develop their own habits, and the handwriting of experienced writers is individual, despite some basic rules governing the stroke order of Chinese characters. Tamaoka and Yamada (2000) also suggested that although knowledge of correct stroke order has been commonly assumed to be fundamental, it may not support character writing.

Although only a few studies have been done on stroke order in relation to L2 Chinese learning, the findings seem to be promising. A few surveys of learners' opinions on L2 Chinese stroke order showed that Chinese as a second language learners would like to pay more attention to character stroke order (Jiang & Zhao, 2001). Learners also relied on stroke-order knowledge while learning characters (Shen, 2005). In addition, some studies supported a positive correlation between correct stroke order and character production. For instance, Li (2006) first reported observations on L2 Chinese learners' character-writing processes. She found that learners who wrote with correct stroke order made fewer character-writing

The effects of stroke-order accuracy on character writing 15

mistakes. Dang (2013) also found a significant correlation between the scores of a Chinese stroke test and several Chinese characters tests.

However, the process of measuring learners' stroke-order accuracy might be problematic in those previous L2 studies (e.g., Dang, 2013). In this process, learners were usually required to write target characters in an unnatural way by dividing a character into component strokes. For example, learners were asked to write "天" in the way shown in Figure 1.1.

That is, each added stroke takes one space. Thus, the character "天" with four strokes in total needs to take four separate spaces to complete the task. This unnatural measurement may not accurately measure learners' ability to write Chinese characters since the learners had to pause by each stroke and had a chance to consciously consider how to write in a correct way. In addition, these previous studies focused on participants in one certain group (e.g., elementary-level L2 Chinese learners), which did not show the learners' developmental trajectory of stroke-order acquisition.

Kang (2011) has made great progress in stroke-order measurement (i.e., using a Smartpen—a state-of-the-art pen-movement tracking device—and a digital camcorder) and participant recruitment (i.e., including 16 beginning- and 12 intermediate-level learners). Her findings showed that the beginning-level participants who followed the correct stroke order made fewer character errors, and the intermediate-level participants with few stroke-sequence errors spent less time writing characters. Yet, one result from her study seemed less convincing: that most intermediate-level participants rarely made stroke-order errors, as that result was not aligned with our class observation. This inconsistency could potentially have resulted from problems in design and analysis. First, the target written characters were not properly controlled. For example, they could be too difficult for the beginners, or too easy for the intermediate-level students. Second, the scores of stroke-order errors were based on each character rather than each stroke. In addition, the proficiency level of the intermediate-level participants in Kang's study is arguable: that is, they may not be intermediate-level learners as the author classified in terms of their actual vocabulary size and learning duration[2]. All these unaddressed questions, thus, need further research.

Taken together, little empirical evidence has shown that incorrect sequencing of strokes would lead to negative effects on character recognition and production in both L1 and L2 studies. The lack of comprehensive understanding apparently exists about effects of stroke-order accuracy on L2 Chinese character writing, particularly in terms of their research methods (i.e., observation and/or questionnaires). Specifically, in most L2 Chinese studies regarding strokes, researchers concluded their findings based on teachers' experience or small-sample questionnaires (e.g., Ke, 1998; Lin, 2009). In addition, a few recent studies seemed not to support the positive relationship between correct stroke order and character writing for L2

Figure 1.1 An example on how to write "天" stroke by stroke

learners (e.g., Hsiung et al., 2017). For instance, Hsiung et al. (2017) investigated 91 L2 Chinese learners and found that the correct stroke order did not significantly affect the effectiveness of recognizing and writing traditional Chinese characters.

Given the importance of stroke-order knowledge as a part of handwriting skill, which directly connects with character writing, the present study focuses on the relationship between stroke-order accuracy and Chinese character-writing efficiency. By examining L2 learners at different language-proficiency levels, we can gain further understanding on how stroke order works for L2 Chinese character production among learners at different language proficiency levels. To shed light on this issue, two research questions were addressed as follows:

(1) What are the differences among L2 learners at the three proficiency levels on stroke-order accuracy and character-writing efficiency?
(2) Does L2 learners' language proficiency affect the relationship between stroke-order accuracy and character-writing efficiency?

Methods

Participants

Sixty-eight adult L2 Chinese learners at one university in Beijing, China initially participated in the study. To minimize the effects from the participants' previous writing experience, Japanese and Korean students were excluded. Therefore, a total of 62 participants from 31 countries were finally involved, including 25 learners (18 males, seven females) at the elementary instructional level of Chinese courses; 17 learners (three males, 14 females) at the intermediate instructional level; and 20 learners (eight males, 12 females) at the advanced instructional level (for convenience, hereafter abbreviated as elementary learners, intermediate learners, and advanced learners). The average formal-learning duration of Chinese language in China for the elementary learners, the intermediate learners, and the advanced learners was eight months, 15 months, and 32 months, respectively. The elementary learners were expected to grasp 2,000 words after one year of learning, and the expected vocabulary sizes were 4,500 and 8,000 for the intermediate and the advanced learners, respectively.

Measures

The participants completed two tasks (i.e., a stroke-order accuracy task and a character-writing task) in this study. In general, it was predicted that a participant with a stronger ability in a task should perform better and receive a higher score.

The stroke-order accuracy task

This task measured participants' ability to write unfamiliar characters with a correct stroke order. There were 20 target characters, which had not been shown in the participants' textbooks or learned in the classrooms. These characters had five different internal structures: four single-component structure characters (e.g., 豸, /zhi4/), four left-right structure characters (e.g., 拢, /long3/), four top-bottom structure characters (e.g., 茎, /jing1/), four enclosed-on-four-sides structure characters (e.g., 囹, /ling2/) and four enclosed-on-two-sides structure characters (e.g., 疟, /nve4/). In addition, all characters were controlled between the low and moderate complexity range (i.e., mean number of strokes is around eight) (See Su & Samuels, 2010), because the number of strokes is an important index for the visual complexity of characters (Zhang et al., 2002). The numbers of the strokes for these characters were from seven to ten, specifically including two seven-stroke characters, eight eight-stroke characters, six nine-stroke characters, and four ten-stroke characters.

The participants were asked to handwrite all these characters one by one following their daily writing habits. Their writing processes were individually videotaped, and the writing duration was timed. Each participant received a score representing his/her stroke-order accuracy, and fewer mistakes in stroke order resulted in higher scores. Specifically, stroke order was scored as a stroke was written: each stroke counted as one point, and a total score of the task was 172. The participants lost one point after each mistake. Two types of mistakes were tracked: internal strokes (e.g., " 丿 " was written as " 丨 ") and between strokes. To avoid repeated deductions, a specific scoring rubric was used: (1) scoring occurs after each stroke is written. For example, "±" should be written as "一, 十, ±" in sequence. If participants' writing order is " 丨, 十, ±", they only lose one point at the first stroke, but earn two points for this character; (2) a mistake of one stroke does not affect scoring of other correct strokes. For example, "国" should be written as " 丨, ㄱ, 玉, 一". If participants write it as " 丨, ㄱ, 一, 玉", they lose one point, rather than five points; (3) a composite stroke cannot be written as two single strokes. For instance, if participants write " ㄱ " as "一, 丨 ", they lose one point. In sum, the different scoring methods ensure consistency across character types.

The character-writing efficiency task

This task measured participants' efficiency (i.e., speed and accuracy, cf. Ke & Koda, 2017) of handwriting Chinese characters in a certain stroke order. All participants were required to handwrite the target characters while reading the character list at the same time (i.e., within five minutes) following their daily writing habits and speed. There were 125 characters in the character-writing task, including 36 seven-stroke characters, 30 eight-stroke characters, 25 nine-stroke characters and 34 ten-stroke characters. Each correct character written was counted as one point. Based on this scoring formula, the participants who wrote characters accurately within five minutes gained more points, whereas those writers with more mistakes within the same time lost more points in this task. The total amount of correctly written characters, therefore, was used to represent participants' character-writing efficiency (Wang et al., 2014).

Results

Table 1.1 shows the means, standard deviations (SDs), minimum scores, and maximum scores in all the tasks for L2 learners at three different language proficiency levels based on their instructional levels (i.e., elementary, intermediate, and advanced) and expected vocabulary size.

To answer Research Question 1: "What are the differences among L2 learners at the three proficiency levels on stroke-order accuracy and character-writing efficiency?", this study conducted one-way ANOVA using language proficiency (three levels: elementary, intermediate, and advanced) as a between-subjects variable. The results showed significant differences among the learners in the three groups on stroke-order accuracy, $F(2, 59) = 3.990, p <.05, \eta^2 = 0.12$. Post hoc tests showed that a significant difference of stroke-order accuracy existed between the elementary and intermediate learners ($p < .05$), and a significant difference existed between the elementary and advanced learners ($p < .05$), whereas no significant difference existed between the intermediate and advanced learners ($p = .727$).

Similarly, another one-way ANOVA was run to investigate whether the learners' character-writing efficiency changed as their language proficiency increased. The results showed that significant differences were found in character-writing efficiency among the learners with different language proficiency, $F(2, 59) = 9.543, p <.001, \eta^2 = 0.24$. Post hoc tests showed that significant differences of character-writing efficiency existed between the elementary and intermediate learners ($p <.01$), and between the elementary and advanced learners ($p <.01$), whereas no significant difference was found between the intermediate and advanced learners ($p = .991$).

The developmental trajectories of stroke-order accuracy and character-writing efficiency were shown in Figures 1.2 and 1.3. The figures clearly showed that the L2 learners' performance on stroke-order accuracy and character-writing efficiency improved significantly from the elementary level to the intermediate level; nonetheless, the developmental pace seemed to stagnate after the learners reached the intermediate level.

To answer Research Question 2: "Does L2 learners' language proficiency affect the relationship between stroke-order accuracy and character-writing efficiency?", three Pearson product-moment correlations were run to determine

Table 1.1 Summary of Participants' Results (N = 62)

Task		Total scores	Mean	SD	Min	Max
Stroke-order accuracy	Elementary level	172	.83	.09	.67	.97
	Intermediate level	172	.89	.09	.66	.98
	Advanced level	172	.90	.06	.78	.98
Character-writing efficiency	Elementary level	125	.46	.15	.26	.85
	Intermediate level	125	.62	.13	.35	.85
	Advanced level	125	.62	.14	.38	.86

Note. Means, SDs, Minimum and Maximum pertain to the proportion of correct item selections in the two tasks.

The effects of stroke-order accuracy on character writing 19

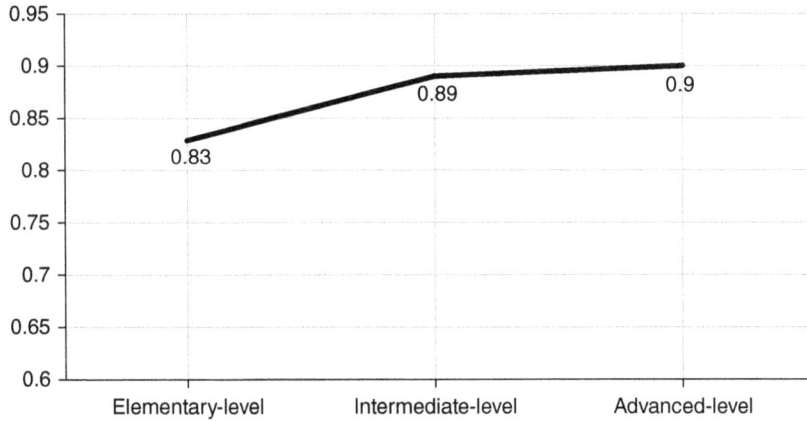

Figure 1.2 Development of learners' stroke-order accuracy

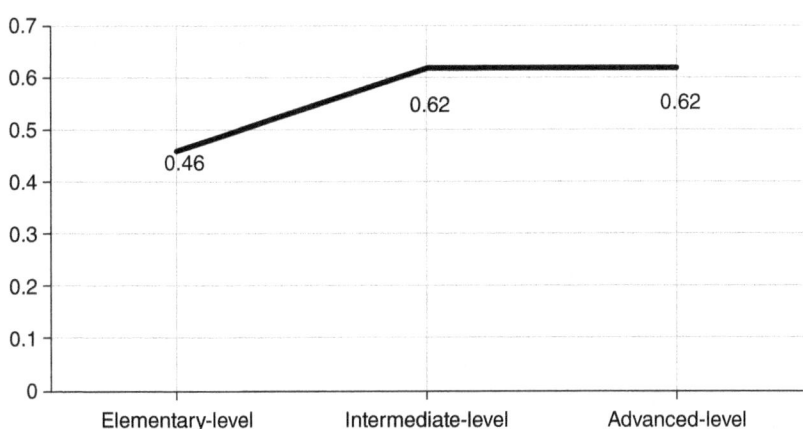

Figure 1.3 Development of learners' character-writing efficiency

the intercorrelations between stroke-order accuracy and character-writing efficiency for L2 learners at different proficiency levels. The results showed that there were significant correlations between stroke-order accuracy and character-writing efficiency in the elementary-level learners ($r = .59$, $p < .01$), in the intermediate-level learners ($r = .57$, $p < .01$), and in the advanced-level learners ($r = .50$, $p < .01$). Following comparisons of correlations showed that correlational differences were not significant between the elementary and intermediate learners (Steiger's $z = .09$, $p = .47$), between the elementary and advanced learners (Steiger's $z = .40$, $p = .35$), or between the intermediate and advanced learners (Steiger's $z = .27$, $p = .39$). In other words, learners with higher stroke-order accuracy had better character-writing efficiency than those who made more mistakes in stroke orders regardless of their Chinese proficiency. This suggests that learners' language proficiency does not affect the relationship between stroke-order accuracy and character-writing efficiency.

Discussion

Knowledge of stroke order includes knowing a set of rules governing how strokes should be written in a specific order and contains the most basic information on how to compose characters (Lo et al., 2015). This study, to some extent, supports the positive relationship between L2 learners' stroke-order accuracy and their character-writing efficiency.

First, the answer to Research Question 1 showed that L2 learners' stroke-order accuracy and character-writing efficiency improved quickly at the initial learning period and seemed to reach a developmental plateau of writing characters as their language proficiency increased (see Figures 1.2 and 1.3). This result indicates that a "sensitive learning period" for stroke-order acquisition seems to exist when L2 learners develop their orthographic system (i.e., how they learn to write characters in correct stroke orders). Specifically, L2 learners rapidly develop their L2 writing system as their orthographic knowledge increases during the initial learning period. As their overall literacy improves, which means they are increasingly familiar with a new language's writing system, L2 learners' speed at which they develop the skill of writing in correct stroke orders slows down. There might be a developmental ceiling of orthographic knowledge for L2 learners; that is, there is not much left for the advanced learners to learn or develop their stroke-order knowledge once it reaches the maximum at a certain learning period (e.g., at the intermediate instructional level in this study). In other words, when L2 learners' linguistic knowledge reaches a certain level (e.g., at the intermediate instructional level in this study), their individual L2 orthographic system might have been set up. This may explain a significant difference in performance between the elementary and intermediate learners on stroke-order accuracy and character writing, while no difference between the intermediate and advanced learners.

Although few previous L2 Chinese studies have reported this possible "sensitive learning period," also called a threshold of L2 linguistic knowledge (see Chen, 2018; Chen et al., 2020), some L1 studies on Chinese children have shown a similar concept of dynamic formation for a new orthographic system (Lo et al., 2015; Shen & Bear, 2000). Su and Samuels (2010) indicated that elementary-level Chinese readers and writers treat Chinese characters following specific and analytical rules, but this progress gradually changes from analytic to holistic as their literacy skills develop. Shen and Bear (2000) also pointed out that as Chinese children develop their orthographic knowledge, they show an increasing understanding of structures within Chinese characters and knowledge of characters' configurations. In other words, the learning period of L1 learners is an important variable affecting their awareness of their writing system (Nagy & Anderson, 1995). Many L1 Chinese children form and even fossilize their own writing habits of stroke orders as their ages and experience of character writing increase, and once such a writing habit is formed, it is difficult to change (Lam & McBride-Chang, 2013).

Since L2 learners' stroke-order development may parallel that of their L1 counterparts, it is reasonable to assume that a "sensitive learning period" exists for L2 learners to develop their orthographic knowledge in a new writing system (e.g., the application of accuracy stroke orders in writing characters in this study). One possibility is that L2 Chinese learners are unfamiliar with a new Chinese orthographic system at the beginning of learning characters. In their attempt to produce correct characters, they struggle and resort to various handwriting tricks, and disregard the officially accepted way of writing stroke by stroke in correct stroke orders. Because the sheer number of recurring components (i.e., semantic and phonetic radicals) in the Chinese writing system is much bigger than in many other languages, such as English, L2 Chinese learners may have to take quite some time to grasp principles and rules that will help them effectively learn, memorize, and compose characters. All these learning processes rely on the acquisition of certain numbers of characters (Ke, 1998). Once L2 learners' individual writing habits are formed, it is difficult to change them, as found in their L1 counterparts. Yet, it is uncertain how long an L2 Chinese learner needs to form his/her individual Chinese writing habits or orthographic preference. Therefore, it might be too hasty to claim the existence of an L2 "sensitive learning period" for the orthographic system's formation before we know more about how it fossilizes. However, this hypothesis is worth exploring in the future.

Moreover, the answer to Research Question 2 is that L2 learners' stroke-order accuracy was significantly correlated with character-writing efficiency regardless of their Chinese proficiency. This finding supports an important role of stroke order in character writing, which is consistent with the previous empirical research (e.g., Kang, 2011) and experienced language instructors' beliefs (e.g., Li, 2013). Specifically, the significant correlations among L2 Chinese learners at all proficiency levels indicate that learners who are able to write characters in a more accurate sequence have better performance in speed and accuracy of character writing. In fact, it is not difficult to understand the positive effect of stroke order on character writing.

First, writing characters in a systematic way can reduce the chance of missing/adding additional strokes caused by random writing, and create an avenue by which learners can gain skills of recognizing Chinese characters. The stroke-order writing is an essential feature in the orthographic representation of Chinese characters in memory (Giovanni, 1994; Luo et al., 2010). In other words, visual representations of words can be facilitated by stroke-order production in learners' memory capacity (Lam & McBride-Chang, 2013). Writing Chinese characters in systematic orders (i.e., correct stroke order) would reduce learners' memorizing burden, and make connections with other higher-level literacy subskills (e.g., radical and character writing).

Second, the correct stroke order has been developed following the economic principle of writing. To be exact, the distance between two adjacent strokes based on the correct stroke order is supposed to be the shortest distance. Clearly, writing

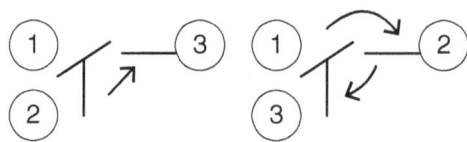

Figure 1.4 An example on how to write the first three strokes of '休'

in the shortest stroke distance means to be more efficient, compared with the longer stroke distance (Ding, 2012). Consider how to write the first three strokes of "休" (/xiu1/, have a rest) as an example. The stroke distance in the first writing order (i.e., the correct stroke order, Figure 1.4a) is closer than its counterpart by the second unconventional writing order (Figure 1.4b).

Despite the benefit of stroke-order knowledge, it should be noted that the emphasis of stroke-order accuracy in character writing in the present study does not indicate that stroke order could directly affect higher-level literacy-related skills. As Lo et al. (2015) indicate, stroke (order) knowledge was a significant predictor of Chinese character spelling (i.e., character writing), but not of word reading. After all, it is unnecessary for Chinese readers to read characters/words following a strict stroke-by-stroke sequence. That might also explain why Hsiung et al. (2017) did not find the effect of stroke order on recognizing traditional characters. In fact, strokes are foundational in writing characters, but might not be a functional unit in other Chinese literacy-related skills (e.g., Chen & Cherng, 2013). Taft and his colleagues' multilevel (interactive) activation framework (Taft & Zhu, 1997; Taft et al., 1999) clearly illustrates the relationships among stroke [order] and other subskills in Chinese literacy. There are four levels (i.e., stroke, radical, character, and word) at this hierarchical framework, among which the stroke and its writing order are at the lowest level. This foundational level of strokes and stroke orders leads to the development of Chinese character and word processing via radicals (e.g., Chen, 2019).

On the other hand, even if stroke order plays a relatively minor role in overall character knowledge (e.g., Tamaoka & Yamada, 2000) and may only indirectly support character production via radicals, this would not weaken the importance of strokes and stroke order at the orthographic level for Chinese writing system. As mentioned previously, L2 learners' Chinese orthographic system is not easily set up in a systematic way without the understanding of how strokes and stroke order work. If L2 learners' literacy development is like the construction of a building, strokes and stroke order can be compared to clay and sand, which are the most important ingredients to make bricks (characters and words). Therefore, correct stroke order in writing characters should be emphasized, particularly in the initial stage of learning characters.

Implications

The present findings are consistent with some previous studies, in which handwriting skills (the ability to convert orthographic structure into a series of writing symbols) have been found as an important skill in predicting text-writing performance (Lo et al., 2015). As a foundation for Chinese handwriting skills, strokes and their writing orders positively affect learners' writing development. After all, when learners constitute a character in a systematic way by following correct stroke orders (as opposed to using a random writing system), learners' cognitive load will be reduced (e.g., Lam & McBride-Chang, 2013).

More importantly, if the hypothesis of a "sensitive learning period" during the development of L2 learners' stroke order could be further verified in the future, Chinese instructors need to consider how to develop the learners' stroke-order knowledge and skills during this critical period. In fact, stroke order is taught in almost all Chinese language classes at the elementary level, but unfortunately, not all instructors pay enough attention to this lowest-level orthographic knowledge. Some Chinese-language instructors believe that as long as a correct character is successfully produced, it is irrelevant and unnecessary to find out whether it is written in a correct way (i.e., following correct stroke orders) or not (e.g., An, 2009; An & Shan, 2007). This might have resulted from the fact that monitoring learners' writing processes is not as easy as judging their writing results. A lack of synchronous monitoring system on students' character-writing process may lead to instructors' ignorance of students' mistakes in stroke orders, which, in turn, prevents them from making efforts to guide learners to write characters in a correct stroke order.

As this study discussed, however, L2 learners' stroke-order writing habits might not be easily changed once they reach a possible "fossilization point" for stroke-order development. Thus, at the initial period of character learning, language instructors should try their best to emphasize the importance of stroke rules and how to use strokes to compose radicals and characters for elementary learners. This study also suggests that Chinese language instructors increase stroke-writing exercises, particularly during the beginning learning period, given that correct stroke order contributes to L2 learners' basic Chinese orthographic system and that a possible, critical phase of stroke-order development exists. Specifically, the exercises should not only include mechanical copying drills, but should also encourage students to identify and analyze the relationships between strokes and radicals (and even radicals and characters). Stroke-by-stroke mechanical copying drills help learners become familiar with Chinese writing rules and cultivate their correct writing habits. Identification and analysis exercises for strokes, stroke order, and radicals within a character help elementary learners develop hierarchical awareness in the Chinese writing system and practice making a connection between a lower-level component (i.e., a stroke and its writing order) and higher-level components (i.e., a radical or character). In a word, compared with intermediate and advanced learners, instruction on stroke order and foundational orthographic knowledge should be conducted more frequently for elementary learners, since these learners do not have sufficient literacy-related knowledge and subskills (e.g., vocabulary knowledge, word recognition ability, and reading comprehension) to build a correct understanding of Chinese writing system. The understanding and knowledge of strokes and their writing orders could help elementary learners realize the relationships among strokes, radicals, and characters, as well as how to write characters in a systematic way.

Conclusions and future directions

In summary, this study showed that (1) L2 learners' performance on stroke order and character writing improved significantly from the elementary level to the intermediate level, while the developmental pace seemed to stagnate after the learners reached the intermediate level; and (2) stroke-order accuracy and character-writing efficiency were significantly correlated with each other for L2 learners at different language proficiency levels; that is, language proficiency did not change the relationship between stroke-order accuracy and character-writing efficiency. The findings support the idea that lacking correct knowledge of strokes may result in an incorrect character-writing order, and consequently may affect the automaticity of writing Chinese characters (Lam & McBride-Chang, 2013). This study re-emphasized the importance of strokes and stroke order, particularly for elementary learners given that the lowest-level orthographic knowledge enables learners to be familiar with the unique Chinese writing system and set up their own writing system.

Admittedly, there are some limitations in this study. First, the participants' proficiency levels were based on the courses they were taking rather than a standardized proficiency test, and there was only one native rater for each task. The research methods should be improved in the future. Second, although this study has found significant correlations between stroke-order accuracy and character-writing efficiency for L2 learners at the different proficiency levels, the correlation does not equal a causal relationship. Thus, it should be cautious to claim that stroke-order accuracy is a predictor of character writing. Similarly, more empirical evidence is needed to test the assumption of a "sensitive learning period" and a "fossilization point" for development of L2 learners' stroke order.

The stroke-order issue, to some extent, is not merely a "Yes/No" question. After all, many Chinese learners and instructors have realized that knowledge of strokes and their writing orders—as Chinese unique and foundational orthographic knowledge—plays an important role in character writing and other literacy-related skills. Yet many more specific issues should be discussed in the future. For example, to what extent does orthographic knowledge of stroke order contribute to character learning and formation of a learner's writing system along with other relatively higher-level subskills (e.g., radical awareness and character recognition)? When do L2 learners gradually set up their own L2 writing system, such as how many characters they know? And which other factors may affect the relationship between stroke-order accuracy and character-writing efficiency?

Notes

1 Funding was provided by the 2021 Research Project on International Chinese Education by Center for Language Education and Cooperation (No. 21YH69D).

2 According to an introduction from a Chinese instructor, who previously worked at the Chinese program at Ohio State University: after two-year intermediate Chinese courses (5 hours/week) at the Ohio State University, where Kang's participants were recruited, the learners are expected to learn around 2,500 words. In contrast, after one-year elementary Chinese courses (20 hours/week) in China, learners are expected to learn more than 2,000 words (e.g., 2,340 words for the participants in this study).

References

An, R. (2009). A study of the foreign students—Writing Chinese characters from a multi-cognitive perspective (in Chinese). *Yunnan Shifan Daxue Xuebao [Journal of Yunnan Normal University]*, *7*(1), 10–15.

An, R., & Shan, Y. (2007). The stroke order issue of CSL learners without character knowledge backgrounds: A case study of Chinese character writing (*in Chinese*), *Yuyan wenzi Yingyong [Applied Linguistic]*, *3*, 54–61.

Burt, J. S., & Tate, H. (2002). Does a reading lexicon provide orthographic representations for spelling? *Journal of Memory and Language*, *46*, 518–543.

Chen, J., & Cherng, R. (2013). The proximate unit in Chinese handwritten character production. *Frontiers in Psychology*, *4*(Article 517), 1–7.

Chen, T. (2018). The contribution of morphological awareness to lexical inferencing in L2 Chinese: Comparing more-skilled and less-skilled learners. *Foreign Language Annals*, *51*(4), 816–830.

Chen, T. (2019). Joint contribution of reading subskills to character meaning retention in L2 Chinese. *Journal of Psycholinguistic Research*, *48*(1), 129–143.

Chen, T., Keiko, K., & Wiener, S. (2020). Word-meaning inference in L2 Chinese: An interactive effect of learners' linguistic knowledge and words' semantic transparency, *Reading and Writing: An Interdisciplinary Journal*. doi:10.1007/s11145-020-10058-w.

Chen, Y. P., Allport, D. A., & Marshall, J. C. (1996). What are the functional orthographic units in Chinese word recognition: The stroke or the stroke pattern? *The Quarterly Journal of Experimental Psychology*, *49A*(4), 1024–1043.

Dang, Y. (2013). *A study about the relationship between stroke feelings and learning Chinese of Thai Middle school students with no basis* (in Chinese) (Unpublished master thesis). Jinan University.

DeFrancis, J. (1984). *The Chinese language: Fact and fantasy*. University of Hawaii Press.

Ding, Y. (2012). *Investigation into the standardization of modern Chinese stroke-order* (in Chinese) (Unpublished master thesis). Shenyang Normal University.

Giovanni, F. B. A. (1994). Order of strokes writing as a cue for retrieval in reading Chinese characters. *European Journal of Cognitive Psychology*, *6*(4), 337–355.

Holmes, V. M., & Carruthers, J. J. (1998). The relation between reading and spelling in skilled adult readers. *Journal of Memory and Language*, *39*, 264–289.

Holmes, V. M., & Castles, A. E. (2001). Unexpectedly poor spelling in university students. *Scientific Studies of Reading*, *5*, 319–350.

Hsiung, H.-Y., Chang, Y.-L., Chen, H.-C., & Sung, Y.-T. (2017). Effect of stroke-order learning and handwriting exercises on recognizing and writing Chinese characters by Chinese as a foreign language learners. *Computers in Human Behavior*, *74*, 303–310.

Jiang, X., & Zhao, G. (2001). A survey on the strategies for learning Chinese characters among CSL beginners (in Chinese). *Yuyan jiaoxue yu yanjiu [Language Teaching and Linguistic Studies]*, *4*, 10–17.

Kang, H. (2011). *Computer-based writing and paper-based writing: A study of beginning-level and intermediate-level Chinese learners' writing* (Unpublished doctoral dissertation). The Ohio State University.

Ke, C. (1998). Effects of strategies on the learning of Chinese characters among foreign language students. *Journal of the Chinese Language Teachers Association, 33*(2), 93–112.

Ke, S., & Koda, K. (2017). Contributions of morphological awareness to adult L2 Chinese word meaning inferencing. *The Modern Language Journal, 101*(4), 742–755.

Lam, S. S., & McBride-Chang, C. (2013). Parent-child joint writing in Chinese kindergarteners: Explicit instruction in radical knowledge and stroke writing skills. *Writing Systems Research, 5*(1), 88–109.

Li, C. K., Yang, C. T., Poon, N. L., & Fung, W. K. (2007). Significance of sequence of strokes in Chinese handwriting examination. *Journal of Forensic Sciences, 52*(2), 467–472.

Li, X. (2006). Investigation into stroke order learning of Chinese characters of CSL elementary learners in Mexico (in Chinese). *Yuyan wenzi yingyong [Applied Linguistic], S2*, 23–25.

Li, Y. (2013). *Chinese character stroke order and teaching Chinese character research—The student of SHNU in junior class as an example* (in Chinese) (Unpublished master thesis). Shanghai Normal University.

Lin, Y. (2009). *Investigation of character teaching and learning among beginner high school students in America* (in Chinese) (Unpublished master thesis). Shanghai International Studies University.

Lo, L., Yeung, P., Ho, C. S., Chan, D. W., & Chung, K. (2015). The role of stroke knowledge in reading and spelling in Chinese. *Journal of Research in Reading*, 1–22.

Luo, Y., Wang, L., Li, X., Chen, M., & Peng, D. (2010). Effects of the number of strokes and the spatial sequence on stroke-form-character in Chinese (in Chinese). *Xinli kexue [Psychological Science], 33*(3), 584–587.

Martin-Chang, S., Ouellette, G., & Madden, M. (2014). Does poor spelling equate to slow reading? The relationship between reading, spelling, and orthographic quality. *Reading and Writing, 27*, 1485–1505.

Nagy, W. E., & Anderson, R. C. (1995). *Metalinguistic awareness and literacy development in different languages*. Center for the Study of Reading. www.ideals.illinois.edu/bitstream/handle/2142/17594/ctrstreadtechrepv01995i00618_opt.pdf?sequence=1

Naka, M. (1998). Repeated writing facilitates children's memory for pseudocharacters and foreign letters. *Memory & Cognition, 26*(4), 804–809.

Shen, H. H. (2005). An investigation of Chinese-character learning strategies among non-native speakers of Chinese. *System, 33*, 49–68.

Shen, H. H., & Bear, D. R. (2000). Development of orthographic skills in Chinese children. *Reading and Writing: An Interdisciplinary Journal, 13*(3), 197–236.

The State Language Commission of China. (1997). *Standard stroke order of frequently used characters in modern Chinese* (in Chinese). Yuwen Press.

Su, Y., & Samuels, S. J. (2010). Developmental changes in character-complexity and word-length effects when reading Chinese script. *Reading and Writing: An Interdisciplinary Journal, 23*, 1085–1108.

Taft, M., & Zhu, X. (1997). Submorphemic processing in reading Chinese. *Journal of Experimental Psychology: Learning, Memory, and Cognition, 23*(3), 761–775.

Taft, M., Zhu, X., & Peng, D. (1999). Positional specificity of radicals in Chinese character recognition. *Journal of Memory and Language, 40*, 498–519.

Tamaoka, K., & Yamada, H. (2000). The effects of stroke order and radicals on the knowledge of Japanese kanji orthography, phonology and semantics. *Psychologia*, *43*(3), 199–210.

Wang, Y., McBride-Chang, C., & Chan, S. (2014). Correlates of Chinese kindergarteners' word reading and writing: The unique role of copying skills? *Reading and Writing*, *27*, 1281–1302.

Yim-Ng, Y. Y., Varley, R., & Andrade, J. (2000). Contribution of finger tracing to the recognition of Chinese characters. *International Journal of Language and Communication Disorders*, *35*(4), 561–571.

Zhang, J., Wang, H., Zhang, M., & Zhang, H. (2002). The effect of the complexity and repetition of the strokes on the cognition of the strokes and the Chinese characters (in Chinese). *Xin li xue bao [Acta Psychologica Sinica]*, *34*(5), 449–453.

2 The more the merrier? A synthesis study of single-coded and dual-coded word learning in theory-driven L2 Chinese instruction

Sihui Ke and Chin-Hsi Lin

Introduction

In recent years, an increasing amount of research on Chinese as a second language (L2) has focused on how students' learning of words can be affected by instructional design (for a review, see Li, 2020). Many of these studies have been based on cognition theories such as Dual Coding Theory (DCT; Paivio, 1971, 2007) and Cognitive Load Theory (CLT; Sweller, 1988; Sweller et al., 2019). Important open questions in this area include: *Should new Chinese words be presented in character strings along with verbal or nonverbal prompts to L2 Chinese learners? How should L2 Chinese instruction sequence the presentation of characters, pinyin, and English translation? Should the learning of new L2 Chinese words be instructor-guided or student-initiated?*

To date, however, no research synthesis has consolidated and evaluated the existing evidence as a means of informing L2 Chinese educators about which instructional methods are optimal for the promotion of word learning. The present study fills that gap. Its two main objectives are: (1) to provide a research synthesis of the instructional designs featured in 15 years' worth of empirical research relating to cognition theories and L2 Chinese word learning; and (2) to synthesize and evaluate the existing evidence about L2 Chinese new-vocabulary teaching methods and their effects on learning. It is hoped that the findings of this synthesis will contribute to theory-driven and evidence-based instructional advancement in L2 Chinese education.

Theoretical background

A brief review of Dual Coding Theory and its relevance in L2 Chinese research

DCT assumes that cognition involves two coding systems: a verbal code for language stimuli (e.g., phonemes, morphemes, words, phrases, and longer linguistic structures) and a nonverbal one for mental imagery: e.g., a picture of a human face (Paivio, 1971, 2007). Sadoski's (2005) review of empirical instructional research suggested that both verbal stimuli and imagery of word meanings may be highly

DOI: 10.4324/9781003029038-4

beneficial to sight word learning in one's first language (L1). In recent years, changes to DCT have included its expansion into a general theory of literacy (Sadoski & Paivio, 2007) and the proposal of bilingual DCT (Paivio, 2010, 2014; Paivio & Lambert, 1981). Bilingual DCT hypothesized that the two language codes have independent and additive effects on novel-word recall.

In a classic instructional experiment, Paivio and Lambert (1981) assigned each member of a group of French-English bilingual learners to one of three learning conditions: (1) writing the English word for each picture; (2) translating French words into English; or (3) copying the target English words. In an unannounced memory post-test, recall performance was best among the verbal-nonverbal dual-coding condition group (i.e., those who had been shown pictures), and worst among the copying group. Notably, when tests were administered in an *unannounced* manner, participants were only informed of one upcoming test, in order to preclude rehearsal. According to Jared et al. (2013), those findings support the bilingual DCT hypothesis.

DCT is also highly relevant in L2 Chinese learning and teaching; previous L2 Chinese research has investigated whether visual codes (i.e., character strings) should be presented along with audio codes like pronunciation or etymology narratives and/or additional visual codes (e.g., stroke animation or handwriting practice) (e.g., Cao et al., 2017; Kuo & Hooper, 2004; Wang, 2005). The findings are further discussed subsequently.

A brief review of Cognitive Load Theory and its relevance in L2 Chinese research

CLT was first developed in the 1980s to examine the relationship between cognitive architecture—which consists of working memory, long-term memory, and the relations between the two—and instructional design (e.g., Sweller & Levine, 1982; Sweller, 1988). More specifically, it aimed to explain "how the information processing load induced by learning tasks can affect students' ability to process new information and to construct knowledge in long-term memory" (Sweller et al., 2019, pp. 261–262). Notably, the learning tasks investigated in the 1980s were not specific to language acquisition, but included computer programming, general mathematics and geometry, among other subjects. The present section will briefly review the key concepts of CLT (i.e., cognitive load, instructional forms and effects, and the relation between CLT and self-regulated learning) based on recent work by Chen and Kalyuga (2020) and Sweller et al. (2019).

Cognitive load refers to the demand that performing a specific task imposes on a learner's cognitive system, and research has shown that excessive cognitive load can impede learning (Sweller, 1988). For this reason, an extensive body of research has examined how various instructional designs affect cognitive loads. For example, Chen and Kalyuga (2020) mentioned about the *working memory resource depletion effect* (meaning that working memory resources become depleted after a period of sustained cognitive exertion, resulting in a reduced capacity to commit further resources), and proposed that simply by increasing the length of the intervals between learning tasks in a series, there will be better learning effects than if the same tasks are performed in quicker succession. Interventions based on this principle are referred to as *spaced designs*. Another major finding of CLT research, often cited in proposals for L2 Chinese instructional designs, is the *split-attention effect* (meaning learners' attention is split when multiple sources of information are distributed in space or time) (e.g., Chung, 2008; Lee & Kalyuga, 2011). Due to this effect, Lee and Kalyuga (2011) recommended that instructional designs integrate multiple supplementary sources of information either spatially or temporally to remove or reduce split attention between characters and pinyin, which may enhance learning Chinese two-character words.

A recent extension of CLT connects it with self-regulated learning (Sweller et al., 2019), on the grounds that both theories involve individuals' monitoring and control of their learning processes, such as allocating cognitive resources, reducing cognitive load, and selecting among multiple activities within a learning task. Effective translation of this extended CLT framework into pedagogical practices, however, will require that language educators have a clear answer to the longstanding question of whether learning should be instructor-guided or student-initiated. In the specific context of L2 Chinese education research, this question was looked at by Kuo and Hooper (2004) and Shen (2004), among others. And there were mixed findings: for example, Kuo and Hooper (2004) found that student-initiated learning was more effective for high school students learning new words in L2 Chinese, whereas Shen (2004) observed that university L2 Chinese learners benefited more from instructor-guided new word learning.

Chinese and its writing system

As noted earlier, unlike with DCT, the development and validation of CLT was not specific to language-learning tasks. Thus, its application to instruction in L2 Chinese has had to be adjusted according to prevailing understandings of the unique properties of Mandarin and its writing system.

According to Perfetti's (2003) Universal Grammar of Reading theory, all written languages encode their corresponding spoken languages. Chinese is no exception, despite its orthography—which lacks the grapheme-phoneme correspondence observed in alphabetic languages—often being described as logographic. To be more precise, the Chinese writing system is *morphosyllabic*: with a character mapped onto a morpheme at the syllable level rather than at the phoneme level. Chinese texts consist of character strings with no spaces inserted, but previous eye-movement research has shown that reading in Chinese—whether as an L1 or an L2—proceeds on a whole-word basis, not character-by-character (for a review, see Li et al., 2014). Words in Chinese vary in the numbers of characters that comprise them: with 6% being single-character words, 72% two-character words, 12% three-character words, and 10% four-character words (Lexicon of Common Words in Contemporary Chinese Research Team, 2008). Yet despite the relative rarity of single-character words, Chinese reading research has predominantly focused on them. Chinese texts can also be presented in *pinyin* (Romanized script of Chinese characters based on their Mandarin pronunciations). To date, the optimal presentation and sequencing of characters, pinyin, and English equivalents in L2 Chinese education remains a topic of debate. Moreover, this is an important issue for both researchers and educators to consider against the COVID-19 backdrop, when online/blended multimedia instructional design involves sequencing language activities based on the inherent cognitive load of each activity type so that student performance and self-efficacy on high cognitive load tasks can be improved (Payne, 2020).

The present study

This study aimed at synthesizing empirical evidence pertaining to instructional design that bootstraps L2 Chinese word learning and clarifying such evidence's implications for researchers and practitioners seeking to use and promote best practices in L2 Chinese pedagogy. It is guided by two research questions (RQs):

RQ1: What are the trends in the selected studies in terms of guided theories, research designs, participant characteristics, L2 Chinese learning contexts, new-word learning conditions, and measurement tasks?

RQ2: Which learning conditions (e.g., single-coding versus dual-coding, simultaneous presentation of characters, pinyin, and English translation versus sequenced presentation, instructor-guided versus student-initiated) are most and least effective for L2 Chinese new-word learning?

Methods

Literature search

A literature search was conducted in May 2020 and proceeded in two steps. In step one, the first author manually screened three systematic reviews of prior research on L2 Chinese teaching and learning or reading conducted between 1976 and 2019 through searches in databases such as China National Knowledge Infrastructure/CNKI, LLBA, ERIC, PsycINFO, Google Scholar, and Web of Science (i.e., Ke, 2020; Li, 2020; Shen, 2013). In step two, given that step one included published articles only, the first author conducted a search of unpublished doctoral dissertations using the ProQuest Dissertation database, with all possible three-keyword combinations of terms from the following three sets: Chinese or Mandarin + second language or foreign language or bilingual or L2 + dual coding or cognitive load. The inclusion criteria for both published and unpublished studies were that they be written in English, include empirical data, and report on learning changes caused by interventions. Ultimately, 20 studies (17 published journal articles and three unpublished doctoral dissertations) produced between 2002 and 2017 were selected, of which one included three independent samples. The authors did not identify any study conducted in the 20th century, partly because cognition theories and their application did not focus on L2 learning during that period. Ultimately, the total number of independent samples was 22, and the grand total of participants was 1,220.

Coding

Coding was conducted by the first author. Its five major categories were: (1) research design (e.g., between- vs. within-subjects design; inclusion of pretests, immediate post-tests, and/or delayed post-tests); (2) participant characteristics (e.g., grade level, L1, or L2 Chinese learning experience levels); (3) L2 Chinese learning context (i.e., country/region; Chinese as a second language/CSL versus Chinese as a foreign language/CFL); (4) conditions of character instruction presentation (i.e., in-class versus out-of-class setting, inclusion of technological mediation, and length of instruction); and (5) L2 Chinese learning measurement tasks (e.g., radical-, character-, and word-level learning). In addition, the sampled studies' summaries of findings about effective learning modes were input manually, along with effect sizes, if available (e.g., Cohen's d, .40 being small, .70 being medium, and 1.00 being large; see Plonsky & Oswald, 2014). The complete coding (Appendix) is available at https://osf.io/sb92p/.

Findings

Trends in the selected studies

As to the theoretical frameworks adopted in the primary studies, nine out of the 22 independent samples were guided by DCT; four were guided by CLT; one combined DCT and CLT (i.e., Chen et al., 2014); six others adopted theories from Second Language Acquisition or Reading research (e.g., the design in Tsai et al., 2012 was guided by Gass & Mackey's, 2006 input-interaction-output hypothesis; and Perfetti's, 2007 lexical quality hypothesis was cited and discussed in Chang et al., 2015); and two were pedagogically motivated. The detailed coding can be found in the Appendix.

About half the sampled studies adopted a between-subjects design ($k = 13$); eight used a within-subjects design; and only one was mixed (i.e., Tsai et al., 2012). Nearly two-thirds of the samples ($k = 14$) adopted testing at all three possible time-points, i.e., used a pretest, an immediate post-test, and a delayed post-test; the rest only included immediate post-tests. The length of the delay varied widely, from as little as three minutes (Lu et al., 2013) to as much as two weeks (e.g., Chung, 2007). While most of the samples adopted short-term designs and made inferences based on behavioral post-test accuracy, one sample adopted a longitudinal design and tracked its participants' performance two years later (Chung, 2008). Another two gathered both behavioral and neurolinguistic data with physiological techniques: i.e., functional magnetic resonance imaging (fMRI) in the case of Cao et al. (2017), and event related potentials (ERPs) in the case of Chang et al. (2015).

Another noteworthy trend is that most of the participant samples ($k = 13$) were of university L2 Chinese learners; of the remaining nine, all were of fourth through ninth graders.

In addition, the vast majority of samples ($k = 19$) were collected in CFL settings, six in Australia and 13 in the United States. Each of the three others was collected in a different CSL setting: i.e., Hong Kong SAR in Sham (2002); Mainland China in Jin (2003), and Taiwan in Chen et al. (2014). To avoid any confounding effects of prior orthographic knowledge in Chinese, the selected studies primarily recruited participants with limited L2 Chinese-learning experience and English as their L1, the only exceptions being Chen et al. (2014) and Zhu and Hong (2005).

In the modes of learning of Chinese characters and words that the sampled studies included, there were notable variations. The number of learning conditions included in a single study ranged from two (e.g., visual and audio vs. audio only, in Chung, 2008) to six (e.g., character—pinyin—English cards; character—English—pinyin cards; pinyin—English—character cards; English—pinyin—character cards; character cards, pinyin cards, and English cards; and picture cards in Chung, 2007). The majority of instruction occurred in out-of-class settings ($k = 19$) and was mediated by various forms of technology ($k = 14$), including Flash, PowerPoint slides, Moodle, and researcher-adapted computer programs. Instruction without technological mediation was delivered via paper cards (Chung, 2002, 2007; Sham, 2002[1]) or during in-class meetings (e.g., Shen, 2004, 2010; Zhu & Hong, 2005).

Finally, there were also notable differences in how the selected studies measured changes in L2 Chinese word learning. Only four reported Cohen's *d* (i.e., small to medium in Chung, 2008; Kuo & Hooper, 2004; medium in Lee & Kalyuga, 2011; and small in Lu et al., 2013). In light of the wider pattern of investigations described earlier, it is perhaps not surprising that the majority of the studies ($k = 15$) measured gains in the learning of single-character words. The remaining seven samples all measured two-character word learning. Also, it should be noted that eight of the selected studies included one outcome only; that is, mapping orthographic forms either to meanings or to pronunciations. A larger number of samples ($k = 14$) examined multiple facets of L2 Chinese ability, such as lexical decision-making, self-rated character familiarity and/or writing characters, as well as mapping of orthography to meaning and/or pronunciation. The next section is therefore organized according to different L2 Chinese new-word learning measurement tasks, within two broad groups of studies: those devoted to character learning or single-character word learning ($k = 15$), and those on two-character word learning ($k = 7$).[2]

Effective instruction in L2 Chinese word learning

Single-character word learning

The findings of the selected studies that examined L2 single-character word learning can be further categorized into four themes: (1) whether dual coding is more effective than single coding; (2) which type of dual/single coding is more effective; (3) whether stroke order matters, and how to best present strokes at the sublexical level; and (4) whether writing or typing is superior to passive reception of multimedia presentations.

With very few exceptions (i.e., Sham, 2002), the selected studies reported that dual coding was more effective than single coding. For instance, Kuo and Hooper (2004) compared the various approaches to learning characters used by high school students, and found that dual coding—in this case, the simultaneous presentation of a character, its English translation, a relevant picture, and a verbal explanation of its etymology—was more effective than single coding. This was the case whether the latter consisted of verbal coding only (as mentioned earlier, but without the picture); visual coding only (as mentioned, but without the etymology); and translation only (just the character and its English translation). Chung (2008) observed more complex patterns. He first found that inexperienced seventh graders had better meaning recall in the dual-coded mode than in the single-coded (visual) mode, but that the effectiveness of these two formats was reversed when the skill being tested was pronunciation recall. However, when he tested the same learners again two years later, he found that they had benefited more from the dual-coded mode, regardless of whether meaning recall or pronunciation recall was being tested. As suggested by an anonymous reviewer, there might be other confounding factors due to the long-time lag (i.e., two years) in Chung (2008)'s study.

Notably, some studies disagreed with one another in their conclusions about which type of dual-coded mode was most effective. L. Wang and Blackwell (2015) compared two types of dual-coded character presentation about character etymology—i.e., animation and verbal narration vs. animation and on-screen texts—and found that the former was more effective for university-level L2 Chinese learners in a delayed post-test (two weeks after intervention). Y. Wang (2015) also compared the same two types of presentation with similar participants, but observed the opposite based on immediate post-test results. Both these studies included two types of characters: pictographs and ideographs. Chuang and Ku (2011) included pictographs only and did not find any significant difference between the same two types of dual-coded presentation in immediate and delayed posttests. In this regard, although the selected research generally concurred on the point that dual coding was more effective than single coding for L2 Chinese character learning in American university zero-beginners, its findings regarding which type of dual-coded presentation of characters was most effective were decidedly mixed, partly due to the various types of characters (e.g., pictographs and ideographs) and post-test administration (e.g., immediate and delayed posttests).

Less than one-fourth of the selected studies investigated the role of stroke presentation in L2 Chinese characters ($k = 5$). Jin (2003) found that instruction focusing on radicals was more beneficial than that focusing on stroke order or pinyin. However, a more recent study by Chen et al. (2014) reported that the mode in which strokes or radicals were presented mattered. The latter authors implemented two types of multimedia instructional presentations (radical-highlighting and stroke-pronunciation), each combined with one or the other of two types of practice (visual cue and voice cue) in a novice-level university course for L2 Chinese learners studying abroad in Taiwan. Their findings suggested that, of the four conditions, stroke-pronunciation with voice cues yielded the best learning results. This was consistent with the bilingual DCT according to which the utilization of two communication channels will lead to additive effects in L2 novel word learning (Paivio, 2010, 2014; Paivio & Lambert, 1981). Chen et al. (2014) also found that radical-highlighting, if used, should be paired with visual cues, because this might help novice learners strengthen their retrieval of previously learned radicals and characters.

As to how strokes should be presented, the findings were again mixed. Tsai et al. (2012) found that animation was more effective than static presentations at helping learners recall characters' meanings and pronunciations, analyze their internal structures, and write them. Lu et al. (2013, p. 4), on the other hand, claimed that their animation learning condition was not as effective as their "embodied animation" one, in which each Chinese character was presented "with a video that not only shows an animation of the character's etymological form changes but also human bodily movements, actions, or gestures that depict both the semantic meaning and written form of the character." Both these studies were conducted with university-level L2 Chinese learners at the novice or beginning level, and measured character recognition and production accuracy based on behavioral testing. Chang et al. (2015) compared the relative effects of character animation and static stroke presentation by administering two different behavioral-accuracy tasks (an old/new judgment task and a form-meaning matching task) and collecting neurolinguistic data (indexed by ERPs). They did not find any significant differences between these two learning approaches based on their behavioral data, but in the neurolinguistic data, they identified positive associations both between character animation and performance on the old/new judgment task, and between static stroke presentation and performance on the form-meaning matching task. In other words, it seemed that character animation led to greater retention of orthographic forms, whereas static stroke presentation was more beneficial to form-meaning mapping.

Similarly, the effect of writing on L2 Chinese-character learning varied according to which learning outcomes were under examination. For example, Xu et al. (2013) compared three ways of learning L2 Chinese characters based on behavioral-accuracy data, and concluded that (1) both writing and character animation facilitated character recognition; (2) writing also, unsurprisingly, predicted learners' ability to produce characters through writing; and (3) reading was most beneficial to character sound-meaning mapping. Cao et al. (2017) compared a handwriting condition against two other learning conditions, phonological repetition and passive viewing, based on both behavioral-accuracy and neurolinguistic/fMRI data. They included two behavioral measures only (writing characters, and character meaning/sound mapping). First, they did not detect any significant difference in behavioral-accuracy rates across the three learning conditions. Second, they found that learning in the handwriting condition elicited a greater activation in the left temporal pole than phonological learning did, and that handwriting and passive viewing led to a greater activation than phonological learning did at the left MFG: a region considered more specific to Chinese reading than to alphabetic reading.

To sum up, the sampled evidence regarding L2 Chinese single-character word learning seemed to indicate that "the more the merrier," that is, dual-coded modes (verbal plus visual) were more effective than single-coded ones (verbal or visual only). However, no conclusion can be drawn as to which exact type of dual coding (e.g., animation plus audio narration of character etymology versus animation plus text narration) is the most effective. In addition, it was generally agreed across the sampled studies that the presentation of stroke order matters. Emerging neurolinguistic evidence suggests that animated vs. static presentations of stroke order play fundamentally different roles: with the former enhancing learners' orthographic representations, and the latter contributing to form-meaning mapping. Finally, when compared against passive viewing of multimedia presentations, handwriting practice was found to be beneficial not only for producing characters but also for character recognition and orthography-phonology mapping.

Two-character word learning

Some of the selected studies that examined L2 two-character word learning also compared the effects of single-coded vs. dual-coded learning conditions (i.e., Shen, 2010; Zhu & Hong, 2005). Others focused on different questions, namely (1) how characters, pinyin, and English translation should be presented and sequenced to optimally promote word retention (i.e., Chung, 2002; Lee & Kalyuga, 2011); (2) whether spaces should be added between characters (Sham, 2002); and (3) whether new-word learning should be instructor guided or student initiated (Shen, 2004).

In contrast to the pattern observed in studies that focused on learning outcomes at the character level, Zhu and Hong's (2005) learning experiment with American first-year L2 Chinese university students reported that, when it came to retention of both single- and two-character words—as measured by a posttest that asked participants to write characters based on their English translations—a single-coded method (characters displayed with pronunciation only) was more effective than a dual-coded one (characters displayed with both pronunciation and stroke animation). Shen (2010), however, contended that such learning effects depend on whether the target word is concrete or abstract. She compared the relative effects of a single-coded instructional condition (verbal coding only) and a dual-coded one (verbal and imagery coding), via a multiple-choice test administered twice (i.e., immediately after and one day after instruction), that asked the participants to select orthographic words that matched English translations. This revealed that the verbal-coding-only instructional condition was associated with greater retention of concrete words, whereas the verbal-plus-imagery method was more effective for the retention of abstract ones.

Lee and Kalyuga (2011) looked at the simultaneous presentation of characters, pinyin, and English translations. They challenged the traditional manner of doing this, i.e., horizontally, and compared the effects of horizontal and vertical presentations via a learning experiment with high school L2 Chinese learners. They found that a vertical presentation—specifically, one following the order of character, pinyin, and English equivalent—had the greatest learning benefits, as measured by a word-recognition posttest. The same study posited that the vertical presentation was more advantageous because it eliminated split attention. Chung (2002), however, studied a similar population of learners and found that sequential rather than simultaneous presentation of characters, pinyin, and English meanings was more effective. Specifically, he recommended that a Chinese character be presented for five seconds before its pinyin and English translation appear. Subsequently, Chung (2007) concluded that the presentation of the Chinese character first and then its pinyin and color-coded English translation was more effective than a non-color-coded equivalent. However, Chung did not compare vertical layouts against horizontal ones in either of these studies.

Sham (2002) investigated the effects of inserting vs. not inserting spaces between two-character words, under two L2 Chinese word-learning conditions: two-character words presented with their English translations, and two-character words presented with relevant pictures. The learning experiment was carried out among sixth graders who were novice-level L2 Chinese learners. A meaning-to-word form mapping posttest revealed that inserting space boosted these children's learning results, regardless of learning condition.

The studies reviewed here were mostly carried out as supplementary learning sessions designed by researchers or instructors, conducted outside of regular class hours. Shen's (2004) study, carried out in a university classroom, compared the effectiveness of three encoding strategies: instructor-guided elaboration, student self-generated elaboration, and rote memorization. It yielded two major findings: (1) that instructor-guided and student self-generated elaboration were more effective than rote memorization when it came to recalling both the sounds and the meanings of two-character words; and (2) that instructor-guided elaboration was significantly more effective than student self-generated elaboration in the short term (i.e., at the time of the immediate posttest), but that this difference had largely disappeared by two days later (i.e., at the time of the delayed posttest). On this basis, Shen posited that instructor-guided and student self-generated elaboration both required deep processing, whereas rote memorization involved shallow processing only.

Discussion

In answer to this study's first RQ, the selected studies were mainly conducted in L1 English-speaking university environments, with L2 Chinese learners at the novice level, and adopted between subjects' pre- and posttest designs that compared the participants' recall performance of word meaning and pronunciation under single-coded or dual-coded instructional conditions. Also, more than half the samples (14 out of 22) were guided by DLT or CLT. In response to RQ2, the effectiveness of the focal instructional designs was found to be subject to the influence of several factors, notably including the number of characters per word, word concreteness versus abstraction, and learner expertise (e.g., Chung, 2008). Taken together, the sampled evidence seems to point to the following three broad conclusions. First, for single-character word learning, dual coding is superior to single coding, but no conclusion can be drawn regarding which type of dual-coded instructional condition is most effective. Second, for two-character word learning, single-coded instruction is more effective for concrete words, while dual-coded instruction is more effective for abstract ones; and sequential presentation of a word for a short period, followed by its pinyin and English equivalent, is recommended—though if characters, pinyin, and English translation are all presented simultaneously, a vertical layout is superior to a horizontal one. Third, there is insufficient evidence to determine whether new-word learning should be instructor-guided or student-initiated.

These findings are partially consistent with the assumptions of (bilingual) DCT and CLT. DCT's hypothesis that dual coding should be superior to single coding, for instance, was found to be broadly true of L2 Chinese novel word learning. But its effectiveness depends on the number of characters in the target new word and whether the word is concrete or abstract. Similarly, the evidence reviewed in this synthesis partially corroborates CLT's predictions regarding the working memory resource depletion and split-attention effects, yet it casts doubt on the connection between CLT and learner self-regulation. Specifically, this was manifested in the contrast between the findings reported by Kuo and Hooper (2004) and those reported by Shen (2004): with the former scholars suggesting that high school L2 Chinese learners who generated their own mnemonics achieved higher performance on a single-character, word-recall posttest, and the latter finding that student self-generated elaboration was *less* effective for two-character, new-word learning than instructor-guided elaboration, at least in the short term. In general, DCT and CLT provide important guidance for effective L2 Chinese multimedia vocabulary instructional design.

Interpretation of these findings should consider the methodologies of the studies that produced them, including measurement effects, item/word characteristics and learner characteristics. First, all the selected studies focused on isolated-word learning, and most of them measured word acquisition via behavioral perception tasks that asked the participants to map orthographic forms onto meanings or pronunciations. Such measurement can be limited, in that it does not tap into vocabulary depth knowledge like the ability to associate a newly learned word with its synonyms or antonyms, to use it in different contexts appropriately, and to produce it at the sentence or discourse level (see also Zhang et al., 2019). Another limitation could be that behavioral paper-and-pencil tests lack the sensitivity to capture changes resulting from interventions. For example, both Cao et al. (2017) and Chang et al. (2015) found inconsistencies between their own behavioral testing and physiological results (i.e., no significant interventional effect was found in the behavioral data; yet there were significant positive interventional effects based on the physiological evidence). More studies using physiological techniques such as fMRI, ERPs, and eye tracking are therefore clearly needed. For example, while Lee and Kalyuga's (2011) study concluded that a vertical layout of characters, pinyin, and English translation was better for word retention than a horizontal one when these three elements were shown simultaneously, a recent eye-movement study by He (2020) reported that a more complex "adjacency" layout (with English translation next to the Chinese characters and pinyin below the Chinese characters), not precisely either vertical or horizontal, might be more effective than either.

A second critical issue involves item characteristics. As noted, the selected studies' conclusions about effective instructional design varied sharply depending on the newly learned words' characteristics. Yet none of these studies included both word length and word concreteness in their instructional designs.

Third, only one selected study (i.e., Chung, 2008) tracked learners' long-term development. It found that the relative effects of single-coded and dual-coded instruction might be subject to learners' L2 Chinese expertise or proficiency level. More research clearly needs to track or compare single-coded and dual-coded instructional conditions among L2 Chinese learners of diverse proficiency levels.

A final puzzle will be whether L2 Chinese word learning should be instructor-guided or student-generated, as we have found contrasting conclusions in the selected studies (i.e., Kuo & Hooper, 2004; Shen, 2004). Perhaps important implications can be drawn from a recent study of L2 Chinese-character learning by Xu and Padilla (2013), who found that a teacher-cued method and familiar student independent work were more effective than a teacher-instructed method and unfamiliar student independent work.

Conclusions and implications

This study synthesized the evidence from 20 studies conducted between 2002 and 2017 that yielded a total of 22 independent samples ($N=1,220$), with the aim of identifying patterns in recent research on single-coded and dual-coded word learning within L2 Chinese instruction, and based on the results, providing evidence-based recommendations for best practices. Based on its findings, future L2 Chinese instruction designers should consider the following: (1) For single-character word learning, a dual-coded mode is more effective than a single-coded mode, yet it is unclear which dual-coded mode is superior. (2) For two-character word learning, a single-coded mode is more effective for learning concrete words, whereas a dual-coded one is more effective for abstract word learning. (3) The temporal and spatial presentation of characters, pinyin, and English translation also matters. It is recommended that characters be presented for a short period before pinyin and English prompts, but if characters, pinyin, and English must be presented simultaneously, a vertical layout is probably superior to a horizontal one. (4) Finally, no conclusions can yet be drawn as to whether instructor-guided or student-initiated learning is more effective.

It should be noted that the scope of this synthesis was limited by the non-inclusion of articles published in Chinese or unpublished conference papers. Future empirical research on this topic should consider the relevancy of DCT, CLT, and other theories across disciplines (e.g., the input-interaction-output hypothesis in Second Language Acquisition research, Gass & Mackey, 2006; and the Lexical Quality Hypothesis in reading science, Perfetti, 2007); include a wide range of word characteristics (e.g., ideographs versus pictographs, single-character words versus two/multi-character words, abstract, and concrete words); gather more longitudinal data; recruit L2 Chinese learners from a wider range of L1 backgrounds and Chinese proficiency levels; and utilize cutting-edge physiological techniques such as fMRI, ERP, and eye tracking.

Notes

1 Three independent samples were used in Sham's (2002) dissertation, which we refer to as Sham (2002a), Sham (2002b), and Sham (2002c) in the coding scheme available here: https://osf.io/sb92p/.
2 Both Chung (2007) and Zhu and Hong (2005) mixed single-character and two-character words in their learning sessions and posttests.

References

*indicates a study selected for review.

Cao, F., Sussman, B. L., Rios, V., Yan, X., Wang, Z., Spray, G. J., & Mack, R. M. (2017). Different mechanisms in learning different second languages: Evidence from English speakers learning Chinese and Spanish. *NeuroImage*, *148*, 284–295. doi:10.1016/j.neuroimage.2017.01.042

Chang, L. Y., Stafura, J. Z., Rickles, B., Chen, H. C., & Perfetti, C. A. (2015). Incremental learning of Chinese orthography: ERP indicators of animated and static stroke displays on character form and meaning acquisition. *Journal of Neurolinguistics*, *33*, 78–95. doi:10.1016/j.jneuroling.2014.09.001

Chen, M. P., Wang, L. C., Chen, H. J., & Chen, Y. C. (2014). Effects of the type of multimedia strategy on learning Chinese characters for non-native novices. *Computers & Education*, *70*, 41–52. doi:10.1016/j.compedu.2013.07.042

Chen, O., & Kalyuga, S. (2020). Cognitive load theory, spacing effect, and working memory resources depletion: Implications for instructional design. In *Form, function, and style in instructional design: Emerging research and opportunities* (pp. 1–26). IGI Global.

Chuang, H. Y., & Ku, H. Y. (2011). The effect of computer-based multimedia instruction with Chinese character recognition. *Educational Media International*, *48*(1), 27–41. doi: 10.1080/09523987.2011.549676

Chung, K. K. (2002). Effective use of Hanyu Pinyin and English translations as extra stimulus prompts on learning of Chinese characters. *Educational Psychology*, *22*(2), 149–164. doi:10.1080/01443410120115238

Chung, K. K. (2007). Presentation factors in the learning of Chinese characters: The order and position of Hanyu pinyin and English translations. *Educational Psychology*, *27*(1), 1–20. doi:10.1080/01443410601061306

Chung, K. K. (2008). What effect do mixed sensory mode instructional formats have on both novice and experienced learners of Chinese characters? *Learning and Instruction*, *18*(1), 96–108. doi:10.1016/j.learninstruc.2007.01.001

Gass, S. M., & Mackey, A. (2006). Input, interaction and output: An overview. *AILA Review*, *19*(1), 3–17. doi:10.1075/aila.19.03gas

He, X. (2020). *Working memory, presentation formats and learning L2 Chinese vocabulary: An eye-tracking study*. Paper accepted to American Association for Applied Linguistics 2020 Conference, Denver, Colorado, United States.

Jared, D., Poh, R. P. Y., & Paivio, A. (2013). L1 and L2 picture naming in Mandarin—English bilinguals: A test of bilingual dual coding theory. *Bilingualism: Language and Cognition*, *16*(2), 383–396. doi:10.1017/S1366728912000685

Jin, H. G. (2003). Empirical evidence on character recognition in multimedia Chinese tasks. *Concentric: Studies in Linguistics*, *29*(2), 36–58.

Ke, S. (2020). Review of research on learning and instruction with specific reference to reading Chinese as an additional language (1976–2018). In Y. Gong & C. Lai (Eds.), *The teaching and learning of Chinese as a second or foreign language (CSL/CFL): The current situation and future directions*. Special Issue in *Frontiers of Education in China*, *15*(1), 14–38. doi:10.1007/s11516-020-0002-z

Kuo, M. L. A., & Hooper, S. (2004). The effects of visual and verbal coding mnemonics on learning Chinese characters in computer-based instruction. *Educational Technology Research and Development*, *52*(3), 23–34. doi:10.1007/BF02504673

Lee, C. H., & Kalyuga, S. (2011). Effectiveness of on-screen pinyin in learning Chinese: An expertise reversal for multimedia redundancy effect. *Computers in Human Behavior*, *27*(1), 11–15. doi: 10.1016/j.chb.2010.05.005

Lexicon of Common Words in Contemporary Chinese Research Team. (2008). *Lexicon of common words in contemporary Chinese* (in Chinese). The Commercial Press.

Li, M. (2020). A systematic review of the research on Chinese character teaching and learning. *Frontiers of Education in China*, *15*(1), 39–72. doi:10.1007/s11516-020-0003-y

Li, X. S., Bicknell, K., Liu, P. P., Wei, W., & Rayner, K. (2014). Reading is fundamentally similar across disparate writing systems: A systematic characterization of how words and characters influence eye movements in Chinese reading. *Journal of Experimental Psychology: General*, *143*, 895–913. doi:10.1037/a0033580

Lu, M. T. P., Hallman Jr, G. L., & Black, J. B. (2013). Chinese character learning: Using embodied animations in initial stages. *Journal of Technology and Chinese Language Teaching*, *4*(2), 1–24.

Paivio, A. (1971). *Imagery and verbal processes*. Holt, Rinehart, and Winston (Reprinted 1979; Lawrence Erlbaum Associates).

Paivio, A. (2007). *Mind and its evolution: A Dual Coding theoretical approach*. Lawrence Erlbaum.

Paivio, A. (2010). Dual coding theory and the mental lexicon. *The Mental Lexicon*, *5*, 205–230. doi:10.1075/ml.5.2.04pai

Paivio, A. (2014). Bilingual dual coding theory and memory. In R. R. Heredia & J. Altarriba (Eds.), *Foundations of bilingual memory* (pp. 41–62). Springer. doi:10.1007/978-1-4614-9218-4_3

Paivio, A., & Lambert, W. (1981). Dual coding and bilingual memory. *Journal of Verbal Learning and Verbal Behavior*, *20*, 532–539. doi:10.1016/S0022-5371(81)90156-0

Payne, J. S. (2020). Developing L2 productive language skills online and the strategic use of instructional tools. *Foreign Language Annals*. https://doi.org/10.1111/flan.12457

Perfetti, C. A. (2003). The universal grammar of reading. *Scientific Studies of Reading*, *7*(1), 3–24. doi:10.1207/S1532799XSSR0701_02

Perfetti, C. A. (2007). Reading ability: Lexical quality to comprehension. *Scientific Studies of Reading*, *11*(4), 357–383. doi:10.1080/10888430701530730

Plonsky, L., & Oswald, F. L. (2014). How big is "big"? Interpreting effect sizes in L2 research. *Language Learning, 64*(4), 878–912. doi:10.1111/lang.12079

Sadoski, M. (2005). A dual coding view of vocabulary learning. *Reading & Writing Quarterly: Overcoming Learning Difficulties, 21*(3), 221–238. doi:10.1080/10573560590949359

Sadoski, M., & Paivio, A. (2007). Toward a unified theory of reading. *Scientific Studies of Reading, 11*(4), 337–356. doi:10.1080/10888430701530714

Sham, D. P. L. (2002). *A dual-coding model of processing Chinese as a second language: A cognitive-load approach* (Unpublished doctoral dissertation). University of New South Wales.

Shen, H. H. (2004). Level of cognitive processing: Effects on character learning among non-native learners of Chinese as a foreign language. *Language and Education, 18*(2), 167–182. doi:10.1080/09500780408666873

Shen, H. H. (2010). Imagery and verbal coding approaches in Chinese vocabulary instruction. *Language Teaching Research, 14*(4), 485–499. doi:10.1177/1362168810375370

Shen, H. H. (2013). Chinese L2 literacy development: Cognitive characteristics, learning strategies, and pedagogical interventions. *Language and Linguistics Compass, 7*(7), 371–387. doi:10.1177/1362168810375370

Sweller, J. (1988). Cognitive load during problem solving: Effects on learning. *Cognitive Science, 12*(2), 257–285. doi:10.1016/0364-0213(88)90023-7

Sweller, J., & Levine, M. (1982). Effects of goal specificity on means—ends analysis and learning. *Journal of Experimental Psychology: Learning, Memory, and Cognition, 8*(5), 463–474. doi:10.1037/0278-7393.8.5.463

Sweller, J., van Merriënboer, J. J., & Paas, F. (2019). Cognitive architecture and instructional design: 20 years later. *Educational Psychology Review, 31*, 261–292. doi:10.1007/s10648-019-09465-5

Tsai, C. H., Kuo, C. H., Horng, W. B., & Chen, C. W. (2012). Effects on learning logographic character formation in computer-assisted handwriting instruction. *Language Learning & Technology, 16*(1), 110–130. doi:10125/44277

Wang, L. (2005). *The impact of multimedia on Chinese learners' recognition of characters: A quantitative and qualitative study* (Unpublished doctoral dissertation). Purdue University.

Wang, L., & Blackwell, A. A. (2015). Effects of dual coded multimedia instruction employing image morphing on learning a logographic language. *Journal of Educational Multimedia and Hypermedia, 24*(3), 281–313.

Wang, Y. (2015). *Applying the modality principle and cognitive load theory to facilitate Chinese character learning via multimedia instruction* (Unpublished doctoral dissertation). Texas Tech University.

Xu, Y., Chang, L. Y., Zhang, J., & Perfetti, C. A. (2013). Reading, writing, and animation in character learning in Chinese as a foreign language. *Foreign Language Annals, 46*(3), 423–444. doi:10.1111/flan.12040

Xu, X., & Padilla, A. M. (2013). Using meaningful interpretation and chunking to enhance memory: The case of Chinese character learning. *Foreign Language Annals, 46*(3), 402–422. doi:10.1111/flan.12039

Zhang, D., Lin, C. H., Zhang, Y., & Choi, Y. (2019). Pinyin or no pinyin: Does access to word pronunciation matter in the assessment of Chinese learners' vocabulary knowledge? *The Language Learning Journal, 47*(3), 344–353. doi:10.1080/09571736.2017.1289237

Zhu, Y., & Hong, W. (2005). Effects of digital voiced pronunciation and stroke sequence animation on character memorization of CFL learners. *Journal of the Chinese Language Teachers Association, 40*, 49–70.

3 Impact of typing vs handwriting on CFL students' character learning

Liu Li

Introduction

Literacy skills in learning Chinese as a Foreign Language (CFL) have been among the most difficult challenges for learners whose first language is based on alphabetic letters. Traditionally, learning Chinese characters involves repeated practice of writing characters stroke by stroke with a pen. With the development of technology, various electronic devices started to take over the role of pen and paper in work and daily life. This change may have a profound impact on CFL learners' literacy development because the input system in most of the electronic devices is based on pinyin, which is alphabetic and drastically different from the traditional stroke-by-stroke handwriting mode.

Some teachers fear, based on their intuition, that the use of electronic devices might be detrimental. They believe such devices actually inhibit or prevent learners from developing their Chinese literacy skills. Some researchers argue that students need to experience the stroke-by-stroke formation of the characters in their fingertips in order to instill the process into their brains (e.g., Tan et al., 2013). Others remain skeptical of this contention because most Chinese learners have already been actively using various electronic devices like computers, tablets, and smartphones, to assist their Chinese reading and writing. These researchers believe that incorporating electronic devices into teaching Chinese can make students feel more at ease and comfortable in reading and writing. Nevertheless, little research exists that investigates this unsolved issue of how different writing modes (typing through electronic devices versus handwriting with a pen) impact students' literacy development. It is necessary to identify which mode of writing is better for the CFL learners' literacy development. The goal of this study, therefore, is to explore the impact of these two writing modes on one important aspect of CFL students' literacy development: reading and writing characters.

Literature review

This section first discusses the complexity of the Chinese orthographic system and how the computer keyboard allows pinyin to become typed characters. Next,

DOI: 10.4324/9781003029038-5

I will discuss several studies about the Chinese orthographic system from the perspective of native speakers. Finally, I will examine studies on CFL learners' character acquisition.

Chinese orthography

The languages of the world are represented by a variety of writing systems that we call "orthographies." Orthographies are the written symbols to represent spoken languages. In other words, an orthography of a certain language consists of the written symbols to turn its spoken language into a written one. Orthographies differ in the size of the sound unit represented by each symbol. For example, in alphabetic orthographies, like English, each symbol represents an individual sound called a phoneme. For example, the /g/ sound in "good" is one phoneme. In non-alphabetic orthographies, such as Chinese, the symbol represents a larger sound unit, like a syllable. For example, "good" in Chinese is a syllable pronounced as "hǎo." and is represented by the orthographic symbol "好." Such orthographic symbols are called Chinese characters.

The Chinese script is often referred to as a pictographic language because people think that the characters are pictures of the words they represent. However, that is a misconception. In fact, very few Chinese characters are actually pictures of the words they represent. Many scholars agree that Chinese writing is logographic, comprising graphemes, the basic graphic units corresponding to the smallest segments of speech in writing, to simultaneously encode the sounds and meaning at the syllable level (Coulmas, 1991; DeFrancis, 2002; Hansell, 2002; Shu & Anderson, 1999; Sun, 2006).

Although all orthographies represent spoken language with written symbols, the portion of spoken language that is coded and the consistency of the mappings between sounds and symbols differ across orthographies. Approximately 80 to 90% of Chinese characters also contain what is called a phonetic radical (DeFrancis, 2002). A phonetic radical is just one part of the character that provides some clue as to how to pronounce the character, but the clue is not necessarily reliable (Sun, 2006).

Written Chinese as a logographic system was developed more than 3,000 years ago. Historically, Chinese students have learned to read and write by learning to associate the visuographic properties of Chinese characters with lexical meaning, typically through handwriting. For Chinese learners, literacy acquisition begins with a demanding visuospatial analysis of characters' graphic forms, composed of strokes and sub-character components that are packed into a square (Leong, 2012; Perfetti, 1985; Perfetti et al., 2005), followed by rote memory of arduous lexical mappings of orthography to phonology, orthography to meaning, and phonology to meaning (Siok et al., 2004; Perfetti et al., 1992). The traditional way to facilitate the development of these mappings is through handwriting, which requires students to repeatedly copy single characters to help them to interpret the visuo-orthographic mapping.

Impact of typing vs writing on Chinese literacy development

Learning to read and write in Chinese in the information age is challenging. Electronic forms of communication via computers, tablets, smartphones, and other devices make information accessible to everyone with internet access, thus enabling education to go beyond pencil and paper to digital media. In recent years, more students of Chinese have learned to use electronic communication devices based on the pinyin input method, which associates phonemes and alphabetic letters with characters. Increasing reliance on electronic modes over handwriting for communications may impact students' literacy skill acquisition, because typing in Chinese is vastly different from typing in English. The input method for English words is straightforward: pronouncing words silently and mapping sounds onto letters, choosing letters on the keyboard, and viewing them on the monitor simultaneously. This method connects phonological and visuographic properties of words and may enhance knowledge of letter-sound correspondences. Written Chinese presents a different case. Its logographic nature makes it difficult to adopt an input method that relies on its orthographic structure (Mackay, 2001).

Most popular Chinese input systems in electronic devices require users to type the phonetic letters of the pinyin system for each character. Pinyin is the short form for Hanyu pinyin (汉语拼音) and is the official Romanization system in the People's Republic of China. It is also the most popular Romanization system of Chinese outside of China, widely taught in schools and used in publications (Chen, 1999). Typing Chinese on electronic devices requires very little training and practice. The pinyin method allows users to input a character (e.g., 梨, pronounced /li/, meaning "pear") by typing its pinyin (li) and then select the appropriate character from a list of characters sharing this pinyin (e.g., 里利力利梨立例丽荔理离礼).

There have been studies on the impact of the input system on the literacy skills in Chinese as a first language. Some studies have found that if students use the pinyin input method early and frequently, particularly before reading skills have been sufficiently acquired, their literacy development could be slowed down (Gabrieli, 2009; Price & Mechelli, 2005; Goswami, 2011; Wolf & Barzillai, 2009; Peterson & Pennington, 2012; Perfetti, 1997). Some researchers (Tan et al., 2013) claim that with pinyin input technique, users type alphabetic letters instead of writing characters' components, such as strokes, components, or radicals, and thus visuospatial properties of characters indispensable to Chinese literacy development are not involved during the typing process. Therefore, they believe, typing with pinyin may hinder the typical reading development processes that start with visuographic analysis of written characters, and then are enhanced by handwriting. In their study, Tan et al. (2013) tested character reading ability and pinyin use by primary school students in three Chinese cities: Beijing (n = 466), Guangzhou (n = 477), and Jining (n = 4,908). The purpose of the test was to find the students with severe reading difficulty, which was defined as those who were normal in nonverbal IQ but two grades (i.e., two years) behind in character-reading achievement. They found that the overall incidence rate of severe reading difficulty appears to be much higher than ever reported on reading in Chinese. They also found that students' reading scores were significantly negatively correlated with their use of the pinyin input method, suggesting that pinyin typing on electronic devices slows down students' reading development. They explained that when students use pinyin to key in letters, their spelling no longer depends on reproducing the visuographic properties of characters that are indispensable to Chinese reading, and thus typing in pinyin may conflict with the traditional learning processes for written Chinese. They concluded the benefits of communicating digitally may come with a cost in proficient learning of written Chinese.

Literacy development among CFL students

Most CFL learners whose first language is English consider learning Chinese writing as the most challenging part of learning Chinese. This is due to the dramatic difference between English and Chinese orthographies. Chinese characters are not transparent compared with alphabetic writing systems such as English. Many CFL Chinese learners view Chinese characters as simply pictographs or ideographs, which they think requires a huge amount of rote memorization. Because learning to read and write Chinese characters are among the biggest obstacles for Chinese learners in the United States, most beginning-level learners often do not go beyond the introductory level (Xu & Jen, 2005). This stern reality makes teaching Chinese characters a core task of Chinese literacy instruction. The difficulty of learning Chinese characters is reflected in the early Chinese literacy acquisition research in the United States. Those early studies debated whether or not teachers should teach Chinese characters to beginning-level learners at all (Chin, 1973). While researchers in the 1970s focused on finding rationales to teach Chinese characters to beginning-level learners, later studies on Chinese literacy acquisition progressed further to investigate the best approaches and methods of teaching characters to learners. During the 1990s, Chinese literacy research shifted to character recognition and the effectiveness of teaching various character learning strategies (Ke, 1998; Shen, 2005). In these studies, experiments were conducted on Chinese learners to identify which character learning strategies they were using. These researchers concluded that learners who utilized character learning strategies performed better in character recognition tests as well. Their results provided pedagogical tools to Chinese teachers to teach Chinese characters. However, a limitation of these studies is that they did not examine the use of electronic technology in Chinese literacy acquisition, possibly because typing Chinese with electronic devices was not yet common among learners at that time. Currently, in addition to these questions, Chinese teachers also debate about how much time should be spent on teaching the Chinese writing system to learners in their curriculum.

In the field of second/foreign language acquisition in general, most studies on using electronic devices deal primarily with the literacy skills in English as a second language or other commonly taught languages based on the Roman alphabet such as Spanish, French, and German (Serrano & Howard, 2007; Thorson, 2000;

Way et al., 2000). Various aspects of literacy skills in Chinese with electronic devices, unlike in English and other Romance languages that have been widely studied, have not been widely addressed for the Chinese language learners. For many CFL learners, like the learners of alphabetic languages, electronic devices have become an indispensable part of their learning. More urgently, the use of electronic devices has become a necessity during global emergencies, such as the outbreak of the pandemic in 2020. However, few studies have investigated the use of computer technology in Chinese literacy acquisition. Among these scant studies, Xu and Jen (2005) compared computer software technologies to those of handwriting on paper in teaching Chinese writing. Despite the differences between computer typing and handwriting, they treated the two sets of writing scores from e-learning and paper-based writing as the same. They found that learners preferred to use computers instead of handwriting. Furthermore, they claimed that the computer input method developed by them helped learners produce more accurate sentences.

A study conducted by Kang (2011) compared two writing modes (typing vs. handwriting) of beginning-level and intermediate-level Chinese learners, investigating how they develop Chinese writing by analyzing their writing errors. This study used methods that combined qualitative and quantitative approaches to examine participants' Chinese writing. The researchers conducted surveys and interviews to examine participants' views of Chinese writing and their attitudes toward computer-based and paper-based writing. Individual writing sessions were arranged with participants to analyze their writing process. Their paper-based writings were recorded using the Smartpen, which is a pen-movement tracking device. Their computer-based Chinese writing was recorded by a computer screen capture program. Two native Chinese teaching assistants graded participants' writing using a 10-point scale to examine their writing with respect to clarity (in terms of character, vocabulary, and grammar error) and organization (in terms of style of writing and use of linking words). The survey data revealed that participants regarded Chinese writing as "handwriting of Chinese characters." They thought that they would write Chinese better with computer typing because of the complexity involved in writing Chinese characters stroke by stroke with a pen. Different from participants' perceptions on computer-based writing, paired t-test results of intermediate-level participants' writings indicated that they wrote Chinese essays better with paper-based writing in terms of clarity and organization. However, typing helped participants produce fewer character errors. When participants wrote unfamiliar genres of writing, there was no difference between computer-based and paper-based writing. In addition, the analysis of the Chinese character writing process indicated that there was a correlation between following correct stroke-sequences and producing correct characters. By analyzing character errors and stroke-sequence errors, the author identified three developmental stages of Chinese character writing: pinyin writing, acquisition of stroke-shapes and rules of compound characters, and matching pronunciations with characters. This groundbreaking study demonstrates that typing with computers allows Chinese learners to produce correct characters.

A study by Zhu et al. (2016) reported the performance and attainment of 32 students from overseas studying elementary Chinese as a foreign language (CFL) in a Chinese university. With an AB-BA design, they were asked to use two forms of writing media to present two essays: one a word-processed essay entitled "My Favorite Female" and the other a conventional hand-written essay entitled "My Favorite Male." The essays were graded by experienced Chinese language experts. Questionnaires and interviews were conducted to collect learners' opinions on each mode of writing. Inferential statistics showed that the students performed significantly better when using a word processor, and they thought that completing writing tasks using pencil-and-paper and word processors were drastically different. Most of them felt that their writing was more professional when produced on a word processor. A small number of students considered handwriting to be beautiful and artistic. Most of the students preferred the convenience of writing electronically, because using a computer could help them write more characters correctly. In conclusion, the study showed that word processors are the preferred writing medium for CFL learners at the beginning level.

Lyu et al. (2021) published a synthesis review on 27 empirical studies comparing the effects of handwriting versus typing in Chinese. They found that typing has a greater effect on Chinese learners' phonology recognition and phonology-orthography mapping than handwriting, and this advantage was more salient in Chinese than in English. They also found that handwriting had positive effects on Chinese learners' orthography recognition and orthography-semantic mapping at both the character and lexical levels. However, the effects of typing on Chinese writing performance were mixed. The findings suggest that the effects of typing and handwriting might manifest differently in English and Chinese. At the end of the review, the authors called for differential theorization of the cognitive impact of typing on English and Chinese language processing. They claimed that such a comparative model would provide nuanced insights into the impact of these two modes of writing on language learning and performance.

Despite these studies, there is still inadequate research that compares students' literacy development by means of electronic devices versus by means of handwriting on paper. Researchers who study different writing modes for Chinese learners have not paid enough attention to the difficulties involved with learning Chinese literacy through electronic devices. Teachers and researchers have not developed a trajectory indicating when learners should start using electronic devices for Chinese reading and writing, nor do they know how the learners feel about using electronic devices to practice their characters. In addition to learning about reading and writing strategies by student observation, researchers and teachers should learn more about how students view Chinese literacy, and how they switch between the pinyin input system and paper-based learning. This will enable researchers and teachers to understand more about learners' literacy development in this new era of information and technology, and thus be able to design appropriate techniques for teaching Chinese literacy. It is essential, therefore, to study the complex processes of Chinese learners' literacy development through the pinyin input system and compare it with paper-based writing.

Research questions

To investigate the impact of Chinese learners' input system on literacy development, this study aims to answer the following research questions:

1. Is there any difference between the typing group and the handwriting group on the scores of quizzes to read characters at the beginning and intermediate level?
2. Is there any difference between the typing group and the handwriting group on the scores of quizzes to produce characters at the beginning and intermediate level?
3. How much time does each group spend on studying Chinese after class?
4. What are the learners' views on different writing modes: typing, handwriting, and a combination of both, after a semester's study?

The findings from the first two research questions will aid in determining whether the use of different modes of Chinese writing by learners at the two different levels, beginning and intermediate, will result in any difference in recognizing and producing Chinese characters. The results will enable researchers to develop suitable teaching materials and approaches to meet the learners' needs. The findings from the third and fourth questions can provide more information for researchers on students' learning activities and attitudes when comparing writing with the pinyin input system with writing with a pen.

Methodology

The first goal of this study is to compare the learning outcome of Chinese learners using the pinyin input system and handwriting at the beginning level and intermediate level. This study also attempts to find out the students' learning time and attitudes toward these two writing modes. In order to capture a better picture of the learners' literacy development, I employed two methods to conduct this research: tests and surveys. In this part, I will discuss the rationale for my methods and describe the participants and the procedure of data collection.

Participants

The research took place at a public university in the Midwest of the United States. The Chinese program at this university offered Chinese major and minor programs to undergraduate students. A total of 67 college students in beginning and intermediate Chinese classes participated in this study. Table 3.1 is the number of the students in each class.

The age range of the participants was 18–21 years old. The beginning-level students had finished Chinese 101 or its equivalent before taking Chinese 102. The intermediate-level students had finished Chinese 101, 102, and 201 or their equivalents before taking Chinese 202. All the participants were taught in a

Table 3.1 Number of Students in Each Class

Class	Pinyin input class	Handwriting class
Chinese 102	19	20
Chinese 202	15	13

traditional face-to-face classroom setting, and they were required to do their written assignments by handwriting with pen and paper in their previous Chinese classes.

Among the participants, no one was a heritage learner (there were three heritage speakers in these classes. But their data were not included in this study). The participants were all CFL learners. English was their first language, except for one English-Japanese bilingual and three English-Spanish bilinguals. The bilingual participants were born and grew up in the United States. They spoke their original non-English language primarily at home. They all studied and used English at school. They all rated themselves as competent readers in English.

Testing batteries and procedure

At each level, the same instructor taught both the handwriting groups and the typing (with pinyin input) groups. At each level, both groups used the same textbook and had the same assignment. The only difference between the two groups is the handwriting groups did all the written assignments, quizzes, and tests with pen and paper, and the typing (with pinyin input) groups used electronic devices like computers or tablets to type when doing their written assignments, quizzes, and tests.

The testing batteries evaluate two skills: recognizing and writing characters. The reading section consists of six character-recognition quizzes. The writing section consists of six character-production quizzes.

The data was collected throughout the whole spring academic semester. Based on their schedule, all four classes needed to learn six lessons in their textbooks in the spring semester. There was a character quiz for each lesson. Each character quiz consisted of two parts: 10 items of the character recognition task and 10 items of the character production task. In the character recognition task, there were 10 words in Chinese and students needed to write/type the English translation for each item. In the character production task, there were 10 English words/phrases, and students had to write/type the corresponding Chinese characters/words. Each correct item would be awarded one point. The quizzes were strictly textbook-based. All the words/phrases of each quiz were chosen from the corresponding lesson in the textbook.

At the end of the previous fall semester, students took an identical written final exam at each level. The final exam sections included listening, grammar, reading comprehension, and writing sections to measure their learning in the target language. The listening section comprised 20 multiple-choice questions

Table 3.2 Mean Scores for the Tests in the Previous Semester

Learning mode	Beginning level		Intermediate level	
	Mean Score	Standard Deviation	Mean Score	Standard Deviation
Handwriting group	76.9	0.24	78.4	0.91
Pinyin input group	78.1	0.39	77.8	0.38

based on 10 mini-dialogues and one dialogue. The grammar section included 30 multiple-choice questions. The reading section contained two passages, each of which had five multiple-choice questions. The writing section required students to write a paragraph using given grammar structures. A two-tailed independent t-test was conducted to determine whether there were differences between students from the two classes at each level in their scores on the tests (grammar, reading, composition, and oral exam). The mean scores of written tests are shown in Table 3.2. There were no significant differences between the two groups of students at the beginning level ($t = 1.92$, $p = .087$) and intermediate level ($t = 1.03$, $p = .180$)

The participants also completed a background questionnaire to gather information on the students' demographics, including their age, major, native language, and exposure to other languages. The questionnaire also collected information concerning their previous input system experience and the use of various electronic devices, especially focusing on the ratio of their work and recreational time with electronic devices. The students were similar in terms of experience and comfort with technology and access to electronic devices.

Results

Results of the students' character recognition quizzes

We first compared the beginning-level students' mean scores of the character recognition task in the six quizzes. Table 3.3 summarizes the statistical descriptions of the mean scores for the character recognition task. Two-tailed independent t-tests were adopted to make comparisons. The test results do not show a significant difference ($t = 8.050$, $p = .148$) on the overall mean scores of the two groups. Also, further t-tests on the scores of each quiz show no significant differences between the two groups.

We then compared intermediate-level students' mean scores of the character recognition task in the six quizzes. Table 3.4 summarizes the statistical descriptions of the mean scores for the character recognition task. The test results do not show a significant difference ($t = 17.097$, $p = 1.872$) on the overall mean scores of the two groups. Also, further t-tests on the scores of each quiz show no significant differences between the two groups.

Third, we compared beginning-level students' mean scores of the character production task in the six quizzes. Table 3.5 summarizes the statistical descriptions

Table 3.3 Statistical Description of the Character Recognition Task for Beginning-Level Students

Quiz #	Learning mode	Mean Score	Standard Deviation
Quiz 1	Typing Group	8.1	0.73
	Handwriting Group	8.0	0.78
Quiz 2	Typing Group	8.3	0.89
	Handwriting Group	8.1	0.54
Quiz 3	Typing Group	8.6	0.94
	Handwriting Group	8.5	0.82
Quiz 4	Typing Group	8.4	0.44
	Handwriting Group	8.5	0.21
Quiz 5	Typing Group	8.7	0.87
	Handwriting Group	8.5	0.92
Quiz 6	Typing Group	8.0	0.74
	Handwriting Group	8.2	0.83

Table 3.4 Statistical Description of the Character Recognition Task for Intermediate-Level Students

Quiz #	Learning mode	Mean Score	Standard Deviation
Quiz 1	Typing Group	9.3	0.92
	Handwriting Group	9.1	0.78
Quiz 2	Typing Group	9.0	1.01
	Handwriting Group	9.1	0.89
Quiz 3	Typing Group	9.2	0.72
	Handwriting Group	9.3	0.82
Quiz 4	Typing Group	9.4	0.41
	Handwriting Group	9.4	0.29
Quiz 5	Typing Group	9.2	0.74
	Handwriting Group	9.3	0.91
Quiz 6	Typing Group	9.6	0.87
	Handwriting Group	9.7	0.97

Table 3.5 Statistical Description of the Character Production Task for Beginning-Level Students

Quiz #	Learning mode	Mean score	Standard deviation
Quiz 1	Typing Group	7.8	0.38
	Handwriting Group	7.4	0.22
Quiz 2	Typing Group	8.5	0.34
	Handwriting Group	7.1	0.98
Quiz 3	Typing Group	8.6	0.11
	Handwriting Group	7.2	0.43
Quiz 4	Typing Group	8.8	0.78
	Handwriting Group	6.8	0.10
Quiz 5	Typing Group	7.9	0.91
	Handwriting Group	7.3	0.14
Quiz 6	Typing Group	8.5	0.68
	Handwriting Group	6.1	0.56

Table 3.6 Statistical Description of the Character Production Task for Intermediate-Level Students

Quiz #	Learning mode	Mean score	Standard deviation
Quiz 1	Typing Group	9.1	0.89
	Handwriting Group	8.8	0.34
Quiz 2	Typing Group	8.7	0.92
	Handwriting Group	6.8	0.23
Quiz 3	Typing Group	9.1	0.67
	Handwriting Group	6.2	0.44
Quiz 4	Typing Group	8.9	0.89
	Handwriting Group	6.4	0.93
Quiz 5	Typing Group	8.6	0.41
	Handwriting Group	7.0	0.98
Quiz 6	Typing Group	8.9	0.33
	Handwriting Group	6.6	0.46

of the mean scores for the character production task. Students in the typing with pinyin input class received higher mean scores than did their counterparts in the handwriting class. Two-tailed independent t-tests were adopted to make comparisons. The test results show the typing group were significantly higher ($t = 0.250$, $p = .013$) on the overall mean scores of the two groups. Also, further t-tests on the scores of the pinyin input group were significantly higher than the handwriting group in Quiz 2, 3, 4, and 6.

Finally, we compared intermediate-level students' mean scores of the character production task in the six quizzes. Table 3.6 summarizes the statistical descriptions of the mean scores for the character recognition task. Students in the typing class received higher mean scores than did their counterparts in the handwriting class. Two-tailed independent t-tests were adopted to make comparisons. The test results show the pinyin input group performed significantly better ($t = 0.097$, $p < 0.01$) on the overall mean scores of the two groups. Also, further t-tests on the results of each quiz show that the pinyin input group scores were significantly higher in Quizzes 2, 3, 4, 5, and 6.

Results of the survey

Next, we sought to elucidate how much time each group used to study Chinese and their attitude toward handwriting and typing with pinyin. We asked the students to participate in a survey study, which asked questions about (1) the average time they spent each week on Chinese homework; (2) the average time they spent each week practicing Chinese reading and writing in addition to homework; and (3) whether they preferred studying Chinese through handwriting or electronic devices with which they can use pinyin input to type. We coded the time data in the questionnaire: students who spent less than an hour were given a score of 1; an hour, a score of 2; about 2 hours, a score of 3; about 3 hours, a score of 4; 4 hours, a score of 5, and so on.

Table 3.7 Average Time Spent on Homework

Proficiency level	Learning mode	Mean score	Standard deviation
Chinese 102	Typing Group	2.1	0.89
	Handwriting Group	3.8	0.34
Chinese 202	Typing Group	2.2	0.89
	Handwriting Group	2.6	0.20

Table 3.8 Average Time Spent on Practice

Proficiency level	Learning mode	Mean score	Standard deviation
Chinese 102	Typing Group	2.5	0.90
	Handwriting Group	0.8	0.65
Chinese 202	Typing Group	1.2	0.72
	Handwriting Group	1.0	0.39

We first calculated the total time that students spent on homework. Table 3.7 shows the results for the first and second survey question.

For the students at the beginning level, the average time spent each week on homework was 2.1 hours for the typing group and 3.5 hours for the handwriting group. The difference is significant: t =2.32, p = 0.04. At the intermediate level, the typing group also spent less time on homework each week than the handwriting group, but the difference is not statistically significant: t = 14.82 and p =0.091.

We then calculated the total time that students spent on practice on reading and writing (excluding the time for homework). Table 3.8 shows the results for the first and second survey question.

At the beginning level, the typing group on average spent much more time on practicing than the handwriting group each week; the difference is significant: t =14.67 and $p < 0.01$. At the intermediate level, the two groups spent similar time on practice, and there is no statistically significant difference between the two groups: $t = 9.47, p = 0.390$.

For Question 3, 16 out of 19 participants in the typing group at the beginning level reported favoring typing in learning Chinese. Three participants preferred to use both typing and handwriting. None of the students still preferred using paper-based writing only. Contrary to the typing group, 12 of 20 students in the handwriting group preferred to use both writing modes, even though they had to handwrite all the assignments and tests during the semester. Four students said that if they could choose, they would prefer typing. And four, including the English-Japanese bilingual participant, preferred handwriting.

For the intermediate-level students, four out of 15 participants in the typing group reported favoring typing to learn Chinese. Eight participants preferred to use both typing and handwriting. Three of the students preferred using paper-based writing only. Contrary to the typing group, two students in the handwriting group said that if they could choose, they would prefer typing. Eight students preferred to use both writing modes. And four participants preferred handwriting only.

Discussion

We asked four research questions at the beginning of the study:

1. Is there any difference between the typing groups and the handwriting groups on the quiz scores of reading characters?
2. Is there any difference between the typing groups and the handwriting groups on the quiz scores of producing characters?
3. How much time does each group spend studying Chinese after class?
4. What are the learners' views on the writing modes after a semester's study?

As for the first question, we did not find any statically significant difference between the typing group and the handwriting group on the quiz scores of reading characters at either level. That is, at both the beginning and intermediate levels, the typing group and the handwriting group performed similarly well in terms of character recognition. This indicates that learning through typing with pinyin is as effective as the handwriting approach in character recognition.

As for the second question, we found both typing groups performed significantly better than the handwriting groups in producing characters in some of the quizzes. This indicates that typing is more effective in helping students produce correct characters, which confirms the findings in previous studies (Kang, 2011; Zhu et al., 2016). We also found the difference to be more pronounced at the beginning level, indicating that typing is more effective in helping beginners produce correct characters. There are likely several reasons for the differences between the beginning level and the intermediate level. First, the pinyin input enables the learners to choose the correct word from a group of candidates with the same pronunciation. This way, typing with pinyin is more like doing a word-recognition task in the format of multiple-choice questions. As for the handwriting group, writing characters with a pen is a pure production task that they must start from scratch, stroke by stroke, for every character. Therefore, handwriting with a pen is more difficult for students than choosing characters from a pool of candidates. This is particularly difficult for beginners, because they are less experienced and have less knowledge of the components and structures of the characters. Another reason for the lower scores from the handwriting group is the grading method for the quiz. A character is considered wrong even if it is partially correct. For example, "师" is considered the correct character, but "帅" is considered a wrong character in the quiz, even though "帅" is very close to the correct answer, "师." This is a common mistake among the beginners in the handwriting group, but it didn't happen in the typing group, because although these two characters are similar in form, they are completely different in pronunciation. When a student types the pinyin for "师," "帅" will not appear as a candidate for the student to choose, thus the student avoids the making a mistake of choosing/writing a very similar character.

Our findings for Question 1 and 2 confirm what have been found in some previous studies (Kang, 2011; Xu & Jen, 2005; Zhu et al., 2016), but are different from Tan et al. (2013), in which the researchers claimed the use of electronic devices is detrimental, because they found that children's Chinese character-reading performance significantly decreases with the utilization of the pinyin input method and electronic devices in general. Tan et al. (2013) argued that pinyin typing interferes with Chinese reading acquisition, which is characterized by fine-grained analysis of visuographic properties of characters. Handwriting, however, enhances children's reading ability. But they also pointed out that there might have been other unknown factors associated with the high percentages of poor readers in China. For example, Chinese language textbooks may be difficult for primary school children. Reduction of handwriting time in primary schools might be another possible contributor. Primary school teachers encourage students to guess the meaning of characters rather than decoding characters as a fine-grained unit, which is inconsistent with contemporary psycholinguistic theories of reading acquisition (Perfetti, 1985). In addition, their reading tests might be difficult, although characters used in the major sections of the tests were from the textbooks. It is also difficult to formally equate the criteria for poor reading across time because there is no standardized reading test in China.

Our study is different from Tan et al. (2013) in several significant ways. First, unlike their participants, who were native speakers of Chinese at elementary schools, our participants were adult learners studying a second/third language. They were all competent readers in English. It is easy for adult learners to transfer their reading skills and metalinguistic awareness to the study of an additional language (Koda, 2005). Second, unlike Tan et al's study, all the characters in our quizzes were strictly from the textbooks. The quizzes were not too difficult for the students. Third, the participants' first language, English, is an alphabetic language. All the participants in the current study had already been skillful at typing alphabets before they started to type pinyin for Chinese. Pinyin input as a way to produce characters is very similar to typing alphabetic letters. The major difference is that pinyin input has an additional visual layer of character recognition, so students need to know not only the pronunciation of the characters, but also how to choose the correct characters from the group of homophones (characters sharing the same pronunciation). They can accomplish this if they have sufficient declarative knowledge of the Chinese characters' orthography. Different from typing with the pinyin input system, writing Chinese characters with a pen may require procedural knowledge. This could be more demanding for English native speakers who do not have much prior knowledge about how to write characters stroke by stroke. This effect is more obvious for beginners. After learners become more skillful at writing Chinese characters, handwriting could be almost as efficient as typing. Yet, at the beginning level, typing with pinyin input still has a big advantage.

From the survey results, we found that for the beginners, the typing group spent significantly less time than the handwriting group in order to finish the same amount of homework, indicating handwriting with a pen may be more difficult for beginners. Typing potentially could save students a large amount of time. But at the intermediate level, the benefit of typing in this regard is less obvious. Although the typing group finished their homework faster, the difference is not statistically significant. The reason could be the students at the intermediate level were much more skillful learners of Chinese, and they could write characters faster after more than three semesters' study of Chinese. Based on the findings, it seems the benefit of typing is less pronounced when the learners are becoming more skillful with handwriting.

Interestingly, we found that although the typing group at the beginning level finished their homework in less time, they spent significantly more time on additional practice in reading and writing to improve their Chinese proficiency. Overall, the two groups spent a similar amount of time studying Chinese (homework + additional practice). It is possible that from their previous study in Chinese 101, they understood how much time would be needed to study Chinese well. Therefore, in Chinese 102, even though they had finished homework earlier, they spent additional time on reading and typing Chinese. This additional effort may also explain why they did better in the character production task. As for the handwriting group at the beginning level, doing homework already consumed a large amount of their time after class. So little additional time was devoted to additional practice in reading and writing in Chinese.

At the intermediate level, both the typing group and the handwriting group spent similar time on homework and other practice, which again indicates that the mode of writing has less effect on more skilled learners.

Finally, the results from the survey show that at the beginning level, an overwhelming majority of students prefer typing or the combination of typing and handwriting. At the intermediate level, a majority of students would still choose typing or the combination of typing and handwriting. This indicates that the new generation of students, as skillful learners using electronic devices in learning and social life, have a strong propensity toward using pinyin input as a way to produce Chinese characters. Their motivation in this area could serve them well in learning Chinese. If we as instructors could use pinyin properly, it could guide students to learn more effectively and efficiently.

Pedagogical implications

As mentioned before, one of the most challenging problems for CFL learners, especially for beginners, is reading and writing in Chinese. Most beginning-level learners often do not go beyond the introductory level of Chinese (Xu & Jen, 2005). Yet from our study, we found that typing with a pinyin input system could be combined with handwriting to make beginners feel more comfortable with literacy study. In this study, the outcome of typing is at least as good as the handwriting group in terms of the character recognition. Typing could also increase the accuracy rate in character writing. These could potentially boost the beginners' interest and confidence in learning Chinese.

In implementing the pinyin input learning approach, we also faced a set of distinct challenges and learned valuable lessons. First, a single approach, whether it is the pinyin input approach or handwriting approach, may not be a good fit for all, as different students have different learning styles. So, a better approach would be to provide options to students and let them choose what fits them best.

In designing a Chinese course, the instructor should have a general sense of the kind of problems students might encounter when engaging with a specific writing mode, though some problems are hard to predict at the design phase. Additional time and technological support might be required for instructors to solve all kinds of unexpected problems during teaching.

Lastly, additional learning material should be provided to students as optional assignments. The typing with pinyin input learning approach is most effective when students have sufficient recourse for additional learning and practice at the beginning level. As the beginners could finish homework much faster than the handwriting group, additional practice would ensure that they have sufficient contact with the target language.

Conclusion

In this study, we attempted to find out if there is any difference between the typing with pinyin input learning approach and the handwriting approach at the beginning level and the intermediate level for CFL students. The results show that the typing group could read Chinese characters as well as the handwriting group at both levels. We also found that students in the typing class outperformed those in the handwriting class in character production quizzes at both levels. The pattern of our findings indicates that students' Chinese character-reading performance is not affected by the mode of writing at the beginning and intermediate levels. But students' character production was significantly better for the typing groups at both levels. As students use the pinyin input method (and electronic tools in general), pinyin typing appears to be beneficial for CFL students, at least at the character production tasks.

The end-of-the-semester survey results also indicate that the typing with pinyin input learning approach did not decrease students' engagement. Although the typing groups at the beginning level finished their homework faster, they spent additional time studying reading and writing in Chinese. Also, on the survey, the majority of the students preferred typing with pinyin or the combination of typing and handwriting.

This study, though limited in scope, is meant to stimulate discussion of pinyin input learning in foreign languages generally and in Chinese particularly. In the future, data from a wider range of courses at different levels will provide fruitful ground to explore a variety of issues, such as the seamless integration of the two modes of writing for better adaptation to the pinyin input learning approach. Research on these issues will help us continue to adjust to various challenges of using the pinyin input approach in the field of CFL instruction.

References

Chen, P. (1999). *Modern Chinese: History and sociolinguistics*. Cambridge University Press.

Chin, T. (1973). Is it necessary to require writing in learning Chinese characters? *Journal of the Chinese Language Teacher Association*, 8, 167–170.

Coulmas, F. (1991). *The writing systems of the world*. Basil Blackwell.
DeFrancis, J. (2002). The ideographic myth. In M. S. Erbaugh (Ed.), *Difficult characters: Interdisciplinary studies of Chinese and Japanese writing* (pp. 1–20). National East Asian Language Resource Center, Ohio State University.
Gabrieli, J. (2009). Dyslexia: A new synergy between education and cognitive neuroscience. *Science, 325*(5938), 280–283.
Goswami, U. (2011). A temporal sampling framework for developmental dyslexia. *Trends of Cognitive Science, 15*(1), 3–10.-Format maybe?
Hansell, M. (2002). Functional answers to structural problems in thinking about writing. In M. S. Erbaugh (Ed.), *Difficult characters: Interdisciplinary studies of Chinese and Japanese writing* (pp. 124–176). National East Asian Language Resource Center, Ohio State University.
Kang, H. (2011). *Computer-based writing and paper-based writing: A study of beginning-level and intermediate-level Chinese learners' writing* (Unpublished doctoral dissertation). The Ohio State University.
Ke, C. (1998). Effects of strategies on the learning of Chinese characters among foreign language students. *Journal of the Chinese Language Teachers Association, 33*(2), 93–112.
Koda, K. (2005). *Insights into second language reading: A cross-linguistic approach*. Cambridge University Press.
Leong, C. K. (2012). Learning to read modern Chinese. In P. T. Daniels (Ed.), *The world's writing system* (pp. 38–67). Oxford University Press.
Lyu, B., Lai, C., Lin, C.-H., & Gong, Y. (2021). Comparison studies of typing and handwriting in Chinese language learning: A synthetic review. *International Journal of Educational Research, 106*(2), 101740. doi:10.1016/j.ijer.2021.101740
Mackay, A. L. (2001). Character-building. *Nature, 410*(6824), 19–31.
Perfetti, C. A. (1985). *Reading ability*. Oxford University Press.
Perfetti, C. A. (1997). The psycholinguistics of spelling and reading. In C. A. Perfetti, L. Rieben, & M. Fayol (Eds.), *Learning to spell: Research, theory, and practice across languages* (pp. 21–38). Lawrence Erlbaum Associates.
Perfetti, C. A., Liu, Y., & Tan, L. H. (2005). The lexical constituency model: Some implications of research on Chinese for general theories of reading. *Psychological Review, 112*(1), 43–59.
Perfetti, C. A., Zhang, S., & Berent, I. (1992). Reading in English and Chinese: Evidence for a "universal" phonological principle. In R. Frost & L. Katz (Eds.), *Orthography, phonology, morphology, and meaning* (pp. 227–248). North-Holland.
Peterson, R. L., & Pennington, B. F. (2012). Developmental dyslexia. *Lancet, 379*(9830), 1997–2007.
Price, C. J., & Mechelli, A. (2005). Reading and reading disturbance. *Current Opinion on Neurobiology, 15*(2), 231–238.
Serrano, R., & Howard, E. (2007). Second language writing development in English and in Spanish in a two-way immersion program. *International Journal of Bilingual Education & Bilingualism, 10*(2), 152–170.
Shen, H. (2005). An investigation of Chinese-character learning strategies among non-native speakers of Chinese. *System, 33*, 49–68.
Shu, H., & Anderson, R. C. (1999). Learning to read Chinese: The development of metalinguistic awareness. In J. Wang, W. Albrecht, & H. C. Chen (Eds.), *Reading Chinese script: A cognitive analysis* (pp. 1–18). Lawrence Erlbaum Associates, Inc.
Siok, W. T., Perfetti, C. A., Jin, Z., & Tan, L. H. (2004). Biological abnormality of impaired reading is constrained by culture. *Nature, 431*(7004), 71–76.

Sun, C. (2006). *Chinese: A linguistic introduction*. Cambridge University Press.
Thorson, H. (2000). Using the computer to compare foreign and native language writing process: A statistical and case study approach. *The Modern Language Journal*, *84*(2), 155–170.
Tan, L. H., Xu, M., Chang, C. M., & Siok, W. T. (2013). China's language input system in the digital age affects children's reading development. *PNAS*, *110*(3), 1119–1123.
Way, D. P., Joiner, E. G., & Seaman, M. A. (2000). Writing in the second foreign language classroom: The effects of prompts and tasks on novice learners of French. *The Modern Language Journal*, *84*(2), 171–184.
Wolf, M., & Barzillai, M. (2009). The importance of deep reading. *Education Leadership*, *66*(6), 32–37.
Xu, P., & Jen, T. (2005). Penless Chinese language learning: A computer-assisted approach. *Journal of the Chinese Language Teachers Association*, *40*(2), 25–42.
Zhu, Y., Shum, S. M., Tse, S. B., & Liu, J. J. (2016). Word-processor or pencil-and-paper? A comparison of students' writing in Chinese as a foreign language. *Computer Assisted Language Learning*, *29*(3), 596–617.

4 Effects of timed dictation on Chinese character writing

A preliminary study in beginning-level CFL learners

Siyan Hou and Atsushi Fukada

Introduction

The Chinese language has been widely recognized as one of the most difficult foreign languages to learn due to its complex writing system. There have been many studies investigating such topics as optimal timing of introducing characters in Chinese as a foreign language (CFL) courses (Allen, 2008; Dew, 2007; Swihart, 2004; Unger et al., 1993; Ye, 2011, 2013; Zhang, 2007); whether typing should replace handwriting (Allen, 2008; He, 2005; Jen & Xu, 2000; Wang & East, 2020); and how technology can be adopted to help with character instruction and to facilitate student learning (Chen et al., 2013; Hsiao et al., 2015; Jin, 2006; Kou & Hooper, 2004; Ren et al., 2013). However, there have been no studies exploring new ways to assist CFL learners in their character writing practice. The main focus of this chapter is to investigate the effects of an innovative character writing activity, Timed Dictation, on beginning-level CFL learners' character writing fluency and accuracy. Learners' perceptions of the timed dictation activity and character copying will also be examined.

Literature review

Challenges of learning Chinese characters

Due to their morphographic nature, learning to write Chinese characters, or *Hanzi*, has long been a formidable challenge for CFL learners whose native languages are phonographic, like English, Spanish, and modern Korean (Allen, 2008; DeFrancis, 1984; Guder, 2005; McGinnis, 1999; Ye, 2013). A Chinese character has three components: pronunciation, form, and meaning (Y. Li, 2020). The meaning component is what makes Chinese characters morphographic. The form of a character does not readily indicate how it is pronounced, which adds to the complexity of the writing system. For instance, the Chinese character for *person, people* is written as "人". Its pronunciation in *pinyin*, the Romanized phonetic writing system for Chinese characters, is "rén." Learners of Chinese need to remember all three aspects of Chinese characters simultaneously, which requires a significant amount of effort.

DOI: 10.4324/9781003029038-6

Another complexity of Chinese characters is the number of strokes. Strokes are the basic orthographic component of a character. For example, the character "谢"(xiè, *to thank*), one of the characters that is introduced in almost all elementary-level CFL courses, contains 12 strokes. According to Zhao and Baldauf (2008), the average number of strokes for the 2000 most used characters is 9.18. In contrast, the Roman alphabetic letter that has the largest number of strokes is the letter "E," with only four strokes in it.

Another factor that adds to the difficulty is the sheer number of characters. While the Roman alphabet contains 26 letters (52 if lower-case and upper-case are counted separately), an authoritative Chinese character dictionary called "Hanyu Da Zidian" (汉语大字典) lists 54,678 characters. While educated Chinese speakers are estimated to know about 8,000, the Office of Chinese Language Council International (*Hanban*) recommends that beginning- to intermediate-level CFL learners should master 2,000–2,200 most-commonly-used Chinese characters (D. Li, 1998).

Lastly, CFL learners also need to deal with 18 different ways compound characters are formed (Kan et al., 2018). For instance, "尖"(jiān, *sharp*) is made up of two components: "小" (small) at the top and "大" (big) at the bottom. These two parts are visually different in the compound character from when they are used independently. According to Qian et al. (2018), this variation is due to the rule that each character, no matter how many strokes or orthographic components it has, must occupy the same space. This "spatial inconsistency" (p. 58) can pose further challenges for beginning learners in terms of character recognition.

Educators, researchers, and CFL learners have previously expressed how difficult it is to learn Chinese characters. In a narrative study, Bell (1995), reflecting on her experience of being a CFL learner, stated that an early part of the experience was very stressful in that "I was devoting all my waking hours (and considerable amounts of my dream time) to the task and yet failing to achieve any measure of success that I could recognize" (p. 694). As one of the earliest scholars of the Chinese language, DeFrancis (1984) concluded in his book that "Learning to speak Chinese is about five percent more difficult than learning to speak French, whereas learning to read Chinese is about five times as hard as learning to read French" (p. 52). The Foreign Service Institute (FSI) has made a similar conclusion. In their list of languages and the approximate time needed to learn those languages, FSI categorized Chinese as a "Category IV Language." They explained this category as "super-hard languages, which are exceptionally difficult for native English speakers" ("FSI's Experience with Language Learning," from www.state.gov/foreign-language-training/). To achieve "Speaking 3/Reading 3" on the Interagency Language Roundtable Scale, a native English speaker, as estimated by FSI, needs about 88 weeks or 2,200 class hours for Chinese, while (s)he only needs about 24–30 weeks or 600–700 class hours for Category I languages like French, Spanish, and Italian. Dew (2007) and Guder (2005) further commented that it is its complex writing system that makes Chinese such a "distant language" (p. 15).

Issues in teaching Chinese characters

Timing of introducing Chinese characters

Considering the demanding nature of learning Chinese characters, scholars have long debated when to introduce characters in CFL courses (Allen, 2008; Everson, 1988, 1994; McGinnis, 1999). There are mainly two camps: the "delayed character introduction (DCI)" camp and the "immediate character introduction (ICI)" camp (Ye, 2013). Grounded in the perspective of speech primacy theory, scholars supporting DCI suggest that at the beginning stage, instructors should adopt *pinyin* to assist learners in establishing a firm foundation in aural and oral skills and to help them gain confidence (Dew, 2007; Jorden & Walton, 1987; Swihart, 2004; Unger et al., 1993; Zhang, 2007). Zhang (2007) argued in a conference presentation that "不会说中国话，当然学不好汉字。学文字要以学语言为基础" ("If you cannot speak Chinese, of course you cannot learn characters well. Learning characters is based upon a background of speaking") (p. 89). Thus, he proposed that especially for learners with alphabetic language backgrounds, listening and speaking should be learned ahead of reading and writing.

Nevertheless, the ICI perspective seems to dominate the CFL pedagogical field in that the most popular CFL textbooks all introduce characters from the very beginning of instruction (Allen, 2008). Among the scholars who favor ICI, Liu's (1983) point of view seems to be widely acknowledged. He argued that "the characters should be taught at the very beginning because the sound, the syntax, and the characters are interrelated in a higher-level structure and they should be integrated from the first lesson" (p. 66).

It is worth mentioning, though, that more and more scholars in the ICI camp have questioned the necessity of handwriting characters, arguing in favor of typing (Allen, 2008; He, 2005; Jen & Xu, 2000; Wang & East, 2020, Chapter 3 of this book). Typing characters may be a realistic and arguably desirable direction in the COVID-19 pandemic era, when all the CFL courses had to be transitioned to the distance mode. As Wang and East (2020) mentioned, considering the heavy workload of CFL instructors and the burden that character learning imposes on the learners, more effective teaching approaches and technologies are needed to continue implementing the character-based curriculum, with an eye on a possible curriculum reform of adjusting the importance of handwriting skills in the digital age.

Technology-blended teaching and learning Chinese characters

The earliest computer technology used in learning Chinese characters dates back to the 1970s, when some commercial Chinese language programs were designed for this purpose (Yao, 2009). With the development of technology, how it can help instructors to teach and students to learn Chinese characters has been investigated by many researchers (Bai, 2003; Bourgerie, 2003; Chen, 2005; Yao, 2009; Williams, 2013; Xie, 2001).

Among the studies on technology and character writing, the use of multimedia has been investigated broadly by scholars (Chen et al., 2013; Jin, 2006; Kou & Hooper, 2004; Ren et al., 2013; Shei & Hsieh, 2012; Zhan & Cheng, 2014). In these studies, animation is the most commonly adopted tool for presenting radicals and stroke order sequences. One major finding is that computer-based multimedia is effective in facilitating CFL learners' character recognition. In one such study, Jin (2006) investigated the effects of multimedia presentation, orthography, and processing experience on recognition of Chinese characters. One-hundred-twenty CFL learners with various language backgrounds experienced learning 36 Chinese characters through two instructional modes: computer-based multimedia presentations of radicals, stroke orders, and *pinyin;* and traditional printouts with pinyin and English translations. The results suggested that participants in the multimedia group, regardless of their language backgrounds, performed better in an immediate recall task than did the participants in the traditional group. Furthermore, within the multimedia group, the effects of radical presentation were stronger than those of stroke order presentation and *pinyin*.

Apart from research on teaching Chinese characters, some scholars also explored how technology, such as stroke order animation, could be used as a tool for the learning of characters (Hsiao et al., 2015; Jin, 2006; Zhu & Hong, 2005). Xu et al. (2013) studied the effects of three character-learning conditions: reading the form—sound and meaning only, reading plus stroke order animation, and reading plus writing down the target characters from memory three times. The participants were 36 L1 English CFL learners. With a pretest and posttest design, the authors found that animation provided participants with reading and writing practice, which enhanced the acquisition of form, sound, and meaning of the characters. Similar results were found in other studies (Hsiao et al., 2015; Jin, 2006; Zhu & Hong, 2005) as well. Hsiao et al. (2015) further commented that CFL learners not only performed better with computer-based learning tools, but they also showed a high degree of satisfaction with and interest in learning Chinese characters.

Hsiung et al. (2017), however, showed different results. This study also used stroke order animation to see what effects it had on CFL learners' *Hanzi* learning. Using a pretest and posttest design with 91 participants, the study found that although stroke order presentation positively impacted the participants' stroke order learning, it had no significant effect on their ability to correctly produce *Hanzi* and to recognize the pronunciation and meaning of *Hanzi*.

Hsiao et al. (2015) developed the Chinese Character Handwriting Diagnosis and Remedial Instruction (CHDRI) system, and conducted a study with 65 participants to investigate its efficacy. The CHDRI system is capable of detecting incorrect stroke orders and providing individualized remedial instruction on stroke order and spatial structure through animation. The study compared a group that used the system with another group that used paper-based materials of the same content. Both groups took a pretest and posttest on stroke order and spatial structure. The results showed that the CHDRI group significantly outperformed the paper-based group from the pretest to the posttest, suggesting the efficacy of the CHDRI system.

As the use of tablet devices and smartphones has become more common in recent years, language educators have also started to develop apps to help with the teaching and learning of characters. Lin and Lien (2012) investigated Chinese learning apps for iPad and classified them into three categories based on their main functions. Among them, apps for character learning include *Pleco, Dian-Hua Dictionary, Trainchinese, Dictionary & Flash Cards*, and *Hanyu Chinese Dictionary*. Apps for character recognition and writing include, for example, *EZi Test Chinese, Chinese Writer*, and *Estroke*.

While numerous studies have been conducted in the field of character teaching and learning, we have not found any studies exploring effective types of activities for practicing characters. Based on our personal experience and informal interviews with instructors from other schools and institutions, it seems that character copying is the most frequently used activity by instructors to help learners practice writing characters. Character copying refers to the paper-based activity in which learners copy characters following models initially stroke by stroke and then as a whole. It is a common activity widely adopted in elementary schools in China for native-Chinese-speaking pupils' character acquisition. Despite character copying's widespread use, learners typically do not find it an enjoyable activity. This is also seen clearly in the complaints from previous learners in our Chinese program (which can be seen from the student perception survey reported later in this chapter).

To summarize, the foregoing review shows that the complexities of Chinese characters present difficulties to learners, and to make matters worse, the most widely practiced approach to learning characters can be tedious and demotivating. Furthermore, the copying activity for character writing could add too much workload to the instructors, especially in the online teaching mode (Miyamoto et al., 2018; Wang & East, 2020). We have found ourselves in a dire need of innovative ways for CFL learners to practice writing Chinese characters.

Timed dictation

Nation (1991) defined dictation as "a technique in which learners receive some spoken input, hold this in their memory for a short time, and then write what they heard" (p. 12). Dictation has been utilized both as a testing tool and a learning tool. In the 1970s scholars started to explore dictation as a testing tool, and many studies found a strong correlation between dictation and language proficiency test scores such as TOEFL (Test of English as a Foreign Language) (Irvine et al., 1974; Jafarpur & Yamini, 1993; Oller, 1971; Oller & Streiff, 1975). Studies have also found that dictation, as a learning tool, could help improve learners' listening and writing skills (Pappas, 1977; Sawyer & Silver, 1961).

As a type of dictation activity, timed dictation (TD) refers to the activity in which instructors limit the time for learners to write down what they heard. Learners need to write as quickly as possible while maintaining accuracy (Okada, 2016).

In a recent study investigating the effects of TD on katakana (one of the two syllabaries in Japanese) acquisition among L2 Japanese learners, Okada (2016) found that, although participants in the TD group did not outperform participants in the traditional writing group on a timed katakana test, the TD group produced more accurate writing, i.e., the TD activity had a positive effect on learners' writing accuracy. Furthermore, more than half of the participants showed positive attitudes toward TD, and those participants who enjoyed TD also tended to achieve higher scores on the katakana test.

TD, as the name implies, places emphasis on both writing speed and fluency, while traditional *Hanzi* instruction tends to emphasize accuracy only. Yan et al. (2012) conducted a study on Chinese children's compositions and found that *Hanzi* writing speed/fluency was strongly predictive of overall composition quality. This finding suggests that a focus on *Hanzi* writing fluency may be particularly helpful for fostering general writing skills.

The present study

In light of the need to explore innovative ways to help learners practice writing Chinese characters and the positive results of previous studies on dictation and TD, the current study adopted TD as a new approach to character learning and evaluated its effectiveness. As a quasi-experimental study, it sought to compare beginning-level Chinese learners' character writing fluency and accuracy under two different character practice conditions: TD and character copying. Learners' perceptions about both TD and character copying were also investigated. Our research questions for this study were:

1. Which is more effective, TD or character copying, in the classroom setting?
2. Do TD in an online course and character copying in a face-to-face (F2F) course foster comparable character writing abilities?
3. How do students perceive TD and character copying activities?

Methods

Participants

The participants of this study were 42 first-year CFL learners in CHN 102 face-to-face (F2F) classes and a distance/online class at a research university in the U.S. Midwest. It was their second semester learning Chinese. All heritage speakers were excluded from the study. The textbook adopted was *New Practical Chinese Reader* (*2nd Edition*), Book 1 (Liu, 2010). All participants had learned the first six chapters during their first semester of Chinese learning. The participants were divided into three groups based on their intact classes: F2F-TD group, Online-TD group, and control group (COPY). Table 4.1 shows the characteristics of the three groups.

Table 4.1 Characteristics of Three Groups

Classes	Groups	Assignment type	L1 background
F2F class 1 (n=14)	Experimental group 1 (TD-F2F)	Timed dictation	English: 7 Korean: 5 Japanese: 0 Indonesian: 1 Others: 1
Distance class (n=11)	Experimental group 2 (TD-OL)	Timed dictation	English: 2 Korean: 6 Japanese: 1 Indonesian: 2 Others: 0
F2F class 2 (n=17)	Control group (COPY)	Character copying homework	English: 12 Korean: 3 Japanese: 1 Indonesian: 0 Others: 1

Treatment materials

Lists of key sentences

For TD training, we developed a list of 10-13 sentences for each chapter. The sentences were carefully selected from those listed as key sentences in the course textbook (*New Practical Chinese Reader, Book 1*, Liu, 2010), making sure to include all new vocabulary words of the chapter. Each sentence was allotted time for writing. To determine an appropriate amount of time for each sentence, we measured the writing times of two native speakers writing neatly and added their writing times together. Figure 4.1 is an example list the TD participants received.

Dictation training website

Timed Dictation Player was an online platform developed by Dr. Fukada in 2015. It was utilized for participants' practice and chapter dictation tests. It is an online platform for instructors to upload and edit TD audio files and for students to conduct their writing practice. Native speakers of Chinese read aloud and audio-recorded the key sentences of each chapter. Then these recordings were uploaded to the TD platform through its instructor portal, which allowed instructors to segment each audio file into sentences and specify pausing durations (See Figure 4.2).

Each sentence was played twice with two pauses. For instance, sentence 1 in Figure 4.2 would be played in the following order: sentence 1 ⇨ 15-second pause ⇨ repeating sentence 1 ⇨ 10-second pause.

Once instructors completed editing the audio files for a chapter, a URL link to the practice site was generated automatically for instructors to share with the participants (see Figure 4.1). Figure 4.3 shows the student portal that participants

Lesson 9 第九课

Timed Dictation 限时听写

1. 祝你生日快乐！(25s)*
2. 他今年多大？(20s)
3. 星期日是一月二十四号。(35s)
4. 明天上午你有没有课？(40s)
5. 你属什么？我属羊。(35s)
6. 我很喜欢吃北京烤鸭。(45s)
7. 宋华一九八二年十月二十七日出生，今年三十四岁。(60s)
8. 我再买一瓶红葡萄酒，怎么样？(65s)
9. 我们下午有一个聚会，庆贺他的生日。(65s)
10. 我的好朋友们都去，你参加不参加？(65s)
11. 林娜家有一只漂亮的小猫。(50s)
12. 中国人过生日的时候吃寿面，还吃蛋糕。(70s)

*25s stands for 25 seconds. It means you are expected to write down Sentence 1 with the correct form and characters in 25 seconds.

Audio link: http://nell.cla.purdue.edu/dict/today.php?fn=C103_13

Figure 4.1 Example list of key sentences

utilized to prepare for the TD test on their own. Participants could also choose to randomize the sentences as well as change the pause durations, as shown in Figure 4.4.

Dictation practice test

On the fourth day after the beginning of each chapter, participants received a separate audio file with 10 selected sentences from the key sentences list. The audio was recorded by the same native speakers of Chinese, with two pauses for each sentence. Participants were required to listen to the audio file and write down the sentences they heard within the given time as homework. Then the instructors

Edit an existing timed dictation activity

Instructions: Edit the form and submit.
Editing: C102_L9

	BEGIN	END	PAUSE1	PAUSE2
1	01	06	15	10
2	07	12	10	10
3	13	22	20	15
4	24	33	25	15
5	34	41	20	15
6	42	51	25	20
7	53	71	35	25
8	73	80	35	30
9	82	94	35	30
10	96	104	35	30
11	112	120	30	20
12	132	144	40	30
13				

Figure 4.2 Example of creating TD activity on Timed Dictation Player

Timed Dictation Practice

Practice your dictation as many times as you want here. You can control the duration of passes. You can initially make in longer and gradually work up to the speed expected in the actual test. You can make it shorter than the test, too. You can choose whether or more to randomize the items.

Pause control: [Same as test ∨]   ☐ randomize items

[Start the audio]

Status: [   ]
Question No. [   ]

Figure 4.3 Student portal of Timed Dictation Player

collected their dictations, corrected mistakes as necessary, and returned them to the participants. The purpose of this dictation practice test was twofold: to provide the participants with feedback on their handwriting and an opportunity for them to check on the progress they had made on TD.

Timed Dictation Practice

Practice your dictation as many times as you want here. You can control the duration of passes. You can initially make in longer and gradually work up to the speed expected in the actual test. You can make it shorter than the test, too. You can choose whether or more to randomize the items.

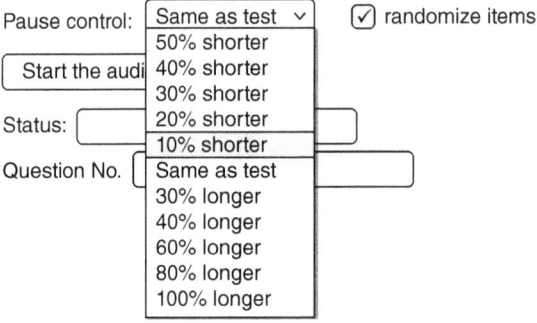

Figure 4.4 Pause duration options

Chapter dictation test

A dictation test for each chapter was created by selecting six sentences from the key sentence list. A separate audio file for the test was created on the TD website.

Treatment procedures

Both TD-F2F and TD-OL groups received TD activities throughout the entire semester. At the beginning of each new chapter, a list of key sentences was distributed. Participants practiced writing the key sentences at their own pace and with their preferred learning strategies. They took a practice test on the fourth or fifth day and received detailed feedback on their handwriting. Participants received regular instruction on *Hanzi* for each chapter. The content of *Hanzi* instruction is based on the *Hanzi* section of each chapter in the textbook and includes rules of stroke order, basic Chinese characters, and culture.

The COPY group received the same *Hanzi* instruction for each chapter as the other groups. Instead of TD activities, this group completed character copying homework, in which they were required to copy each new character five times and each dialogue twice. They received instructors' feedback on their handwriting the next day.

Testing materials and procedures

Timed Hanzi test for measuring accuracy and fluency

At the end of the semester after completing all new chapters, all three groups took a timed *Hanzi* test. The test included 15 sentences selected from the textbook, covering important new characters and grammar points of the semester. There were 180 *Hanzi* on the test. The sentences were presented in *pinyin*. Participants were instructed to write down the corresponding *Hanzi* for all the sentences within 15 minutes. The time limit was determined by adding the two native speakers' writing times together. To ensure that this time limit was reasonable, it was piloted with students in Chinese 201 prior to the administration of the test. Character writing accuracy and fluency were measured by counting the number of correct characters participants produced within the allotted time. (The full version of this test is in Appendix 4.1.)

Perception survey

Participants completed a perception survey after finishing the timed *Hanzi* test at the end of the semester. The survey contained 14 items, with 11 Likert scale questions and three open-ended questions (Appendix 4.2).

Coding and scoring

The *Hanzi* test was graded by two instructors of Chinese. One point was granted for each correctly-formed *Hanzi*. The total possible score for the *Hanzi* test was 180. Cohen's kappa was computed to see how much the two graders agreed on the binary decision of "correctly formed" vs. "incorrectly formed" for each character the participants produced. Cohen's kappa was .91, indicating strong inter-rater reliability. For the perception survey, a mean score was calculated for each Likert-scale item, and the open-ended questions were analyzed qualitatively.

Statistical analyses

SPSS version 23 was utilized for statistical analyses. For the inter-rater reliability of the timed *Hanzi* test, Cohen's kappa was computed to see how much the two graders agreed on the binary decision of "correctly formed" vs. "incorrectly formed" for each character the subjects produced. A two-tailed t-test was conducted to detect where there was a significant difference between the mean *Hanzi* test score of the TD-F2F group and that of the COPY group, and also between the TD-OL group and the COPY group.

Results

Testing for homogeneity

The first chapter test of the semester was used to check if the TD-F2F group and the COPY group were homogeneous. The test was entirely in written format, and more than half of the questions required responses in *Hanzi*. Table 4.2 shows the descriptive statistics of the test scores of the two groups.

An independent sample t-test was run to see if there was a significant difference between the two group means, and the result was non-significant ($t = -1.94$,

Table 4.2 Descriptive Statistics of the First Chapter Test Scores

	Mean	Standard deviation	Max	Min
TD-F2F (n = 14)	92.01	3.59	97.75	83.25
COPY (n = 17)	94.12	3.28	98.00	88.00

$p = .06$). It can thus be inferred that the Chinese levels of the two groups were similar at the beginning of the semester.

The TD-OL group had performance-based assessments rather than paper-based chapter tests, and therefore it was impossible to compare their *Hanzi* writing ability with that of the other groups using the first chapter test. However, since both TD-F2F and TD-OL groups took the same chapter dictation test, an independent samples t-test was run on the scores of that test to check if there was a significant difference between the two groups, and the result was non-significant ($t = 0.04$, $p = .97$). Therefore, it was concluded that the writing ability among the three groups was roughly at the same level.

Comparing results of the timed Hanzi *test*

Table 4.3 shows the descriptive statistics of the *Hanzi* test administered to all three groups at the end of the semester. The maximum possible score was 180.

A two-tailed t-test showed that the TD-F2F group significantly outperformed the COPY group ($t = 3.39$, $p = .004$). The difference between the TD-OL group and the COPY group was not significant ($t = 1.96$, $p = .06$). This lack of significance could be due to the small sample size. The data indicated that participants who experienced TD activities were able to write more fluently as well as accurately within the given time than did those who engaged in character copying.

Results of the perception survey

The results of this statistical comparison would not be a fair comparison if the TD-F2F group participants had spent more time practicing writing *Hanzi* than the other groups. For this reason, we asked in Question 2 of the perception survey (see Appendix 4.2) for the approximate number of hours participants spent each day on learning and practicing *Hanzi*. Table 4.4 shows that the majority of the participants in all three groups spent no more than two hours per day on practicing and learning *Hanzi*.

When asked in Question 3, on a 10-point Likert scale, how beneficial TD/copying was for their learning of characters, both the TD-F2F and the TD-OL group indicated a positive attitude toward TD, while the COPY group was neutral about character copying (See Table 4.5).

Sixteen participants in the TD-F2F and TD-OL group responded that TD was beneficial for their learning of *Hanzi*. What follows are a couple of them explaining why in Question 4:

Effects of timed dictation on Chinese character writing 73

Table 4.3 Descriptive Statistics of the Timed Hanzi Test Scores

	Mean	SD	Max	Min
TD-F2F (n = 14)	120	26.96	173	78
TD-OL (n = 11)	106.55	23.65	133	62
COPY (n = 17)	86.81	28.69	150	29

Table 4.4 Participants' Self-report on Time Spent on Learning and Practicing Hanzi

	0–1 hr	1–2 hrs	2–3 hrs	3–4 hrs	More than 4 hrs
TD-F2F (n = 14)	9 (64%)	3 (22%)	1 (7%)	0	1 (7%)
TD-OL (n = 11)	2 (18%)	5 (46%)	2 (18%)	0	2 (18%)
COPY (n = 17)	8 (47%)	8 (47%)	1 (6%)	0	0

Table 4.5 Descriptive Statistics on Participants' Perceptions on TD/Copying

	TD-F2F (n = 14)		TD-OL (n = 11)		COPY (n = 17)	
	Mean	SD	Mean	SD	Mean	SD
Question 3	7.14	2.41	7.27	2.20	5.18	2.40
Question 5	6.86	2.14	8.00	2.00	6.65	2.09
Question 6	6.00	2.39	7.45	2.16	6.94	2.44
Question 7	7.21	1.63	7.45	2.46	4.29	2.49
Question 8	7.50	2.44	7.72	1.90	3.06	2.04
Question 9	5.00	2.80	6.45	2.81	3.06	1.78
Question 12	5.86	2.82	6.82	2.52	2.76	1.82

"*It does a good job of helping us learn how to write Hanzi quickly and clearly.*"

(TD-F2F_11)

"*I can review the characters that were learned through the chapter.*"

(TD-OL_6)

Nine participants indicated that although TD was beneficial in general, it had shortcomings, including that it was difficult to maintain the phrases in memory, the time provided for each sentence was too short, and the format of the TD test was too difficult. A couple of the participants even mentioned that they would prefer the character copying activity, as one of them responded:

"*Writing out the characters, for me, was much more beneficial.*"

(TD-F2F_2)

In the same open-ended question, eight participants in the COPY group stated that copying homework was not helpful at all. As shown in these examples, a main reason they presented was that when copying characters, they could not fully engage in the activity:

> "*The fact that it is given as homework, I tend to do it mindlessly.*"
> (COPY_7)

> "*I feel it's just tiring, because I'm just trying to finish my homework.*"
> (COPY_13)

> "*Sometimes I don't pay attention to what I am copying.*"
> (COPY_15)

Other reasons included that character copying was time-consuming and boring. One participant called for more learner autonomy in terms of learning style with respect to *Hanzi* learning:

> "*Let me figure it out myself. I can study on my own.*"
> (COPY_12)

Interestingly, the foregoing view related to learning style was not representative of everyone in the COPY group. According to another COPY group participant:

> "*Repetition is the best way for me to engrave the Hanzi in my head.*"
> (COPY_2)

Although we observed some statistically significant differences among the three groups on the *Hanzi* test, their perceptions on how helpful TD/copying was in improving their speed and accuracy of writing *Hanzi* did not vary much (Questions 5 and 6). Only the TD-OL group showed a somewhat higher mean score of 8.00 in perceiving TD to be helpful in improving their speed of writing (see Table 4.5).

When asked in Questions 7–9 how much TD/copying helped improve their grammar, listening, and speaking skills, participants of both TD groups showed markedly more positive perceptions on all three skill areas. The COPY group, on the other hand, rated character copying as providing a limited amount of help in the mentioned language skills (see Table 4.5). This is not surprising, since the TD activity required participants to not only know how to write individual characters in a sentence, but also know how to put together sentences with specific structures. The format of the dictation activity undoubtedly also provided the TD groups plenty of listening practice, which can also be helpful in boosting their speaking skills.

At the end of the survey in Questions 12 and 13, we asked participants whether they enjoyed TD/copying or not, and why. Both TD groups responded positively with respect to TD, while the COPY group's responses were clearly in the negative territory (see Table 4.5). Comments favoring the TD activity from the TD groups included compatibility with their personal learning style, comparatively less work than character copying but more beneficial, and beneficial effects on other language skills like listening and grammar. Several participants in the TD groups, however, expressed their dislike of the TD activity by commenting that the time provided for writing was too short and that TD gave them too much pressure. Here are examples of the comments:

> *"Compared to the practice we did in 101 I feel TD has benefited me more."*
> (TD-F2F_1)

> *"I personally enjoy having time crunches, so the tests were quite fun for me."*
> (TD-F2F_11)

> *"I thought I was motivated to learn characters well because otherwise I would do poorly on TD. If you only have a sneaky grasp of characters, you can still do alright on exams, but not TD."*
> (TD-OL_14)

> *"There's a lot of pressure to write quickly, which may make it hard to write accurately."*
> (TD-F2F_4)

All participants but one in the COPY group commented that the copying homework was not enjoyable at all. Their main complaint was that the copying homework was tedious and not efficient. A couple of the participants called for more learner autonomy and new ways to achieve the goal:

> *"It forces me to study a certain way. Let me study on my own."*
> (COPY_12)

> *"Instead of copying the words, do something else that will improve grammar and understanding of the characters. Copying is very unhelpful."*
> (COPY_6)

> *"Seems tedious and I feel like there must be more beneficial ways to spend time in order to improve Chinese skills."*
> (COPY_14)

Discussion

This study examined the effects of TD on beginning-level CFL learners' character writing fluency and accuracy. With a pretest and posttest design, the results showed that the TD group outperformed the COPY group in a character writing test in the classroom setting. TD also functioned well in the online setting. In addition, participants showed a strong preference for TD compared to the traditional copying exercise. In this section, we answer the three research questions and discuss the results.

RQ 1. Which is more effective, TD or character copying, in the classroom setting?

The statistical comparison showed that the TD-F2F group significantly outperformed the COPY group. The TD-F2F students became able to write characters with greater fluency and accuracy than did the COPY group students. Therefore, we can conclude that TD is more effective than character copying. This finding is consistent with Okada's (2016) study, where TD was found to have facilitative effects on JFL learners' katakana writing accuracy. To help rule out a possibility that the participants' greater accuracy and fluency might be attributed to their having had more character practice than the COPY students, we asked the participants to self-report in the perception survey on the number of hours they spent on character practice. The reports did not reveal a noticeable difference between the TD groups and the COPY group. In designing the character copying homework and the TD test for each chapter, we strove to ensure that students in the three groups would produce roughly the same amount of work. The self-reports appeared to indicate that we were successful in achieving that goal. Admittedly, self-reported results may not be precise, which could be a limitation of the study.

RQ 2. Do TD in an online course and character copying in a face-to-face (F2F) course foster comparable character writing abilities?

Since writing is presumably harder to coach in an online environment, we wanted to see whether TD could foster comparable character writing abilities in the online students. Although the statistical comparison between the TD-OL group and the COPY group did not reach significance, there was a clear tendency ($p = .06$) to favor TD. This suggests that TD could be an attractive alternative to character copying in the online environment as well.

It should be noted that thus far, we have tested and discussed character copying and TD as two distinct activities; in the reality of classroom *Hanzi* teaching, however, these two activities are perhaps both indispensable and could not be precisely separated. Before students can engage in TD, they must learn each character by following a model stroke by stroke, just as students do in a character copying condition. This initial stroke-by-stroke practice phase is indispensable and is common to both methods.

RQ 3. How do students perceive TD and character copying activities?

The perception survey revealed deeper information about TD and character copying from the students' perspectives. In Question 3, the TD students thought TD was beneficial, while the COPY students did not have the same positive perception of character copying. Some of the TD students, however, pointed out a few shortcomings of TD; those shortcomings had actually been addressed in the design of the Timed Dictation Player, specifically in light of its feature to adjust the duration of pauses between sentences. That feature was designed with the exact purpose to lessen the kind of frustration and pressure that participants reported in this study. Those complaints of some TD students perhaps suggested that we could have taken time to explain that feature to them more thoroughly. One advocate of character copying in the TD-F2F group and the several students unhappy about character copying in the COPY group have reminded us of the importance of paying attention to individual learning styles. In other words, TD, despite showing positive results in this study, may not be suitable for everyone.

Questions 12 and 13 addressed the enjoyability aspect of the activities. Related to learning style, one student found TD to be a "fun" activity (TD-F2F_11). With an imposed time limit, TD may have a game-like appeal to some students. Overall, however, the TD groups' perceptions were in the *somewhat* enjoyable range rather than the *highly* enjoyable range (5.86 and 6.82 for the TD-F2F and the TD-OL group, respectively). The COPY group's perceptions on character copying, on the other hand, were decidedly negative. They did not find it enjoyable at all. Words like "time-consuming," "tedious," "mindless," and "boring" were used to describe the character copying activity. This confirms our discussion earlier in this chapter on character copying and the general beliefs about character copying held by CFL instructors.

This study also revealed that students seemed to recognize TD's spillover effect on other skill areas, most obviously listening. Our use of key sentences was deliberate in this regard since they contained important vocabulary words and key grammar points. We wanted students to produce something meaningful and intended to give them a feeling of actively producing language through TD rather than pure attention to character forms in character copying.

Conclusion

We began this chapter by examining the complexities of Chinese characters that make them difficult to learn, and then discussed issues in teaching/learning Chinese characters. We then introduced Timed Dictation, an innovative method that we had used for improving CLF learners' acquisition of Chinese character writing skills, and reported a quasi-experimental study that aimed to test the effect of the method on beginning-level CFL learners' character writing accuracy and fluency. The results of this preliminary study were encouraging; not only was TD more effective than character copying for character writing accuracy and fluency, but it also showed a potential to improve grammar, listening, and speaking skills. These findings corroborate those of Sawyer and Silver (1961) and Pappas (1977) that dictation could help improve learners' listening and writing. TD was also perceived as more enjoyable and beneficial than copying. The findings of this study also shed light on how to conduct Chinese character training in online courses to help reduce the "excessive workload" (Sun et al., 2013) of instructors and achieve teaching goals.

The study admittedly has a few limitations. It was a preliminary, small-scale study with a small sample of 42 CFL learners. A larger-scale, follow-up study is clearly needed to solidify the conclusions on the positive effects of TD. A separate and better pretest could have been conducted to measure the starting character writing ability of the students and check the compatibility of the three groups. In the current study, we used only the result of the first chapter test. Although the chapter test required students to write characters, it was not intended specifically as a test to measure character writing ability. In addition, a delayed posttest could be administered to investigate long-term retention of the experimental effect.

References

Allen, J. R. (2008). Why learning to write Chinese is a waste of time: A modest proposal. *Foreign Language Annals, 41*, 237–251.

Bai, J. (2003). Making multimedia an integral part of curricular innovation. *Journal of the Chinese Language Teachers Association, 38*(2), 1–15.

Bell, J. S. (1995). Relationship between L1 and L2 literacy: Some complicating factors. *TESOL Quarterly, 29*, 687–704.

Bourgerie, D. (2003). Computer aided language learning for Chinese: A survey and annotated bibliography. *Journal of the Chinese Language Teachers Association, 38*(2), 17–47.

Chen, D. (2005). Empowering Chinese language via technology. *Global Chinese Journal on Computer in Education, 3*, 159–182.

Chen, H., Hsu, C., Chang, L., Lin, Y., Chang, K., & Sung, Y. (2013). Using a radical-derived character e-learning platform to increase learner knowledge of Chinese characters. *Language Learning & Technology, 17*(1), 89–106.

DeFrancis, J. (1984). *The Chinese language: Fact and fantasy*. University of Hawaii Press.

Dew, J. E. (2007). Language is primary, script is secondary: The importance of gaining a strong foundation in the language before developing major efforts to character recognition. In A. Guder, X. Jiang, & Y. Wan (Eds.), *The cognition, learning and teaching of Chinese characters* (pp. 451–462). Beijing Language & Culture University Press.

Everson, M. E. (1988). Speed and comprehension in reading Chinese: Romanization vs. characters revisited. *Journal of the Chinese Language Teachers Association, 23*, 1–15.

Everson, M. E. (1994). Towards a process view of teaching reading the second language Chinese curriculum. *Theory into Practice, 33*(1), 4–9.

Guder, A. (2005). *Struggling with Chinese: New dimensions in foreign language teaching*. Paper presented at the International and Interdisciplinary Conference, University of Mainz, Germersheim, Germany.

He, W. (2005). *Teaching Chinese written scripts with a new computer approach*. Paper presented at the International and Interdisciplinary Conference, University of Mainz, Germersheim, Germany.

Hsiao, H., Chang, C., Chen, C., Wu, C., & Lin, C. (2015). The influence of Chinese character handwriting diagnosis and remedial instruction system on learners of Chinese as a foreign language. *Computer Assisted Language Learning, 28*(4), 306–324.

Hsiung, H.-Y., Chang, Y.-L., Chen, H.-C., & Sung, Y.-T. (2017). Effect of stroke-order learning and handwriting exercises on recognizing and writing Chinese characters by Chinese as a foreign language learners. *Computers in Human Behavior, 74*, 303–310.

Irvine, P., Atai, P., & Oller, J. W. (1974). Cloze, dictation, and the test of English as a foreign language. *Language Learning, 24*(2), 245–252.

Jafarpur, A., & Yamini, M. (1993). Does practice with dictation improve language skills? *System, 21*, 359–369.

Jen, T., & Xu, P. (2000). Penless Chinese character reproduction. *Sino-Platonic Papers, 102*, 1–15.

Jin, H. (2006). Effects and Chinese character processing: An empirical study of CFL learners from three different orthographic backgrounds. *Journal of the Chinese Language Teachers Association, 41*(3), 35–56.

Jorden, E. H., & Walton, A. R. (1987). Truly foreign languages: Instructional challenges. *The Analysis of the American Academy, 490*, 110–149.

Kan, Q., Owen, N., & Bax, S. (2018). Researching mobile-assisted Chinese-character learning strategies among adult distance learners. *Innovation in Language and Teaching, 12*(1), 56–71.

Kou, M., & Hooper, S. (2004). The effects of visual and verbal coding memories on learning Chinese characters in computer-based instruction. *Educational Technology Research and Development, 52*(3), 23–38.

Li, D. (1998). 从汉语的两个特点必须切实重视汉字教学 (Discussing the importance of teaching Chinese characters from the two characteristics of Chinese language). *Journal of Peking University, 3*(35), 128–132.

Li, Y. (2020). *The Chinese writing system in Asian: An interdisciplinary perspective.* Routledge.

Lin, C. H., & Lien, Y. J. (2012). Teaching and learning Chinese with an iPad. *Journal of Technology and Chinese Language Teaching, 3*(2), 47–63.

Liu, I. (1983). The learning of characters: A conceptual learning approach. *Journal of the Chinese Language Teachers Association, 18*(2), 65–76.

Liu, X. (2010). *New practical Chinese learners* (2nd ed.). Beijing Language and Culture University Press.

McGinnis, S. (1999). Students' goals and approaches. In M. Chu (Ed.), *Mapping the course of the Chinese language field* (*Chinese language teachers association monograph series: Vol. III*) (pp. 151–188). Chinese Language Teachers Association.

Miyamoto, M., Suzuki, N., Fukada, A., Huang, Y., Hou, S., & Hong, W. (2018). Teaching languages online: Innovations and challenges. In R. Sell (Ed.), *Purdue e-Pubs.* https://docs.lib.purdue.edu/plcc/purduelanguagesandculturesconference2017/translationalideas/3/

Nation, I. S. P. (1991, October). Dictation, dicto-comp and related techniques. *English Teaching Forum, 29*, 12–14. www.wgtn.ac.nz/lals/resources/paul-nations-publications/paul-nations-publications/publications/1991-Dictation.pdf

Okada, A. (2016). *Effects of a timed dictation activity in the introductory course in Japanese focusing on the accuracy and fluency of writing Katakana.* (Publication No. 10146956) [Master's thesis, Purdue University]. ProQuest.

Oller, J. W. (1971). Dictation as a device for testing foreign-language proficiency. *ELT Journal, 25*(3), 254–259.

Oller, J. W., & Streiff, V. (1975). Dictation: A test of grammar-based expectancies. *ELT Journal, 30*(1), 25–36.

Pappas, G. S. (1977). You mean you still give dictation? *Language Arts, 54*(8), 936–939.

Qian, K., Owen, N., & Bax, S. (2018). Researching mobile-assisted Chinese-character learning strategies among adult distance learners. *Innovation in Language and Teaching, 12*(1), 56–71.

Ren, X., Ren, F. X., & He, W. H. (2013). The design and implementation of CAI software used in Chinese character components in the process of teaching Chinese as a foreign language. *Journal of Yunnan University, 35*(S1), 123–128.

Sawyer, J., & Silver, S. (1961). Dictation in language learning. *Language Learning, 11*(1–2), 33–42.

Shei, C., & Hsieh, H. (2012). Linkit: A CALL system for learning Chinese characters, words, and phrases. *Computer Assisted Language Learning, 25*(4), 319–338.

Sun, M., Chen, Y., & Olson, A. (2013). Developing and implementing an Online program: A case study. In B. Zou, M. Chen, Y. Wang, M. Sun, & C. Xiang (Eds.), *Computer-assisted foreign language teaching and learning: Technological advances* (pp. 160–187). IGI Global.

Swihart, D. W. (2004). *Success with Chinese, level 1: Listening & speaking*. Cheng & Tsui Company.

Unger, J., Lorish, F., Noda, M., & Wada, Y. (1993). *A framework for introductory Japanese language curricula in American high schools and colleges*. The National Foreign Language Center.

Wang, D. P., & East, M. (2020). Constructing an emergency Chinese curriculum during the pandemic: A New Zealand experience. *International Journal of Chinese Language Teaching, 1*(1), 1–19.

Williams, Z. (2013). *The use of multimedia material in teaching Chinese as a second language and pedagogical implications* (Master's thesis). University of Massachusetts Amherst. https://scholarworks.umass.edu/cgi/viewcontent.cgi?article=2073&context=theses

Xie, T. (2001). e-Generation's Chinese language teachers: Meet the new challenges. *Journal of the Chinese Language Teachers Association, 36*(3), 75–80.

Xu, Y., Chang, L., Zhang, J., & Perfetti, C. A. (2013). Reading, writing, and animation in character learning in Chinese as a foreign language. *Foreign Language Annals, 46*(3), 423–444.

Yan, C. M. W., McBride-Chang, C., Wagner, R. K., Zhang, J., Wong, A. M. Y., & Shu, H. (2012). Writing quality in Chinese children: Speed and fluency matter. *Reading and Writing, 25*(7), 1499–1521.

Yao, T. (2009). The current status of Chinese CALL in the United States. *Journal of Chinese Language Teachers Association, 44*(1), 1–23.

Ye, L. (2011). *Teaching and learning Chinese as a foreign language in the United States: To delay or not delay the character introduction* (Doctoral dissertation). Georgia State University. https://scholarworks.gsu.edu/cgi/viewcontent.cgi?article=1021&context=alesl_diss

Ye, L. (2013). Shall we delay teaching characters in teaching Chinese as a foreign language? *Foreign Language Annals, 46*(4), 610–627.

Zhan, H., & Cheng, H. J. (2014). The role of technology in teaching and learning Chinese characters. *International Journal of Technology in Teaching and learning, 10*(2), 147–162.

Zhang, T. R. (2007). 中国集中识字教学的认知机制 (The cognitive system of focus-on-literacy pedagogy in China). In A. Guder, X. Jiang, & Y. Wan (Eds.), *The cognition, learning and teaching of Chinese characters* (pp. 451–462). Beijing Language & Culture University Press.

Zhao, S., & Baldauf, R. (2008). *Planning Chinese characters: Reaction, evolution or revolution?* Springer.

Zhu, Y., & Hong, W. (2005). Effects of digital voiced pronunciation and stroke sequence animation on character memorization of CFL learners. *Journal of the Chinese Language Teachers Association, 40*(3), 49–70.

Appendix 4.1
Chinese characters written test

*Instruction: Please write down each sentence in Hanzi according to the Pinyin. You will have **15 minutes** to finish writing.*

1. wǒ zài mǎi yì píng hóng pútao jiǔ, zěnme yàng?

2. wǒmen xiàwǔ yǒu yígè jùhuì, zhùhè tā de shēngrì.

3. wǒ hěn xǐhuān chī kǎoyā.

4. yígòng shíliù kuài qián, nín gěi wǒ èrshí, wǒ zhǎonín sì kuài.

5. shīfu, yì jīn xiāngjiāo duōshǎo qián?

6. qǐng wèn, xiànzài jǐ diǎn? chà yíkè bā diǎn.

7. nǐ wǎnshàng jǐ diǎn shuìjiào?

8. jīntiān tiānqì hěn lěng, nǐ yào duō chuān diǎnr yīfu.

9. nǐ nǎr bù shūfu?

10. nǐ sǎngzi yǒu diǎnr fā yán, hái yǒu diǎnr fā shāo, shì gǎnmào.

11. wǒ xiǎng gàosu nǐ yí jiàn shìr.

12. wǒ xiǎng zū yítào yǒu chúfáng hé cèsuǒ de fángzi.

13. wǒ gěi wǒ péngyou dǎ gè diànhuà, ràng tā lái bāngzhù nǐmen.

14. bù hǎo yì si, zāng yīfu wǒ xiǎng xīngqī liù yìqǐ xǐ.

15. wǒ xiǎng qù ōuzhōu lǚxíng, kěshì wǒ de péngyǒu xiǎng qù shànghǎi.

Appendix 4.2
A survey on learning Chinese characters for TD groups

Gender: Male   Female
First language: _____
Additional language(s): _____
Age group: 18–24   25–34   Above 34

1. How important do you think learning Chinese characters is?
   Not at all Very important

   1   2   3   4   5   6   7   8   9   10

2. Approximately how many hours do you spend each day on learning/practicing Chinese characters?

   1. 0–1   B. 1–2   C. 2–3   D. 3–4   E. More than 4 hours

3. Overall, how beneficial is Timed Dictation to your learning of characters?
   Not at all Very beneficial

   1   2   3   4   5   6   7   8   9   10

4. Please explain why you think it is or is not beneficial.

5. Do you think Timed Dictation is helpful in improving your speed of writing characters?
   Not at all Very helpful

   1   2   3   4   5   6   7   8   9   10

6. Do you think Timed Dictation is helpful in improving your accuracy of writing characters?
   Not at all Very helpful

   1   2   3   4   5   6   7   8   9   10

7. Do you think Timed Dictation is helpful in learning grammar/sentence structure?
   Not at all Very helpful

   1   2   3   4   5   6   7   8   9   10

8. Do you think Timed Dictation is helpful in improving your listening skills?
   Not at all Very helpful

   1   2   3   4   5   6   7   8   9   10

9. Do you think Timed Dictation is helpful in improving your speaking skills?
   Not at all Very helpful

   1   2   3   4   5   6   7   8   9   10

10. Do you think Timed Dictation will be beneficial in 101 level as well?
    Not at all Very beneficial

    1   2   3   4   5   6   7   8   9   10

11. Do you think Timed Dictation will be beneficial in 201 level as well?
    Not at all Very beneficial

    1   2   3   4   5   6   7   8   9   10

12. Overall, did you enjoy Timed Dictation?
    Not at all Enjoyed very much

    1   2   3   4   5   6   7   8   9   10

13. Please specify why you enjoyed/did not enjoy Timed Dictation:

14. Any other comments or suggestions for Timed Dictation?

谢谢你的参与！
Thank you for your participation!

Part II
Reading comprehension subskills and readers' identity

5 The role of character-recognition skills in shallow and deep reading comprehension

Wei-Li Hsu

Introduction

Reading is a skill that is essential for functioning in contemporary society, as it allows us to understand the various types of texts like signs, text messages, news headlines, emails, captions of foreign movies, novels, and technical reports, that can be encountered in day-to-day life. In a foreign-language context, although language courses emphasize learning to read, a primary goal is often the acquisition of linguistic forms based on selected written texts. Although the curriculum often requires learners to comprehend a written text, the content could already be familiar to the learner in their first or dominant language. Deep and meaningful comprehension is often overlooked or even assumed. The emphasis on linguistic forms is contradictory to principles of communicative language learning in which the primary focus of instruction is on meaning rather than on form (Canale & Swain, 1980).

Given that language learning should aim for real-world language use, research on second language (L2) reading and reading pedagogies should consider real-world reading with different purposes, in which both the emphasis on meaning and form are important (Bachman & Palmer, 1996). Accordingly, L2 reading research should consider different levels of comprehension and their pedagogical and testing implications on L2 reading (Grabe, 2009). For example, for L2 readers, a superficial understanding, based on mere word recognition, would be sufficient for browsing shop signs; but a deep understanding, which requires cognitive skills, vocabulary knowledge, and background knowledge, among others, would be necessary for reading a science textbook. The present study aimed to understand better how L2 Chinese readers, especially advanced L2 Chinese readers, adjust their reading processes and skills for different reading purposes where the level of comprehension involved differs.

Literature review

Levels of text comprehension

While there are many ways to categorize the levels of text comprehension or levels of mental representations of textual information, the three main levels are: the surface structure, propositional textbase, and the situation model (Grabe, 2009; Kintsch, 1988; Kintsch & van Dijk, 1978; McNamara & Magliano, 2009). The level of surface structure, which is the shallowest level of comprehension, refers to the mental representation of words and syntactical relationship between them in decoded texts. An example characterized by surface reading is proofreading a text when the purpose is to check and correct spelling and grammatical errors without attention to the meaning behind what is read.

The second level of comprehension is the propositional textbase; the propositional knowledge encoded in the textbase is simple and not detailed. Propositions are units of meaning networks which are activated in working memory during text comprehension. As decoded information from the surface structure is processed in working memory, more propositions are formed and activated. The propositions that get activated more often become central within the semantic network, as the less activated or deactivated propositions become excluded from the network. Textbase comprehension is simple and general, and requires a limited degree of background knowledge, such as the knowledge enabling the recognition that *Anne* is a female name while *Tom* is a male name.

To construct the third level, a situation model, readers are required to extract meaningful representations of a text, incorporate more background knowledge, and make inferences beyond the text. Although propositional textbase and situation model are complementary and not exclusive layers of comprehension (Kintsch, 1998), Grabe (2009) concluded that there are three advantages of distinguishing the textbase and the situation model in teaching and testing L2 reading. He argues that the two-model framework is better at explaining both reading different texts in different ways for different purposes and individual differences in reading comprehension. However, instructors would be more interested in how well readers can construct a mental "situation" representing the temporal, causal, spatial, or motivational relationships depicted in a text. Therefore, an alternative way of assessing different levels of comprehension would be to examine levels of shallow and deep comprehension. While shallow comprehension represents explicit content of a text, deep comprehension requires inferencing to build the referenced and implicit aspects of a text (McNamara & Kendeou, 2011; McNamara & Magliano, 2009).

There are two common types of inferences guiding a situation model, which are bridging and knowledge-based inferences (McNamara & Magliano, 2009). Bridging references refer to the semantic "bridges" connecting propositions that are not made explicit within a text. To obtain coherence in comprehension, readers need to generate bridging inferences that link a piece of new information to its referent in a previous clause, such as connecting *tea* in one subordinate clause with *drink* in a previous main clause. Compared to bridging inferences concerning co-reference connections, knowledge-based inferences connect textual propositions with prior knowledge. L2 readers, like L1 beginner-level readers, were found to be more likely than proficient L1 readers to encounter challenges in inferential comprehension (Barry & Lazarte, 1995; Carrell, 1985), suggesting that inferencing is influenced by both cognitive and linguistic subskills, such as word

Role of character-recognition skills in reading comprehension 91

recognition, syntactic processing, discourse knowledge, and prior knowledge (Barry & Lazarte, 1995; Carrell, 1985; Hudson, 2007; Perfetti & Stafura, 2014).

Character recognition and Chinese script

Among the linguistic subskills interacting with inferencing, character recognition (CR), as a word-recognition subskill in Chinese reading, has been reported as a major challenge to L2 readers, especially beginning readers (Everson & Ke, 1997; Shen, 2013). CR has been found to be fundamental in reading development in L1 and L2 Chinese reading (e.g., Everson, 1998; Lü & Koda, 2011; McBride-Chang & Kail, 2002; Shen, 2000; Shen & Ke, 2007; Tong & McBride-Chang, 2010). The challenges of CR are related to the nature of Chinese script, which usually comprises three aspects: orthography, phonology, and morphology (Perfetti & Tan, 1999). Accordingly, the features of Chinese script, which are fundamental to CR, are discussed here based on these three constituents.

Regarding orthography, most Chinese characters, as the basic unit of Chinese script, encode both phonetic and semantic information (Ho et al., 2003); and such characters are termed as compound characters. Two common patterns of these compound characters are: left-right and top-bottom (Ho et al., 2003; Shen & Bear, 2000). For the left-right pattern, the *phonetic component* is typically, but not always, on the right-hand side of the host character, while the *semantic component* or *radical* is generally located on the left-hand side. For the top-bottom pattern, the positioning of the sub-character components is more versatile than the left-right pattern, in that the semantic radical can be either on the top or the bottom of a character. However, each semantic radical usually occupies a specific position in the host character. For instance, the regular positions of semantic radicals 木, 欠, 艹, and 灬 are on the left, the right, the top, and the bottom of characters, respectively. Since the typical position of 欠 is on the right of a character, placing it on the left, the top, or the bottom violates the rules of positional regularity, which is a subcategory of orthographic knowledge (Cheung et al., 2007; Taft & Zhu, 1997; Taft et al., 1999; X.-L. Tong & McBride-Chang, 2010). Therefore, as orthographic knowledge develops, Chinese readers refine their knowledge from more general orthographic patterns to more specific radical positions (Shu et al., 2000; X.-H. Tong et al., 2017).

Unlike in alphabetic languages, which directly encode pronunciation in graphemes/letters, the phonetic component in a Chinese compound character provides only partial pronunciation of the character. For example, in the character 松 (*sōng* in pinyin, "pine"), the phonetic component 公 (*gōng* "fair, equitable, public") provides only the rime *ōng* of the character. In another compound character, 訟 (*sòng* "accuse, argue, litigate"), the phonetic component 公 provides the same rime as that in the character 松. Between the two compound characters, 松 and 訟, the different semantic radicals, denoting their semantic categories of the host characters. Namely, 木 and 言 mean "trees, woods" and "words, speech, speak," respectively.

On the morphology of Chinese in the context of reading, a Chinese character is typically a morpheme and most Chinese words are composed of two morphemes, or two characters, although a word can consist of one to six characters (Shen & Bear, 2000). Take 松树 (*sōngshù*, "pine tree") and 訴訟 (*sùsòngshù*, "lawsuit") as examples. While the radicals 木 and 言 offer the broad semantic categories of their respective host character, the characters 松, 树, 訴, and 訟 reflect more precise meanings of the words, which are "pine," "trees," "accuse," and "litigate," respectively. In a study of the reading development of L1 Chinese first and fourth graders (W. Li et al., 2002), morphological skill was found to be the best predictor and to play an increasingly important role as readers grew older. In a more refined study of CR development, X.-L. Tong (2008) examined the relationship between phonology, orthography, morphology, and sub-character processing skills. The results of the Structural Equation Modeling analysis suggested that for pre-readers, the four variables loaded into two groups: one group tested orally and the other one tested through print. For later readers, morphology, orthography, and sub-character skills loaded on one factor; and phonological skills were found to function differently from the three other types. Therefore, as reading ability progresses, phonological skills are likely to function differently from the other CR subskills in reading processing.

For the purpose of the present study, CR subskills are divided into three categories: ortho-phonology, ortho-semantics, and morphology. The first two skills reflect sub-character components and their corresponding CR subskills. Their roles in L1 and L2 reading are first reviewed here, followed by those of morphological skill in the development of CR and Chinese reading (Dong et al., 2020; Ku & Anderson, 2003; W. Li et al., 2002; X.-L. Tong, 2008; X.-L. Tong & McBride-Chang, 2010; D. Zhang, 2017a, 2017b; D. Zhang & Ke, 2020).

Ortho-phonological skill

Ortho-phonological skill (PS) refers to the ability to analyze the phonetic components of characters and to apply the knowledge, or the analyzed information, for CR (Shu et al., 2000). Chinese L1 children begin to develop PS as early as the age of six, when they start to become able to apply PS to unfamiliar characters (W. Li et al., 2002; Shu & Anderson, 1999; Tan & Perfetti, 1997; X.-L. Tong, 2008). In a regression-analysis study, Cheung et al. (2007) found that PS is a significant predictor of reading comprehension for L1 children aged between nine and 11.6 years old, explaining approximately 5% of the unique variance in Chinese reading comprehension. PS's small but essential role in CR has been explained in a study (Hung et al., 2014); their results indicate that PS is more crucial than ortho-semantic skill at the early stage of decoding novel or unfamiliar characters.

Studies of bilingual Chinese readers (X.-L. Tong, 2008; X.-L. Tong et al., 2016; X.-L. Tong & McBride-Chang, 2010; H.-W. Zhang & Roberts, 2019) also revealed PS's significant contribution to Chinese reading comprehension. However, PS is considered less predictive than ortho-semantic and morphological skills, due to the low grapheme-phoneme correspondence (GPC) of Chinese script (X.-L. Tong, 2008; X.-L. Tong & McBride-Chang, 2010). Regarding differences in GPC between L1 and L2 orthographies, X.-L. Tong and colleagues (2016) found that

PS has a lower effect on CR for English-speaking L2 Chinese readers than for Korean- and Japanese-speaking L2 Chinese readers. Other studies (Everson & Ke, 1997; Lee-Thompson, 2008; W.-W. Wong, 2011) found that, while English-speaking L2 Chinese readers can apply PS for the weak-GPC Chinese script, they rely less on PS than on ortho-semantic skill.

Ortho-semantic skill

Ortho-semantic skill, or radical skill (RS), refers to the ability to analyze semantic radicals in characters and apply the knowledge to CR (Shu & Anderson, 1997). While studies have found that beginner-level L1 Chinese readers rely more on PS than RS (X.-H. Tong et al., 2017; X.-L. Tong & McBride-Chang, 2010; Y. Wang et al., 2015), RS remains a significant predictor of CR, with its contribution increasing as reading ability develops. Young, beginner-level L1 Chinese children between the ages of four and six, were observed to actively apply RS to determine the meaning of a character when reading an unfamiliar character and when reading sentences (X.-H. Tong et al., 2017; X.-L. Tong & McBride-Chang, 2010; Y. Wang et al., 2015). For older bilingual readers, between the ages of nine and 12, Cheung and colleagues (2007) found that the contributions of PS and RS in Chinese reading comprehension and the correlations of PS and RS with Chinese reading comprehension are similar, with all contributions and correlations being statistically significant. For advanced L1 Chinese readers who are older than university students, scholars (Feldman & Siok, 1999; Zhou et al., 2013) found that semantic information is processed at multiple levels, such as at the sub-character, character, and word levels; and RS is more likely to be activated for less-frequent characters than for frequent ones.

For adult L2 readers, RS is also a significant predictor of word reading (X.-L. Tong et al., 2016; X.-L. Tong & Yip, 2015). English-speaking L2 readers tend to rely more on RS than on PS because of the challenge of transferring the ortho-semantic skill from English to Chinese. Furthermore, pedagogy-oriented studies (Shen & Ke, 2007; W.-W. Wong, 2011; Xu et al., 2014) reported the advantage of introducing and grouping semantic radicals for learning new characters, thus suggesting the RS effect on reading development.

Morphological skill

Morphological skills often refer to the skills that are used to determine the character meanings in compounding words and among homophones (Dong et al., 2020; Kuo & Anderson, 2008; H. Li et al., 2017; X.-L. Tong, 2008; D. Zhang et al., 2019; H.-M. Zhang, 2014). Morphological skills can be assessed through tasks for morpheme recognition, morpheme discrimination, compound structure, meaning selection, and morpheme production (see Ke & Xiao, 2015 for a review). However, this study focuses on the morpheme-discrimination skill, which is used to test whether readers understood that the same character may have different meanings in different words. Studies found that morpheme-discrimination skill is positively and significantly correlated with word reading, character and vocabulary knowledge, and reading comprehension (Ku & Anderson, 2003; D. Zhang, 2017a; H.-M. Zhang, 2016), and that morpheme-discrimination skill is a predictor of reading comprehension (Cheng, Zhang, Wu et al., 2016; D. Zhang et al., 2019).

In a meta-analysis of studies that examined the relationship among RS, MS, orthographical skill, and reading comprehension in L1 Chinese readers, MS was reported to be the strongest predictor of reading comprehension (Dong et al., 2020). Studies of L1 and bilingual Chinese readers (Kim et al., 2020; D. Zhang, 2017a; D. Zhang et al., 2019; H.-M. Zhang, 2014) reported that MS directly and/ or indirectly contributes to reading comprehension, with indirect paths sometimes being mediated by vocabulary knowledge and word recognition abilities. Path/ regression coefficients for direct contributions ranged from 0.18 to 0.51 and those for indirect contributions ranged between 0.05 and 0.34. They indicated a wide range of MS contributions, which can perhaps be attributed to which MS aspects were measured in those studies and how they were measured. For example, the largest and smallest direct contributions were reported by D. Zhang (2017a), which measured MS contributions using a morpheme-discrimination task, a compound-structure task, and a meaning-selection task; and the tasks were read aloud to the participants. However, H.-M. Zhang (2014) found that MS only indirectly but significantly contributed to reading comprehension, with direct contribution not being statistically significant. In this study, MS was measured using a morpheme-discrimination task, a compound-structure task, and a morpheme-recognition task, and the tasks were presented on paper. In other words, in addition to the aspects measured, MS contribution could also be influenced by the tasks used and the ways the tasks were administered.

J. Zhang et al. (2014) explains MS's importance in light of morphology being a larger processing unit and henceforth the releasing of working memory for vocabulary learning and reading comprehension. Following this study, Cheng and others (Cheng, Zhang, Li et al., 2016; Cheng, Zhang, Wu et al., 2016) found MS's reciprocal relationship with word reading. Through the reciprocal relationships, MS both directly and indirectly facilitates reading comprehension, which may lead MS to be the CR subskill most predictive of reading comprehension.

Research questions

The objective of the present study was to find out to what extent the three CR subskills contribute to both shallow and deep reading comprehension for L2 Chinese readers. Accordingly, the two research questions are:

1. To what extent do the three CR subskills correlate with shallow and deep reading comprehension?
2. To what extent do the three CR subskills predict shallow and deep comprehension?

Method

Participants

Recruiting emails were sent out to Chinese language instructors in Canada, Singapore, and the United States through associations and discussion forums for Chinese language teachers and personal connections. The emails asked recipients to distribute a recruiting flyer to their students who met five requirements, with particular emphasis on the fifth requirement regarding their language background. To participate in the study, participants had to be 1) at least 16 years old, 2) have English as their native or dominant language, 3) be able to read Chinese articles with more than 250 Chinese characters (either in simplified or traditional characters), and 4) have English-speaking or Chinese-speaking parents.

To reflect the multi-lingual, multi-lectal (multidialectal) contexts where many Chinese language learners lived/studied, language background was chosen as the fifth requirement. In this study, language background is defined as home exposure, or a lack of it, to the target language (He & Xiao, 2008; Wiley, 2009; K.-F. Wong & Xiao, 2010; L. Zhang, 2014 for detailed reviews on Chinese heritage language learning). The fifth requirement for participating in the study was to be members of one of the following four groups:

1. Singaporean Chinese Mother-Tongue Language Learners[1] (Singaporean CMTLLs): participants who were born and raised in Singapore, were native speakers of English, and whose parents were both native speakers of English;
2. Chinese Foreign Language Learners (CFLLs): participants who were born and raised in Canada or the U.S., were native speakers of English, and whose parents were both native speakers of English;
3. Mandarin-Speaking Heritage Language Learners (Man-HLLs): participants who were born and raised in Canada or the U.S., whose strongest language was English, and whose parents were both native speakers of Mandarin; or
4. Cantonese-Speaking Heritage Language Learners (Can-HLLs): participants who were born and raised in Canada or the U.S., whose strongest language was English, and whose parents were both native speakers of Cantonese.

In this study, the group of CFLLs represent the "typical" Chinese language learners, Man-HLLs represent the heritage learners with home exposure to the Chinese dialect taught in class and Can-HLLs represent the heritage learners with home exposure to a common Chinese dialect as learners' home language. Singaporean CMTLLs are included to represent a relative multilingual context in which the target language enjoys a certain official status, which is not the case for Chinese in Canada and the United States.

After screening the data, 85 participants were included in the final sample. The mean lengths of Chinese learning in different contexts are 3.54 years for those attending Chinese weekend schools ($SD = 4.58$), 2.58 years for those attending middle schools and high schools ($SD = 3.58$), and 1.15 years for those at university ($SD = 1.23$). There were 14 Singaporean CMTLLs, 19 CFLLs, 38 Man-HLLs, and 14 Can-HLLs. The age of the participants ranged from 16 to 52 ($M = 22.99$ years, $SD = 7.34$). The average age of the four groups ranged from 18.00 to 24.03 years, with the Singaporean CMTLLs being the youngest of the four groups ($M = 18.00$, $SD = 0.85$ for Singaporean CMTLLs; $M = 21.85, SD = 8.02$ for CFLLs; $M = 24.03$, $SD = 7.19$ for Man-HLLs; $M = 22.93, SD = 4.95$ for Can-HLLs).

Instruments

Shallow and deep comprehension were measured with a fill-in-the-blank cloze subtest and a multiple-choice passage-comprehension subtest, respectively. The cloze subtest was designed to assess shallow comprehension, that is, comprehension accessible through surface structure and local co-references only. Inter-sentential and inter-paragraph connections were not necessary to fill in the blanks (Shanahan et al., 1982).[2] The passage-comprehension subtest was designed to assess deeper comprehension, including bridging and knowledge-based inferences. The MS, RS, and PS, the three character-recognition skills, were measured with three corresponding subtests (in Table 5.1).

All subtests were piloted twice, once with five educated native speakers of Mandarin and once with readers of Chinese as a second language who had a similar level of proficiency in Chinese. After the first pilot test, only the items that received the same responses from the five native speakers remained. The items that received contradictory responses were later revised and retested with the same native speakers. Considering that the format of the cloze subtest was fill in the blank, all responses provided by the native speakers were regarded as correct. After the second pilot test, when less than 30% of the participants correctly answered a particular item or more than 80% of the participants correctly answered a specific item, the items were deleted because the items were too easy or too difficult for the participants. Thus, the percentage of participants correctly answering the item represents item difficulty; and when 30% of the participants correctly answer the item, the item difficulty is 0.3. This approach is different from that of traditional classroom-based assessment. This was chosen because the current study aimed at items that could elicit greater individual differences in the target's skill. As a result, the number of items in each subtest was relatively low,

Table 5.1 Average Performances

Subtests	K	α	M	SD
Cloze	12	0.91	0.42	0.36
Passage-comprehension	7	0.67	0.59	0.28
PS	4	0.69	0.58	0.32
RS	4	0.61	0.56	0.33
MS	5	0.60	0.65	0.29

which also led to lower reliabilities for some of the subtests. All questions were presented with both simplified and traditional characters.

Shallow comprehension

The cloze subtest consisted of two passages. Both passages contained approximately 130 Chinese characters. One passage was a descriptive text and the other an expository text. The topics of the two articles were scenic attractions in China and highway systems. The cloze subtest was designed in the format of fill in the blanks. The first blank targeted the eighth character of each passage, and there were seven characters between each blank. After deleting items that were too easy and too difficult, 12 blanks remained. Participants received a point when their answer was one of the responses provided by the native speakers during the first pilot test.

Deep comprehension

The passage-comprehension subtest consisted of five passages, each ranging from 340 to 430 characters. Text types included descriptive, narrative, and expository. The topics were an email to parents, a news article about higher education in China, job-searching by overseas returnees to China, Chinese mythology, and scientific exploration in Antarctica. Bridging inferencing was operationalized as the ability to identify answers by connecting explicit details in different sentences; knowledge-based inferencing was operationalized as the ability to identify answers by connecting background knowledge with details that were not specified in the passages. Item examples of the two kinds of inferences are 1) "what does Peter usually do on Wednesday afternoon" for bridging inferencing when Peter's activities on other weekdays were mentioned and 2) "what can we know about scientific expedition in Antarctica" for knowledge-based inferencing, which required connecting background knowledge of science and Antarctica and bridging inferences made from the text. Initially, 30 items were developed, and seven items remained after the two pilot tests. Among the 10 items, seven items targeted bridging and knowledge-based inferencing.

Character recognition

Character-recognition skills were measured with the PS, RS, and MS subtests. In the PS subtest, a pseudo-character made up of two real characters was presented at the beginning of each item, and participants were asked to choose the option from three options with the closest pronunciation to it. A correct answer was the phonetic component of the pseudo-character. One distractor was the semantic radical of the pseudo-character, with the other distractor being a character with a similar shape to that of the target pseudo-character (see Figure 5.1).

In the RS subtest, a drawing of something that does not exist in the real world was presented at the beginning of each item. Participants were then asked to

Figure 5.1 Example of the PS subtest

Figure 5.2 Example of the RS subtest

choose the option that best described it. The drawings were targeted at the radicals of insects, wooden objects, and luminous or flaming objects. Each item included three options, each of which was a pseudo-character made up of two real characters (see Figure 5.2). To complete this subtest, a participant would need to know the semantic radicals representing the drawing and their positions as semantic radicals. Again, two distractors were presented in the options: 1) a pseudo-character with the same sub-character components as the correct answer but which violated the rules of positional regularity; and 2) a pseudo-character containing the same character as the phonetic component of the correct answer.

The MS subtest was designed to assess the participants' knowledge of the multiple meanings of characters. Each item consisted of three two-character words that shared one character. This target character was located in the same position within the three options. Participants were asked to identify the option whose shared character contained the meaning that differed the most from those of the other two options. For example, the three words in one item were 开始 (kāishǐ, "to start"), 开学 (kāixué, "school opening"), and 开车 (kāichē, "to drive"). The correct answer was 开车 (kāichē, "to drive") because the 开 in this word does not mean "to start," as it does in the other two words.

Data analysis

Before analyzing the data, test scores from the cloze, the passage-comprehension, the PS, RS, and MS subtests were screened to ensure that they met the assumptions of multiple regression analysis. Data-screening procedures recommended by Tabachnick and Fidell (2012) were followed. Three stages of data analysis were undertaken. First, descriptive statistics of the five subtests were analyzed. Second, correlational analyses were conducted to determine the magnitude of the relationships between measures of reading comprehension and character recognition. Third, two stepwise multiple regression models were built to quantify the degree to which character-recognition subtests contributed to the prediction of the variance observed within the cloze and passage-comprehension scores.

Results

Descriptive statistics

The mean and standard deviations of the subtest scores are listed in Table 5.1. All scores are represented as percentages for easier comparisons across subtests. Because items in the pilot study with a difficulty level lower than 0.3 and higher than 0.8 were removed from the study, the difficulty level of the five subtests for participants was within a reasonable range. However, the removal of items after the pilot study also led to lower reliability.

In the cloze subtest, the two passages showed similar difficulty (0.44 for the first passage and 0.41 for the second passage). The greater difficulty with the cloze subtest may be related to its test format in that it was the only fill-in-the-blank subtest, with the other subtests containing multiple-choice items. Unlike multiple-choice items targeting receptive skills, the fill-in items required both receptive and productive skills, leading to the higher difficulty of the cloze subtest.

Participants' performance in the passage-comprehension subtest was at a medium level, and the items of bridging inferences were easier than items of knowledge-based inferences (0.61 for bridging inference and 0.52 for knowledge-based inferences). Note, however, that although knowledge-based inferences are regarded as a deeper level of comprehension than bridging inferences, the comprehension level does not equal item difficulty, which can be influenced by other factors, like how questions are presented in a task.

Participants' performance on the PS and MS subtests suggested they had some knowledge of the positioning and function of phonetic and semantic components in compound characters. Participants hypothetically would score highest in the PS and RS subtests, out of the three CR subtests, owing to the relatively simple rules of Chinese orthography. This, however, was not the case. Their scores on the PS and RS subtests were lower than that on the MS subtest, indicating that they may rely more heavily on processing morphological information than on the orthographical information related to phonetic and semantic access.

Correlations between reading comprehension and CR skills

To answer the first research question, correlations between CR subskills and the two levels of reading comprehension were examined through bivariate correlations using IBM SPSS software. The intercorrelation matrix is shown in Table 5.2. All correlation coefficients were statistically significant ($p < 0.05$). Most coefficients showed medium ($r > 0.3$) to large ($r > 0.5$) effect sizes. The correlation between the two comprehension subtests showed a large effect size and was also the largest of all correlations ($r = 0.62$, $p < 0.001$) in Table 5.2, suggesting that the two comprehension subtests shared many reading subskills.

All correlations between CR subskills are significant. The highest was between RS and MS ($r = 0.44$, $p < 0.001$). In comparison to MS's relationship to RS, the correlations between MS and PS and between PS and RS were much lower and showed a small effect size ($r = 0.24$, $p < 0.05$ for both correlations). MS showed a stronger relationship with both comprehension subtests, especially the passage subtest, than did the two other CR subtests. PS's and RS's correlations with the two comprehension subtests were also significant, and their correlations with the passage subtest appeared larger than those with the cloze subtest.

In summary, the three CR subskills significantly correlated with both shallow and deep reading comprehension. Among the three CR subskills, MS showed the strongest correlation with the two levels of reading comprehension, implying that MS's greater importance in both shallow and deep comprehension. Moreover, all three CR subskills demonstrated higher correlations with deep reading comprehension than with shallow reading comprehension.

Predictors of reading comprehension

To answer the second research question, two sets of hierarchical regression analyses were carried out to determine which of the three CR subskills was a unique,

Table 5.2 Intercorrelation Matrix

	Cloze	*Passage*	*PS*	*RS*	*MS*
Cloze		.62***	.33**	.35***	.54***
Passage			.33**	.45***	.57***
PS				.24*	.24*
RS					.44***
MS					

* $p < .05$, ** $p < .01$, *** $p < .001$

significant predictor of shallow and deep reading comprehension. The first set of analysis was conducted with the cloze test scores as the dependent variable (DV) and with the three CR subskills as the independent variables (IVs). The second set was performed with the passage-comprehension test scores as the DV and the same CR subskills as the IVs. Tables 5.3 and 5.4 show the steps taken to enter the IVs into the hierarchical regression models and the results of the two sets of analyses, respectively. In each of the two analyses, three models were conducted to evaluate the unique contributions of the three CR subskills to the cloze and the passage-comprehension scores. CR subskills that explain cloze or passage scores were entered in two steps. In Step 1, two of the three CR skills were the IVs, and in Step 2, the change of R^2 from that of Step 1 indicated the unique contribution of the remaining IV entered in Step 2.

As shown in Table 5.3, the three CR subskills collectively explained about 34.8% of the variance in the cloze subset. Based on the standardized regression coefficient (β) of the three models, MS was the strongest predictor of the three, βs = .447, .199, and .110 for MS, PS, and RS, respectively. More specifically, Model 1 showed that RS and PS as the first two variables entered into the regression equation explained about 19.1% of the variance. Over and above RS and PS,

Table 5.3 Hierarchical Regression of the Cloze Subtest

Model 1	Variable	B	SE	R^2	R^2 change	F change	Sig.
Step 1				0.191	-	9.650	<0.001
	RS	0.290	0.110				<0.01
	PS	0.265	0.114				<0.05
Step 2				0.348	0.157	19.532	<0.001
	RS	0.110	0.109				0.280
	PS	0.199	0.104				<0.05
	MS	0.447	0.125				<0.001
Model 2	Variable	B	SE	R^2	R^2 change	F change	Sig.
Step 1				0.311	-	18.545	<0.001
	MS	0.481	0.126				<0.001
	RS	0.142	0.110				0.168
Step 2				0.348	0.036	4.514	<0.05
	MS	0.447	0.125				<0.001
	RS	0.110	0.109				0.280
	PS	0.199	0.104				<0.05
Model 3	Variable	B	SE	R^2	R^2 change	F change	Sig.
Step 1				0.338	-	20.957	<0.001
	MS	0.491	0.115				<0.001
	PS	0.214	0.103				<0.05
Step 2				0.348	0.01	1.185	0.280
	MS	0.447	0.125				<0.001
	PS	0.199	0.104				<0.05
	RS	0.110	0.109				0.280

Table 5.4 Hierarchical Regressions of the Passage-Comprehension Subtest

Model 1	Variable	B	SE	R^2	R^2 change	F change	Sig.
Step 1				0.255	-	14.040	< 0.001
	RS	0.392	0.082				< 0.001
	PS	0.239	0.085				< 0.05
Step 2				0.400	0.145	19.580	< 0.001
	RS	0.219	0.081				< 0.05
	PS	0.176	0.077				0.054
	MS	0.429	0.093				< 0.001
Model 2	Variable	B	SE	R^2	R^2 change	F change	Sig.
Step 1				0.372	0.049	6.451	< 0.05
	MS	0.459	0.094				< 0.001
	RS	0.247	0.082				< 0.05
Step 2				0.400	0.028	3.829	0.054
	MS	0.429	0.093				< 0.001
	RS	0.219	0.081				< 0.05
	PS	0.176	0.077				0.054
Model 3	Variable	B	SE		R^2 change	F change	Sig.
Step 1				0.362	0.040	5.126	< 0.05
	MS	0.518	0.087				< 0.001
	PS	0.206	0.078				< 0.05
Step 2				0.400	0.038	5.119	< 0.05
	MS	0.429	0.093				< 0.001
	PS	0.176	0.077				0.054
	RS	0.219	0.081				< 0.05

MS explained additional 15.7% of the variance, which was statistically significant ($p < .001$). Model 2 showed the unique contribution of PS. After controlling for MS and RS, PS uniquely and statistically significantly explained about 3.6% of the variance ($p < .05$). Finally, as shown in Model 3, over and above MS and PS, a significant and unique effect of RS did not surface. It only added about 1% to the total variance explained of the cloze subset ($p > 0.05$). To sum up, the results of the three models revealed that MS and PS, as opposed to RS, were significant and unique contributors to the cloze. The effect of MS was the strongest, followed by that of PS.

In Table 5.4, the three CR subskills collectively explained 40% of the variance in the passage subset. Based on the β-values of the three CR subskills in the full regression model, MS was also the strongest predictor of the three, βs = .429, .219, and .176 for MS, RS, and PS, respectively. The three models showed MS and RS were significant and unique contributors to the passage subset, explaining 14.5% ($p < .001$) and 3.8% ($p < 0.05$) of the total variance, respectively, while PS did not surface as a significant IV and added about 2.8% of the total variance ($p > 0.05$). In sum, MS also emerged as the strongest contributor to the passage subtest along with RS as the second significant contributor.

Discussion

The current study investigated the relationships of three CR subskills, which are RS, PS, and MS, with the two levels of reading comprehension (shallow vs. deep) in English-dominant L2 Chinese readers, through bivariate correlation analyses and two sets of hierarchical regressions analyses.

The relationships between MS and the two levels of reading comprehension

The results found that MS, among the three CR subskills, was the strongest predictor of both shallow and deep comprehension. MS demonstrated the largest correlation with both comprehension-levels and also explained the largest amount of unique-variance. This finding corroborates those in existing studies of L1 and L2 Chinese reading (e.g., Dong et al., 2020; Kim et al., 2020; H. Li et al., 2017; D. Zhang et al., 2019; D. Zhang & Ke, 2020; H.-M. Zhang, 2014; Zhao et al., 2019). In a meta-analysis study, Dong and other scholars (2020) demonstrated that MS's correlation with L1 reading comprehension was strong and that its dominant importance in L1 Chinese reading could be related to the low GPC of Chinese script. Whereas as a result of the high GPC, readers of alphabetic orthographies often prioritize phonological skills in reading acquisition, the low GPC of Chinese script, and its morphosyllabic nature, reasonably leads readers to rely more on MS to process the morphosyllable information than on phonological skill or PS. Moreover, MS's importance in reading comprehension can also be understood in light of its indirect contribution through other related skills. Previous studies (Kim et al., 2020; D. Zhang, 2017a; H.-M. Zhang, 2014, 2017) found that MS indirectly contributed to reading comprehension through listening comprehension, vocabulary knowledge, and word reading for L1 and L2 Chinese readers.

Comparing MS's contribution to the two levels of comprehension, the results of the current study indicated that MS may play a more important role in deep comprehension than in shallow comprehension. Although the hierarchical regression models found that the unique variance explained of deep comprehension by MS (14.5%) was smaller than that of shallow comprehension (15.7%), deep comprehension could activate more character level of semantic processing than could shallow comprehension regarding MS's correlations with the cloze and passage subtests. Previous studies (Cain & Oakhill, 2014; Perfetti & Stafura, 2014; Singer et al., 1992) found that vocabulary knowledge and word recognition, especially word meaning, were central for inferencing. The depth of word knowledge and the speed of accessing semantic information, which are also related to MS and other CR subskills, are critical to release more cognitive resources for generating and updating real-time inferences (Oakhill et al., 2015). This finding suggests the central role of semantic processing at the lexical level in inferencing. As a result, the paths among MS, word reading, vocabulary knowledge, and inferencing may be more active in deep comprehension than in shallow comprehension.

The relationship of RS to shallow and deep comprehension

Radical knowledge refers to the ability to access orthographic and semantic information of semantic radicals in CR. RS contributed a significant amount of the variance only in deep comprehension, but not in shallow comprehension. The finding is compatible with a study for bilingual children in Hong Kong (Cheung et al., 2007). The intercorrelations matrix in Table 5.2 showed that RS had a higher correlation with deep comprehension than with shallow comprehension. From the regression models presented in Tables 5.3 and 5.4, RS can further be seen to have played a more critical role in deep comprehension than in shallow comprehension. Similar to the importance of MS for deep comprehension discussed earlier, RS's significant contribution to deep comprehension may also relate to the complex interactions between semantic processing, especially that at the word level, and inferencing, as suggested by existing studies of reading (Oakhill et al., 2015; Perfetti & Stafura, 2014). Considering that inferencing actively mediates the effect of access to word meaning and vocabulary knowledge to reading comprehension, RS may also make an indirect contribution to reading comprehension (Shen, 2000; Shu & Anderson, 1997; D. Zhang, 2017a). This may also explain RS's significant but small contribution to deep comprehension.

The relationship of PS to shallow and deep comprehension

PS is a skill that maps orthographic components to phonological knowledge acquired from oral vocabulary. The current study examined PS's correlations with shallow and deep comprehension. Both correlations were significant and medium-sized (see Table 5.2). This finding is compatible with previous research examining L1 and L2 Chinese reading (Cheung et al., 2007; Dong et al., 2020; Song et al., 2016; H.-W. Zhang & Roberts, 2019). After controlling for the contribution of MS and RS, PS significantly explained 3.6% of the variance in shallow comprehension (see Table 5.3), but not in deep comprehension (see Table 5.4).

In the present study, although the contribution of PS to reading comprehension appears very small, it is still a significant predictor of shallow comprehension. Previously, X.-L. Tong and colleagues (2016) found that English-speaking CSL readers applied PS for encoding new characters. In fact, in the present study, when examining participants' responses to the cloze subtest, many responses that were marked as incorrect were typed in pinyin,[3] indicating that participants accessed their oral vocabulary. The findings may suggest that PS was activated for retrieving oral vocabulary and phonetic knowledge for unfamiliar and new words in shallow comprehension, when processing local comprehension outweighs global comprehension. Moreover, beginner-level readers may rely more on PS, before gradually relying more on RS as their reading proficiency increases (Joshi et al., 2012; X.-L. Tong et al., 2016; Yeung et al., 2016).

PS's significant contribution to shallow comprehension, however, did not surface in other studies (Dong et al., 2020 for L1; H.-W. Zhang & Roberts, 2019 for L2). H.-W. Zhang and Roberts (2019), for example, conducted a path analysis and found that PS directly explained 1.44% of the CR variance for both Arabic- and English-speaking CSL readers ($p > 0.05$, not statistically significant). On closer examination, however, English-speaking readers showed a higher correlation between PS and CR than did their Arabic-speaking counterparts. Thus, the contribution of PS to CR could increase and possibly become significant in any separate path analysis for only English-speaking readers.

The significant but small relationship between PS and shallow comprehension could be related to beginner-level bilingual and L2 Chinese readers being able to apply PS for CR to some degree (Cheung et al., 2007; H.-W. Zhang & Roberts, 2019). Phonological information in Chinese characters, however, is not consistently reliable. PS's relatively low importance in Chinese reading could be related to the low GPC in Chinese script. Although it has been reported that phonological skill significantly predicts reading in both Chinese and English (Dong et al., 2020; Ho & Bryant, 1997; Huang & Hanley, 1995; McBride-Chang & Kail, 2002; Song et al., 2016; H.-W. Zhang & Roberts, 2019), its role is usually smaller in reading Chinese.

Conclusion

The present study examined the contribution of three CR subskills to deep and shallow comprehension in L2 Chinese readers. Notably, it was found that MS was the strongest unique predictor of both levels of comprehension. RS and PS, however, only significantly and uniquely predicted deep comprehension and shallow comprehension, respectively. The findings should be interpreted with the following limitations in mind. First, although four groups of participants were chosen to reflect the diversity in L2 Chinese learners, the Singaporean participants were from a more multilingual context and education system than other participants. It would be interesting to investigate how the four groups may differ in L2 reading development in further research with a larger sample of each group. Second, only part of the range of CR skills and comprehension subskills were included. Other subskills related to reading processes, such as compounding morphological awareness and listening comprehension, are also considered to be crucial in Chinese reading comprehension, but were not included in this study. Third, the two levels of comprehension were measured with different test formats, which could introduce a task effect to the results. Fourth, the reliabilities of the CR subtests were relatively low due to the small number of items included in each CR subtest.

Despite these limitations, the findings make a valuable contribution to the literature on L2 Chinese reading comprehension. First, the results showed that CR subskills were activated to a greater extent in deep comprehension than for comprehension at the shallow level. Second, the findings suggested the essential role of morphological knowledge and processing for both shallow and deep comprehension, particularly for deep comprehension. Furthermore, the results showed that semantic processing, i.e., MS and RS, contributed more to deep comprehension than to shallow comprehension. Taken together, these findings suggested that constructing a coherent situation model requires greater semantic processing than for a textbase understanding, which may result in differences in the contribution of RS to shallow and deep comprehension.

Pedagogically, the findings on different levels of comprehension suggested that CSL reading instruction should consider different reading purposes, expanding from reading for linguistic acquisition to include reading for diverse meaning-focused purposes, like browsing through shop signs, obtaining new information, and reading between the lines. Likewise, reading assessments need to involve multiple reading purposes and to obtain a more nuanced understanding about how students engage in reading for those purposes. Many researchers emphasize the role of CR subskills, especially MS, in reading comprehension and thus suggest that reading instruction should underscore those skills. However, this study suggested that the relationship between CR skills and reading comprehension can be quite complex. The effect of the former on the latter can be modulated by reading tasks or levels. The fact that MS and RS had a greater role in deep comprehension suggests that students may benefit from explicit instruction in applying MS and RS to inferencing, like building local bridging inferences with semantic radical clues.

Notes

1 In Singapore, although English is the official language for all Singaporeans, there are three other "mother tongue" languages for students to learn at school (Ministry of Education, Singapore, 2020). In other words, the term "mother tongue" in the Singaporean setting does not necessarily indicate the participants' L1 or home language. However, considering the large proportion of ethnic Chinese living in Singapore (Department of Statistics Singapore, 2020), it would be safe to assume that Mandarin Chinese would be accessible outside of classes. For the Singaporean participants who identified themselves and their parents as native speakers of English, Mandarin in Singapore would be different from a foreign language. As such, the term Singaporean CMTLLs is used to reflect the unique multilingual context of Singapore.
2 While some scholars (c.f. Chihara et al., 1994; Cziko, 1994; Trace, 2020) argue that cloze tests can also evaluate inter-sentential comprehension, they also comment that some passages are not ideal to create cloze tests evaluating comprehension beyond sentence-level. As for the current study, the inter-sentential blanks were deleted after the pilot study and only blanks requiring local comprehension remained.
3 All the pinyin responses, coincidentally, denoted incorrect characters.

References

Bachman, L. F., & Palmer, A. S. (1996). *Language testing in practice: Designing and developing useful language tests*. Oxford University Press.
Barry, S., & Lazarte, A. A. (1995). Embedded clause effects on recall: Does high prior knowledge of content domain overcome syntactic complexity in students of Spanish? *The Modern Language Journal*, *79*(4), 491–504.
Cain, K., & Oakhill, J. (2014). Reading comprehension and vocabulary: Is vocabulary more important for some aspects of comprehension? *LAnnee Psychologique*, *114*(4), 647–662.
Canale, M., & Swain, M. (1980). Theoretical bases of communicative approaches to second language teaching and testing. *Applied Linguistics*, *1*, 1–47.
Carrell, P. L. (1985). Facilitating ESL reading by teaching text structure. *TESOL Quarterly*, *19*(4), 727–752.

Cheng, Y., Zhang, J., Li, H., Wu, X., Liu, H., Dong, Q., Li, L., Nguyen, T. P., Zheng, M., Zhao, Y., & Sun, P. (2016). Growth of compounding awareness predicts reading comprehension in young Chinese students: A longitudinal study from Grade 1 to Grade 2. *Reading Research Quarterly, 52*(1), 91–104.

Cheng, Y., Zhang, J., Wu, X., Liu, H., & Li, H. (2016). Cross-lagged relationships between morphological awareness and reading comprehension among Chinese children. *Frontiers in Psychology, 7*, 1–12.

Cheung, H., Chan, M., & Chong, K. (2007). Use of orthographic knowledge in reading by Chinese-English Bi-scriptal children. *Language Learning, 57*(3), 469–505.

Chihara, T., Oller, J. W., Jr., Weaver, K. A., & Chavez-Oller, M. A. (1994). Are cloze items sensitive to constraints across sentences? In J. W. Oller Jr. & J. Jonz (Eds.), *Cloze and coherence* (pp. 135–148). Associated University Presses.

Cziko, G. A. (1994). Another response to Shanahan, Kamil, and Tobin: Further reasons to keep the cloze case open. In J. W. Oller Jr. & J. Jonz (Eds.), *Cloze and coherence* (pp. 197–206). Associated University Presses.

Department of Statistics Singapore. (2020). *Resident population by ethnic group, age group and sex dashboard*. www.singstat.gov.sg/find-data/search-by-theme/population/population-and-population-structure/visualising-data/resident-population-by-ethnic-group-age-group-and-sex-dashboard

Dong, Y., Peng, S.-N., Sun, Y.-K., Wu, S. X.-Y., & Wang, W.-S. (2020, February). Reading comprehension and metalinguistic knowledge in Chinese readers: A meta-analysis. *Frontiers in Psychology, 10*, 1–15.

Everson, M. E. (1998). Word recognition among learners of Chinese as a foreign language: Investigating the relationship between naming and knowing. *Modern Language Journal, 82*(2), 194–204.

Everson, M. E., & Ke, C. (1997). An inquiry into the reading strategies of intermediate and advanced learners of Chinese as a foreign language. *Journal of the Chinese Language Teachers Association, 32*(1), 1–20.

Feldman, L. B., & Siok, W. W. T. (1999). Semantic radicals contribute to the visual identification of Chinese characters. *Journal of Memory and Language, 40*(4), 559–576.

Grabe, W. (2009). *Reading in a second language: Moving from theory to practice*. Cambridge University Press.

He, A. W., & Xiao, Y. (Eds.). (2008). *Chinese as a heritage language: Fostering rooted world citizenry*. National Foreign Language Resource Center.

Ho, C. S., & Bryant, P. (1997). Phonological skills are important in learning to read Chinese. *Developmental Psychology, 33*(6), 946–951.

Ho, C. S., Yau, P. W.-Y., & Au, A. (2003). Development of orthographic knowledge and its relationship with reading and spelling among Chinese kindergarten and primary school children. In C. McBride-Chang & H.-C. Chen (Eds.), *Reading development in Chinese children* (pp. 51–71). Praeger.

Huang, H. S., & Hanley, J. R. (1995). Phonological awareness and visual skills in learning to read Chinese and English. *Cognition, 54*(1), 73–98.

Hudson, T. (2007). *Teaching second language reading*. Oxford University Press.

Hung, Y. H., Hung, D. L., Tzeng, O. J. L., & Wu, D. H. (2014). Tracking the temporal dynamics of the processing of phonetic and semantic radicals in Chinese character recognition by MEG. *Journal of Neurolinguistics, 29*(1), 42–65.

Joshi, R. M., Tao, S., Aaron, P. G., & Quiroz, B. (2012). Cognitive component of componential model of reading applied to different orthographies. *Journal of Learning Disabilities, 45*(5), 480–486.

Ke, S., & Xiao, F. (2015). Cross-linguistic transfer of morphological awareness between Chinese and English. *Language Awareness*, *24*(4), 355–380.

Kim, Y.-S. G., Guo, Q., Liu, Y., Peng, Y., & Yang, L. (2020). Multiple pathways by which compounding morphological awareness is related to reading comprehension: Evidence from Chinese second graders. *Reading Research Quarterly*, *55*(2), 193–212.

Kintsch, W. (1988). The use of knowledge in discourse processing: A construction-integration model. *Psychological Review*, *95*, 163–182.

Kintsch, W. (1998). *Comprehension: A paradigm for cognition*. Cambridge University Press.

Kintsch, W., & van Dijk, T. A. (1978). Toward a model of text comprehension and production. *Psychological Review*, *85*(5), 363–394.

Ku, Y. M., & Anderson, R. C. (2003). Development of morphological awareness in Chinese and English. *Reading and Writing*, *16*(5), 399–422.

Kuo, L.-J., & Anderson, R. (2008). Conceptual and methodological issues in comparing metalinguistic awareness across languages. In K. Koda & A. M. Zehler (Eds.), *Learning to read across languages* (pp. 39–67). Routledge.

Lee-Thompson, L.-C. (2008). An investigation of reading strategies applied by American learners of Chinese as a foreign language. *Foreign Language Annals*, *41*(4), 702–721.

Li, H., Dronjic, V., Chen, X., Li, Y., Cheng, Y., & Wu, X. (2017). Morphological awareness as a function of semantics, phonology, and orthography and as a predictor of reading comprehension in Chinese. *Journal of Child Language*, *44*(5), 1218–1247.

Li, W., Anderson, R. C., Nagy, W., & Zhang, H. (2002). Facets of metalinguistic awareness that contribute to Chinese literacy. In W. Li, J. S. Gaffney, & J. L. Packard (Eds.), *Chinese children's reading acquisition: Theoretical and pedagogical issues* (pp. 87–111). Kluwer Academic.

Lü, C., & Koda, K. (2011). The impact of home language and literacy support on English Chinese biliteracy acquisition among Chinese heritage language learners. *Heritage Language Journal*, *8*(2), 44–80.

McBride-Chang, C., & Kail, R. V. (2002). Cross-cultural similarities in the predictors of reading acquisition. *Child Development*, *73*(5), 1392–1407.

McNamara, D. S., & Kendeou, P. (2011). Translating advances in reading comprehension research to educational practice. *International Electronic Journal of Elementary Education*, *4*(1), 33–46.

McNamara, D. S., & Magliano, J. (2009). Toward a comprehensive model of comprehension. In B. Ross (Ed.), *Psychology of learning and motivation* (Vol. 51, pp. 297–384). Elsevier.

Ministry of Education, Singapore. (2020). *Mother Tongue languages policy*. www.moe.gov.sg/primary/curriculum/mother-tongue-languages

Oakhill, J., Cain, K., & McCarthy, D. (2015). Inference processing in children: The contributions of depth and breadth of vocabulary knowledge. In E. J. O'Brien, A. E. Cook, & R. F. Lorch, Jr. (Eds.), *Inferences during reading* (pp. 140–159). Cambridge University Press.

Perfetti, C. A., & Stafura, J. (2014). Word knowledge in a theory of reading comprehension. *Scientific Studies of Reading*, *18*(1), 22–37.

Perfetti, C. A., & Tan, L. H. (1999). The constituency model of Chinese word identification. In J. Wang, A. W. Inhoff, & H.-C. Chen (Eds.), *Reading Chinese script: A cognitive analysis* (pp. 115–134). Lawrence Erlbaum Associates.

Shanahan, T., Kamil, M. L., & Tobin, A. W. (1982). Cloze as a measure of intersentential comprehension. *Reading Research Quarterly*, *17*(2), 229–255.

Shen, H. (2000). Development of orthographic skills in Chinese children. *Reading and Writing*, *13*(3/4), 197–236.

Shen, H. (2013). Chinese L2 literacy development: Cognitive characteristics, learning strategies, and pedagogical interventions. *Language and Linguistics Compass*, *7*(7), 371–387.

Shen, H., & Bear, D. R. (2000). Development of orthographic skills in Chinese children. *Reading and Writing: An Interdisciplinary Journal*, *13*, 197–236.

Shen, H., & Ke, C. (2007). Radical awareness and word acquisition among nonnative learners of Chinese. *Modern Language Journal*, *91*(1), 97–111.

Shu, H., & Anderson, R. C. (1997). Role of radical awareness in the character and word acquisition of Chinese children. *Reading Research Quarterly*, *32*(1), 78–89.

Shu, H., & Anderson, R. C. (1999). Learning to read Chinese: The development of metalinguistic awareness. In J. Wang, A. W. Inhoff, & H.-C. Chen (Eds.), *Learning to read Chinese script: A cognitive analysis* (pp. 1–18). Lawrence Erlbaum Associates.

Shu, H., Anderson, R. C., & Wu, N. (2000). Phonetic awareness: Knowledge of orthography-phonology relationships in the character acquisition of Chinese children. *Journal of Educational Psychology*, *92*(1), 56–62.

Singer, M., Andrusiak, P., Reisdorf, P., & Black, N. L. (1992). Individual differences in inference processes. *Memory and Cognition*, *20*(5), 539–548.

Song, S., Georgiou, G. K., Su, M., & Hua, S. (2016). How well do phonological awareness and rapid automatized naming correlate with Chinese reading accuracy and fluency? A meta-analysis. *Scientific Studies of Reading*, *20*(2), 99–123.

Tabachnick, B., & Fidell, L. (2012). *Using multivariate statistics* (6th ed.). Pearson Education.

Taft, M., & Zhu, X. (1997). Submorphemic processing in reading Chinese. *Journal of Experimental Psychology: Learning, Memory, and Cognition*, *23*, 761–775.

Taft, M., Zhu, X., & Peng, D. (1999). Positional specificity of radicals in Chinese character recognition. *Journal of Memory and Language*, *40*, 498–519.

Tan, L., & Perfetti, C. (1997). Visual Chinese character recognition: Does phonological information mediate access to meaning? *Journal of Memory and Language*, *37*, 41–57.

Tong, X.-H., Tong, X.-L., & McBride, C. (2017). Radical sensitivity is the key to understanding Chinese character acquisition in children. *Reading and Writing*, *30*(6), 1251–1265.

Tong, X.-L. (2008). *The development of Chinese word reading: Relations of sub-character processing, phonological awareness, morphological awareness, and orthographic knowledge to Chinese-English biscriptal reading*. (Doctoral dissertation). ProQuest Dissertations and Theses (Order No. 3363236).

Tong, X.-L., Kwan, J. L. Y., Wong, D. W. M., Lee, S. M. K., & Yip, J. H. Y. (2016). Toward a dynamic interactive model of non-native Chinese character processing. *Journal of Educational Psychology*, *108*(5), 680–693.

Tong, X.-L., & McBride-Chang, C. (2010). Developmental models of learning to read Chinese words. *Developmental Psychology*, *46*(6), 1662–1676.

Tong, X.-L., & Yip, J. H. Y. (2015). Cracking the Chinese character: Radical sensitivity in learners of Chinese as a foreign language and its relationship to Chinese word reading. *Reading and Writing*, *28*(2), 159–181.

Trace, J. (2020). Clozing the gap: How far do cloze items measure? *Language Testing*, *37*(2). 235–253.

Wang, Y., Yin, L., & McBride, C. (2015). Unique predictors of early reading and writing: A one-year longitudinal study of Chinese kindergarteners. *Early Childhood Research Quarterly*, *32*, 51–59.

Wiley, T. G. (2009). Chinese "dialect" speakers as Heritage language learners: A case study. In D. M. Brinton, O. Kagan, & S. Bauckus (Eds.), *Heritage language education: A new field emerging* (pp. 91–105). Routledge.

Wong, K.-F., & Xiao, Y. (2010). Diversity and difference: Identity issues of Chinese heritage language learners from dialect backgrounds. *Heritage Language Journal*, *7*(2), 314–348.

Wong, W.-W. C. (2011). *The learning of Chinese orthography and its centrality in learning Chinese as a foreign language* (Thesis). University of Hong Kong, Hong Kong SAR.

Xu, Y., Chang, L.-Y., & Perfetti, C. A. (2014). The effect of radical-based grouping in Character learning in Chinese as a foreign language. *The Modern Language Journal*, *98*(3), 773–793.

Yeung, P.-S., Ho, C. S., Chan, D. W., & Chung, K. K. (2016). A componential model of reading in Chinese. *Learning and Individual Differences*, *45*, 11–24.

Zhang, D. (2017a). Multidimensionality of morphological awareness and text comprehension among young Chinese readers in a multilingual context. *Learning and Individual Differences*, *46*, 13–23.

Zhang, D. (2017b). Word reading in L1 and L2 learners of Chinese: Similarities and differences in the functioning of component processes. *Modern Language Journal*, *101*(2), 391–411.

Zhang, D., & Ke, S. (2020). The simple view of reading made complex by morphological decoding fluency in bilingual fourth-grade readers of English. *Reading Research Quarterly*, *55*(2), 311–329.

Zhang, D., Koda, K., Leong, C. K., & Pang, E. (2019). Cross-lagged panel analysis of reciprocal effects of morphological processing and reading in Chinese in a multilingual context. *Journal of Research in Reading*, *42*(1), 58–79.

Zhang, H.-M. (2014). Morphological awareness in literacy acquisition of Chinese second graders: A path analysis. *Journal of Psycholinguistic Research*, *45*(1), 103–119.

Zhang, H.-M. (2016). Does morphology play an important role in L2 Chinese vocabulary acquisition? *Foreign Language Annals*, *49*(2), 384–402.

Zhang, H.-M. (2017). Development of morphological awareness in young Chinese readers: Comparing poor comprehenders and good comprehenders. *Reading and Writing Quarterly*, *33*(2), 187–197.

Zhang, H.-W., & Roberts, L. (2019). The role of phonological awareness and phonetic radical awareness in acquiring Chinese literacy skills in learners of Chinese as a second language. *System*, *81*, 163–178.

Zhang, J., Lin, T. J., Wei, J., & Anderson, R. C. (2014). Morphological awareness and learning to read Chinese and English. In X. Chen, Q. Wang, & Y. C. Luo (Eds.), *Reading development and difficulties in monolingual and bilingual Chinese children* (pp. 3–22). Springer.

Zhang, L. (2014). College Chinese Heritage language learners' implicit knowledge of compound sentences. *Heritage Language Journal*, *11*(1), 45–75.

Zhao, Y., Wu, X., Sun, P., Xie, R., Feng, J., & Chen, H. (2019). The relationship between morphological awareness and reading comprehension among Chinese children: Evidence from multiple mediation models. *Learning and Individual Differences*, *72*, 59–68.

Zhou, L., Peng, G., Zheng, H. Y., Su, I. F., & Wang, W. S. Y. (2013). Sub-lexical phonological and semantic processing of semantic radicals: A primed naming study. *Reading and Writing*, *26*, 967–989.

6 Development of morphological awareness and its impact on reading among young learners of Chinese as a heritage language

*Yanhui Zhang, Keiko Koda,
Chin-Lung Yang and Chan Lü*

Introduction

There has been increasing interest among reading researchers and applied linguists in morphological awareness—the ability to identify, analyze, and manipulate a word's internal structure and its morphological components (Carlisle, 2003; Nagy et al., 2014). Given the unique feature of the Chinese writing system as well the corresponding lexical and syntactic formation rules, however, the notion of morphological awareness adopted in the current study extends to a large spectrum of skills to include not only radical recognition and exploitation but also morpheme discrimination and word compounding (for instance, Li et al., 2002; X. Chen et al., 2009 for similar adoption). On the other hand, although an implicit grasp of morphological structure evolves from spoken language, its explicit understanding develops primarily through decoding and encoding morphological information in print during word reading and spelling. The critical issue thus is what happens to morphological awareness and literacy when either input is insufficient. Since the particular aspects underlying word learning and reading entail a clear insight into how morphological information is graphically represented, we can assume that their formation relies heavily upon print exposure and experience. Therefore, systematic examinations of how limited print exposure affects morphological awareness formation are vital in understanding literacy development in a non-societal language. Heritage language (HL) learners provide a unique case to look into this issue.

Consequently, the current study explores scenarios involving school-age children learning to read Chinese as a heritage language (CHL) in the United States. These children typically speak their mother tongue at home, receive primary literacy instruction in English at school, and pursue ancillary literacy in Chinese in a weekend school. Thus, their primary literacy in English builds on limited oral language exposure, and their secondary literacy in Chinese on duly developed oral language proficiency and heavily restricted print input. Remarkably, their experience is distinct from their counterparts in China and those learning to read Chinese as a second language (L2). CHL learners' literacy learning in the heritage language offers a unique opportunity to dissect the specific contributions stemming from oral language proficiency and print exposure. In essence, the study's

DOI: 10.4324/9781003029038-9

primary goals are two-fold: (a) illuminating the nature and development of morphological awareness among young CHL learners in the United States compared to those among children in China, and (b) exploring how morphological awareness relates to reading development in Chinese as a heritage language.

Background and research framework

Roles of morphological awareness in reading

Reading literacy in all languages necessitates linking the spoken languages and their writing systems (Kieffer et al., 2013; Nagy & Anderson, 1999; Perfetti & Liu, 2005). First, children must recognize which language elements are encoded in the writing system and then uncover the specific ways of encoding. Morphological awareness contributes to the latter stage of reading acquisition. Next, children must deduce precisely how language elements correspond with units of graphic symbols by enabling them to analyze words according to their morphological constituents. Such analysis, in turn, helps them develop the critical skills to map these constituents onto units of graphic symbols.

Morphological awareness is a multi-faceted and developmental construct involving a range of capabilities attuned, over learning, to morphemes' functional and structural properties in a particular language. In English, for example, children must become able to distinguish affixes from base morphemes and know where each affix can be placed within a word (before or after the base) to manipulate morphological information. Nevertheless, morphological awareness is not an isolated skill. Strong relationships between morphological awareness and reading have been reported. Skilled readers are more sensitive to a word's morphological structure than less experienced readers (e.g., Chilant & Caramazza, 1995; Fowler & Liberman, 1995; Taft, 1991; Taft & Zhu, 1995). Children with low reading ability commit far more errors of affix omissions in their writing and speaking (e.g., Duques, 1989; Rubin, 1991). Moreover, morphological information's efficient use distinguishes competent and less competent high school readers (e.g., Tyler & Nagy, 1989, 1990). There is also evidence from longitudinal studies that morphological awareness and reading are developmentally interdependent (Manolitsis et al., 2019; D. Zhang et al., 2019).

Morphological awareness in Chinese

In contrast to English, the basic unit of character formation in Chinese are radicals (e.g., Y. Chen et al., 1996; Shu & Anderson, 1997), referring to the recurrent stroke patterns used in characters. Many radicals are single-unit characters, used as independent lexical morphemes and as components in other characters. Some radicals, however, lack lexical status, thus serving only as character components. Although there are several character-formation procedures, semantic-phonetic compounding is, by far, the most dominant formation, used in roughly 80–90% of multiple-unit characters (H. Zhang, 1994). There are approximately 700 phonetic radicals, many of which have lexical status. Therefore, their readings as a single-unit character are used to read the compound characters containing them. Hence, in principle, the multiple-unit characters can be pronounced by extracting their phonetic radicals' phonological information. In contrast, semantic radicals, roughly 140 in use, provide a guide to characters' meanings.

Though helpful, semantic radical information is restricted to the general semantic category or common attribute of the character's referent. Thus, the relationship between the semantic radical information and the whole-character meaning is not always transparent, as in the case of the "water" radical (氵) used in the character 治, which means "to control" and has little to do with "water." Moreover, semantic radical information captures only aspects of the meaning of the character serving as a radical. For some characters, the connection between the radical information and the meaning of its original character is clear and straightforward. This, however, is not always the case. For example, when the character for "gold," 金, is used as a radical, it indicates that the characters containing this radical refer to anything metallic, as in 鎖 (chain), 鎧 (armor), and 針 (needle). Although the radical information is consistent across these characters, the semantic connection between the radical information and the source character's meaning is less transparent.

In summary of these observations, morphological awareness in Chinese should entail, broadly, an integrated understanding that graphic components provide, yet possibly only partial, information on the whole-character meaning, and that characters with shared semantic radicals are generally semantically related but radical information alone may not be sufficient for meaning identification. As such, lexical or even higher layers of linguistic experiences are often indispensable for a thorough morphological knowledge of the Chinese language. Indeed, a considerable number of researchers have endorsed not only the critical role of morphological awareness in Chinese literacy development but also the multifacetedness of morphological awareness and the mutual mediating effects played by morphological awareness and other additional linguistic and cognitive factors (X. Chen et al., 2009; Kuo & Anderson, 2006; Li et al., 2002; D. Zhang, 2013; D. Zhang & Koda, 2014; D. Zhang et al., 2016). For instance, Kuo and Anderson (2006) provided strong evidence that radical awareness, or grapho-morphological awareness, plays an essential role in character recognition and reading acquisition in Chinese. Li et al. (2002) documented that morphological awareness was more significantly a factor in comparison to phonological skills, for the development of reading proficiency among average Chinese school children in the first and fourth grades. X. Chen et al. (2009) focused on the compounding rules in Chinese morphology and showed the significance of compound awareness in Chinese children's vocabulary acquisition. Finally, as shown by Shu and Anderson (1997), it is noteworthy that different aspects of morphological awareness typically develop according to different timelines among children. In particular, Ku and Anderson (2003) argued that acquiring compounding awareness typically is earlier than that of derivational morphology among Chinese children.

Morphological awareness among second language learners

There have been increasing research studies recently on morphological awareness among L2 learners of Chinese, as well as investigations on the learning mechanisms therein (X. Chen et al., 2009; Kuo & Anderson, 2006; Li et al., 2002; D. Zhang, 2013, 2016; D. Zhang & Koda, 2014; D. Zhang et al., 2016). For example, Pasquarella et al. (2011) demonstrated the interconnectedness between morphological awareness and the early development of word reading for L2 learners of Chinese. Cross-language transfer has been evidenced by a strand of empirical studies (Pasquarella et al., 2011; Wang et al., 2006; D. Zhang & Koda, 2014) as a workable mechanism to explain the facilitating role of the L1 morphological knowledge in the development of L2 morphological awareness. For example, D. Zhang (2013) studied and showed the facilitating power of morphological awareness in L1 Chinese on lexical inference ability in L2 English learning. Specifically, such facilitating power was demonstrated as more significant for compound word learning than for derived words. By analyzing the reading acquisition in Chinese among a group of college-level heritage Chinese learners, H. Zhang and Koda (2016) suggested that transferred subskills need to undergo a modification process to accommodate the target language properties, and that the benefits of cross-language transfer are limited by skill specificity.

In addition, findings in many existing studies directly addressing the roles of morphological awareness in character learning and processing among second-language learners of Chinese (as opposed to CHL learners) show that beginning-level learners rarely engage in morphological (radical) decomposition when encountering unfamiliar characters (e.g., Everson, 1998; McGinnis, 1995). However, higher-proficiency learners at the intermediate and advanced levels learn to be more attentive to radical information during character recognition and inference (Everson & Ke, 1997; Mori & Nagy, 1999). These findings imply that adult second-language learners are sensitized to the basic properties of radicals and rely on their understanding of learning new characters and retrieving stored information. Moreover, such sensitivity readily develops with far less exposure and processing experience (about 300–500 characters) among metalinguistically adroit adult second-language learners. This contrasts sharply with native Mandarin-speaking children necessitating approximately 2,000 characters to form similar metalinguistic insights (Shu & Anderson, 1999).

Caution is necessary, however. Despite the reported rapidity in acquisition, morphological awareness among second-language learners could be less attuned to radical properties' specific details because of the restricted input. If so, their morphological awareness may be less serviceable in character learning and processing than that among native character users. An empirical justification to such caution was provided by Lü et al. (2015), where they examined how and to what extent the properties of Chinese sub-lexical morphemes affect character learning and processing among adult L2 learners of Chinese. The results demonstrated that the facilitative effect of radical functional salience was highly associated with radical knowledge, suggesting that second-language learners' evolving morphological awareness has yet to reach the level of radical properties' specific details for an efficient maneuvering of such knowledge in real-time linguistic processing. In another example, in Kanji, Koda and Takahashi (2003) tested a similar hypothesis directly by contrasting the effects of radical information validity on character meaning extraction among second-language learners and native Japanese readers. While native Japanese readers were selective in incorporating only valid radical information, second-language learners could not distinguish valid from invalid radicals. To sum up, limited print exposure, although not delaying the understanding of general radical properties, possibly impedes the refinement of basic awareness.

Hypotheses and research questions

In this study, HL learners are operationally defined as a group of school-age children with Chinese ancestry, who (a) grew up in Chinese-speaking homes in the United States, (b) have developed sufficient oral proficiency for daily communication in Mandarin or a related dialect, (c) attend American schools during the week, and (d) are enrolled in a weekend Chinese school. One apparent disparity separating HL learners from children in China is that their literacy learning is subservient to literacy development in another language, English. Although the disparity involves several corollary factors affecting heritage literacy learning, including literacy achievement in English, oral Mandarin proficiency, and print exposure in Chinese, the present study focused on the impact of limited print exposure/experience on the development of morphological awareness in Chinese, as well as its relationship to character recognition and reading comprehension.

Presumably, limited print exposure should have harmful effects on morphological awareness among HL learners. Since many of the characters introduced in the early grades subsequently become radicals and are then used as components in the more complex characters taught in later grades (Shu & Anderson, 1999), children are seriously handicapped if they do not learn these basic characters. Without an adequate perceptual base, it is also unlikely that children will become sensitive to those characters' internal structure. It is then virtually impossible to recognize individual radicals' basic function when well-established sound-symbol and meaning-symbol linkages are absent. As shown, for instance, in Shen (2003), the textbook-based input available to HL learners is exceedingly limited, providing only a slim—if any—base for forming the morphological awareness reflecting the specific details of radical properties. It was hypothesized, therefore, that morphological awareness of HL learners is restricted to radical formation's general properties and remains undefined.

The most predictable consequence of underdeveloped morphological awareness is that character learning becomes heavily dependent upon rote memorization rather than radical analysis. Memorizing symbols is far from easy for anyone, but especially for HL students, particularly because they are learning to read two vastly different languages simultaneously. Hence, it seems irrational to expect these children to expand their character knowledge steadily and cumulatively over time as they advance in their Chinese school. Consequently, a second hypothesis is that systematic increment does not occur in character knowledge among heritage language learners.

Moreover, heavy reliance on rote memorization involves neither character segmentation nor radical analysis, making character learning an all-or-nothing process. In the absence of radical analysis, it is highly improbable that children extract partial information from strange characters and use it to infer their meanings. Limited lexical inference capacity, in turn, makes it challenging to fill semantic gaps created by the unknown characters encountered during text reading, thereby seriously impairing text comprehension. Hence, the final hypothesis is that no systematic relationships exist between morphological awareness and reading comprehension among heritage learners. To test the hypotheses mentioned earlier, the following questions were posed:

1. How does morphological awareness among HL learners differ from that among Chinese children in China?
2. Does morphological awareness among HL learners increase over time?
3. Do character knowledge and reading comprehension subskills among HL learners increase over time?
4. Does morphological awareness systematically relate to character knowledge and reading comprehension among heritage learners?

The study

Participants

Participants were 59 Chinese children at the Pittsburgh Chinese School. The school is a non-profit organization, a weekend regional school that promotes cultural understanding and Chinese literacy. Classes range from kindergarten to the 12th grade. All classes are held on Sundays for three hours. The first two hours are devoted to language instruction to develop four language skills, particularly Chinese literacy. During the final hour, students engage in extracurricular activities designed to promote interest in Chinese culture. Seventy percent of the participants were born in the United States, and 30 percent of them came to the United States at around four to 11 years of age. Of these children, 23 were in the 3rd grade (mean age, 9:4), 20 were in the 4th grade (mean age, 10:7), and 16 in the 5th grade (10:10). Table 6.1 provides general demographic information for the participating students.

Three batteries of tasks were administered: (a) morphological awareness, (b) character knowledge, and (c) reading comprehension. The morphological awareness tasks were adopted, with some modifications, from a large-scale Chinese literacy study by Li et al. (2002). Based on the Chinese school's language curriculum and textbooks, the character knowledge and reading comprehension tests were designed for the study.

Table 6.1 Background Information of the Participating Students

		Grade 3	Grade 4	Grade 5
Age (year: month)		9:4	10:7	10:10
Gender	Male	56%	40%	56%
	Female	44%	60%	44%
Place of Birth	China	31.3%	80%	22.2%
	U.S.A.	68.8%	20%	77.8%
Age of Arrival in the U.S.A. (year: month)		4:6	4:10	5:8
Years of Chinese School		2.2	2.8	3.9
No. of Siblings	0	25%	50%	11%
	1	56%	50%	89%
	2	19%	0	0
Home Language	English	19%	10%	11%
	Chinese	81%	90%	89%
Non-Chinese Parents		0	0	0

Morphological awareness tasks

Five tasks were administered. Each had 12 items, and students were given 30 minutes to complete the entire test. Except for the Radical Formation task, eight items were adopted from Li et al. (2002), with minor modifications. Four items were newly constructed based on the rationales provided by Li et al. (2002). Table 6.2 provides examples of each task. Reliability coefficients (Cronbach's alpha) ranged from .75 to .93 across the five subtests and three grades.

Radical meaning

This task was designed to understand that the whole character's meaning can be inferred from the semantic radical's information. The task was to choose the appropriate character from a pool of four to substitute for the target character's Pinyin part. Because the four characters in the multiple-choice pool share the same phonetic radical while differing in their semantic radicals, the task requires students to make their selection based on semantic radical information.

Morpheme discrimination

This task assessed that two-character compound words containing the same character do not always share the same meaning. Students were presented with four two-character words in the task and asked to identify the one with a different meaning from the others.

Radical form

This task was designed to measure an understanding of how the meaning of a Chinese character relates to the meaning of its semantic radical, and to measure an

Table 6.2 Examples of the Graphic-Morphological Tasks

Task	Example	Answer
Radical meaning	**Instruction:** The leftmost is a Chinese word with one of its characters as Pinyin. Please choose the appropriate character from the four characters at the right to substitute with the Pinyin part of the target item. **Example:** xué xiào ___ 校 [school]（1）垦　（2）峃　（3）栄　（4）学	(4)
Morpheme discrimination	**Instruction:** You will see some words in a row. Each row has four words (listed from left to right) that share a character. Please select the word where the character has a different meaning from the other three words in the same row. **Example:** shāmò　　shātān　　shāfā　　shāqiū （1）沙漠　（2）沙滩　（3）沙发　（4）沙丘	(3)
Radical form	**Instruction:** The rightmost target character without parentheses is composed of a few radical parts. Please select one answer which has most of the meaning of the target character. **Example:** (hǎi) yáng (海)洋　（1）氵　（2）主　（3）羊　（4）王	(1)
Radical formation	**Instruction:** There are two different radicals on the left. Please select one of the four choices at the right that best represents **the most possible and accurate** combination for these two radicals. **Example:** "见" and "扌"　（1）觉　（2）见扌　（3）抈　（4）觉	(3)
Radical explanation	**Instruction:** Please select the best meaning of the radical part (in parentheses) of the target character based on how the radical part provides meaning to the meaning of the whole character. **Example:** gāo　(mǐ)　dàmǐ　　miànfěn　liángshí　miànbǐng 糕　(米)　(1) 大米　(2) 面粉　(3) 粮食　(4) 面饼	(3)

ability to recognize the particular graphic component that contributes to the meaning of the whole character. In the task, students were given a multiple-unit character and asked to select the graphic component, providing information related to the character's meaning.

Development of morphological awareness and its impact on reading 119

Radical formation

The task was used to assess sensitivity to structural constraints on character formation (understanding that particular radicals appear only at specific locations). Students were shown two radicals and then asked to choose their correct placement from a pool of four possible combinations.

Radical explanation

This task was designed to assess how the semantic radical contributes to the overall meaning of the whole character. In particular, it measures sensitivity to meaning alterations of characters when they are used as semantic radicals. The task was to select from a pool of four descriptions that best described the radical's meaning in the target character.

Character knowledge

The following two tasks were designed to assess students' character knowledge. Reliability coefficients (Cronbach's alpha) ranged from .78 to .91 across the two subtests and three grades.

Character meanings

In this task, students were asked to write in English the meaning of each character. They were given five minutes for completion. The number of test items varied in each grade: (a) 10 characters in the grade 3 test (all items randomly selected from the grade 3 textbook); (b) 15 in the grade 4 test (six grade 3 items taken from the grade 3 test and nine grade 4 items randomly selected from the grade 4 textbook); and (c) 20 in the grade 5 test (six grade 3 items used in the grade 3 tests, six grade 4 items taken from the grade 4 test, and eight grade 5 items randomly selected from the grade 5 textbook).

Character pronunciations

Students were asked to write, within a five-minute time limit, the pronunciation of a set of characters in Pinyin, with which the students were highly familiar through systematic instruction in the weekend school. The number of test items also varied, depending on school grades in the same way as the character meaning tests: 10 characters in the grade 3 test, 15 in the grade 4 test, and 20 in the grade 5 test.

Reading comprehension

The reading comprehension test was designed to measure five comprehension subskills: (a) retrieving context-appropriate word meanings (vocabulary); (b) inferring text meaning based on word knowledge (lexical-based inference); (c) integrating text information across sentences through identifying the referent of pronouns (co-referential resolution); (d) detecting the main idea of the passage (gist detection); and (e) inferring text meaning based on contextual information (text-based inference). Thirty minutes were allowed to complete the entire reading test.

Eight reading passages on general topics were adapted from Chinese storybooks and modified to be syntactically and lexically appropriate for grades 3 to 5 HL students. Four passages were adjusted to grades 3 and 4 students (Level I) based on the grade 3 textbook, with two degrees of difficulty within this level. The remaining four passages were made appropriate for grades 4 and 5 students based on the grade 4 textbook (Level II), again with two degrees of difficulty within this level. Each student read two versions (character only and Pinyin aided) of four passages: grade 3 students read four Level I passages; grade 4 students two Level I difficult passages and two Level II easy passages; and grade 5 students read four Level II passages. In this way, two overlapping passages between grades 3 and 4 students and those between grades 4 and 5 allowed direct comparisons of comprehension subskills across grade levels without compromising grade-level appropriateness of reading passages. Reliability coefficients (Cronbach's alpha) of the reading test ranged from .77 to .95 across the five subtests and three grades.

Task administration and rating

The tasks were organized into two text booklets and administered in class during the language instruction period. The first booklet contained the morphological awareness test and the first set of reading comprehension, and a background survey. The second included the character-knowledge test and the second set of reading comprehension. In addition, the teachers of the grades 3, 4, and 5 classes at the Chinese school were asked to rate each student's Chinese language oral language competence, using a five-point scale, ranging from "Far Below Average" (point 1) to "Far Above Average" (point 5). The teacher ratings were used as an independent index of general language proficiency in correlation analyses.

Results and discussion

Morphological awareness among CHL and native Chinese-speaking children

Figure 6.1 presents the means and standard deviations of the morphological awareness subtest scores (presented in percentage of correct responses) for grades 3–5 CHL learners. Figure 6.2 compares their average scores with grade 4 native Chinese-speaking children taken from the Li et al. (2002) study. Not surprisingly, native speakers scored considerably higher than heritage learners on most, but not all, of the subtests. Given the limited linguistic exposure, particularly in print, it is astonishing that heritage learners performed well above the chance level (.25) on all tasks but one (Radical Explanation). The overall results would indicate that

Development of morphological awareness and its impact on reading 121

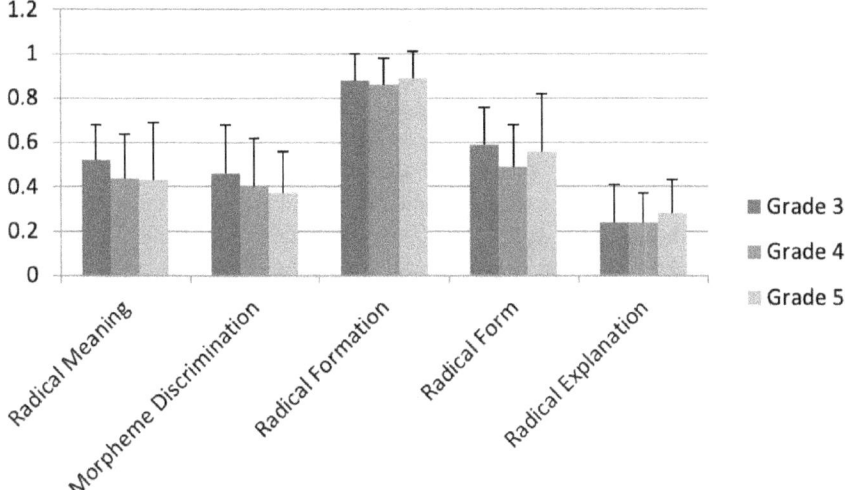

Figure 6.1 Means and standard deviations of the morphological awareness subtest scores (% correct) for CHL learners

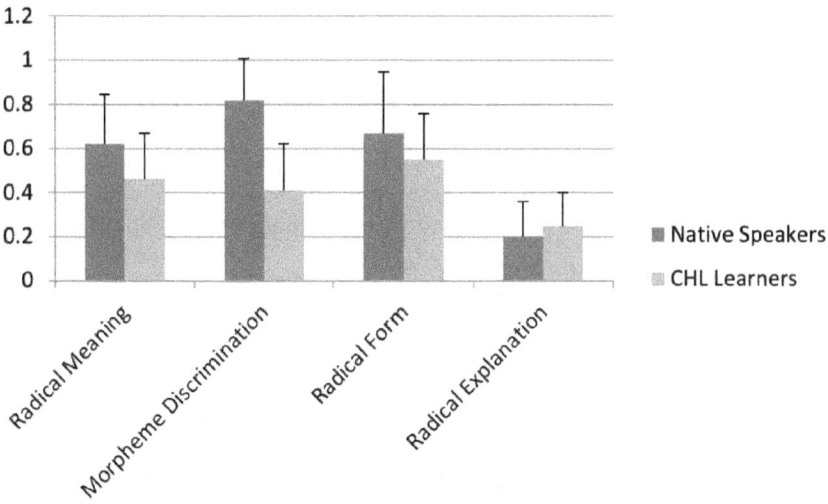

Figure 6.2 Comparison of means and standard deviations of the morphological awareness subtest scores (% correct) for native Chinese (Li et al., 2002) and CHL learners

heritage learners become sensitized to Chinese characters' internal morphological structure by the 3rd grade and utilize this sensitivity during character processing, despite the heavily limited print exposure. However, it is important to note that performance differences among heritage and native Chinese-speaking children vary widely across the tasks. The most notable disparity occurred in the

Morpheme Discrimination task, in which students were expected to differentiate the meaning of a component character shared in four two-character compound words.

In contrast, the groups' performance gap was far less pronounced in the Radical Form task, designed to assess an understanding of the constraints on semantic radicals' placement. These discrepancies indicate that varying facets of morphological awareness necessitate differential amounts of character exposure for their acquisition. Given that those heritage students performed on radical formation at the near-ceiling level, it seems reasonable to suggest that sensitivity to radicals' structural properties develops with far less input than understanding their functional/semantic properties. Moreover, native Chinese and heritage-language learners both performed equally poorly on Radical Explanation. Significantly, this implies that what is required for successful completion of this task is a late-developing capacity, yet to be acquired even by native Chinese-speaking grade 4 children after having learned nearly 1,700 characters. Viewed collectively, the present results suggest that various morphological awareness facets in Chinese develop at disparate rates both among native and heritage Chinese learners. Seemingly, sensitivity to structural constraints evolves earlier than the understanding of functional properties. Even more critically, the acquisition of more abstract and character-specific facets of morphological awareness depends on substantially more input and exposure to morphologically complex characters, suggesting that morphological awareness and character knowledge are closely intertwined in their development and refinement.

Of the most noteworthy significance, however, our data demonstrate that grades 3–5 heritage learners can form the basic facets of morphological awareness despite the heavily restricted input. Given that grade 1 children in China typically do not exhibit sensitivity to the character-internal structure (Shu & Anderson, 1999), it is reasonable to interpret the present findings as indicating that in addition to print exposure and experience, other related factors play a role in the development of morphological awareness among heritage language learners. Given that Chinese literacy among heritage learners is subservient to their primary literacy in English, and also that literacy skills, including metalinguistic competencies, transfer across languages (e.g., Gholamain & Geva, 1999; Wang et al., 2005), it is feasible that non-language-specific aspects of morphological awareness, such as the ability to detect structural and functional regularities in print input (developed through primary literacy in English) may have facilitated the acquisition of the basic facets of Chinese morphological awareness.

Development of morphological awareness among CHL learners

Our second research question addresses systematic increments of morphological awareness among HL learners. The experiments' results (see Figure 6.1) appeared to show that grade 3 children generally scored higher than the older cohorts. Still, score differences across the three grade levels were consistently negligible in all tasks. Subsequent one-way ANOVAs performed separately on each of the morphological awareness subtests, with grade as the between-subject variable, indicated no significant main effects of grade in all subtests. As predicted, the result suggested no systematic increments of morphological awareness among grades 3–5 HL learners.

This contrasts sharply with the developmental patterns reported in earlier studies involving native English (Bear et al., 1995; Carlisle, 2003) and Chinese-speaking children (Ku & Anderson, 2003; Shu & Anderson, 1999). Given the developmental reciprocity between morphological awareness and print exposure/experience, the absence of incremental changes in morphological awareness among heritage language learners seems attributable to both quality and quantity of character input in their literacy instruction. As noted, of the 118 single-unit characters introduced in the grades 1 and 2 textbooks, only small proportions of these characters reappear as radicals in later grades. Seemingly, the limited input makes it prohibitive for HL learners to gain reliable insights into radicals' structural and functional properties. Lacking such insights, it seems improbable that HL learners organize incoming input—roughly 150 characters per year—by radicals.

Moreover, the non-componential lexical organization is likely to keep them from analyzing and constructing character information based on constituent radicals. This being the case, non-analytical and non-constructive approaches, such as rote memorization, can predominate their character learning and remembering. Using such inefficient and taxing procedures, it is unlikely that heritage learners can systematically and effectively expand their character knowledge.

Development of character knowledge and reading comprehension subskills among CHL learners

Table 6.3 shows the means and standard deviations of the two-character knowledge tests (meaning and pronunciation) by grade. The table reveals no systematic increments in either character meaning or pronunciation scores across the grade levels. As discussed earlier, underdeveloped morphological awareness does not permit analytical approaches to character learning and remembering, making it

Table 6.3 Means and Standard Deviations (in Parentheses) of the Character Knowledge Subtest Scores (% correct)

	Meaning		
	G3 Characters	*G4 Characters*	*G5 Characters*
Grade 3	.35(.22)	N.A.	N.A.
Grade 4	.18(.29)	.25(.25)	N.A.
Grade 5	.37(.29)	.26(.19)	.39(.28)
	Pronunciation		
	G3 Characters	G4 Characters	G5 Characters
Grade 3	.50(.21)	N.A.	N.A.
Grade 4	.21(.23)	.26(.24)	N.A.
Grade 5	.30(.22)	.22(.18)	.35(.27)

124 Yanhui Zhang et al.

difficult to accumulate and organize character information in a systematic fashion. The current results, by and large, are following these speculations. Grades 4 and 5 HL learners performed at roughly the same level across the test items sampled from multiple grade textbooks. These findings would seem to suggest that the learners retain a somewhat fixed number of characters in their lexical memory at any given point in time—with little expansion in their knowledge base, indicating that character knowledge development among native and heritage Chinese learners may take considerably different paths.

Figure 6.3 provides the means and standard deviations of the five reading comprehension subtest scores. Unlike morphological awareness and character knowledge, grade 5 students outperformed the lower-grade cohorts in all subtests. Similar escalation, however, did not occur on reading comprehension among grades 3 and 4 students. To more fully examine reading comprehension subskills development across grade levels, a series of t-tests was performed on each of the five comprehension subtest scores on the two sets of overlapping passages: (a) two Level I difficult passages administered to grades 3 and 4 students; and (b) two Level II easy passages given to grades 4 and 5 students. As shown, none of the t-tests on the Level I difficulty passages was found significant, suggesting that there were no reliable gains or losses in the measured reading comprehension subskills among grades 3 and 4 students. In contrast, three out of the five subtest scores among 5th-grade students were significantly higher than those among 4th-grade students.

Viewed collectively, the results would seem to imply that comprehension subskills substantially increase between 4th and 5th grades, but no such growth occurs between 3rd and 4th grades. Considering the complete absence of increments in

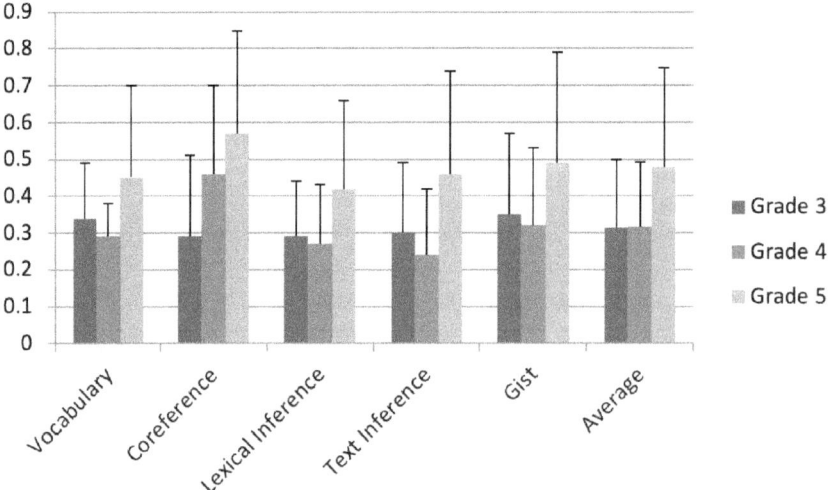

Figure 6.3 Means and standard deviations of the reading comprehension subtest scores (% correct)

morphological awareness and character knowledge, other literacy experience in English seems one plausible factor explaining the noticeable gains in reading skills among 5th-grade students. First, since virtually all students who participated in the study indicated that they rarely read Chinese books, other than the textbooks, outside the school, it is implausible that HL learners accumulate adequately high text processing experience in Chinese. Second, many literacy studies involving bilingual learners have demonstrated that reading skills, once developed in one language, transfer across languages (e.g., Durgunoglu et al., 1993; Gholamain & Geva, 1999; Koda, 2008; Wang et al., 2005). Therefore, it is plausible that HL learners rely upon the comprehension skills acquired through their primary literacy when reading heritage language.

Further, since the primary focus of reading comprehension shifts from "learning to read" to "reading to learn" in the middle grades, comprehension skills—such as inference and coherence building—among grades 3 and 4 students are still developing, and thus may not be ready for transfer. This likely explains the observed upsurge of comprehension performance only among the 5th-grade students. Hence, the current findings point to an interesting possibility—unique to bilingual learners—that heritage language learners' reading development may rely upon capabilities acquired in another language, resources unavailable to native-speaking, monolingual learners. This said, it goes against our hypothesis to overemphasize the benefit of heritage in reading acquisition for L2 learners. The picture would be more impartial when compared with a larger spectrum of results of studies involving more diversified backgrounds. As a matter of fact, according to H. Zhang and Koda (2016), adult heritage learners were reported to have outperformed pure L2 learners of Chinese on oral vocabulary, morphological discrimination, and lexical inference, but not on print vocabulary or reading comprehension. Given that the tests in H. Zhang and Koda (2016) were based on adult heritage learners and that the accurate amount of print exposure and learning of Chinese among those adult learners prior to the test is not available, it is premature to draw another conclusion. In a juxtaposition of results in H. Zhang and Koda (2016) and the current study, what is clear is that reading constitutes a core but more demanding skill that early exposure of spoken communication or

Table 6.4 Means and Standard Deviations (in Parentheses) of the Reading Comprehension Test Scores (% correct) for Overlapping Passages

	Grade 3		Grade 4		t	Grade 4		Grade 5		t
Vocabulary	.27	(.19)	.37	(.16)	−1.80	.21	(.16)	.39	(.32)	−2.14*
Coreference	.29	(.26)	.43	(.30)	−1.59	.50	(.25)	.58	(.36)	−.73
Lexical Inference	.32	(.18)	.30	(.27)	.34	.24	(.21)	.28	(.26)	−.57
Text Inference	.32	(.28)	.27	(.27)	.61	.22	(.23)	.44	(.36)	−2.07*
Gist	.38	(.29)	.35	(.28)	.25	.28	(.23)	.50	(.33)	−2.24*
Total Composite	.32	(.16)	.34	(.18)	−.53	.29	(.13)	.44	(.26)	−2.11*

* $p < .05$

Table 6.5 Correlations among Character Knowledge, Morphological Awareness, Oral Language Skills, and Reading Comprehension

	Grade 3			Grade 4			Grade 5		
	RC	CK	OLP	RC	CK	OLP	RC	CK	OLP
MA	.54*	.10	.09	.04	.27	−.32	.2	.26	−.24
RC	—	.26	.33	—	.49	.22	—	.43	.52
CK	—	—	.60**	—	—	.09	—	—	.61*

Note. RC: Reading Comprehension; CK: Character Knowledge; OLP: Oral Language Proficiency; MA: Morphological Awareness.
* $p < .05$; ** $p < .01$

familiarity of the morphological system do not provide sufficient premium advantage to reading development without systematic and purposive drills.

Interaction between morphological awareness, character knowledge, and reading comprehension

To examine the relationships among them, composite scores of the three constructs—morphological awareness, character knowledge, and reading comprehension—were computed by adding the subtest scores. Teacher ratings on students' spoken Chinese were an independent index of overall oral language proficiency. The correlations among the three constructs are provided in Table 6.5, yielding interesting patterns of interconnections. As shown, reading comprehension correlates moderately with character knowledge and oral language proficiency, but not with morphological awareness except for the 3rd-grade data. Moreover, while character knowledge and oral language proficiency are strongly related in the 3rd- and 5th-grade data, the two are entirely distinct in the 4th-grade data. In general, as predicted, reading and character knowledge development among HL learners seem to occur independently of morphological awareness, but apparently, both build on general language competence acquired through oral language interactions at home.

Further discussion and conclusion

The present study explored morphological awareness among grades 3–5 CHL learners and its impacts on character knowledge and reading sub-skill development. The results demonstrate that (1) HL learners performed well above the chance level on all but one morphological awareness tasks, but their performance was visibly worse than that among native Chinese-speaking children except in radical explanation; (2) there were no differences in any of the morphological awareness subtest scores among grades 3–5 heritage language learners; (3) although character knowledge did not differ across the grade levels, reading comprehension performance of grade-5 students was significantly superior to that of the younger cohorts; and (4) morphological awareness among heritage language learners was not systematically related either with character knowledge or with reading comprehension. Several important implications stemmed from these results.

First, heritage learners' performance on the morphological awareness tasks—low but non-random—indicates that they are sensitized to certain formation regularities in Chinese characters and utilize the sensitivity, though not always successfully, during character processing. Interestingly, such rule-governed behaviors were not observable among native Chinese-speaking 1st-grade children (Shu & Anderson, 1999) who had learned roughly the same number of characters as the children in the present study. Other than print input and exposure, factors contribute to the formation of morphological awareness among heritage language learners. Future research, perhaps, should focus on these additional factors. Knowing that certain aspects of morphological awareness are shared across languages (Koda, 2005), we can speculate that the non-language-specific awareness capabilities, acquired through primary literacy, may provide substantial facilitation, both directly and indirectly, in the development of morphological awareness in a heritage language.

Second, the performance variance across the morphological awareness tasks implies that various awareness facets are acquired at disparate rates. Those pertaining to structural constraints develop earlier, with less input than those related to character-specific semantic/functional properties. Significantly, the present data demonstrated that no perceptible increments occurred in character knowledge among grades 3–5 heritage language students. Also, no systematic relationship existed between morphological awareness and character knowledge. Because of these results, it seems plausible to suggest that (1) understanding the structural properties is far from sufficient for character-knowledge development; and (2) systematic increments in this knowledge are heavily dependent upon the awareness facets to be highly attuned to the language-specific, functional, properties. Given that even 3rd-grade students can detect and use structural regularities of characters, it also seems likely that heritage language learners benefit greatly from explicit instruction on functional and distributional properties of radicals, designed to promote effective use of the information in character learning and processing. Moreover, it will be highly beneficial to determine to what extent such metalinguistic training compensates for heavily limited character input and exposure in character-knowledge development among HL learners.

Third, the present study revealed that clear gains occurred only in comprehension subskills and only among grade 5 students. The seemingly peculiar patterns of developments suggest the involvement of non-language-specific factors—presumably unaffected by limited print exposure and experience—in HL literacy learning. Given that reading comprehension requires highly specialized subskills and that these skills are acquired primarily through extensive text information processing, it is highly plausible that 5th-grade students use their comprehension subskills developed through primary literacy English. Since cross-language transfer is a common phenomenon in L2 learning, the transfer of comprehension subskills among upper-grade HL learners should warrant more comprehensive research. Ideally, the reading subskills in the dominant language should be measured for a more accurate assessment of the effect of such transfer. In this regard, we acknowledge one limitation of the current study. To date, biliteracy research has focused mainly on the transfer of lower-level reading skills like phonological awareness and decoding development. Undoubtedly, systematic examinations of cross-linguistic relationships in comprehension subskills, particularly those directly involved in academic content learning, will significantly contribute to biliteracy theory and practice.

Additionally, literacy learning in an HL differs from that in the first language. It occurs with heavily restricted print exposure and experience and is distinct from that in a second language because it typically builds on adequately developed oral language competence. Pedagogically, enhancing literacy learning experiences requires an in-depth understanding and analysis of the contributing factors to oral proficiency and reading acquisition. In particular, the underlying mechanism accounting for how morphological skills of heritage language learners are developed may well likely be multidimensional. As such, research endeavors are recommended to be invested in the classic psycholinguistic domain and neighborhood fields. For instance, Pellicer-Sánchez and Schmitt (2010), Bruton et al. (2011), and Y. Zhang and Li (2016) demonstrated that optimally designed incidental-learning strategies might enhance the learning efficiency in L2 learning. Several studies also tended to support the role of social-cultural interactions in formal and informal settings in boosting the morphological awareness for heritage language learners at various ages (S. Chen et al., 2021; He, 2010; Tigert, 2020; Xiao, 2013). Nevertheless, a clearer understanding of the complex functional interconnections between morphological awareness and other metalinguistic skills among L2 learners of Chinese is needed in building new agendas for future literacy studies and pedagogical practices.

References

Bear, D. R., Invernizzi, M., & Templeton, S., & Johnston, F. (1995). *Words their way: Word study for phonics vocabulary, and spelling instruction*. Merrill.

Bruton, A., Lopez, M. G., & Mesa, R. E. (2011). Incidental L2 vocabulary learning: An impracticable term? *TESOL Quarterly, 45*, 759–768.

Carlisle, J. F. (2003). Morphology matters in learning to read: A commentary. *Reading Psychology, 24*, 291–322.

Chen, S. H., Zhou, Q., & Uchikoshi, Y. (2021). Heritage language socialization in Chinese American immigrant families: Prospective links to children's heritage language proficiency. *International Journal of Bilingual Education and Bilingualism, 24*, 1193–1209.

Chen, X., Hao, M., Geva, E., & Shu, H. (2009). The role of compound awareness in Chinese children's vocabulary acquisition and character reading. *Reading and Writing, 22*(5), 615–631.

Chen, Y. P., Allport, D. A., & Marshall, J. C. (1996). What are the functional orthographic units in Chinese word recognition: The stroke or the stroke pattern? *The Quarterly Journal of Experimental Psychology, 49*(A), 1024–1043.

Chilant, D., & Caramazza, A. (1995). Where is morphology and how is it processed? The case of written word recognition. In L. B. Feldman (Ed.), *Morphological aspects of language processing* (pp. 55–76). Erlbaum.

Duques, S. L. (1989). Grammatical deficiencies in writing: An investigation of learning disabled college students. *Reading and Writing, 1*, 309–325.

Durgunoglu, A. Y., Nagy, W. E., & Hancin, B. J. (1993). Cross-language transfer of phonemic awareness. *Journal of Educational Psychology, 85*, 453–465.

Everson, M. E. (1998). Word recognition among learners of Chinese as a foreign language: Investigating the relationship between naming and knowing. *Modern Language Journal, 82*, 194–204.

Everson, M. E., & Ke, C. (1997). An inquiry into the reading strategies of intermediate and advanced learners of Chinese as a foreign language. *Journal of the Chinese Language Teacher Association, 32*, 1–20.

Fowler, A. E., & Liberman, I. Y. (1995). The role of phonology and orthography in morphological awareness. In L. B. Feldman (Ed.), *Morphological aspects of language processing* (pp. 157–188). Erlbaum.

Gholamain, M., & Geva, E. (1999). The concurrent development of word recognition skills in English and Farsi. *Language Learning, 49*, 183–217.

He, A. W. (2010). The heart of heritage: Sociocultural dimensions of heritage language learning. *Annual Review of Applied Linguistics, 30*, 66–82.

Kieffer, M. J., Biancarosa, G., & Mancilla-Martinez, J. (2013). Roles of morphological awareness in the reading comprehension of Spanish-speaking language minority learners: Exploring partial mediation by vocabulary and reading fluency. *Applied Psycholinguistics, 34*(4), 697–725.

Koda, K. (2005). *Insights into second language reading: A cross-linguistic approach*. Cambridge University Press.

Koda, K. (2008). Impacts of prior literacy experience on learning to read in a second language. In K. Koda & A. M. Zehler (Eds.), *Learning to read across languages: Cross—linguistic relationships in first- and second-language literacy development* (pp. 68–96). Routledge.

Koda, K., & Takahashi, T. (2003). *Role of radical awareness in lexical inference in Kanji* (Unpublished Manuscript).

Ku, Y-M., & Anderson, R. C. (2003). Development of morphological awareness in Chinese and English. *Reading and Writing: An Interdisciplinary Journal, 16*, 399–422.

Kuo, L. J., & Anderson, R. C. (2006). Morphological awareness and learning to read: A cross-language perspective. *Educational Psychologist, 41*, 161–180.

Li, W., Anderson, R. C., Nagy, W., & Zhang, H. (2002). Facets of metalinguistic awareness that contribute to Chinese literacy. In W. Li, J. S. Gaffney, & J. L. Packard (Eds.), *Chinese children's reading acquisition: Theoretical and pedagogical issues* (pp. 87–106). Kluwer Academic.

Lü, C., Koda, K., Zhang, D., & Zhang, Y. (2015). Effects of semantic radical properties on character meaning extraction and inference among learners of Chinese as a foreign language. *Writing Systems Research, 7*(2), 169–185.

Manolitsis, G., Georgiou, G. K., Inoue, T., & Parrila, R. (2019). Are morphological awareness and literacy skills reciprocally related? Evidence from a cross-linguistic study. *Journal of Educational Psychology, 111*(8), 1362–1381.

McGinnis, S. (1995). *Student attitudes and approaches in the learning of written Chinese*. Paper presented at the Annual Conference of the American Association for Applied Linguistics.

Mori, Y., & Nagy, W. (1999). Integration of information from context and word elements in interpreting novel Kanji compounds. *Reading Research Quarterly*, *34*, 80–101.

Nagy, W. E., & Anderson, R. C. (1999). Metalinguistic awareness and literacy acquisition in different languages. In D. Wagner, R. Venezky, & B. Street (Eds.), *Literacy: An international handbook* (pp. 155–160). Westview Press.

Nagy, W. E., Carlisle, J. F., & Goodwin, A. P. (2014). Morphological knowledge and literacy acquisition. *Journal of Learning Disabilities*, *47*, 3–12.

Pasquarella, A., Chen, C., Lam, K., Luo, Y. C., & Ramirez, G. (2011). Cross-language transfer of morphological awareness in Chinese-English bilinguals. *Journal of Research in Reading*, *34*, 23–42.

Pellicer-Sánchez, A., & Schmitt, N. (2010). Incidental vocabulary acquisition from an authentic novel: Do things fall apart? *Reading in a Foreign Language*, *22*, 31–55.

Perfetti, C. A., & Liu, Y. (2005). Orthography to phonology and meaning: Comparisons across and within writing systems. *Reading and Writing*, *18*, 193–210.

Rubin, H. (1991). Morphological knowledge and writing ability. In R. M. Joshi (Ed.), *Written language disorders* (pp. 43–69). Kluwer Academic.

Shen, H. H. (2003). A comparison of written Chinese achievement among heritage learners in homogeneous and heterogeneous groups. *Foreign Language Annals*, *36*(2), 258–266.

Shu, H., & Anderson, R. C. (1997). Role of radical awareness in the character and word acquisition of Chinese children. *Reading Research Quarterly*, *32*, 78–89.

Shu, H., & Anderson, R. C. (1999). Learning to read Chinese: The development of metalinguistic awareness. In A. Inhuff, J. Wang, & H. C. Chen (Eds.), *Reading Chinese scripts: A cognitive analysis* (pp. 1–18). Lawrence Erlbaum.

Taft, M. (1991). *Reading and the mental lexicon*. Erlbaum.

Taft, M., & Zhu, X. P. (1995). The representation of bound morphemes in the lexicon: A Chinese study. In L. B. Feldman (Ed.), *Morphological aspects of language processing* (pp. 109–129). Erlbaum.

Tigert, J. M. (2020). Vanilla sauce and songs: Literacies in a heritage language school. *Language Culture and Curriculum*, *33*(1), 100–113.

Tyler, A., & Nagy, W. (1989). The acquisition of English derivational morphology. *Journal of Memory and Language*, *28*, 649–667.

Tyler, A., & Nagy, W. (1990). Use of derivational morphology during reading. *Cognition*, *36*, 17–34.

Wang, M., Cheng, C., & Chen, S. W. (2006). Contribution of morphological awareness to Chinese-English biliteracy acquisition. *Journal of Educational Psychology*, *98*, 542–553.

Wang, M., Perfetti, C. A., & Liu, Y. (2005). Chinese-English biliteracy acquisition: Cross-language and writing system transfer. *Cognition*, *97*, 67–88.

Xiao, Y. (2013). Effect of home background on advanced heritage language learning. *Chinese as a Second Language Research*, *2*(2), 193–220.

Zhang, D. (2013). Linguistic distance effect on cross-linguistic transfer of morphological awareness. *Applied Psycholinguistics*, *34*, 917–942.

Zhang, D. (2016). Morphology in Malay-English biliteracy acquisition: An intervention study. *International Journal of Bilingual Education and Bilingualism*, *19*(5), 546–562.

Zhang, D., & Koda, K. (2014). Awareness of derivation and compounding in Chinese—English biliteracy acquisition. *International Journal of Bilingual Education and Bilingualism*, *17*, 55–73.

Zhang, D., Koda, K., & Leong, C. K. (2016). Morphological awareness and bilingual word learning: A longitudinal structural equation modeling study. *Reading and Writing*, *29*, 383–407.

Zhang, D., Koda, K., Leong, C. K., & Pang, E. (2019). Cross-lagged analysis of reciprocal effects of morphological awareness and reading in Chinese in a multilingual context. *Journal of Research in Reading*, *42*(1), 58–79.

Zhang, H. C. (1994). Some studies on the recognition of Chinese characters. In Q. Jing, H. Zhang, & D. Peng (Eds.), *Information processing of Chinese language* (pp. 1–11). Beijing Normal University Press.

Zhang, H. C., & Koda, K. (2016). Word-knowledge development in Chinese as a heritage language learners: A comparative study. *Studies in Second Language Acquisition, 40*(1), 201–223.

Zhang, Y., & Li, R. (2016). The role of morphological awareness in the incidental learning of Chinese characters among CSL learners. *Language Awareness*, *25*(3), 179–196.

7 Developmental interdependence between word decoding, vocabulary knowledge, and reading comprehension in young L2 readers of Chinese

Dongbo Zhang and Xiaoxi Sun

Text comprehension necessitates simultaneous execution of a number of cognitive and psycholinguistic processes (Cain & Barnes, 2017; Grabe, 2009; Perfetti, 1999; Perfetti et al., 2005). Notably, for smooth comprehension of a text, readers need to rapidly identify words in the text and access the meanings of those words (Perfetti, 2010; Perfetti et al., 2005). Reading comprehension development thus depends on lexical development, including word decoding and vocabulary knowledge (Duke & Carlisle, 2011). Conversely, lexical development also depends on reading experience and comprehension (Nagy, 2005; Nagy & Scott, 2000). Developmentally, written texts are a fundamental source of information for exposure to new sound-grapheme patterns and consolidation of knowledge of existing patterns; understanding the context where unknown words appear is also important for incidental learning of those words and vocabulary expansion.

The aforementioned insights are encapsulated in many models of reading, including the verbal efficiency theory (Perfetti, 1985) and the lexical quality hypothesis (Perfetti, 2007). Perfetti (2010) characterizes the complex relationships between word decoding (D), vocabulary knowledge (V), and reading comprehension (C) in light of "*the Golden Triangle of Reading Skill*" (hereafter, the DVC triangle). Although the DVC triangle is not intended as a reading *development* model, the theoretical outlining does imply some developmentally interdependent relationships between the component skills, which have been supported by some longitudinal evidence. Yet, the evidence is not always consistent, and has been largely on monolingual or L1 reading. In the L2 literature, the evidence was mostly based on *concurrent* correlations (Jeon & Yamashita, 2014). Longitudinal relationships, particularly how the growth in L2 word decoding and vocabulary knowledge may be predicted by reading comprehension, have rarely been tested on L2 readers. Additionally, existing longitudinal studies have focused primarily on alphabetic languages; little longitudinal research has sought to test developmental interdependence between lexical competence and reading comprehension in readers of Chinese in general, and L2 readers of Chinese in particular.

The present study aimed to fill this research gap. Three waves of data were collected across a year, from grade 3 to grade 4, from a group of children in Singapore who had English as the dominant home language and learned Chinese through

Developmental interdependence in young L2 readers of Chinese 133

school instruction. The data were fitted to a trivariate, cross-lagged panel model and analyzed through path analyses where the longitudinal effects of decoding and vocabulary on reading comprehension, and those of reading comprehension on decoding and vocabulary, were tested and compared across time points.

"The golden triangle of reading Skill"

Perfetti's (2010) DVC triangle (see Figure 7.1) aims to disentangle the complex interaction between word decoding, vocabulary knowledge, and reading comprehension. To begin with, it underscores bidirectional, causal relationships between vocabulary knowledge and reading comprehension. On the one hand, comprehending a text requires the "ability to access the meaning of the word, as it applies in the context of this particular text" (p. 293). This instrumentalist view on the importance of vocabulary knowledge for reading comprehension has long been recognized (Anderson & Freebody, 1981). On the other hand, the reader needs to understand the discourse context where an unknown word appears—that is, comprehension—for lexical inferencing or incidental learning of that word to happen (Nagy, 2005). In this respect, comprehension "can cause the reader to learn something about the meaning of that word" (p. 293).

The DVC triangle also contends that there are bi-directional causal relationships between decoding and vocabulary. As Perfetti (2010) argues, successful word decoding during text reading triggers the retrieval of meanings for familiar words and hence strengthens or consolidates form-meaning connections that have been formed in the mental lexicon. Additionally, it can "establish context-dependent links between unfamiliar words and meaning-bearing contexts" (p. 292). Conversely, vocabulary knowledge also affects decoding because "decoding a word whose meaning is known strengthens the connection between the word's orthographic form (its spelling) and its meaning" (p. 292). In this respect, decoding and vocabulary strengthen each other toward high-quality lexical representations (phonology, orthography, morphology, and semantics).

The DVC triangle does not, however, hypothesize any causal relationship between decoding and reading comprehension. Instead, it highlights a pivotal, mediating role of vocabulary. Perfetti (2010) argues that "the effects of decoding

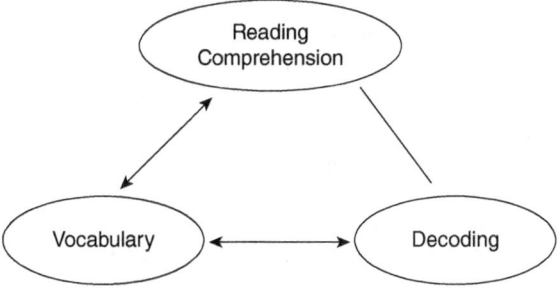

Figure 7.1 The DVC reading skill triangle (based on Perfetti, 2010, p. 293)

on comprehension are mediated by knowing the meaning of the decoded words." In other words, decoding words in a text, while serving as the initial basis for comprehending that text, will not in itself result in comprehension unless the meanings of those words are activated and subsequently integrated. Conversely, the effect of comprehension on decoding is "mediated by achieving enough meaning from the text to verify the identity of a decoded word" (p. 294). Perfetti further argues that the assumption about the lack of "decoding-comprehension effects" in the DVC triangle "rests on the logic of cognitive event sequences in reading and not on correlations of skill assessments" (p. 294).

The DVC triangle serves as a heuristic for understanding complex interaction between lexical processes and reading comprehension in skilled reading. It is unclear, though, how the hypothesized relationships based on "cognitive event sequences" may be *developmentally* valid. In other words, how may the relationships be manifested in developing readers, and how may any interdependent relationships change across stages of reading development? Additionally, the DVC triangle is largely contextualized in monolingual English reading. How the three skills may be developmentally related as such in L2 readers of Chinese remains to be explored.

In what follows, we review some longitudinal studies that shed light on developmental relationships between decoding, vocabulary, and reading comprehension.[1] Because of the purpose of this study, the relationships between decoding and vocabulary are not a focus of the review. Whereas some studies focused only on one direction of developmental effects, such as Lervåg and Aukrust (2010), which tested only the effects of decoding and vocabulary on growth in reading comprehension, others examined reciprocal or bi-directional relationships, such as Verhoeven and van Leeuwe (2008). For clarity of discussion, the review is divided into two separate sections: the first is on the impact of decoding and vocabulary on reading comprehension development; and the second, on that of reading comprehension on the development of decoding and vocabulary.

Decoding and vocabulary in L2 Reading comprehension development

This section focuses on reviewing longitudinal effects of decoding and vocabulary on reading comprehension, including those in L2 readers. Based on cross-lagged panel analysis, Santos et al. (2019) found that Portuguese-speaking children's grade 2 decoding significantly predicted grade 3 reading comprehension over and above grade 2 reading comprehension (i.e., the autoregressor); this longitudinal effect was similarly found from grade 3 to grade 4. Quinn et al. (2015) found significant growth of both vocabulary knowledge and reading comprehension in English-speaking children from grade 1 to grade 4. The researchers' latent change score modeling analysis revealed that children's initial vocabulary scores as well as the speed of vocabulary growth significantly predicted the growth speed of reading comprehension. Verhoeven and van Leeuwe (2008) tracked the development of decoding, vocabulary (and listening comprehension), and reading comprehension in Dutch-speaking children throughout the six years of elementary school. Cross-lagged panel analyses revealed that, controlling for grade 3 reading comprehension (and grade 3 decoding), grade 3 vocabulary knowledge significantly predicted grade 4 reading comprehension. A similar effect was found from grade 5 to grade 6. Yet, it did not surface from grade 2 to grade 3 and from grade 4 to grade 5. For decoding, the only unique longitudinal effect was found from grade 5 to grade 6. Over and above grade 5 reading comprehension (and grade 5 vocabulary knowledge, for which ® = .33), grade 5 decoding had a significant, yet small effect (® = .04) on grade 6 reading comprehension.

A few studies also examined the longitudinal effects in L2 readers (e.g., Lam et al., 2012; Lervåg & Aukrust, 2010). In Lervåg and Aukrust (2010), L1 and L2 readers of Norwegian were first tested on word decoding, vocabulary knowledge, and reading comprehension when they had received formal instruction in Norwegian for four months in school, and subsequently further tested on reading comprehension three more times with an interval of six months. The initial level of both decoding and vocabulary was a unique, significant predictor of the intercept (or initial level) of two different comprehension measures in both L1 and L2 readers. Yet when the criterion variable was the slope or growth speed, some discrepancy was found between decoding and vocabulary. For both groups, particularly L2 readers, controlling for decoding, vocabulary was a unique, significant predictor of the growth in reading comprehension, suggesting that those who had greater initial vocabulary knowledge tended to show faster growth in reading comprehension. This effect, however, did not surface for decoding; and this was consistently the case for the L2 readers across the two comprehension measures.

These findings suggested that vocabulary, compared to decoding, tended to have a more consistent and salient effect on reading comprehension development in young, developing readers, which seems to support its pivotal role underscored in the DVC triangle. The evidence, however, was all based on alphabetic readers (e.g., English, Portuguese, Dutch, and Norwegian). Different from alphabetic languages, Chinese is a morphosyllabic language based on character/morpheme-syllable mapping (DeFrancis, 1989; Taylor & Taylor, 2014). Most Chinese characters (about 80–90%) are semantic-phonetic compounds composed of a semantic and a phonetic radical. These two orthographic components have varied spatial configurations and canonical positions (e.g., left/right, top/bottom, surrounding, and half surrounding). A phonetic radical provides clues to the host character's pronunciation, while a semantic radical provides clues to the meaning of that character. For example, in 梅 /méi/ (plum), the left component 木 (wood) is the semantic radical, which indicates that 梅 is related to wood; the right component 每 /měi/ (every) is the phonetic radical, which has the same pronunciation (except the tone) of 梅, but has nothing to do with its meaning. Many Chinese characters, however, are unlike the near-perfect illustration in 梅 in that the phonetic information in a phonetic radical is often not reliable (the same holds true for the semantic information in the semantic radical as well) (Zhou, 1978). For example, in 海 /hǎi/ (ocean), while 氵 suggests that 海 is related to water, 每 does not at all provide any clue to the sound of 海.

Another unavoidable issue for examining word knowledge in Chinese is what constitutes a word in the language. A character is typically a morpheme. Many characters are free morphemes or words themselves. There are, however, only a few thousand commonly used characters in modern Chinese (Zhao & Zhang, 2007); Chinese words are mostly multi-morphemic and formed largely through compounding. In written texts, those words are represented in multiple characters and are not spaced as in English (Taylor & Taylor, 2014). For example, in 篮球是一项很受欢fl的体育运动 (*Basketball is a popular sport*), 篮球 /lánqiú/ (basketball) is a two-morpheme/character compound word where both 篮 and 球 are a semantic-phonetic compound character and mean *basket* and *ball*, respectively.

The properties briefly outlined of Chinese orthography and lexis suggest that word decoding based on phonological recoding, which characterizes alphabetic languages, does not often pertain to Chinese. The utility of phonetic strategies is very restricted in Chinese, and orthographic processing is far more important (Leong, 2015; Perfetti et al., 2013). Developmentally, this suggests that, unlike the limited effect reviewed earlier on alphabetic readers, the decoding component of the DVC triangle may have a far more salient role in Chinese. This should perhaps pertain to all developing readers and may particularly be the case in L2 readers, for whom characters are typically learned in a way where meaning and form (e.g., pronunciation, stroke order, and orthographic structure) are taught together. Due to this instructional effect, decoding a character, which relies on visual-orthographic processing (Leong, 2015), should be expected to activate the meaning of that character (Everson, 1998; Zhang et al., 2019). A learner not knowing 篮 /lán/, for example, is likely unable to decode it; conversely, correct decoding of 篮 implies that the learner knows its meaning.

The aforementioned analysis on form-meaning co-activation during decoding should not be interpreted to mean that decoding individual characters is the entirety of the lexical support required for reading comprehension and its development in L2 Chinese. Tens of thousands of words in modern Chinese are formed based on a few thousand common characters (Zhao & Zhang, 2007). The ability to decode the constituent characters of a word (e.g., 业务), and the knowledge of the respective meaning of each character (业 and 务), does not in itself represent a knowledge of the whole word—at least not a precise knowledge. Decoding individual characters without vocabulary support would cause the inability to deal with the challenge of word segmentation required of reading Chinese texts. In summary, while theoretically decoding is fundamental for Chinese text reading and its effect on comprehension may be more salient than in alphabetic languages, vocabulary knowledge should also be expected to play a distinct role, as in alphabetic languages.

Little longitudinal research has directly examined the effects of decoding and vocabulary on reading comprehension development in Chinese. The limited evidence nonetheless lends some support to the earlier analysis. Yeung et al. (2016) aimed to construct a componential model of reading in Chinese. Informed by the simple view of reading (SVR) (Gough & Tunmer, 1986), the authors collected two waves of data from native Chinese-speaking elementary school students in Hong

Kong. Children were first tested in grade 1 on a number of oral (word definition and listening comprehension) and reading skills (word decoding, reading fluency, and sentence and passage comprehensions). Two years later (grade 3), their sentence and passage comprehensions were tested a second time. Among the many findings, grade 1 decoding predicted grade 3 sentence comprehension, controlling for grade 1 sentence comprehension and other related skills; a similar effect was found on grade 1 reading fluency on grade 3 passage comprehension. Overall, the findings provided some longitudinal evidence on the importance of decoding for reading comprehension development in native Chinese-speaking children. There was, however, no evidence on the longitudinal effect of vocabulary, and the relative longitudinal effects of vocabulary and decoding. The word definition measure did tap children's oral vocabulary knowledge; however, because of the authors' concern about its unsatisfactory reliability, it was not included in any statistical modeling.

Given its focus on L2 readers of Chinese, Wong (2017) is a notable study. Also informed by the SVR, Wong measured twice, from grade 4 to grade 5, ethnic minority children learning L2 Chinese in Hong Kong on character decoding, listening comprehension, and reading comprehension. Cross-lagged path modeling showed that grade 5 decoding (® = .41) and listening comprehension (® = .20) both uniquely predicted grade 5 reading comprehension, controlling for grade 4 reading comprehension, and decoding seemed to have a larger effect. However, the study did not consider vocabulary knowledge. Considering that vocabulary should strongly underpin listening comprehension, it may be inferred that decoding and vocabulary were both important predictors of change in reading comprehension; and decoding might have played an even greater role. In terms of longitudinal modeling, the study has a notable limitation; that is, the crossed-effect predictors would need to be grade 4 measures.

Impact of comprehension on L2 lexical development

The DVC triangle hypothesizes that comprehension is fundamental for incidental learning of vocabulary through reading. Developmentally reading comprehension should predict vocabulary growth in that better comprehenders would be more likely to pick up new words from reading experience. Poor readers, compared to good readers, tend to be less motivated to read and thus would lose learning opportunities that reading can offer (Stanovich, 1986). Theoretically, the dependence of vocabulary development on reading experience and comprehension should pertain to any language and any reader, particularly L2 readers (esp. foreign language learners), because written texts could be a dominant source of (lexical) input. Empirical evidence, however, is limited and often inconsistent.

Quinn et al. (2015), as reviewed earlier, found an effect of vocabulary knowledge on English-speaking children's reading comprehension growth from grade 1 to grade 4. Conversely, however, no significant effect was found of the initial reading comprehension level and its growth speed on the growth speed of vocabulary knowledge. The authors cautioned that the finding should not be interpreted to mean that reading is unimportant for vocabulary development; instead, they argued that developmental effects may depend on how sensitive literacy measures are to change. Verhoeven and van Leeuwe (2008) reported that Dutch-speaking children's grade 2 reading comprehension (® = .61) significantly predicted grade 3 vocabulary knowledge, controlling for grade 2 vocabulary knowledge. A much smaller yet significant effect was found from grade 4 to grade 5 (® = .06). Similar effects, however, did not surface during other periods of elementary school.

Chen et al. (2019) tracked the development of vocabulary and reading comprehension for a year in three cohorts (grades 1, 3, and 5) of native Chinese-speaking children in China. Vocabulary knowledge was measured through explaining the meanings of orally presented words. Cross-lagged panel analysis revealed a significant effect of earlier reading comprehension on later vocabulary knowledge (controlling for the autoregressor) in the older two cohorts as opposed to the youngest cohort. The authors explained the discrepancy between the cohorts in light of their different developmental stages. The older cohorts, compared to the youngest one, were transitioning to learning to read, at which stage they tended to read more independently and the texts they read were also more complex and diverse, which should have provided a greater opportunity for their incidental learning and vocabulary expansion.

The DVC triangle hypothesizes that any effect of reading comprehension on decoding should be mediated by vocabulary. If this contention holds for developmental relationships, in that the effect of reading comprehension on decoding development is fully mediated by vocabulary knowledge, then in longitudinal modeling, reading comprehension should not be expected to directly predict change in decoding, particularly in the presence of vocabulary. Few studies have aimed to test these relationships. In Verhoeven and van Leeuwe (2008), controlling for earlier decoding, earlier reading comprehension was never a significant predictor of later word decoding across six elementary school years. This result might be related to Dutch being a transparent orthography. In other words, growth in decoding may well be a manifestation of gradual mastery of the alphabetic principle rather than a function of reading comprehension. Wong (2017) examined the developmental independence between character decoding, listening comprehension, and reading comprehension in ethnic minority children learning Chinese in Hong Kong. In addition to the finding reviewed earlier on the effect of decoding on reading comprehension, grade 4 reading comprehension also significantly predicted grade 5 decoding, over and above grade 4 decoding. The discrepancy in the findings of the two studies might indicate that reading comprehension may have a notable role to play in decoding development in (L2) readers of Chinese as opposed to alphabetic readers.

The present study

Longitudinal research on developmental relationships between decoding, vocabulary, and reading comprehension is limited. While there seemed to be consistent evidence on the effect of vocabulary on reading comprehension development, existing findings on the effect of decoding seemed to differ between alphabetic languages and Chinese on the one hand and between L1 and L2 readers on the other. Conversely, regarding the effect of reading comprehension on decoding and vocabulary development, the evidence was even more limited and inconsistent. With a notable exception of Wong (2017), little research has addressed those issues with a focus on L2 readers of Chinese. Drawing upon the data of a large project that examined Singaporean children's biliteracy development, the present study aimed to address this gap and explore how decoding, vocabulary, and reading comprehension may be developmentally interdependent in young L2 readers of Chinese. It aimed to answer the following three questions:

1. How do word decoding and vocabulary knowledge (relatively) predict developmental change in reading comprehension in young L2 readers of Chinese?
2. Do the (relative) longitudinal effects of word decoding and vocabulary knowledge change over time?
3. Reciprocally, does reading comprehension predict developmental change in word decoding and vocabulary knowledge?

Method

Participants and dataset

This study was based on a large, longitudinal project that examined Singaporean children's biliteracy development (Zhang, 2017a; Zhang et al., 2016, 2017). In that project, a battery of tests was administered three times over a year: at end of grade 3 (Time 1), in the middle of grade 4 (Time 2), and at the end of grade 4 (Time 3), to measure children's reading and its related skills in English as well as their respective ethnic language. In addition, a questionnaire was administered to parents at Time 1 to elicit patterns of home language use. For the purpose of this study, we drew upon the three waves of data on Chinese word decoding, vocabulary knowledge, and reading comprehension in those children with English as the dominant home language.

Singapore is a multilingual country in Southeast Asia with four official languages, including English and the languages of the three major ethnic groups: Chinese of the Chinese, Malay of the Malays, and Tamil of the Indians (Shepherd, 2005). Chinese is the largest ethnic group, accounting for about 75% of the population. Singapore adopts a bilingual education policy. Students of all ethnic groups are required to learn their respective ethnic language (locally called the mother tongue or MT) as a school subject while also developing proficiency in English, which is the medium of school instruction. Over the past few decades, the globalized influence of English as a lingua franca has had strong ramifications on the sociolinguistic milieu in Singapore. A significant one is the gradual home language shift from MT to English, which is particularly true of the Chinese group (Zhao & Liu, 2010). As a result, though all ethnic Chinese children learn Chinese in school, they bring diverse experiences into the process of learning. While some Chinese families still use Chinese (Mandarin and/or a dialect of Chinese, like Hokkien, Teochew, or Cantonese) as the dominant home language, in many other families, children grew up using English as the sole or dominant home language. The latter group usually have had no, or very limited, oral language and print experience in Chinese prior to formal schooling. They essentially learn to read Chinese as an L2.

When the longitudinal, biliteracy project mentioned earlier first started in grade 3, the three participating schools' records showed that a total of 677 students were studying in 19 classes, and 415 of them were studying Chinese as the MT subject. (Not all participated initially or stayed on, however.) Among those Chinese-studying students, a large majority were ethnic Chinese born in Singapore; there were also a small number of non-ethnic Chinese who were immigrants from other countries (e.g., South Korea or Thailand). The participants for the study reported here were ethnic Chinese children with English as the dominant home language. They were purposively selected from the 415 Chinese-studying students following these steps. To begin with, 66 students were first removed from the list, because their parents either did not consent for them to participate in the project (in other words, they were not tested at all throughout the project) or did not complete the questionnaire. Among the 349 students who remained on the list, a variety of home language patterns were revealed. Only those ethnic Chinese children from an English-dominant family, in which both parents used English as the dominant language, were selected. This step left 123 students in the dataset. The final step was to adopt listwise deletion so that only those with data on decoding, vocabulary, as well as reading comprehension in all three waves were retained. The final dataset for the present study included 89 ethnic Chinese children with English as the dominant home language. Their mean age was 9.4 years when they were first tested at the end of Grade 3.

Measures

The same battery of tasks described here was administered together with other skills in Chinese (and English), three times with an interval of about six months. The decoding task was administered individually by trained research assistants in a quiet space in the children's respective schools. Vocabulary and reading comprehension were group-tested in their Chinese classes. All tasks had strong internal consistency reliability across all waves (see Table 7.1).

Word decoding

Children were asked to read aloud 30 multi-character words printed on cards. The words were sampled from the textbooks developed by the Singapore Ministry of Education for elementary school students (grades 1 to 6). They included words from textbooks that had been learned by the children at the time of the study as well as those from textbooks that had not been learned (e.g., grades 5 and 6 textbooks). A point would be awarded for a word only if both/all component characters were pronounced correctly.

Table 7.1 Descriptive Statistics, Normality Estimates, and Reliability

	Mean	SD	Skewness	Kurtosis	Reliability (α)
Word Decoding (MSP = 30)					
Time 1	11.830	5.940	0.436	0.488	.925
Time 2	13.970	6.125	0.043	0.153	.940
Time 3	14.640	6.698	−0.051	−0.109	.946
Vocabulary Knowledge (MSP = 60)					
Time 1	35.200	8.116	−0.579	1.468	.877
Time 2	38.720	7.790	−0.846	2.635	.904
Time 3	39.220	9.141	−0.982	1.762	.911
Reading Comprehension (MSP = 15)					
Time 1	4.830	2.773	1.101	1.239	.732
Time 2	5.350	2.370	1.135	1.057	.718
Time 3	5.990	2.830	0.482	0.028	.767

Notes. MSP: Maximum Score Possible; Time 1: end of grade 3; Time 2: mid of grade 4; Time 3: end of grade 4

Vocabulary knowledge

Oral, receptive vocabulary knowledge was measured with a researcher-developed picture-selection task modeled after the form of the PPVT-IV (Dunn & Dunn, 2007). It included five sets of 12 multisyllabic words of various frequency levels based on the Modern Chinese Frequency Dictionary (Beijing Language Institute, 1986). All 60 words were read aloud to children, and they were asked to circle the number of the picture, from among four, that represented the meaning of a word.

Reading comprehension

Reading comprehension was measured with a researcher-developed multiple-choice passage-comprehension task, which included three passages, including one narrative and two informational texts, with a mean length of about 350 characters. Each passage was followed by five questions that tested different subskills of comprehension (e.g., resolution of co-referential relationships, inferential comprehension, and gist); and each question was followed by four choices. Altogether, there were 15 questions.

Cross-lagged panel and path analysis

The three-wave data were fitted to a trivariate, cross-lagged panel (CLP) with the developmental relationships analyzed using path analysis (Newsom, 2015; Selig & Little, 2012). Figure 7.2 shows a simple CLP model with two observed variables (A and B) measured at three time points (indicated by the subscripts 1, 2, and 3, respectively). In the model, for crossed effects, A_1 predicts B_2 (c1) and A_2 predicts B_3 (c2); and conversely, B_1 predicts A_2 (d1) and B_2 predicts A_3 (d2). Additionally, a variable's earlier performance also predicts its immediately

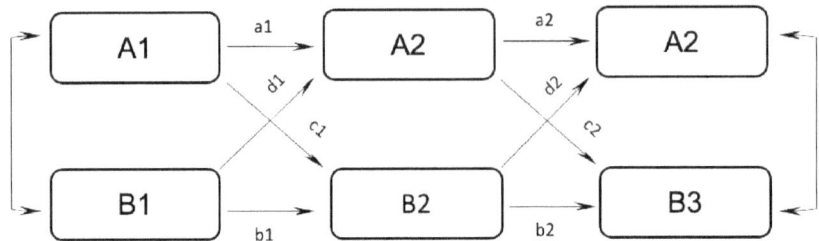

Figure 7.2 Cross-lagged panel analysis with three-wave data

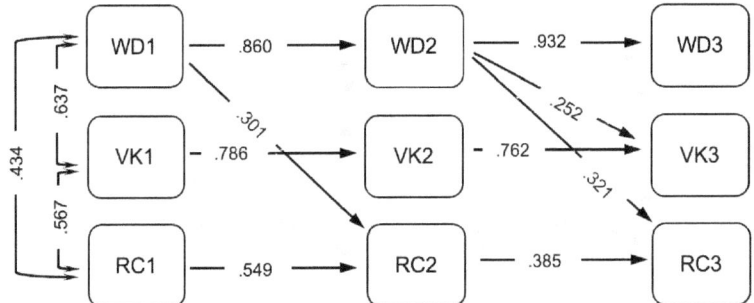

Figure 7.3 Cross-lagged path analysis on developmental interdependence between word decoding, vocabulary knowledge, and reading comprehension

Notes. Significant path coefficients are shown in black solid lines (all $ps < .001$); paths not statistically significant shown in gray dash lines. WD: word decoding; VK: vocabulary knowledge; RC: reading comprehension. Subscripts 1, 2, and 3 represent Times 1, 2, and 3, respectively.

later performance, that is, a1 and a2; and b1 and b2, which are lagged effects or autoregressive control. In this way, CLP modeling allows for testing developmental interdependence or prediction of each other's change over time between two or more variables.

Specifically for the present study, each reading skill at Time 2 was predicted by all three skills (decoding, vocabulary, and reading comprehension) at Time 1. Likewise, each skill at Time 3 was predicted by all three skills at Time 2. Residual covariances were also estimated for both Times 1 and 3. The model shown in Figure 7.3 was tested on M*plus* 8 (Muthén & Muthén, 1998–2017) with Maximum Likelihood estimation. As suggested by Hu and Bentler (1999), we reported Comparative Fit Index (CFI), Root Mean Square Error of Approximation (RMSEA), and Standardized Root Mean Square Residual (SRMR) for evaluating the goodness of model fits. Cutoff values of CFI ≥ .95, RMSEA ≤ .06, or SRMR ≤ .08 indicated good model fits.

Results

Descriptive statistics and estimates of normality and reliability

Table 7.1 shows children's performance on the three skills at the three times with the skewness and kurtosis estimates of each skill at each time. Those estimates were generally lower than the rule-of-thumb values for univariate normality (i.e., ±2 for both skewness and kurtosis); they were also below the critical values found to result in significant deviation from multivariate normality (i.e., ±2 for skewness and ±7 for kurtosis) (Curran et al., 1996).

A series of repeated ANOVA was conducted to compare children's performance across the three times. A statistically significant time difference was found for all three skills. For decoding, $F(1, 88) = 108.46, p < .001$. Post-hoc pairwise comparisons with Bonferroni adjustment showed that decoding at Time 1 was significantly lower than that at Times 2 and 3 ($p < .001$); and Time-2 decoding was also lower than Time-3 decoding ($p = .011$). For vocabulary knowledge, $F(1, 88) = 54.342, p < .001$. Post-hoc comparisons showed Time-1 vocabulary knowledge was significantly lower than that at Times 2 and 3 ($p < .001$). There was, however, no significant difference between Times 2 and 3 ($p = .694$). Finally, for reading comprehension, $F(1, 88) = 16.979, p < .001$. Post-hoc comparisons showed no significant difference between Times 1 and 2 ($p = .071$); however, the performance at both Time 1 ($p < .001$) and Time 2 ($p = .024$) was significantly lower than that at Time 3.

Concurrent and longitudinal correlations

Table 7.2 shows the bivariate, concurrent as well as longitudinal correlations, which were all significant (all $ps < .001$). Notably, Time-1 decoding ($r = .530$)

Table 7.2 Bivariate Correlations Between Literary Measures at Three Different Times

	1	2	3	4	5	6	7	8	9
Time 1 measures									
1 Word Decoding	—								
2 Vocabulary Knowledge	.637	—							
3 Reading Comprehension	.434	.567	—						
Time 2 measures									
4 Word Decoding	.933	.659	.460	—					
5 Vocabulary Knowledge	.599	.856	.510	.619	—				
6 Reading Comprehension	.530	.488	.671	.529	.515	—			
Time 3 measures									
7 Word Decoding	.926	.634	.416	.948	.594	.523	—		
8 Vocabulary Knowledge	.667	.828	.487	.709	.903	.496	.687	—	
9 Reading Comprehension	.601	.561	.553	.633	.575	.644	.589	.604	—

Notes. All $ps < .001$. Time 1: end of grade 3; Time 2: mid of grade 4; Time 3: end of grade 4.

and vocabulary ($r = .488$) significantly correlated with Time-2 reading comprehension; likewise, Time-2 decoding ($r = .633$) and vocabulary ($r = .575$) also significantly correlated with Time-3 reading comprehension. The longitudinal correlations appeared to become slightly stronger over time. Time-1 reading comprehension also significantly correlated with Time-2 decoding ($r = .460$) and vocabulary ($r = .510$). Likewise, the correlations of Time-2 reading comprehension with Time-3 decoding ($r = .523$) and vocabulary ($r = .496$) were also significant.

Cross-lagged path analysis

Path analysis showed that the CLP model in Figure 7.3 overall had good model fits (see the fit indexes of Model 1 in Table 7.3). Tables 7.4 and 7.5 show the parameter estimates from Time 1 to Time 2 and from Time 2 to Time 3, respectively. As shown in Table 7.4, over and above Time-1 reading comprehension ($ß = .549, p < .001$) and vocabulary, Time-1 decoding significantly predicted Time-2 reading comprehension ($ß = .301, p < .001$). This unique effect, however, did not surface for Time-1 vocabulary ($ß = .015, p = .890$). Altogether, the three Time-1 predictors explained about 52.1% of the variance in Time-2 reading comprehension. The pattern of the longitudinal effect of decoding on reading comprehension appeared similar from Time 2 to Time 3. As shown in Table 7.5, controlling for Time-2 reading comprehension ($ß = .385, p < .001$) and vocabulary, Time-2 decoding significantly predicted Time-3 reading comprehension ($ß = .321, p < .001$). The unique effect of vocabulary, however, was only marginally significant ($ß = .181, p = .056$). The three Time-2 predictors, including the autoregressor, explained about 54.7% of the variance in Time-3 reading comprehension.

Table 7.3 Goodness-of-Fit Indexes of Path Models Comparing Effects Across Predictors and Times

	$\chi^2(df)$	p	χ^2/df	CFI	RMSEA (95% CI)	SRMR
Model 1	20.754(12)	.054	1.730	.989	.091(.000 .154)	.017
Constrained Models for Comparing Effects of Decoding and Vocabulary						
Model 2a	24.897(13)	.024	1.915	.985	.101(.036, .161)	.023
Model 2b	22.231(13)	.052	1.710	.989	.089(.000, .151)	.019
Constrained Models for Comparing Effects Across Times						
Model 3a	20.979(13)	.073	1.614	.990	.083(.000, .146)	.017
Model 3b	23.043(13)	.041	1.773	.988	.093(.019, .154)	.020

Notes. Model 1: baseline model; Model 2a: equivalence constraint on the paths from Time-1 decoding and vocabulary to Time-2 reading comprehension; Model 2b: equivalence constraint on the paths from Time-2 decoding and vocabulary to Time-3 reading comprehension; Model 3a: equivalence constraint on the paths from Time-1 decoding to Time-2 reading comprehension and from Time-2 decoding to Time-3 reading comprehension; Model 3b: equivalence constraint on the paths from Time-1 vocabulary to Time-2 reading comprehension and Time-2 vocabulary to Time-3 reading comprehension.

Table 7.4 Parameter Estimates of Cross-Lagged Panel Analysis Testing Developmental Interdependence Between Measures from Time 1 to Time 2

Time 2 Criterion Variables	Time 1 Predictors	R^2 (p)	β	p
Reading Comprehension		.521 (<.001)		
	Reading Comprehension		.549	<.001
	Word Decoding		.301	<.001
	Vocabulary Knowledge		.015	.890
Word Decoding		.879 (<.001)		
	Word Decoding		.860	<.001
	Vocabulary Knowledge		.090	.088
	Reading Comprehension		.035	.438
Vocabulary Knowledge		.738 (<.001)		
	Vocabulary Knowledge		.786	<.001
	Word Decoding		.086	.224
	Reading Comprehension		.027	.688

Table 7.5 Parameter Estimates of Cross-Lagged Panel Analysis Testing Developmental Interdependence Between Measures from Time 2 to Time 3

Time 3 Criterion Variables	Time 2 Predictors	R^2 (p)	β	p
Reading Comprehension		.547 (<.001)		
	Reading Comprehension		.385	<.001
	Word Decoding		.321	<.001
	Vocabulary Knowledge		.181	.056
Word Decoding		.900 (<.001)		
	Word Decoding		.932	<.001
	Vocabulary Knowledge		.002	.970
	Reading Comprehension		.029	.477
Vocabulary Knowledge		.852 (<.001)		
	Vocabulary Knowledge		.762	<.001
	Word Decoding		.252	.224
	Reading Comprehension		.029	.557

Conversely, with the autoregressive control considered, the longitudinal effect of reading comprehension on neither decoding nor vocabulary was significant. Later decoding was largely a function of earlier decoding rather than earlier reading comprehension. This was similarly the case for vocabulary knowledge. Specifically, over and above Time-1 decoding (® = .860, $p < .001$) and vocabulary, Time-1 reading comprehension did not significantly predict Time-2 decoding (® = .035, $p = .438$). The effect of Time-2 reading comprehension on Time-3 decoding was similar (® = .029, $p = .477$). Likewise, controlling for Time-1 vocabulary (® = .786, $p < .001$) and decoding, Time-1 reading comprehension did not significantly predict Time-2 vocabulary (® = .027, $p = .688$). This pattern also appeared similar for the effect of Time-2 reading comprehension on Time 3 vocabulary (® = .029, $p = .557$).

Comparing path coefficients

The standardized path coefficients presented in Tables 7.4 and 7.5 seem to suggest that compared to vocabulary, decoding had a greater longitudinal effect on reading comprehension during both periods, that is, from Time 1 to Time 2 and from Time 2 to Time 3. Additionally, whereas the longitudinal effect of decoding on reading comprehension appeared similar across the two periods, that of vocabulary on reading comprehension appeared to have strengthened. To statistically test the relative effect of decoding and vocabulary on reading comprehension on the one hand, and also whether the effect of either lexical predictor changed across the two periods, four additional path models were run with equivalence constraints imposed on coefficients of interest.

To compare the relative longitudinal effect of decoding and vocabulary on reading comprehension, the coefficients of the paths from Time-1 decoding to Time-2 comprehension and from Time-1 vocabulary to Time-2 comprehension were first constrained to be the same. As shown in Table 7.3, this new, constrained model (Model 2a) overall showed good model fits, yet it significantly deviated from the baseline model (Model 1): $\otimes \chi^2(1) = 4.143$, $p = .041$, which means the null hypothesis should be rejected and a conclusion be made that Time-1 decoding had a significantly larger effect on Time-2 reading comprehension than did Time-1 vocabulary.

As the next step, the equivalence constraint was placed on the coefficients of the paths from Time-2 decoding to Time-3 comprehension and from Time-2 vocabulary to Time-3 comprehension. This constrained model (Model 2b) showed good model fits and did not significantly deviate from the baseline model (Model 1): $\otimes \chi^2(1) = 1.477$, $p = .224$. The null model should thus be retained. In other words, different from the previous period, the unique, longitudinal effect of decoding and vocabulary on reading comprehension, from Time 2 to Time 3, did not show any significant difference.

Two additional models with equivalence constraints were run to test whether the unique, longitudinal effect of either decoding or vocabulary on reading comprehension changed across the two periods. In Model 3a (see Table 7.3), the path coefficient of Time-1 decoding to Time-2 reading comprehension and that of Time-2 decoding to Time-3 reading comprehension were constrained to be the same. Model 3a showed good model fits and did not differ from Model 1 significantly: $\otimes \chi^2(1) = .225$, $p = .635$. The null model was thus retained, which means there was no significant change in the unique effect of decoding over time.

Likewise, in Model 3b, equivalence constraint was placed on the path coefficients of Time-1 vocabulary to Time 2 reading comprehension and Time-2 vocabulary to Time-3 reading comprehension. Model 3b also showed good model fits, and it did not differ from Model 1 significantly: $\otimes \chi^2(1) = 2.289$, $p = .130$. This model comparison result again suggests that the null model should be retained; and an inference was thus made that there was no significant change in the unique effect of vocabulary on reading comprehension over time.

Discussion

This study aimed to explore developmental interdependence between decoding, vocabulary, and reading comprehension in L2 readers of Chinese. To answer the three research questions, decoding, as opposed to vocabulary knowledge, surfaced as a unique, longitudinal predictor of reading comprehension; its effect on change in reading comprehension was similar over time. From Time 1 to Time 2, the effect of decoding was also stronger than that of vocabulary; from Time 2 to Time 3, however, there was no significant difference between the two lexical predictors. Finally, no significant effect was found of reading comprehension on change in decoding or vocabulary for both periods.

Longitudinal effects of decoding and vocabulary on reading comprehension

Earlier decoding consistently predicted later reading comprehension with autoregressive control considered. From Time 1 to Time 2, decoding also had a greater effect than did vocabulary knowledge on change in reading comprehension. Overall decoding seemed to have a more salient effect on reading comprehension development. This finding differs notably from previous longitudinal studies on alphabetic readers, including L2 readers (e.g., Lervåg & Aukrust, 2010), where vocabulary, as opposed to decoding, tended to have a more consistent and salient effect on growth in reading comprehension. Considering how decoding prioritizes subskills differentially in alphabetic languages and Chinese (Leong, 2015; Perfetti et al., 2013), the finding on decoding did not seem to be a surprise in the present study. Decoding in Chinese relies heavily on orthographic processing, and phonetic strategies have very restricted utility. This should be the case for any readers of Chinese, including L2 readers. L2 character learning typically involves integrated teaching of form and meaning; successful decoding of a character tends to suggest that the learner "knows" the character and there is meaning activation during decoding. In Everson's (1998) study on beginning university learners of L2 Chinese in the United States, there was a near-perfect correlation ($r = .96$) between saying Chinese words out loud (i.e., decoding) and explaining their meanings in English. It was also estimated that when participants were able to pronounce a word correctly, there was a probability of 90.7% that they would be able to give the meaning of the word. This implies that for L2 readers, character decoding ability entails a constellation of skills including, importantly, knowledge of character meanings, which are fundamental for text reading and comprehension. In this respect, it is not surprising that in both the present study and Wong (2017), decoding was an important longitudinal predictor of reading comprehension in L2 readers of Chinese.

What is puzzling is why vocabulary knowledge did not surface as a unique predictor. As discussed earlier in this chapter, decoding constituent characters of words alone should not be sufficient to meet the various requirements for text comprehension. Notably, text reading in Chinese requires proper word segmentation, which necessitates the support of vocabulary knowledge. In addition, being able to sound out (and activate the meanings) of the common characters that make up a multi-character word does not in itself suggest that the reader knows the meaning of the *whole* word. For understanding 这/家/公司的/业务/很/广泛, for example, a learner may successfully decode 公 and 司 because s/he might have learned the two characters respectively from the words 公园 and 司机 from the textbook; likewise, s/he may successfully decode 业 and 务, because s/he might have learned them respectively from 作业 and 服务. Yet the meanings learned of those individual characters in other lexical contexts may not translate into those of the new, whole words, despite potential help from morphological/compound awareness (Zhang, 2017b). This semantic gap would not only in itself impair the construction of a propositional meaning but pose a challenge for correct word segmentation. In a nutshell, vocabulary should hypothetically have predicted change in reading comprehension in this study.

Instead of concluding that vocabulary was unimportant for reading comprehension development in L2 readers of Chinese, we argue that in this study, the lack of a unique effect of vocabulary in the presence of character/word decoding in the model may only temporarily characterize L2 reading development at an early stage. In other words, in the early stage of L2 reading, decoding may tend to have a more crucial influence on text reading and comprehension development. As learners pass the initial stage (able to recognize a number of common characters and start to read more complex texts), vocabulary may gradually emerge as an important—if not more important than decoding—unique predictor of developmental change in reading comprehension. In fact, from Time 2 to Time 3, vocabulary had a marginally significant effect on reading comprehension (see Table 7.5) and its effect did not significantly differ from that of decoding. Presumably, had the longitudinal project gone further to the rest of the participants' elementary school years (grades 5 and 6), a unique and more salient effect of vocabulary might have emerged; and the relative effects of decoding and vocabulary might have further changed, showing a greater effect of vocabulary. That would show convergence with the many findings in the general L1 and L2 reading literature that meaning gradually plays a far more important role than code-based skills in reading comprehension and its development (García & Cain, 2014).

Longitudinal effects of reading comprehension on decoding and vocabulary

This study did not find any significant longitudinal effect of reading comprehension on vocabulary knowledge. Although this finding seems to corroborate some previous studies (e.g., Quinn et al., 2015), it came as a surprise. The DVC triangle (Perfetti, 2010) contends that comprehension is essentially for incidental learning of vocabulary during reading. To unlock the meaning of a word in a text, the reader needs to understand at least the local discourse and obtain contextual clues (Nagy, 2005). Good comprehenders, compared to poor comprehenders, are thus better word learners (e.g., Cain et al., 2003). This could be even more salient in Chinese, as learners need contextual support to segment words properly and establish the lexical identity for an unknown word. Developmentally, comprehension should thus be expected to predict vocabulary development.

Previous studies sometimes explained the lack of a developmental effect found of comprehension on vocabulary development considering how sensitive literacy measures may be to change (e.g., Quinn et al., 2015). Although this explanation may pertain to this study as well, we argue that our finding may be attributed to the short interval between waves of data in specific and the short duration of the project in general. Specifically, although participants' skills were measured three times, the intervals were only about half a year (and the three waves only spanned about a year). Readers would perhaps need to read widely over a sufficiently long period of time, over and above learning the school curriculum, to realize the potential benefit of comprehension for incidental word-learning and vocabulary expansion. Even though good comprehenders possess an advantage for incidental learning, if they do not read widely and create opportunities for that learning to happen, there would be little to expect of that advantage for vocabulary growth. Chen et al. (2019) explained the developmental effect of reading comprehension on vocabulary in the older cohorts (grades 3 and 5), as opposed to the youngest cohort (grade 1), based on the older cohorts' independent reading and exposure to complex and diverse texts. Note, however, that Chen et al.'s participants were native Chinese-speaking children in China, where the medium of school instruction is Chinese. It is questionable that those authors' characterization of reading experience would similarly hold for the third/fourth graders of the present study, who learned Chinese primarily through classroom instruction in an English-medium educational system. In other words, the participants of this study might not have read (sufficiently) widely during the project periods for any potential effect of comprehension on vocabulary expansion to emerge. Constrained exposure to written texts or extracurricular reading experience would unlikely result in any effect of comprehension on lexical growth.

This study also did not find any longitudinal effect of reading comprehension on word decoding. While the earlier explanation for vocabulary may hold for decoding as well, we speculate that this result might be because L2 readers learn characters primarily through classroom instruction where pronunciation, together with orthographic features and meaning, is taught. In other words, L2 Chinese decoding could primarily be the result of classroom instruction. Unless written texts are annotated with *pinyin* (the alphabetic system used for initial learning to read in Chinese) or the learner looks up a character dictionary for the pronunciation of an unknown character, reading would not result in incidental learning of character sound. While self-teaching of sound-letter mapping patterns through reading is a possible mechanism for learning to read or decoding development in English (Share, 1995), it is hardly the case for Chinese (Leong, 2015; Perfetti et al., 2013). In other words, individual differences in L2 Chinese decoding may well be a manifestation of learners' differential effects of learning a curriculum. In fact, the words in the decoding task for this study were all sampled from the elementary school textbooks that children had learned or would learn in upper grades.

Limitations and future research

The present study has a few limitations. To begin with, the study was conducted in Singapore, where Chinese-studying students were almost all ethnic Chinese. Our participants were all ethnic Chinese children with English as their dominant home language. There were actually a small number of non-ethnic Chinese students who were L2 learners of Chinese as well, such as immigrant children from South Korea or Thailand. They were excluded for this study because compared to their ethnic Chinese peers, there was a qualitative difference in home language patterns, not to mention distinctions in view of sociocultural factors for learning Chinese in Singapore. It would be interesting in the future to study those learners and compare them with the ethnic Chinese L2 learners. Likewise, future research could also consider learners of Chinese in other contexts, like young foreign language learners in Chinese immersion programs in a place like the United States (Lü, 2019). It would also be interesting to compare how the patterns of relationships may or may not hold for native Chinese-speaking children.[2]

Another limitation is the relatively short period for a longitudinal study. The short duration might have constrained the insights generated in several ways. For example, as discussed earlier, had the project lasted longer, a more salient role of vocabulary knowledge might have begun to appear. Additionally, reading experience might have been accumulated to a level for an effect of comprehension on vocabulary development to emerge.

More refined consideration for measuring skills might produce a more nuanced insight into developmental patterns. For example, as L2 readers progress in Chinese learning, decoding fluency, as opposed to basic accuracy of decoding, may better represent the decoding component of the DVC triangle for exploring developmental relationships. Although it was discussed earlier that L2 readers' decoding development may be primarily a function of classroom learning, extra-curricular text reading should provide contextualized experiences for consolidating the learned connections between sound (and other formal features like orthographic structure) and meaning. In this respect, decoding fluency may better manifest the quality of lexical representations (Perfetti, 2007); change in decoding fluency, as opposed to that in basic accuracy, may be more sensitive to reading experience and comprehension.

There are many conceptual discussions about how reading is important for lexical development. As hypothesized in the DVC triangle (Perfetti, 2010), comprehension "causes" learning of new words. However, developmentally, nobody—no matter how good they are at comprehension at a particular time point—is able to benefit from incidental learning for vocabulary expansion if reading experience is not there! For research, this means that to obtain a more nuanced understanding about the mechanism of developmental change, like the Matthew effect in reading ("the rich get richer and the poor become poorer" in reading development)

(Stanovich, 1986), it would be important to consider individual differences in the quantity and quality of learners' reading experience (Bast & Reitsma, 1998).

Finally, a limitation pertains to the use of CLP and path analysis to examine developmental interdependence. CLP has the advantage for testing developmentally reciprocal effects between two or more variables. However, it has a limitation in that it focuses only on individual differences (i.e., inter-individual variability). "Although the parameters of the panel model are affected by intraindividual change," they are not "sensitive to the type of individual-level change" (Selig & Little, 2012, p. 267). It will thus be desirable for further research to adopt longitudinal modeling methods, like latent growth curve modeling (Newsome, 2015), that can account for both inter- and intra-individual variability.

Conclusions

This study explored developmental interdependence between decoding, vocabulary, and reading comprehension in young L2 readers of Chinese. To our knowledge, it is the first of its kind that aimed to directly test this issue in L2 readers. Despite its relatively short period as a longitudinal study, it has generated some interesting findings. For example, decoding was consistently an important longitudinal predictor of reading comprehension; there was also emergence of vocabulary knowledge as a unique lexical predictor of reading comprehension development as well. The study also sheds light on some important issues for further research with a longer duration and more rigorous methodological considerations.

To guide the present study, the DVC triangle was referred to as the conceptual basis for discussing the relationships between decoding, vocabulary, and reading comprehension. We explored how the DVC triangle, which intends to outline the complex interaction between lexical processes and reading comprehension in skilled reading and is largely contextualized in monolingual English reading, may explain developmental associations in L2 readers of Chinese. Although limited empirical evidence has prevented us from a sound evaluation of the developmental validity of the DVC triangle, it is noteworthy that decoding played a critical role in L2 Chinese reading comprehension development; and there was no evidence to suggest that any developmental effect of decoding on reading comprehension would have to go through the mediation of vocabulary in L2 Chinese readers. Another insight was that any conceptualization of the effect of comprehension on lexical development would perhaps need to consider learners' reading experience and the instructional context.

Notes

1 Longitudinal studies are defined here as those where more than one wave of data is collected from a same cohort(s) of readers; additionally, statistical inference involves more than concurrent correlational relationships. In particular, data analysis should include the effect of a predictor (e.g., decoding and/or vocabulary knowledge) on the change or growth of a criterion variable (e.g., reading comprehension). This developmental effect could be based on controlling for an autoregressor (e.g., earlier reading comprehension)

or predicting the growth of a criterion variable (e.g., the slope in latent growth curve modeling analysis). Compared with studies based on concurrent correlations obtained from one or more groups/cohorts of students, longitudinal research so defined is particularly limited. Yet it is longitudinal evidence that directly informs *change* or *development* and is of immediate interest here.

2 We actually explored the DVC developmental interdependence in children who had Chinese (as opposed to English) as the dominant home language. Although those children were essentially bilingual readers (that is, Chinese and English) and thus unlike those native Chinese-speaking children in places like China (e.g., Chen et al., 2019), and they were not included in this paper given the study's L2 focus, the same CLP modeling revealed some interestingly different findings. Notably, from Time 1 to Time 2 as well as from Time 2 to Time 3, both decoding (® = .153, p = .020 and ® = .288, p < .001, respectively) and vocabulary (® = .171, p = .008 and ® = .208, p < .001, respectively) were each a unique longitudinal predictor of reading comprehension. The oral language experience those children had at home, which distinguished them from the participants of the study reported in this chapter, could perhaps explain the presence of a significant, unique effect of oral vocabulary (and more balanced effects between decoding and vocabulary) during both periods. In fact, and unsurprisingly, those children also significantly outperformed their L2 peers on all three skills at all the three times. Taking into consideration the trend of vocabulary emerging as a significant, unique predictor from Time 2 to Time 3 in the L2 readers, these findings together perhaps suggest that, whether an effect of vocabulary would appear, over and above decoding, on developmental change in Chinese reading comprehension might involve complex reader (L1 vs. L2) X time (or learning/developmental stage) interaction. The CLP modeling on those from Chinese-dominant families, conversely, found the same pattern that reading comprehension did not significantly predict change in either decoding or vocabulary. This might be similarly explained by the constrained reading experience discussed earlier of the L2 readers. After all, although those children used Chinese as the dominant home language, the medium of instruction in Singapore is English and English was, as expected, their primary literacy in grades 3 and 4. Those children, like their peers from English-dominant families (but likely unlike those native-speaking peers in a monolingual society like China), might not highly value reading in Chinese, beyond the learning of the school curriculum.

References

Anderson, R. C., & Freebody, P. (1981). Vocabulary knowledge. In J. T. Guthrie (Ed.), *Comprehension and teaching: Research reviews* (pp. 77–117). International Reading Association.

Bast, J., & Reitsma, P. (1998). Matthew effects in reading: A comparison of latent growth curve models and simplex models with structured means. *Multivariate Behavioral Research, 32*, 135–167.

Beijing Language Institute. (1986). 现代汉语频率词典 (*Modern Chinese frequency dictionary*). Beijing Language Institute Press.

Cain, K., & Barnes, M. A. (2017). Reading comprehension: What develops and when? In K. Cain, D. L. Compton, & R. K. Parrila (Eds.), *Theories of reading development* (pp. 257–282). John Benjamins Publishing.

Cain, K., Oakhill, J., & Elbro, C. (2003). The ability to learn new word meanings from context by school-age children with and without language comprehension difficulties. *Journal of Child Language, 30*, 681–694.

Chen, H., Zhao, Y., Wu, X., Sun, P., Xie, R., & Feng, J. (2019). The relation between vocabulary knowledge and reading comprehension in Chinese elementary children: A cross-lagged study. *Acta Psychologia Sinica, 51*, 924–934.

Curran, P. J., West, S. G., & Finch, J. F. (1996). The robustness of test statistics to nonnormality and specification error in confirmatory factor analysis. *Psychological Methods*, *1*, 16–29.

DeFrancis, J. (1989). *Visible speech: The diverse oneness of writing systems*. University of Hawaii Press.

Duke, N. K., & Carlisle, J. F. (2011). The development of comprehension. In M. L. Kamil, P. D. Pearson, E. B. Moje, & P. Afflerbach (Eds.), *Handbook of reading research Volume 4* (pp. 199–228). Routledge.

Dunn, L. M., & Dunn, D. M. (2007). *Peabody Picture Vocabulary Test* (4th ed.). Pearson Assessments.

Everson, M. (1998). Word recognition among learners of Chinese as a Foreign Language: Investigating the relationship between naming and knowing. *The Modern Language Journal*, *82*, 194–204.

García, J. R., & Cain, K. (2014). Decoding and reading comprehension: A meta-analysis to identify which reader and assessment characteristics influence the strength of the relationship in English. *Review of Educational Research*, *84*, 74–111.

Grabe, W. (2009). *Reading in a second language: Moving from theory to practice*. Cambridge University Press.

Gough, P. B., & Tunmer, W. E. (1986). Decoding, reading and reading disability. *Remedial and Special Education*, *7*, 6–10.

Hu, L.-Z., & Bentler, P. M. (1999). Cutoff criteria for fit indexes in covariance structure analysis: Conventional criteria versus new alternatives. *Structural Equation Modeling*, *6*, 1–55.

Jeon, E. H., & Yamashita, J. (2014). L2 reading comprehension and its correlates: A meta-analysis. *Language Learning*, *64*, 160–212.

Lam, K., Chen, X., Geva, E., Luo, Y. C., & Li, H. (2012). The role of morphological awareness in reading achievement among young Chinese-speaking English language learners: A longitudinal study. *Reading and Writing: An Interdisciplinary Journal*, *25*, 1847–1872.

Lervåg, A., & Aukrust, V. G. (2010). Vocabulary knowledge is a critical determinant of the difference in reading comprehension growth between first and second language learners. *Journal of Child Psychology and Psychiatry*, *51*, 612–620.

Leong, C. K. (2015). Functional components of reading with reference to Chinese. In T. Papadopoulos, R. K. Parrila, & J. R. Kirby (Eds.), *Cognition, intelligence, and achievement: A tribute to J. P. Das* (pp. 149–171). Elsevier.

Lü, C. (2019). *Chinese literacy learning in an immersion program*. Palgrave Macmillan.

Muthén, L. K., & Muthén, B. O. (1998–2017). *Mplus user's guide* (8th ed.). Muthén & Muthén.

Nagy, W. E. (2005). Why vocabulary instruction needs to be long-term and comprehensive? In E. H. Hiebert & M. L. Kamil (Eds.), *Teaching and learning vocabulary: Bring research to practice* (pp. 27–44). Lawrence Erlbaum Associates.

Nagy, W. E., & Scott, J. (2000). Vocabulary processes. In M. Kamil, P. Mosenthal, P. D. Pearson, & R. Barr (Eds.), *Handbook of reading research, Volume III* (pp. 269–284). Lawrence Erlbaum Associates.

Newsom, J. T. (2015). *Longitudinal structural equation modeling: A comprehensive introduction*. Routledge.

Perfetti, C. A. (1985). *Reading ability*. Oxford University Press.

Perfetti, C. A. (1999). Comprehending written language: A blueprint for the reader. In C. Brown & P. Hagoort (Eds.), *Neurocognition of language* (pp. 167–208). Oxford University Press.

Perfetti, C. A. (2007). Reading ability: Lexical quality to comprehension. *Scientific Studies of Reading, 11*, 357–383.

Perfetti, C. A. (2010). Decoding, vocabulary, and comprehension. In M. G. McKeown & L. Kucan (Eds.), *Bridging reading research to life* (pp. 291–303). The Guilford Press.

Perfetti, C. A., Cao, F., & Booth, J. (2013). Specialization and universals in the development of reading skill: How Chinese research informs a universal science of reading. *Scientific Studies of Reading, 17*, 5–21.

Perfetti, C. A., Landi, N., & Oakhill, J. (2005). The acquisition of reading comprehension skills. In M. J. Snowling & C. Hulme (Eds.), *The science of reading: A handbook* (pp. 227–247). Blackwell.

Quinn, J. M., Wagner, R. K., Petscher, Y., & Lopez, D. (2015). Developmental relations between vocabulary knowledge and reading comprehension: A latent change score modeling study. *Child Development, 86*, 159–175.

Santos, S., Cadime, I., Viana, F. L., & Ribeiro, I. (2019). Cross-Lagged relations among linguistic skills in European Portuguese: A longitudinal study. *Reading Research Quarterly, 55*, 177–192.

Selig, J. P., & Little, T. D. (2012). Autoregressive and cross-lagged panel analysis for longitudinal data. In B. Laursen, T. D. Little, & N. A. Card (Eds.), *Handbook of developmental research methods* (pp. 265–278). Guilford Press.

Share, D. L. (1995). Phonological recoding and self-teaching: *Sin qua non* of reading acquisition. *Cognition, 55*, 151–218.

Shepherd, J. (2005). *Striking a balance: The management of language in Singapore*. Peter Lang.

Stanovich, K. (1986). Mathew effects in reading: Some consequences of individual differences in the acquisition of literacy. *Reading Research Quarterly, 21*, 360–407.

Taylor, I., & Taylor, M. M. (2014). *Writing and literacy in Chinese, Korean and Japanese*. John Benjamins.

Verhoeven, L., & van Leeuwe, J. (2008). Prediction of the development of reading comprehension: A longitudinal study. *Applied Cognitive Psychology, 22*, 407–423.

Wong, Y. K. (2017). Relationships between reading comprehension and its components in young Chinese-as-a-second-language learners. *Reading and Writing, 30*, 969–988.

Yeung, P.-S., Ho, C. S.-H., Chan, D. W.-O., & Chung, K. K.-H. (2016). A componential model of reading in Chinese. *Learning and Individual Differences, 45*, 11–24.

Zhang, D. (2017a). Derivational morphology in reading comprehension of Chinese-speaking learners of English. *Applied Linguistics, 38*, 871–895.

Zhang, D. (2017b). Multidimensionality of morphological awareness and reading comprehension among young Chinese readers in a multilingual context. *Learning and Individual Differences, 53*, 13–23.

Zhang, D., Chin, C.-F., & Li, L. (2017). Metalinguistic awareness Malay-English bilingual children's word reading: A cross-lagged panel study on transfer facilitation. *Applied Psycholinguistics, 38*, 395–426.

Zhang, D., Lin, C.-H., Zhang, Y., & Choi, Y. (2019). *Pinyin* or no *pinyin*: Does access to word pronunciation matter to the assessment of Chinese learners' vocabulary knowledge? *Language Learning Journal, 47*(3), 344–353.

Zhang, D., Koda, K., & Leong, C. K. (2016). Morphological awareness and bilingual word learning: A longitudinal Structural Equation Modeling study. *Reading and Writing, 29*, 383–407.

Zhao, S., & Liu, Y. (2010). Chinese education in Singapore: Constraints of bilingual policy from the perspectives of status and prestige planning. *Language Problem and Language Planning, 34,* 236–258.

Zhao, S., & Zhang, D. (2007). The totality of Chinese characters: A digital perspective. *Journal of Chinese Language and Computing, 17,* 107–125.

Zhou, Y. G. (1978). 现代汉字中声旁的表音功能问题 (To what degree are the phonetics of present-day Chinese characters still phonetic?). *Zhongguo Yuwen, 146,* 172–177.

8 A tale of two less successful CSL readers

A qualitative study of reading difficulties and strategies used

Sha Huang

Introduction

An essential skill in language learning is reading, which is usually learned through instruction (Everson, 2009). Reading is a critical skill for functioning meaningfully in a modern society, and it provides access to information and resources that cannot be obtained through oral communication. However, scholars have commonly acknowledged that reading Chinese is one of the most challenging endeavors for Chinese as a Second Language (CSL) learners (Everson, 2009; Huang, 2018a, 2018b; Lee-Thompson, 2008). A main reason is the linguistic distance between Chinese and alphabetic languages such as English, a difference that results in learners needing more time to get used to the Chinese writing system (Everson, 2009; Huang, 2018a; Ke & Chan, 2017).

It has been commonly accepted that strategies, when used appropriately, enhance reading comprehension (Grabe, 2009; Pressley, 2002a, 2002b, 2006). Thus far, a limited number of studies have been conducted about reading strategies of CSL learners. Most of them have focused on how successful readers applied strategies. Since a purpose of research on reading is to help less successful readers to improve reading, it is equally important if not more so to investigate both the causes of these readers' comprehension breakdown and the effectiveness of their strategies in coping with reading difficulties. In addition, since previous literature has suggested L1 background affects L2 reading (Bernhardt, 2012; Ke & Chan, 2017), it is also important to compare reading difficulties and strategy use of heritage and non-heritage L2 learners. Reading strategy research focusing on less successful readers with different backgrounds will shed light on Chinese reading curriculum and pedagogy for guiding different readers to improve reading proficiency. Such research will also enhance our general understanding about L2 reading and bridge the gaps in previous literature about L2 reading strategy, which focuses mainly on L2 learners of alphabetic languages such as English.

Literature review

In the last several decades, approaches to the study of reading have evolved from viewing reading either as a bottom-up or top-down process to conceptualizing it as an interactive process (Bernhardt, 1991). According to this latter view of reading, readers combine useful resources and elements from both bottom-up processing (e.g., decoding words and sentences) and top-down processing (e.g., strategic processing, inferencing, and using background knowledge) to construct a representation of the information they have read (Grabe, 2009). Based on the interactive model of reading, Bernhardt (2005, 2011) proposed a compensatory model of L2 reading. This model predicts the impact of three dimensions on L2 reading: first language (L1) literacy, which accounts for about 20% variance of L2 reading comprehension; L2 knowledge, which explains about 30% of L2 reading comprehension; and the remaining 50% of variance is attributed to an unexplained dimension, which includes comprehension strategies, engagement, content and knowledge domains, interest, motivation, and so on. Bernhardt emphasized that all three dimensions are not additive, but instead work synchronically and interactively. She also pointed out the need for conducting research on the interplay of these components (Bernhardt, 2005). To extend this model, McNeil (2012) discussed further the contributions of comprehension strategies, predicting that they are greater for students at higher levels than those at lower levels. This prediction suggests the significance of studying L2 reading strategies, and in particular raises a need to study strategy use in lower-level or less successful L2 readers.

Studies on L2 reading strategies

One way to group reading strategies is to define them as global and local strategies, or top-down and bottom-up strategies (Abbott, 2006; Block, 1986; Ke & Chan, 2017; Lee-Thompson, 2008). Top-down strategies are applied to gain a holistic understanding of larger parts of a whole text. They focus on main ideas, discourse organization, and the use of background knowledge (Plakans, 2009). Bottom-up strategies are used to solve difficulties in comprehending smaller linguistic units such as characters, words, phrases, and sentences. Reading strategies can also be defined as cognitive and metacognitive strategies (Phakiti, 2003a, 2003b; Purpura, 1998). Cognitive strategies appear as conscious behaviors that individuals use to process language to understand, learn, or use in some context (Phakiti, 2008). Examples include guessing from context, noting discourse organization, skipping a word, and identifying a main idea (Grabe, 2009). Metacognitive strategies regulate cognitive strategies and other processing (Phakiti, 2008). They usually involve constant monitoring, regulation, and orchestration of cognitive processes to achieve cognitive goals (Phakiti, 2003b). Examples of metacognitive strategies include evaluating reading materials, repairing miscomprehension, evaluating the developing understanding of text, adjusting reading speed, and selecting cognitive strategies accordingly.

These taxonomies are sometimes combined. For example, in a study of CSL readers' strategies, Lee-Thompson (2008) categorized reading strategies into two main groups, bottom-up and top-down strategies, with metacognitive strategies grouped as a subcategory of top-down strategies. This framework was used in the present study.

Many scholars (Block, 1986; Carrell, 1989; Hosenfeld, 1977; Nassaji, 2006; Yayli, 2010; Young & Oxford, 1997) have been interested in comparing types of strategies used among different groups of L2 readers. Some studies (Carrell, 1989; Young & Oxford, 1997) reflected similar trends that low-proficiency participants used more bottom-up strategies, while high-achieving L2 learners used more top-down strategies. Other scholars tried to identify strategies that support reading. Based on the findings of several studies (Pressley, 2002a, 2002b, 2006), Grabe (2009) summarized the strategies that support active comprehension of the text. These strategies include reading carefully in key places, monitoring reading constantly, identifying important information, making guesses about unknown words, using text structure to guide understanding, integrating ideas from different parts of the text, building main idea summaries, and building interpretation of the text while reading. One common finding revealed by several studies (Anderson, 1991; Block, 1986; Sheorey & Mokhtari, 2001) is that compared with less successful readers, successful readers tend to flexibly orchestrate multiple strategies to specific reading contexts, and they are more meta-cognitively aware of why, when, and how to effectively use a specific set of strategies to realize the goals of reading (Grabe, 2009; Pressley & Harris, 2006).

Reading strategies used by CSL readers

Thus far, few studies have investigated how CSL readers process Chinese texts with multiple paragraphs. A study of seven college CSL readers' reading processes (Everson & Ke, 1997) showed that intermediate-level students had many difficulties in character and word recognition. This study was extended by Lee-Thompson (2008), who identified 12 bottom-up and 14 top-down strategies applied by eight CSL learners by using a think-aloud and recall protocol as well as interviews. This study showed that CSL readers at the intermediate level used bottom-up strategies more frequently. Another study (Chang, 2010) examined and compared self-reported reading strategies of 75 college CSL readers at three instructional levels. According to the self-report results, within each instructional level, good readers engaged in more global-level processing activities than not-so-good readers. For instance, at the intermediate level, good readers reported using context more actively to guess the meaning of unknown words; and at the advanced level, that is, level three, good readers believed they had better abilities to understand the overall text meaning and could better recognize the text structure.

In a more recent study, Huang (2018a) identified several strategy clusters and pairs that helped CSL readers infer word meaning, monitor comprehension, and segment words successfully. The study also showed that successful use of strategies in CSL reading usually involves attending to context and multiple linguistic cues; and that vocabulary and grammatical knowledge also play important roles in L2 Chinese reading. Huang (2018b) further focused on strategy use of three readers who successfully comprehended a text. Findings revealed some common strategies the readers used to enhance comprehension, such as using context to decode words, monitoring, identifying important information, and skipping unimportant parts. None of these studies, however, focused specifically on less successful or unsuccessful readers.

Chinese heritage learners and reading

Extant literature suggests that reading strategy is affected by learners' L1 background (Bernhardt, 2012; Ke & Chan, 2017). However, there has been an Anglocentric tendency in L2 reading strategy research, and studies investigating Chinese heritage learners' reading comprehension and strategies are extremely limited. In a notable study that compared language development of heritage and non-heritage learners of Chinese, Xiao (2006) found that heritage learners did significantly better than their non-heritage counterparts in speaking, listening, grammar, and sentence constructions, but not in reading comprehension, vocabulary learning, and Chinese character writing. These results suggest that heritage learners' exposure to spoken Chinese at home does not necessarily lead them to acquire reading and writing skills more quickly than non-heritage learners. In other words, home use of Chinese, which is often restricted to spoken communication, may not support reading comprehension or vocabulary learning if that use does not include sufficient exposure to the orthography.

Ke and Chan (2017) investigated the interrelationships among L2 Chinese learners' use of reading strategies, L1 background, and L2 proficiency. Among many other findings, learners of Chinese Cultural Sphere (CCS) background appeared to have an advantage in decoding compared to students of Non-Chinese Cultural Sphere (NCCS) background. Yet, such an advantage vanished as readers' L2 proficiency level increased. More specifically, both CCS and NCCS readers used similar decoding strategies at the intermediate and advanced levels.

The present study

Most previous studies investigated successful readers' strategy use and reading comprehension or compared strategy-use frequencies of successful and less successful readers. One ultimate goal of L2 reading research is to gain insights into the causes of challenges confronting less successful readers and accordingly provide those readers with targeted instruction to guide them to read more successfully. However, thus far, few studies have focused on less successful readers' difficulties, how they used strategies to cope with these difficulties, and how their background may have affected their comprehension and reading strategies.

To address these gaps, this case study investigated how two less successful CSL readers, one heritage and one non-heritage learner, read a Chinese text, and aimed to answer three groups of research questions: (1) What were the causes of the comprehension breakdown experienced by the two readers? Did these causes differ from one reader to another with different backgrounds? (2) What strategies did they use? How did they use these strategies to cope with comprehension difficulties? (3) Were there similarities and differences in their patterns of strategy use?

Method

Setting and participant selection

This study aimed to explore the causes of comprehension breakdown of two less successful CFL readers and the effectiveness of their strategies when coping with reading difficulties. Therefore, a qualitative case study that focuses on understanding strategy application in the "process" (Bogdan & Biklen, 1997) was conducted, to reveal in-depth information about readers' use of strategies. The data were collected from a Midwest public university where the researcher served as an instructor. Participants of the whole project were 12 students enrolled in a third-year Chinese class, but this chapter reports findings only about two participants who were identified as less successful readers. According to the curriculum of the Chinese language program, they were at the intermediate level of ACTFL guidelines (ACTFL, 2012).

In that class, students met three times every week. On Mondays, they studied new words and characters and practiced using them in context. On Wednesdays, they focused on listening and speaking. On Fridays, they read the text with the guidance of the teacher. Reading strategies were not instructed explicitly in class. After the class, students were given reading assignments online, which required independent reading without the help of the teacher.

The reading tasks designed for the project consisted of two parts, a recall task (with a total score of 87) and short-answer questions (a total score of 40). Based on the total scores of the performances in these two tasks, Linda and Teresa were ranked 11th and 12th among the whole group of 12 participants. They were considered to be less successful readers and thus identified as the participants for the purpose of this chapter. Although these two participants both performed unsuccessfully in the reading tasks, they had very different family backgrounds and home literacy environments.

Linda was a non-heritage learner of Chinese. She had received a bachelor's degree in psychology and biology and an MA degree in speech pathology with a focus on literacy. She is American and her husband is Taiwanese. At home, they mainly used English and occasionally used some phrases in Mandarin Chinese. When the data were collected, she had studied in the Chinese program for two and a half years. She finished the first semester of the third-year class and continued her Chinese study afterward for about three hours per week with private tutors.

Teresa was a learner of Chinese as a heritage language. She double majored in Finance and International Studies. In high school, she studied Chinese for three years. She was studying in the third-year Chinese class when the data were collected. She was born and grew up in the United States. Her parents were Cantonese and did not speak English very well. When Teresa was young, she communicated with her parents in Cantonese. She visited family and friends in China, but had no experience studying Chinese in any language programs there.

Reading materials

The Chinese text used in this study was adapted from an essay called "Chinese Parents and American Parents" included in an online reading program, Chinese Reading World (https://chinesereadingworld.sites.uiowa.edu). The essay compares parenting styles of American and Chinese parents. The first two paragraphs summarize the main differences of American and Chinese parenting styles. The third paragraph provides two examples that demonstrate these differences. In the last paragraph, the author includes a short conclusion. There are 597 characters in the text. This essay is an expository text, which imposed some challenges on readers (Snow et al., 2005) but served the purpose well to elicit strategies the participants used for coping with comprehension difficulties.

The researcher adapted the original text to make it appropriate for the level of the participants. Based on research on linguistic complexity and L2 Chinese reading (Shen, 2005), the text was modified to contain 2% of characters that participants had not learned in the class. This level of difficulty was believed to result in a text that was moderately challenging for eliciting strategies and distinguishing successful readers from less successful ones. According to post-task interviews, readers' average rating of the text difficulty was 2.5 on the scale of 1–5 (with 1 indicating extremely easy and 5 indicating extremely difficult), which confirmed that this difficulty level was moderate and appropriate for the purpose of this study.

Instruments and procedure

Think-aloud protocol or verbal report is a method used extensively in L2 reading research (Cohen, 1986) for obtaining mental data, insights into reading strategies, reader responses and characteristics, as well as the influence of situational variables (Afflerbach, 2000; Smith, 2006). Think-aloud protocols are categorized either as introspective verbalization, which requires readers to report verbally while performing a task, or as retrospective verbalization, which is conducted after processing has taken place (Leow & Morgan-Short, 2004). In this study, an introspective think-aloud method was used, because it is considered to be a better reflection of learners' mental processes (Cohen & Upton, 2007; Ericsson & Simon, 1993).

A recall protocol is another important instrument utilized in the study. Written recall protocol requires readers to read or listen to a passage and then to write everything they can remember. It has been widely used in second language reading research (Chang, 2010; Everson & Ke, 1997; Lee-Thompson, 2008) as a measure of reading comprehension. This type of recall assessment has been recommended over other traditional measures for its multiple benefits, like providing no leading information related to text content, helping readers integrate components of reading passages (Bernhardt, 1991), and identifying readers' comprehension errors (Everson & Ke, 1997).

The researcher met twice with each participant individually to collect the data. At the first meeting, the researcher explained the procedure and provided instruction about the think-aloud protocol. An audio file sample of a think-aloud was played to help participants understand this method. Participants also practiced thinking aloud while reading a short passage in Chinese. Then they were asked to read the text developed for this study in the same manner as they read their reading assignments for class. They were allowed to use a dictionary, mark the text, or take notes. While reading, participants were expected to speak aloud or verbally express their thoughts in English and provide justifications for their actions as thoroughly as possible. If a participant stopped verbalizing for more than 10 seconds, the researcher would ask prompting questions (e.g., "What are you thinking now?"). Participants were allowed to spend as much time as they wanted to read the text. During the think-aloud process, the researcher closely observed participants' behaviors and took notes. After that, participants recalled the content of the text in as much detail as possible and typed it in English on a computer. In this phase, they did not verbally express their thoughts. After the recall task, participants finished seven short-answer questions about the text content. Then, they were interviewed about their rationales for using particular strategies while reading, their background as readers, their commonly used reading strategies, their perceptions of these reading strategies, and their opinions of the think-aloud protocol and the text's difficulty. At the second meeting, the researcher conducted a member check (Merriam, 2009) with the participants by sharing transcripts, preliminary coding, and main themes to elicit their feedback.

Data analysis

Nvivo 10, a qualitative analysis software package, was used to store and manage codes and data. Think-aloud recordings were transcribed and analyzed line-by-line to identify the causes of comprehension breakdown and the reading strategies used. Multiple sources, like participants' think-aloud transcripts, their interview transcripts, and their performances on the recall task and short-answer questions were triangulated to deepen the researcher's interpretation. Strategy terms and taxonomies used in a previous study (Lee-Thompson, 2008) were referred to and adapted to fit the data from this study. The frequency of each strategy was counted.

The recall protocols were analyzed based on the method proposed by Bernhardt (1983). The original text was divided into separate idea units; a point or a half point was awarded for each idea unit from the text that appeared or was implied by the protocol. The weight of each idea unit was decided by considering two factors: the amount of information revealed by the unit and the importance of the information for understanding the text. There were 120 units and the full score for the recall protocol was 87. The total score for the seven short-answer questions was 40. Two scholars, including the researcher, evaluated, discussed, and agreed upon these rubrics. Partial credits were given (e.g., 1/4, 4/6, 4.5/6) for each item if the reader provided partially correct answers. Two raters, including the researcher, rated participants' performance. The interrater reliability calculated by Krippendorff's Alpha Coefficient was 0.94 for the recall protocol and 0.88 for the short answer questions. The researcher chose Krippendorff's Alpha Coefficient because it is a versatile statistic that can measure intercoder agreement with small sample sizes. Disagreement was resolved through discussion.

The researcher focused on the cases of Linda and Teresa, whose comprehension scores, as mentioned earlier, were the two lowest in the whole group of 12 participants (see their scores in the Results section). When analyzing the data of these two less successful readers, the researcher counted the strategy frequencies and then identified and coded the themes that emerged from the data. Constant comparisons were conducted between to identify similarities and differences in their reading difficulties and strategy use. When the preliminary analysis was finished, the researcher implemented a peer review (Merriam, 2009) by inviting a colleague to read the raw data (including parts of the transcripts and all the coding), then discuss and assess the findings. Based on peer review feedback, the researcher made some minor revisions to the codes.

Results

Causes of comprehension breakdown

Linda had a total score of 51% (64.5/127), with 44% (38/87) in the recall task and 66% (26.5/40) in the short-answer questions. Teresa had a total score of 64.5% (82/127), with 58.6% (51/87) in the recall task and 77.5% (31/40) in the short-answer questions. A total of five major causes of comprehension breakdown were identified from the data of the two less successful readers (see their frequencies, descriptions, and examples in Table 8.1).

Table 8.1 Causes of Comprehension Breakdown and Their Frequencies

Code	Total frequency	Frequency of Linda	Frequency of Teresa	Description	Example
Character/ word recognition	89	35	54	Fail to recognize characters/words or confused them with other characters/words with similar shape	他们愿意为孩子 something 最好的something件
Syntax	9	8	1	Have difficulties in identifying the structure of the sentences	和中国父母不一样em . . . Chinese parents, dad and mom are not the same
Ambiguity of character and words	8	6	2	Fail to recall the right meaning when a character/word has multiple meanings	孩子不需要当尖子 They don't have to grow up to be sharp

(*Continued*)

164 Sha Huang

Table 8.1 (Continued)

Code	Total frequency	Frequency of Linda	Frequency of Teresa	Description	Example
Chunk/phrase	2	2	0	Have difficulties in understanding longer phrases or chunks	…在这里不能一一列举 This cannot 一一列举, one example? This cannot be one example?
Word decision	2	1	1	Have difficulties in deciding if one or more characters consist of a word or not	正像一位中国家…长说的那样…

Table 8.1 also shows that although the two readers shared several common causes for comprehension breakdown, the frequencies of the difficulties encountered during the process of reading varied from one reader to another. The major cause of comprehension breakdown for both readers is the difficulty in recognizing characters/words, which means that they both had many difficulties in lexical decoding. As a heritage learner, Teresa encountered difficulty in understanding syntax only once, whereas Linda, as a non-heritage learner, had more difficulties in understanding syntactic structures, comprehending words/characters in different contexts, and understanding longer phrases or chunks. It is also interesting to note that although Teresa encountered difficulties in recognizing words more frequently (54 times), her overall comprehension rate was higher than Linda, which might be attributed to her better syntactic knowledge.

The following section will present how the two readers used reading strategies to cope with these difficulties.

How strategies were used to cope with reading difficulties

The Case of Linda

A complete list of the reading strategies that Linda used is provided in Table 8.2. As shown in the table, Linda's frequency of bottom-up strategies (147) was higher than the group indices, and her frequency of the top-down strategies (16) was lower than the group average. This suggests that, compared to most other participants, she used more bottom-up strategies and fewer top-down strategies. Her frequencies of translating, writing notes about unknown words, checking the dictionary, and decoding characters were higher than the group indices, which reveal her challenges in processing Chinese words and sentences. It is also interesting to note that the only bottom-up strategy that she did not use is grammar knowledge. As for top-down strategies, she monitored her comprehension occasionally and also used other types of top-down strategies such as prior knowledge, title,

Table 8.2 Linda's Reading Strategies

Groups	Code	Frequency	Percentage	Difference from the mean frequency of the 12 participants
Bottom-up Strategies	Translate	34	20.9	26.5
	Write notes	22	13.5	12.2
	Mark	21	12.9	−9.3
	Check dictionary	19	11.7	3
	Decode characters/words	13	8	3.8
	Make inferences	12	7.4	4.2
	Context	11	6.7	5.4
	Mental lexical network	6	3.7	3.6
	Paraphrase	3	1.8	−2.9
	Repeated words	2	1.2	0.3
	Reread	2	1.2	−2.2
	Identify words	2	1.2	1.1
	Grammar knowledge	0	0	–
	Total	147	90.2	43.7
Top-Down Strategies	+Monitor comprehension	8	4.9	4.6
	Prior knowledge	2	1.2	1.2
	Skip	2	1.2	−4.25
	+Identify problem	1	0.6	−0.8
	Foreshadow	1	0.6	0.5
	Title	1	0.6	0
	Summarize	1	0.6	−0.3
	+Identify important information	0	0	–
	+Plan	0	0	–
	Text structure	0	0	–
	+Evaluate text content	0	0	–
	Total	16	9.8	−2.2

Note. +metacognitive strategies

summarize, etc. Her frequency of skipping was much lower than the group figures. She did not use *text structure*, nor did she use the metacognitive strategies such as *identifying important information, planning, and evaluating the text*.

What follows are major patterns that characterized Linda's strategy use. Examples are also given to illustrate how some strategies were used by Linda.

Reliance on word-by-word translation: Difficulty in parsing sentences. One characteristic of Linda's strategy use is her heavy reliance on word-for-word translation. Translation was used 34 times, and it was her most frequently used strategy. In some cases, her English translation was grammatically incorrect or did not make sense in the context. Here is an example:

LINDA: Em . . . 和中国父母不一样[1] (unlike Chinese parents) em . . . Chinese parents, dad and mom are not the same.

This example shows that although Linda recognized every word and character in the sentence, her translation was not accurate, possibly because she was not familiar with the syntactic pattern "和 . . . 不一样" (unlike something/somebody).

She thought "Chinese parents" was the subject, and did not realize that the subject of the sentence would appear in the subsequent segment. Another example is discussed here:

LINDA: 对美国家长来说 (In American parents' opinion), em . . . for American parents, they say . . .

Again, in this case Linda did not recognize the pattern "对 . . . 来说" (for somebody/in somebody's point of view) and translated this segment of the text word-for-word as a subject-verb sentence.

When translating a longer sentence, Linda sometimes did not parse the sentence correctly either, despite her successful decoding of the words and characters in the sentence. In the example, the original sentence (很多美国人的信条是：生命是短暂的) means "The belief of many Americans is that life is short . . ." But Linda wrongly translated it as "Many Americans' beliefs are short lived." She did not realize that "life is short" is the subject complement of the main subject predicate structure "The belief of many Americans is . . ."

LINDA: There have a lot of American people's beliefs are 生 something, something about life is short. Em . . . helped by resetting my dictionary (checking 短暂 in dictionary) . . . 短暂, short, brief. Ok. So their beliefs are short lived.

Data showed that eight cases of Linda's incorrect interpretation were caused by lack of knowledge about syntax or certain sentence patterns. In those cases, word-to-word translation was attempted but did not effectively aid comprehension. In fact, Linda seemed very well aware of what she did during the reading of the text. As shown in the remark she gave at the post-task interview, in many cases, Linda resorted to direct translation only because there was no other choice. As Linda realized, without understanding the syntactic structure, sometimes her ways of putting chunks together were random, which made her interpretation deviate from the text.

LINDA: My expectation eventually for myself would be just I read it and I know it. That's my goal, but at this point when the grammar becomes more complicated it's a lot harder for me to do that.

Heavy reliance on dictionary and character decoding. Table 8.2 indicates that Linda's greatest difficulty in Chinese reading was with unknown characters and words. Her main strategy to cope with this issue was to check the dictionary. She checked the dictionary 19 times in the whole process of reading. In the interview, she confirmed that in her opinion, checking the dictionary is the most helpful strategy. It is interesting to note that she did not use the strategy *grammar knowledge*. Her frequencies of top-down reading strategies in Table 8.1 show that she never used the strategy of identifying "important information" and she seldom skipped parts. When encountering unknown characters or words, most of the time she chose to check the dictionary. She also mentioned in the interview that she tended to figure out the meaning of every character because "If I can't read the individual characters, that's going to be really difficult for me to read the sentence."

One problem of focusing on decoding every character was that it consumed Linda's cognitive resources that could have been used in higher level processing. As shown in the following two examples, she repeatedly mentioned that when reading Chinese, she needed to pay focused attention, but still lost track of the text or forgot the previous content.

LINDA: I think part of it is I lose the thread because you're concentrating on that sentence and then you need to integrate it back to the previous sentence that there's so much translation that still happening for me that I can't pull it up.

LINDA: Just how can that really make sure that my attention is constantly where it's supposed to be which can be very tiring.

Relying on the dictionary and being exhausted by focusing on each character, Linda was not confident in her ability to make inferences. Even though sometimes she made inferences, she was largely unable to confirm, reject, or adjust her previous interpretation.

Diffident to infer. Linda said that she did not trust her lexical inferences and thought they were less reliable than the dictionary. However, her think-aloud transcripts show that she did infer word meaning 12 times when reading for this study, and seven lexical inferences were correct or partially correct. These inferences were usually made by referring to contextual cues or her prior knowledge about Chinese culture. However, her think-aloud transcripts also show that when she was making these inferences, she was uncertain about their accuracy, and she did not include most of them in her final recall product. This uncertainty was revealed in her think-aloud transcripts as shown in the following examples. In these two cases, her inferences of the words 差异 (differences) and the phrase 争尖子 (strive to be the top student) were correct. But because she was not confident about her inferences, she skipped these two parts when she typed out the content of the text.

LINDA: Have a lot of . . . I'll say differences. 差 is like . . . em . . . Because . . . It was up here again or somewhere (tried to refer to the previous passages but did not find the word) Oh, that was the first line, but I am not seeing that. May be in another paragraph. I don't know. Now I am questioning everything here!

LINDA: Just little argument top. Oh, maybe few people fight for the top? Em . . . I don't know.

Although Linda did not trust her ability to make lexical inferences based on contextual clues, she did admit at the post-task interview that she used context to make global inference of the text gist.

LINDA: For inferring words, it (context) is not very helpful, but once I have the words then I can understand that sentence's context and then you can figure out from that the general ideas about that paragraph, and then onto the second paragraph. You introduce the topic in the first paragraph and then give examples, and then conclusion.

This transcript shows that context helped Linda to grasp the main idea of each paragraph. Her awareness of text structure (topic sentence, examples, and then conclusion) also helped her to understand the logic that links paragraphs. However, she still struggled in understanding many sentences and words, thus inhibiting access to important textual information. This may explain her struggle with the recall task, which required understanding important details of the text.

Monitoring: Effective with the help of context. One top-down strategy Linda used multiple times was monitoring. Observable monitoring happened eight times, among which six cases guided her to correct her interpretations.

LINDA: 让孩子享受生活，让他们活得 (Allow their children to enjoy the life, and make them live a full and happy life) . . . 充 . . . 买? . . . buy? To allow them live full buy? That's probably not really . . . 充 . . . em . . . I mean I'm not remembering that character correctly or (check the dictionary). . or 充实.

As shown in this example, when decoding the word 充实 (full, fully), Linda confused the second character 实 with 买 (to buy) because of the orthographic resemblance of the two characters. While she was translating the sentence, she found that her initial interpretation did not make sense in the sentence context. Then, she checked the word in her dictionary and adjusted her interpretation.

Sometimes, Linda used sentence context and her prior knowledge (such as common sense) to monitor her comprehension, as the following example shows.

LINDA: 孩子不需要当尖子 (Their children do not need to be top students). They don't have to grow up to be sharp. Hmm . . . That seems odd to me. Why would a parent be ok with their kids not being smart? (Check the dictionary) Oh, it's not smart. It's outstanding or top. So the top, stands up, top, how interesting relationship.

In this example, the character 尖 has the basic meaning of "sharp." However, the word "尖子" means "top students." Linda translated the word literally as "sharp" multiple times until she reread the previous sentence. When comprehending the word in the context, she found her initial interpretation did not make sense, so she decided to check this word in the dictionary, which led to her final, correct understanding. These examples show that despite Linda's limited L2 knowledge, with the help of context, she could still use the strategy *monitor* effectively, which guided her back to the right track of comprehension.

A summary of Linda's pattern of strategy use. As this analysis has shown, the basic approach Linda used was checking unknown words in the dictionary, translating sentences, and double-checking if the translation fit into the local context. However, due to her limited grammar knowledge, this approach did not work very effectively. Another difficulty she mentioned multiple times was that she kept forgetting prior contexts when focusing on decoding and translating individual characters and sentences. The two difficulties actually were connected with each other. As most of her attention focused on character decoding and ineffective application of translation, she exhausted her cognitive resources that could have been used in higher level processing, such as integrating sentences into previous contexts for construction and maintenance of coherence. Nevertheless, Linda still managed to use, although to a much lesser extent than those bottom-up strategies, some top-down strategies such as monitoring, context, and prior knowledge to help with comprehension.

The case of Teresa

Although Teresa's percentage of unknown words (14.72%) was higher than that of Linda (10.22%), her overall reading performance was better. Her better performance on short-answer questions suggests that she did a better job in comprehending the main ideas than the details. The following table shows her reading strategies and their frequencies.

Like Linda, Teresa's frequency of bottom-up strategies was higher than the group average, which reveals her heavy reliance on bottom-up strategies. Frequent decoding of characters/words reveals her difficulties in lower-level processing. The frequencies of her use of the dictionary (12) and inferring about small units (six) show that, when she tried to figure out the meaning of unknown words, she relied more on the dictionary than inference. She skipped much more frequently than other group members. She skipped 15 times, which was 8.75 points higher than the mean frequency of the whole group. As in the case of Linda, Teresa also used top-down strategies such as *monitor*, *prior knowledge*, and *text structure*, but did not use the metacognitive strategies *plan* and *identify problems*. The following summarizes the major patterns of strategy use found in Teresa's case.

Frequent skipping. Teresa skipped 15 times during the reading session. Because of her frequent skipping, she failed to retrieve many important details when doing the recall task. The following excerpt from her think-aloud transcripts shows how she skipped.

TERESA: 在中国文化里 (In Chinese culture)... something (良 good) 好是不 ... something（够 enough）的. .正向一位中国家长说的那样，每个人都可以做到... something (良 good) 好 ...

In this transcript, Teresa skipped three words in this single sentence. Although the unknown character 良 appeared twice, she did not stop to check it but chose to continue reading. Likewise, as shown in the following example, Teresa encountered four unknown characters/words in such a short sentence. She did not stop but chose to skip them and went on reading.

TERESA: 生 something (命 life) 是 something (短暂 short)的 ... 要 something (充 fully) 分... something (享受 enjoy) 它 ...

When asked about why she chose to skip, Teresa explained:

TERESA: If I can read probably 60% of it, I will probably choose to skip . . . if I have got the main idea about what it's talking about, I may choose to skip. . . . if I have no idea and I have to circle every other word . . . like this . . . I will mostly likely check.

Her explanation shows that a main factor that determined how she dealt with unknown words was the rate of comprehension. If she could understand 60% of the sentence she was reading, she felt comfortable in skipping the unknown words. If there were so many unknown words and phrases that she could not understand the main idea, she had no choice but to check the dictionary.

Obviously, Teresa seemed to be able to tolerate more ambiguity and pay more attention to the main idea while reading. Unlike Linda, who struggled in understanding every single character, Teresa felt satisfied in merely understanding 60% of the text. However, because of frequent skipping, Teresa missed many important details in the text. In addition, when deciding whether to skip, she never considered whether the skipped parts were important for comprehending the text. Her pure reliance on the ongoing assessment of her level of understanding each sentence/clause to decide her strategy choice may have led to missing key information and time wasted on unimportant words and characters.

Too many unknown words: Hard to infer without enough context cues. Like Linda, Teresa did not infer word meaning very frequently. As she explained in the interview, "If I have enough context clues, then I usually just guess it. But because there can be so many unknown words, I have to look up." Similar to Linda, Teresa did not trust her ability to infer when there was not enough context available, which was usually the case due to a lack of word knowledge. When there were enough contextual cues, she chose to make inferences. She made four accurate inferences out of a total of six. In most of these successful cases of inferencing, she used contextual cues. As the examples in the following excerpt indicate, when inferring the phrase 举个例子 (for instance), Teresa used both the local contextual cues (the meaning of 例子), as well as the context revealed by the subsequent sentences.

TERESA: . . . For 例子 (example) is like case . . . and then 举个 (hold up a . . .) is like to hold up to . . . to raise . . . although there is a variance, I ignore that . . . but to act as an example . . . I find that kind of make sense . . . it makes sense in the context . . .

Focusing on the main ideas. Compared with the recall task, Teresa did a better job in the short answer questions (77.5%) which focused more on the main ideas of the passages. When talking about reading strategies, Teresa stressed the importance of grasping the main ideas: "Like if I don't have the main idea . . . if I have no idea what it's talking about then it's like I don't know where to begin . . ." When asked how she usually grasped the main ideas, she talked about paying special attention to the title and the topic sentences of each paragraph.

She also summarized and monitored her comprehension by paying attention to the text structure and integrating different parts of the text. As Table 8.3 shows, summarizing and monitoring were observed twice and text structure was used once to facilitate her comprehension of the main ideas. The following are two examples. In the first example, Teresa summarized the main idea of the first paragraph. The second example shows that she used text structure clues to monitor her comprehension of the main ideas of the passage.

TERESA: Just to get the general idea of what the paragraph is about . . . and this one is about Chinese parents and American parents . . . their thoughts about their children and education.

TERESA: I wonder if that make sense because I thought they are comparing . . . so this part is the American students . . . and then this part is about Chinese students' parents.

Table 8.3 Teresa's Reading Strategies

Group	Code	Frequency	Percentage (%)	Difference from the mean frequency of the whole group
Bottom-up Strategies	Mark	61	32.1	30.7
	Write notes	36	18.9	26.2
	Decode characters/words	13	6.8%	3.8
	Check dictionary	12	6.3	−4
	Translate	9	4.7	1.5
	Paraphrase	7	3.7	5.9
	Reread	7	3.7	5.9
	Context	6	3.2	0.4
	Infer about small units	6	3.2	−1.8
	Repeated words	3	1.6	1.3
	Mental Lexicon	2	1.05	−0.4
	Grammar knowledge	2	1.05	0.7
	Identify words	1	0.5	0.1
	Radical	0	0	–
	Total	165	87	61.7
Top-Down Strategies	Skip	15	7.9	8.75
	+Important information	2	1.05	0.7
	+Monitor comprehension	2	1.05	−1.4
	Summarize	2	1.05	0.7
	+Evaluate text content	1	0.5	0.75
	Prior knowledge	1	0.5	0.2
	Text structure	1	0.5	0.6
	Title	1	0.5	0
	+Identify problem	0	0	–
	+Plan	0	0	–
	Foreshadow	0	0	–
	Total	25	13	6.8

Note. +metacognitive strategies

Advantages as a heritage learner: Daily input, prior knowledge, knowledge about syntax and phrases. As a heritage learner with family members speaking Chinese, Teresa had some advantages in reading Chinese, one of which was the Chinese input she received in her daily life. When decoding unfamiliar words, Teresa usually activated her mental lexicons with the help of the context, and many of those mental lexicons were acquired from daily Chinese input. For example, when she first read the word "奖励" (to reward), she did not recall its meaning immediately because she was unfamiliar with the written form of this word. She read the sentence again, trying to understand the sentence's context. Then during the second reading, she pronounced and interpreted the word correctly. When asked how she did it for the second time, she said:

> 'Cause they are buying items or gifts . . . that's the first thing that comes to my mind when I read that . . . I know the pronunciation . . . I don't always look at the characters . . . this (奖励 *reward*) is familiar, but I don't know what it is.

The context implied to Teresa that the unfamiliar word 奖励 might mean "to reward." Although she did not recognize the written form of this word, she knew how to pronounce it in Chinese. So, the context helped her retrieve the pronunciation of the word.

Teresa also mentioned in the interview that the daily input provided by her family members and Taiwanese television drama helped her to retrieve her mental lexicons: ". . . it is just come to my mind . . . sometimes when I read . . . because I do have a little bit Chinese background . . . I'm Cantonese. My parents speak Cantonese at home . . . and I watch a lot of Taiwanese drama."

As a heritage learner, Teresa had some prior knowledge about the Chinese parenting style. To some extent, this background knowledge helped her interact with the given text and evaluate the text content. When reading the two scenarios of different parenting styles, she gave such comments as, "It's so true." In the interview, she explained the reasons for her comment as follows:

> Because my background is Chinese also, so I can compare to, even though I grew up in the United States, my parents are still very, almost traditional in the sense of typical Chinese parents . . . I can compare it (the text) to my own life and my own parents; that's why I said it's so true.

She also mentioned that her family background gave her some advantage in understanding Chinese sentence structure:

> I speak Chinese. We have similar language structure, and then, like, me watching a lot of Taiwanese dramas that it does help like if I read it.

Table 8.3 shows that grammar problems only occurred once in her whole reading process. Unlike Linda, who frequently got lost despite the help of the dictionary, Teresa seldom had problems in parsing sentences. Other evidence of her better knowledge of grammar is her use of translation. Compared with Linda, who translated 33 times, Teresa translated less frequently (nine times). Teresa seldom applied direct translation, and most of her translations (seven out of nine translations) were correct.

A summary of Teresa's patterns of strategy use. This analysis shows that because Teresa struggled with word recognition, she usually found it difficult to make word level inference. She felt difficulty in making word level inferences based on context, and in many cases, she chose to skip unknown words. Frequent skipping caused gaps in text comprehension. However, her use of multiple strategies such as rereading, summarizing, and monitoring helped her to grasp the main idea of the text and compensated, to some extent, for her lack of vocabulary knowledge. As a heritage learner, she had more daily Chinese input, which gave her some advantages in using mental lexicons and understanding Chinese sentence structure.

Similarities and differences in difficulties and strategy use

Both readers' major difficulties were in word and character recognition. However, compared to Teresa, Linda had more problems in comprehending longer phrases and parsing sentences, and selecting the right meaning of words and characters in the context.

As for strategy use, both readers relied heavily on bottom-up strategies and occasionally used top-down strategies (e.g., text structure, monitor, summarize, and prior knowledge), which helped them fill comprehension gaps and grasp the main idea of the text. It is interesting to note that neither of the two readers trusted their ability to infer word/character meaning, nor did they put selective attention to unknown words/characters based on the importance of the unknown parts. Linda checked almost every unknown character and word, which gave her a heavy cognitive burden and made it hard for her to retrieve previous context. On the contrary, Teresa skipped most unknown words, which caused loss of important details and factual information in the text. Both readers used translation as a lower-level processing strategy. Due to the lack of the grammar knowledge, Linda relied heavily on word-by-word translation, which was usually ineffective, whereas Teresa, with her Chinese heritage background and daily language input, better understood sentence structures and translated much more accurately.

Discussion

This study supports and expands the Compensatory Model of L2 Reading (Bernhardt, 2005, 2011), by revealing how components of the model interplay during text reading and comprehension process. Due to limited word knowledge, both less successful readers did not trust their lexical inferences. Linda, due to the lack of grammar knowledge, could not understand the context well for lexical inference or apply the translation strategy effectively. These findings demonstrate how L2 linguistic knowledge affects strategy choice and effectiveness of use. On the other hand, despite their difficulties with some lower-level processes, the two readers managed to apply some helpful strategies identified in the previous literature (Grabe, 2009; Pressley, 2006). Top-down strategies such as context, monitoring, prior knowledge, and text structure helped the two readers to grasp the gist of the text, which suggests that effective use of strategies can help to compensate, to some extent, for comprehension gaps caused by limited language knowledge.

This study also supports and expands the literature by showing how learners' background can affect their L2 reading process, particularly their use of reading strategies. Both less successful readers experienced a common challenge in lexical decoding, yet the frequencies of reading difficulties varied from one reader to another. Notably, Linda had more difficulties in parsing sentences and understanding grammar of longer phrases, whereas Teresa barely had such problems. This finding corroborates those of previous studies (Ke & Chan, 2017; Xiao, 2006) that heritage learners had advantages over non-heritage learners in grammar. However, if a heritage learner's domestic linguistic input did not include sufficient exposure to a Chinese script system, s/he did not necessarily have advantages over non-heritage learners in vocabulary learning and reading comprehension when they advanced to higher levels. It is interesting to observe that the two readers' strategies to deal with reading difficulties also differed. Linda focused on unknown words and characters, which seemed to exhaust her cognitive resources, whereas Teresa skipped most unknown parts that might contain key information or textual details, trying to focus on the main idea of the text. A possible explanation for Teresa's unique approach could be her heritage background. She might be more used to paying attention to general messages because of her exposure to spoken Chinese input at home.

Another significant finding is the importance of syntactic parsing in comprehending Chinese text. Although Linda recognized more characters and words (with the help of the dictionary) than Teresa, due to her lack of ability to conduct syntactic parsing, her overall comprehension rate was lower than Teresa. This finding corroborates previous research, revealing the critical role of syntactic parsing in L2 Chinese reading (Chen et al., 2018; Huang, 2018a). The effects of syntactic parsing in Chinese reading may be unique due to characteristics of the Chinese writing system. Unlike English, Chinese does not have boundaries between words, which makes word segmentation the third component of lower-level processing of Chinese in addition to character recognition and lexical access (Shen & Jiang, 2013). This component makes syntactic analysis even more challenging in Chinese than in other languages. Without guidance and training, learners whose first language is English may feel it is difficult to understand the sentence structure, which can result in comprehension breakdown even if they know most of the characters in a sentence.

The findings of this study provide several pedagogical suggestions. First, the interplay between L2 knowledge and reading strategies suggests the need to emphasize both language knowledge and reading strategy training in classroom instruction so that the two components can work together better to contribute to comprehension. Second, in light of the two readers' different difficulties and differing use of strategies, the instruction needs to be differentiated depending on learners' background. The study also demonstrated that the think-aloud task was useful in revealing the unique difficulties each reader faced and can thus be used as a diagnostic assessment tool to provide individualized guidance for readers. In addition, this study revealed the critical role of grammar knowledge in comprehending Chinese text. This finding suggests the need to design learning activities to improve learners'—particularly non-heritage learners'—awareness of Chinese sentence structure and ability to practice syntactic analysis.

This study is a preliminary step to investigate the reading difficulties and strategies of less successful CSL readers and compare two readers with distinct backgrounds. More studies are needed to expand the findings of this study. More qualitative and quantitative research needs to be conducted with less successful readers of different language and family backgrounds (e.g., heritage and non-heritage learners) to reveal their similarities and differences in reading difficulties and strategy use. Intervention studies may be implemented along with learning activities to address the challenges faced by less successful readers. In particular, studies may diagnose those readers' distinct difficulties and provide individualized instruction. The effect of these interventions on learners' strategy use and reading proficiency development can be evaluated.

Conclusion

Through think-aloud and recall protocols, interviews, and close observations, this study revealed that although the two less successful readers shared a common major reading difficulty, frequencies of difficulties that occurred in the process of reading varied greatly from one reader to the other. As for strategy use, both readers heavily relied on bottom-up strategies, and they were both reluctant and unconfident to infer unknown words. Despite these similarities, the two readers differed in strategies and approaches in coping with comprehension breakdown. While the non-heritage learner focused on decoding every character and struggled in parsing sentences and comprehending the text globally, the heritage learner, with a better understanding of grammar and text structure, focused on understanding the gist of the text as opposed to textual details. These findings revealed the differences in reading difficulties and strategy use among less successful readers and point to the importance of analyzing each case when providing instructional suggestions. They also suggest the important role of grammar knowledge in comprehending Chinese texts. More qualitative and quantitative research is needed to investigate less successful readers' challenges and strategy use to yield useful pedagogical implications to improve the L2 Chinese reading curriculum.

Note

1 English translation is provided in the parenthesis.

References

Abbott, M. L. (2006). ESL reading strategies: Differences in Arabic and Mandarin speaker test performance. *Language Learning*, *56*(4), 633–670.

ACTFL. (2012). *ACTFL proficiency guidelines 2012*. American Council on the Teaching of Foreign Languages.

Afflerbach, P. (2000). Verbal reports and protocol analysis. *Handbook of Reading Research*, *3*, 163–179.

Anderson, N. J. (1991). Individual differences in strategy use in second language reading and testing. *The Modern Language Journal*, *75*(4), 460–472.

Bernhardt, E. B. (1983). Testing foreign language reading comprehension: The immediate recall protocol. *Die Unterrichtspraxis/Teaching German*, *16*(1), 27–33.

Bernhardt, E. B. (1991). *Reading development in a second language: Theoretical, empirical, and classroom perspectives*. Ablex.

Bernhardt, E. B. (2005). Progress and procrastination in second language reading. *Annual Review of Applied Linguistics*, *25*, 133–150.

Bernhardt, E. B. (2011). *Understanding advanced second-language reading*. Routledge.

Bernhardt, E. B. (2012). What do we know about L2 reading? *ADFL Bulletin*, *42*(1), 31–42.

Block, E. (1986). The comprehension strategies of second language readers. *TESOL Quarterly*, *20*(3), 463–494.

Bogdan, R. C., & Biklen, S. K. (1997). *Qualitative research education: An Introduction to theories and methods*. Pearson Education Inc.

Carrell, P. L. (1989). Metacognitive awareness and second language reading. *The Modern Language Journal*, *73*(2), 121–134.

Chang, C. (2010). See how they read: An investigation into the cognitive and metacognitive strategies of nonnative readers of Chinese. In M. E. Everson & H. H. Shen (Eds.), *Research among learners of Chinese as a foreign language (Chinese Language Teachers Association Monograph Series, vol. 4)* (pp. 93–116): National Foreign Language Resource Center.

Chen, X., Li, H., & Gui, M. (2018). Instructional effects of syntactic parsing on Chinese college students' EFL reading rates. *Journal of Education and Training Studies*, *6*(11), 176–185.

Cohen, A. D. (1986). Mentalistic measures in reading strategy research: Some recent findings. *English for Specific Purposes*, *5*(2), 131–145.

Cohen, A. D., & Upton, T. A. (2007). I want to go back to the text: Response strategies on the reading subtest of the new TOEFL. *Language Testing*, *24*(2), 209–250.

Ericsson, K., & Simon, H. (1993). *Protocol analysis: Verbal reports as data*. Bradford Books.

Everson, M. E. (2009). Literacy development in Chinese as a foreign language. In M. E. Everson & Y. Xiao (Eds.), *Teaching Chinese as a foreign language: Theories and applications* (pp. 97–112). Cheng & Tsui Company.

Everson, M. E., & Ke, C. (1997). An Inquiry into the reading strategies of intermediate and advanced learners of Chinese as a foreign language. *Journal of the Chinese Language Teacher Association*, *32*(1), 1–10.

Grabe, W. (2009). *Reading in a second language: Moving from theory to practice*. Cambridge University Press.

Hosenfeld, C. (1977). A preliminary investigation of the reading strategies of successful and nonsuccessful second language learners. *System*, *5*(2), 110–123.

Huang, S. (2018a). Effective strategy groups used by readers of Chinese as a Foreign Language. *Reading in a Foreign Language, 30*(1), 1–28.

Huang, S. (2018b). A qualitative case study of CSL learners' reading strategies. *Chinese as a Second Language: The journal of the Chinese Language Teachers Association, USA, 53*(2), 131–162.

Ke, S., & Chan, S.-D. (2017). Strategy use in L2 Chinese reading: The effect of L1 background and L2 proficiency. *System, 66*, 27–38.

Lee-Thompson, L.-C. (2008). An investigation of reading strategies applied by American learners of Chinese as a foreign language. *Foreign Language Annals, 41*(4), 702–721.

Leow, R. P., & Morgan-Short, K. (2004). To think aloud or not to think aloud: The issue of reactivity in SLA research methodology. *Studies in Second Language Acquisition, 26*(1), 35–57.

McNeil, L. (2012). Extending the compensatory model of second language reading. *System, 40*(1), 64–76.

Merriam, S. B. (2009). *Qualitative research: A guide to design and implementation.* Jossey-Bass.

Nassaji, H. (2006). The relationship between depth of vocabulary knowledge and L2 learners' lexical inferencing strategy use and success. *The Modern Language Journal, 90*(3), 387–401.

Phakiti, A. (2003a). A closer look at gender and strategy use in L2 reading. *Language Learning, 53*(4), 649–702.

Phakiti, A. (2003b). A closer look at the relationship of cognitive and metacognitive strategy use to EFL reading achievement test performance. *Language Testing, 20*(1), 26–56.

Phakiti, A. (2008). Construct validation of Bachman and Palmer's (1996) strategic competence model over time in EFL reading tests. *Language Testing, 25*(2), 237–272.

Plakans, L. (2009). The role of reading strategies in integrated L2 writing tasks. *Journal of English for Academic Purposes, 8*(4), 252–266.

Pressley, M. (2002a). Comprehension strategy instruction: A turn-of-the-century status report. In C. Block & M. Pressley (Eds.), *Comprehension instruction: Research-based practices* (pp. 11–27). Guilford Press.

Pressley, M. (2002b). Metacognition and self-regulated comprehension. In A. E. Farsrup & S. J. Samules (Eds.), *What research has to say about reading instruction* (3rd ed., pp. 291–309). International Reading Association.

Pressley, M. (2006). *Reading instruction that works: The case for balanced teaching.* Guilford Press.

Pressley, M., & Harris, K. R. (2006). Cognitive strategies instruction: From basic research to classroom instruction. In P. A. Alexander & P. H. Winne (Eds.), *Handbook of educational psychology* (pp. 265–286). Routledge.

Purpura, J. E. (1998). Investigating the effects of strategy use and second language test performance with high-and low-ability test takers: A structural equation modeling approach. *Language Testing, 15*(3), 333–379.

Shen, H. H. (2005). Linguistic complexity and beginning-level L2 Chinese reading. *Journal of Chinese Language Teachers Association, 40*(3), 1–28.

Shen, H. H., & Jiang, X. (2013). Character reading fluency, word segmentation accuracy, and reading comprehension in L2 Chinese. *Reading in a Foreign Language, 25*(1), 1–25.

Sheorey, R., & Mokhtari, K. (2001). Differences in the metacognitive awareness of reading strategies among native and non-native readers. *System, 29*(4), 431–449.

Smith, L. A. (2006). Think-aloud mysteries: Using structured, sentence-by-sentence text passages to teach comprehension strategies. *The Reading Teacher, 59*(8), 764–773.

Snow, C., Griffin, P., & Burns, S. (2005). *Knowledge to support the teaching of reading.* Jossey Bass.

Xiao, Y. (2006). Heritage learners in the Chinese language classroom: Home background. *Heritage Language Journal, 4*(1), 47–56.

Yayli, D. (2010). A think-aloud study: Cognitive and metacognitive reading strategies of ELT department students. *Eurasian Journal of Educational Research, 38*, 234–251.

Young, D. J., & Oxford, R. (1997). A gender-related analysis of strategies used to process written input in the native language and a foreign Language. *Applied Language Learning, 8*(1), 17–29.

9 Literacy environment and heritage language learner's literacy identity

Liu Li

Introduction

Chinese and English scripts vary drastically. Chinese has a morphosyllabic writing system in which most of the basic unit, the character, represents a morpheme as well as a syllable. Reading Chinese depends on skills that differ from reading alphabetic scripts like English. Compared with the heritage learners of other alphabetic languages in the United States, learning to read in Chinese presents a bigger challenge for young heritage language learners of Chinese due to the greater divergence between Chinese and English writing.

This study investigates the sociocultural context of a young Heritage Language (HL) learner's individual pathway to Chinese literacy in a cultural and linguistic background distinct from most American families. Through the examination of the sociocultural factors that may affect his reading development in Chinese, we hope to provide a more complete picture of Chinese literacy development among Heritage Language Learners (HLL). Moreover, a case study like this can provide informative and insightful descriptions of HLL's language and literacy acquisition from an emic stance of inquiry (Lincoln & Guba, 1985). This means that we will focus on the intrinsic learning patterns and distinctions from an "insider's" perspective. Through such a case study, commonality and difference found in the case can provide detailed descriptions of context, with which people can judge whether such findings are transferrable (Stake, 1994, 1995, 2005). In this study, we hope to find certain insights into heritage learners' Chinese literacy development by examining the case of an 11-year-old boy learning to read in both Chinese and English.

The participant of this case study was a typical Chinese American boy, Adam, who studied Chinese as a Heritage Language (CHL). We explored his journey of becoming biliterate in English and Chinese while living in the United States. Drawing on a "literacy as social practices" perspective (Barton & Hamilton, 2000; Barton, 2006), we examined how home environment and community resources influenced Adam's identity, which in turn would affect his biliteracy development.

The data was collected from multiple sources, including 1) the researcher's observation of the community; 2) class observation and interviews with the teachers in Chinese weekend schools; 3) observation, conversation, and interviews

DOI: 10.4324/9781003029038-12

with Adam as well as his parents; and 4) questionnaires for Adam's parents. We hope the findings provide both theoretical and practical implications for the literacy education of CHL learners inside and outside the United States.

Literature review

Literacy as a social practice

Social and cultural approaches to literacy have been developed by researchers and practitioners as a reaction to cognitive psychological literacy models that have dominated literacy instruction (Lankshear & Knobel, 2003). Researchers in this group (e.g., Barton & Hamilton, 2000; Cope & Kalantzis, 2009; Lankshear & Knobel, 2003; Luke, 2004; Street, 2004, 2005) went beyond a psychological approach by examining the contextual nature of literacy and the way literacy is inextricably embedded within particular sociocultural contexts. A sociocultural perspective toward literacy viewed literacies as always situated within specific social practices within specific discourses (Gee, 1996, 2000). In this theory, literacy is considered to be a basic skill, which is context embedded, used to achieve social goals, and imbued with the policies and ideologies of the social settings in which it occurs (Street, 1993). Also, literacy is viewed as a socially constructed practice, in which individuals are seen as active agents co-constructing meaning as well as developing perceptions, values, goals, and purposes about the ways in which literacy is used (Carrington & Luke, 1997; Muspratt et al., 1997). Such a perspective on literacy offers a way of understanding what human agents think they are doing when they practice literacy in the social world.

When literacy is viewed as a social practice, the acquisition of literacy is viewed as a part of what people do when they practice literacy in a social context. Accordingly, literacy learning is understood as a process by which individuals participate in specific literate communities for gaining group membership (identity) and, in turn, co-construct the social practices of these communities (Gee, 1990; Luke, 2004). Rather than a set of static, decontextualized, and discrete skills, literacy learning is always contextualized, dynamic, situated, and multifaceted through local practices (Street, 2004), and is closely related to group membership, that is, the identity of the literacy learners.

From CHL learners' perspective, Chinese literacy learning is also a social practice, which is deeply intertwined and influenced with social interactions around them. In this study, we will examine through a case study the intertwined relationship between social community, home, CHL learners' identity, and their CHL literacy development.

Community and home environment on CHL literacy development

Previous studies have not reached consensus on whether sociocultural factors may have an impact on CHL learners' acquisition of literacy skills. For example, Xiao (2006) compared Chinese language development of heritage students who had a home background in Chinese language and culture with those who did not. This study found that heritage learners did significantly better than their non-heritage counterparts in speaking, listening, grammar, and sentence constructions, but not in reading comprehension, vocabulary learning, or Chinese character writing. These results suggest that heritage learners' oral exposure to their home language does not necessarily lead them to acquire reading and writing skills more quickly than non-heritage learners. Home background knowledge of Chinese may not support reading comprehension or vocabulary learning if that knowledge does not include sufficient exposure to the Chinese script system.

However, several other studies have found that community and home literacy environments play a positive role in CHL learners' literacy development. For example, Zhang and Koda (2011) examined young Heritage Language (HL) learners' home literacy environment and its impact on HL word-knowledge development. They focused on a group of Chinese-English bilingual children learning to read in Chinese as a Heritage Language in the United States and found a significant positive correlation between parents' language use and learners' HL vocabulary breadth. The learners' schoolwork-related reading practice was also positively correlated with HL word knowledge. However, the research observed no significant relationships between independent and shared reading unrelated to schoolwork and the learners' word knowledge.

Lü and Koda (2011) investigated the effect of home language and literacy support on crucial literacy skills, including oral vocabulary knowledge, phonological awareness, and decoding skill in English and Chinese, among Chinese HL learners. They found that speaking Chinese at home supported children's language and literacy skills in Chinese, especially their oral vocabulary knowledge, and that support of learning Chinese at home did not hinder children's acquisition of literacy skills in English.

Luo and Wiseman (2000) also examined familial influences on Chinese HL speakers' HL maintenance. They found that family parental attitude toward Chinese HL maintenance, parents-child cohesion, and grandparents-child cohesion were correlated to learners' Chinese HL speakers' Chinese fluency and their attitudes toward Chinese HL maintenance. They also found that parents' attitudes toward HL were positively associated with immigrant children's HL preservation. Moreover, the researchers found a positive correlation between grandparents-child cohesiveness and child's HL maintenance. They argued that grandparents could be the best resource for the knowledge of their ethnic culture and language.

Although these studies on community and home learning environments explored the relations between learning and environment, little is known yet about the relationship between community/home literacy environments and CHL learners' identity construction and evolutions, and how such identity affects literacy development. The current study attempts to address these questions.

Heritage learners' identity

Identity is about "belonging" (Weeks, 1990, p. 88). Hall (1994) viewed identity as an ever-evolving production, which is never complete, always in process, and always constituted within, not outside, representation. Wenger (1998) defined identity as the combination of negotiated experience, community membership, and learning process. A language learner's identity can be understood with reference to larger inequitable social structures, which are produced and reproduced in daily social interactions (Peirce, 1995).

Ding (2013) pointed out there was a lack of research on CHL learners' identities. While HL learners of other languages, such as Korean, Japanese, and Spanish, have been intensively studied regarding their ethnic identity and cultural identity, the studies on CHL learners rarely touched the identity issues, especially the identity as a HL reader.

Among the limited number of CHL studies on identities, He (2004) took a linguistic anthropological perspective, and viewed identity as indexical with specific sets of acts and stances, which in turn are constructed by specific language forms. Based on sequential and grammatical analyses of data from Chinese heritage language classes, He argued that identity is dynamic, constantly unfolding along with interaction, and thus has the potential to shift and mutate. In her view, identity is emerging through co-participants' responses and reactions and thus as an intersubjective and reciprocal entity. It further suggests that identity construction significantly affects heritage language learning.

In another article, He (2006) proposed an identity theory of CHL development, based on the characteristics of the CHL learner and drawing insights from Language Socialization, Second Language Acquisition, and Conversation Analysis. In her study, she considered that CHL development takes place in a three-dimensional framework with intersecting planes of time, space, and identity. According to her theory, both communities and history play important roles in HL learners' construction of their identity. In terms of time, CHL development could connect history with the future by recontextualizing the past, transforming the present and pre-contextualizing the future. This might help HL learners to develop an identity of a rooted world citizenry with appreciation of and competence in Chinese language and culture. In terms of space, HL could transform local, seemingly independent communities into global, interdependent communities. Therefore, He concludes that a learner's CHL development depends on the degree to which s/he can find continuity and coherence in multiple communicative and social worlds in time and space and to develop hybrid, situated identities and stances. He's identity theory of HL development explained the relationship between sociocultural factors and identity during the process of CHL learning.

Wong and Xiao-Desai (2010) in their study explored the identity constructions of Chinese heritage language students from different dialect backgrounds. Their study was based on 64 interviews with Mandarin learners from various Chinese dialect backgrounds. They found that HL learners' experiences in learning Mandarin as a "heritage" language—even though it is spoken neither at home nor in their immediate communities—could showcase how identities are produced, processed, and practiced in this postmodern world. They also found the identity constructions of the dialect speakers could be explained from the perspectives of imagined community to globalization and investment.

Although some recent studies in CHL literacy development have begun to move beyond the individual's cognitive development to explore the social context of literacy learning, this is a potentially significant void. If we view children's literacy practice not as a product of reading or writing sentences but as a discourse that is produced through social practices, multiple factors of literacy learning need to be combined under an overarching configuration of literacy development in order to explore how bilingual learners interact with their social worlds through literacy learning. Yet few studies in Chinese heritage speakers' reading and writing have captured this domain of literacy learning.

As CHL learners are ethnically Chinese while many of them also have the nationality of the host country, there may exist clashes and conflicts between the different aspects of their identities. Research addressing these issues will help us to better understand the socio-psychological complexities of these learners and to better accommodate them in their language learning. In our study, we try to find out how a CHL learner acted on his "agency"—to assume or resist particular identities in certain sites and times, and how these identities have affected his Chinese literacy learning. To be more specific, we adopt this sociocultural view of literacy to analyze the impact of social (specifically, home and community) environment on the construction and evolution of a CHL learner's identity, and whether such impact would in turn affect his literacy acquisition of Chinese as a heritage language.

The current study

The current study investigates sociocultural factors that may have an impact on the subject's Chinese literacy development. The first theme to form the guiding framework of this study is "literacy is social practice" (Barton & Hamilton, 1998), which proposes that the development of literacy is influenced by the personal history of the child and his/her family, and the social contexts available for learning. This notion can capture the complex and multifaceted processes of literacy development and serve as a productive conceptual tool within which we can examine the intersection of the individual and the community. While locating literacy learning in social and cultural contexts, we can explore the heritage speakers' adoption of different ways with printed words within different sociocultural contexts (Gee, 2000). With this theory, we would like to look at literacy as social practice that is rooted in conceptions of identity, knowledge, and being. As such, it is constantly being redefined by individuals and social groups (Gee et al., 1996). Accordingly, the acquisition of literacy implies acquisition of the values and uses associated with literacy.

The current study also draws on He's identity theory of CHL development (2006): that CHL development takes place in a three-dimensional framework with intersecting planes of time, space, and identity. As He (2006) explains, CHL learners' development depends on the ability to find continuity and coherence in multiple communicative and social worlds in time and space and to develop hybrid, situated identities and points of view.

Research questions

Based on the theoretical framework, we asked two specific research questions in this study:

(1) Do community factors have an impact on the subject's identity as a Chinese literacy learner?
(2) Do home literacy environments and family literacy practice have an impact on the subject's Chinese literacy development?

Methodology

Participants

In qualitative research, purposeful sampling is frequently used to discover the unique characteristics inherent in a population (Patton, 1990). Rather than working with large samples, this study focuses on studying a single person, with the aim of capturing a multifaceted view of the participant's literacy development in more depth. In this study, sampling was purposeful. Purposeful sampling is employed when researchers intend to obtain in-depth, detailed information about selected cases (Patton, 1990).

The subject in this study was an 11-year-old bilingual boy whom we named Adam (a pseudonym). Although Adam was born and brought up in Pittsburgh with Chinese as the home language, he picked up English almost simultaneously in his daycare. The boy's mother was an instructor in the Chinese program at a prestigious university in Pittsburgh. She and her whole family had been making efforts to develop the boy's bilingual and biliteracy skills as soon as he began to talk. The boy had been making steady progress in his English reading after he entered the school, where English was the language for instruction and the communication between students. Despite unfavorable conditions for Chinese literacy learning, the boy had kept making progress in Chinese literacy development, as well.

As a Chinese-English bilingual, Adam was fluent in spoken Chinese, although his oral Chinese was limited in certain areas. For example, he did not know the formal word for "dad" in Chinese, which is equivalent to "father" in English. His English literacy development was excellent—he had always been the top student in the class. However, his Chinese literacy lagged behind. His reading vocabulary was very limited, but he was good at Pinyin. He quit Chinese weekend school that semester partly because he was not happy with the learning environment and his performance was considered only mediocre in the class.

Adam represents a typical case of heritage learner's literacy development among the American-born Chinese (ABC) children. Compared with their English literacy development, which excels in their peers, their Chinese literacy progress remains somehow stagnant or develops too slowly. An exploration into Adam's case from the social-cultural perspective can provide some insights into the factors of literacy development affecting Chinese children in the United States.

Instruments and data collection

There were four parts in the data collection procedure: the researcher's observation, informal chats with the subject and his parents, semi-structured interviews with the subject and his parents, and a questionnaire for the subject's parents. The researcher's observations included observation of the language practice in Pittsburgh at the various community levels, class observations in Chinese schools, and observation of Adam's Chinese and English language skills in general.

The chats and interviews were held between the researcher and Adam's mother in her office, and between the researcher, Adam, and his parents at the researcher's home. In the semi-structured interviews, the researcher asked how the boy learned simultaneously two typologically different languages—English and Chinese. Questions also included difficulties in simultaneous biliteracy learning and family influence.

The third part was a questionnaire, which covered four areas regarding the home literacy environment influence:

(1) Demographic background of the family,
(2) Materials in the home,
(3) Parents' affective variables toward their children's literacy learning, and
(4) Literacy-related activities between parents and children.

The mother was asked to answer the questionnaire following the instructions.

Parents' affective variables contained 40 questions. The first seven questions were on parents' expectation for their children's reading development, and how they view themselves and their children as a reader. The 33 other questions were adopted from an interview guide developed by Anderson (1995). These 33 questions focus on the parents' views on learning literacy in general.

Part 4 was also a questionnaire, dealing with literacy-related activities, adopted from Saracho (2000), which provides information on what kinds of materials and activities the parents provide for the development of their children's literacy development. This part has 60 items in nine subdivisions on family elements.

Results

Community-wise literacy practice

From the researchers' observation, chats, and interviews with Adam's parents, it was found that in the community where Adam lived, both Carnegie Mellon University (CMU) and University of Pittsburgh offered a Chinese language program. The East Asia Language and Literature in University of Pittsburgh had a long history and was well established. The Chinese program in CMU was also immensely popular among students, as evidenced by its rapidly increasing student numbers in each year. Worthy of note is that a Chinese class and the study abroad program had been offered in Grove City College—a private, comparatively small liberal arts college. Two Chinese weekend schools also played important roles in language maintenance and intergenerational transmission. In one of the schools, there were more than 230 students. Most of them were young heritage students who came to school regularly to learn Chinese language and culture. Some of them continued to study Chinese arts for one more hour after the two hours of language class.

In the two Chinese churches of the Pittsburgh area, there were several reading and writing classes for both adults and children. Chinese programs had also been set up recently in some highly rated high schools. The instructors were experienced teachers who used to teach at the college level in China.

Signs in Chinese in public places in the Pittsburgh area like banks, bus terminals, hospitals, airports, and supermarkets were increasingly visible. Public awareness of Chinese culture and tradition seemed more and more evident. Around the Chinese traditional New Year's Day, the radio stations and TV channels broadcast special programs celebrating the event. An increasing number of English-speaking people were familiar with a few greetings in Chinese, such as "nihao" (hello) and "xiexie" (thanks). During the traditional Chinese holidays, business organizations like banks sent special greeting letters to their Chinese customers as a token of appreciation for their business and their Chinese culture. The annual Drag Boat Festival was an important event to bring together the Chinese community and disseminate their culture. These activities normally provided more motivation and input for the heritage students' literacy development.

Although the community of Pittsburgh overall had become increasingly supportive of learning Chinese language and culture, the community resources for learning Chinese literacy were still not sufficient.

This insufficient community-wide literacy practice had a negative influence on Adam's Chinese literacy development. Adam was an excellent English reader, but when it came to reading in Chinese, he was far behind his peers in China, as were many other heritage speakers in his weekend school. By examining Adam's case, we found that Chinese input in written form in the community was still minimal. There was no Chinese TV station, nor were there many Chinese video programs in the area. Through observation and chat, we found that Adam showed more interest and motivation in learning Japanese, as he had watched Japanese cartoons and played computer games designed in Japan. He complained that the library did not have any Chinese books for him to read. From Adam's point of view, Chinese was less practical, thus his identity as a Chinese reader was not strong.

The lack of reading materials in Chinese had a severe impact on Adam's learning to read in Chinese. Although he had previously attended a weekend Chinese school every week, Adam complained about the scarcity of Chinese books in both number and variety in the community: he couldn't find anything in Chinese to read. As an avid young reader thirsty for knowledge, he had to put all his passion for reading toward English books. English reading led Adam to perceive himself as an American boy without much difference from other students in his school. He did not consider himself a Chinese boy who was born in the United States.

Rather, he identified himself with other American boys in the school, although he acknowledged that his ethnic background was slightly different.

Moreover, his success in school helped in the construction of another identity: the top student in the class. Once this identity of being a top student collapsed in the Chinese weekend school, he felt uncomfortable. It seems that the concept of "transfer" is not confined only to cognitive abilities. Social identities are intertwined and can sometimes be transferred from one area to another. For example, when Adam's "top reader" identity failed to transfer to his Chinese learning, he chose to give up.

In the interview and chat with Adam, we found that there were several reasons that he was not enthusiastic about his Chinese class in the Chinese weekend school. First, the teachers were not well-trained or certified. In the greater Pittsburgh area, there were only two Chinese weekend schools, which were the main sources for most of the heritage learners to develop their literacy. Although the enrollment kept rising in recent years, the schools had a hard time finding competent teachers. Most of the teachers were volunteers. Despite their passion for the second generation's literacy development, they lacked adequate training in teaching. To address this problem, more importance has been attached to the quality of instruction and curriculum design. A PhD student specializing in second language acquisition at CMU became the education director in one school, and a Chinese instructor working at CMU was the educational advisor for the other school. There was also heightened awareness of the need for collaboration between schools and parents for the children's literacy development recently. However, most classroom instruction in the weekend Chinese schools still followed the traditional teaching style. The class was often teacher-centered. Most teachers taught based on their experience as students in China many years ago. Without proper training, they just copied the teaching methods with which they had been taught reading and writing in Chinese schools. Through class observation, the researcher found that reading aloud by the students was quite frequent in most of the classes. Meaningful communication between peers was severely limited. Compared with the Chinese weekend schools, the normal American K-12 schools had more communicative activities and less rote memorization in class. According to Adam, his teachers in his normal school often provided games to help students learn new words and new concepts. Competition from peers and pressure from teachers in his normal school were also less severe. In the interviews, Adam explicitly expressed his preference for the American classroom, because he did not like the teaching style in the Chinese weekend school.

Still another reason for Adam's lagged development was the inadequate instruction and learning hours for the Chinese class. He usually spent only two hours in weekend school for Chinese learning every week. The homework took him about one hour each week. In addition, teaching materials were monotonous and inadequate. Both the teachers and the students found the textbook boring. The researcher heard complaints from both the teachers and the parents. Adam also expressed some dislike of the textbook.

An additional problem connected with Adam's multifaceted literacy identity was his family origin. Adam's family came from Mainland China. However, the weekend school he attended was operated by a group of Chinese speakers from Taiwan. The school adapted traditional characters and a set phonetic system different from the Pinyin system used in Mainland China. Taught by his mother, Adam was good at Pinyin. He knew nothing about the Taiwanese phonetic system used in his class. Such an experience led to a feeling of being an outsider in the class, which was most annoying to Adam. Furthermore, over time, when Adam practiced traditional Chinese characters at home, he was told by his grandmother, who had come for a visit, that it was useless to learn traditional characters, as no one used them in Mainland China. Such words from his grandmother were powerful. Adam became more averse to the Chinese class since he aligned himself with the Mainlanders.

Home literacy environment

Demographic background information in the questionnaire showed that the socialeconomic status (SES) of the subject family was high. Both parents had received graduate education. The father was a research scientist with a PhD degree. The mother was a university instructor with a master's degree. Adam had only one sibling, a two-year-old sister, who did not have much influence on the boy's literacy development so far.

Through the questionnaire and interview, we found that the materials for reading in Adam's home were abundant. There were more than 300 books, but only 50 of them were in Chinese. About 100 books were for children, but none of them were in Chinese. In addition to the printed books, there was an electronic device that could download books, journals, or magazines. There were three computers in the home, which were used primarily for work, research, and fun. The literacy materials were closely related to the parents' educational background and the family's SES. Since the parents were well-educated and their professions demanded high literacy skills, books had been an indispensable part of their life. In addition, their steady and sufficient income guaranteed that a steady purchase of a certain number of books was not a luxury beyond their means. However, Adam's parents did not engage in any literacy-oriented computer games or stories with Adam, as they were raised without such activities. They didn't realize that such activities could be included in their interaction with their children to promote literacy learning.

As to the affective variables in the questionnaire, the parents had high expectations regarding the child's reading competence. The mother's perception of the child's interest in reading and his own expectations were both high. The parents positioned themselves as educated Chinese people living in the United States, where emphasis is laid on "Chinese." However, they did not encourage their offspring to form the same identity. Rather, they accepted the fact that their children were living in a society where English was the dominant language. They hoped their youngsters would be accepted and assimilated by mainstream society. Although Adam had been taught Chinese from a very young age and Chinese remained the home language, much more emphasis had been put on his school performance, which relied mostly on proficiency in English. Influenced by the parents' attitudes, Adam viewed himself as an American boy with a Chinese ethnical background. The Chinese language was not as indispensable to him as English.

Part of the questionnaire contains the parents' belief of literacy learning (adopted from Anderson, 1995). All the statements were scored on a five-point scale from Strongly Agree to Strongly Disagree, with a higher score given for response that represented a more holistic literacy perspective, and a low score that represented a more skill-training perspective. The score from the subject was 92, indicating that the parents' view toward literacy learning was somewhere around the middle between holistic extreme and skills-training extreme. The parents placed less value on repeated reading of favorite books; emphasized neatness in writing; saw copying texts as a means to learn to write; and believed that only gifted children learn to read and write prior to formal instruction.

At the end of the questionnaire, the parents were asked the following question: "What are the five most important things you are doing to help your child learn to read and write in Chinese?" The answers were "go to Chinese weekend school," "buy Chinese books and cards," "subscribe to Chinese TV programs," "bring them back to China for a visit," and "talk to them about the importance of learning."

Part 4—the category of literacy-related activities—was adopted from Saracho (2000), which provides information on what kinds of materials and activities parents provide for the development of their children's literacy development. There were 60 items in nine subdivisions on family elements. The family's responses indicated the types of literacy activities and materials they used to promote the children's literacy development at home. The result shows that the family engaged in literacy-related activities like watching TV programs and reading newspapers and storybooks, etc. But the family did not play many board games or engage their children with activities like riddles. The result also shows that the parents helped the child read both inside and outside the home, but mostly in English.

Like most of the Chinese parents, Adam's parents were both busy professionals. Although they were motivated to provide better education to the children, they usually did not have time to teach their children reading and writing. Furthermore, unlike in many Asian countries but like many Chinese mothers in the United States, Adam's mother was a professional woman who valued her career, leaving little time for her children. Although she often felt sorry for Adam, she was not willing to sacrifice her career, as women's jobs were also highly valued in contemporary Chinese culture. In addition, in contemporary China, grandparents play a vital role in bringing up and educating the children, as normally parents are often too busy with work. In Adam's case, his grandmother's point of view on learning Chinese had a profound influence on him.

Discussion

From these results, we found that Adam's literacy identity has several layers. He considered himself 1) as an American boy; 2) with Chinese ethnicity background; 3) (family) from Mainland China; 4) excellent in classes taught in English; 5) mediocre in the Chinese class. The most important social-cultural factors affecting Adam's identity were his ethnicity background, schools he attended, and his home environment.

The first research question in this study is whether community environment impacts the subject's identity as a Chinese literacy learner and how. We found that one element of the Chinese literacy environment in the community—the Chinese weekend school—greatly influenced Adam's Chinese literacy development. Although an increasing amount of Chinese language was being used in the community, it was still far from enough for heritage-speaker children to pick up Chinese literacy.

Ethnicity and identity

Adam considered himself an American boy with a Chinese ethnic background. His acceptance of his ethnic background helped motivate him to study Chinese in order to know more about his roots and heritage. His ethnic identity helped him to identify with the Chinese ethnic group and provided the value and emotional significance attached to this membership. This finding conforms with the findings in previous research on heritage language education that ethnic identity plays a crucial role in HL development. For example, Chinen and Tucker (2005) found that Japanese HL learners who held a stronger ethnic identity generally assessed their Japanese proficiency to be higher than those with less strong ethnic identity. Jo (2001) and Kim (2002) reported that the primary reason for a majority of Korean HL learners to take Korean language classes was to learn their ethnic language to recover their roots and identity as Korean, which was irrelevant to the non-HL learners. Like the students in these studies, Adam's recognition of his ethnic identity encouraged him to maintain his heritage language skills, especially in speaking.

However, Chinese ethnicity is a broad concept covering a variety of subcultural groups. When Adam's subcultural identity—a child of a family from Mainland China—clashed with his Chinese weekend school's teaching of traditional Chinese characters and phonetic system, his motivation to learn was severely jeopardized. Adam's case is the opposite of Wong and Xiao-Desai (2010)'s study exploring the identity constructions of Chinese heritage language students from dialect backgrounds. Wong and Xiao-Desai found that CHL learners' experiences in learning Mandarin as a "heritage" language—even though it is spoken neither at home nor in their immediate communities—indicates that heritage learners' identity as Mandarin learners is produced, processed, and practiced through acknowledging similarities among regional languages and subcultures. Unfortunately, Adam's grandparents and the Chinese weekend school both chose to emphasize regional differences rather than embracing the commonalities across the subcultural groups. If they had done things differently, Adam's identity could have been forged differently. For example, if Adam's grandmother would have taught Adam the evolution of Chinese characters, Adam would have been able to appreciate the beauty of the traditional Chinese characters and would probably have continued to learn. Or if the Chinese weekend school had provided options for students to choose between traditional and simplified characters, Adam would have chosen the system he liked and happily continued his learning. Both the home and school could have helped HL learners like Adam to form a more inclusive identity to transcend the regional differences, as found in Wong and Xiao-Desai's s study (2010) that the identity constructions of the dialect speakers could be explained from the perspective of the imagined community of globalization.

Previous studies found that factors such as age, gender and place of birth can influence the level of ethnic/cultural identity found in individual HL learners (e.g., E.J. Kim, 2004; E. J. Kim, 2006; Lee, 2002). In this study, we found that an HL learner's identity with a particular region could be a similar factor affecting his/her identity as a learner. Both learners' homes and schools should approach this problem with more care to avoid possible identity conflicts.

Chinese weekend school and identity

Adam didn't have a positive attitude toward the Chinese weekend school he had attended. In fact, his negative attitude eventually led him to quit the Chinese school. This finding is consistent with some previous studies, which found HL learners' attitudes toward the heritage school link to their heritage-related identity formation. Chinen and Tucker (2005), for example, investigated Japanese HL learners' attitudes toward the supplementary heritage school they were attending and found that learners' ethnic identity rating was positively correlated to their attitude toward the school and their HL proficiency level.

Some previous studies (Xiao, 2006; Li, 2006; Francis et al., 2008; Creese et al., 2006) found that Chinese weekend schools have a few common features. For example, Chinese weekend schools receive little or no funding from the government. Instead, they are supported by the Chinese community. Teachers are either volunteers or employed staff with very low salaries. Some of them are parents of students and do not have any teaching background. Adam's Chinese weekend school also had similar features, which created significant problems for him. First, many teachers in the school used outdated teacher-centered instructional methods in class. Learning in this way was not interesting enough to motivate young students like Adam to continue the painstaking journey of Chinese literacy learning. Second, the school failed to create a pan-Chinese identity to meet the needs of people from different Chinese-speaking regions. They could have been more flexible and open-minded toward students' choices in which written system the students would like to use. Instead, their curriculum was too rigid to accommodate the diverse needs among different subcultural groups. Therefore, Adam's identity as a child from a Mainlander family clashed with the school's teaching of traditional characters and another phonetic system that are no longer used in Mainland China. Third, the school failed to address students' identity conflicts created by the imbalance of students' Chinese and English proficiency. Adam was a top student in all his classes taught in English, but he couldn't accept being mediocre in his Chinese class. This means that his identity as a "top student in English" crushed his identity as a "mediocre student in Chinese." Gradually, he lost confidence and interest in developing Chinese literacy skills. If the teachers could tell the students that this unbalanced development was very common, Chinese heritage learners like Adam probably would be less frustrated. They need to be made aware of the gap between the proficiency levels of the two languages and thus encouraged by the teachers and parents to focus on the process of learning, rather than the test scores. Then, heritage learners like Adam would probably be more confident about learning to read and write in Chinese. Eventually, these three problems resulted in his negative attitude toward the school.

The second research question is whether home environment has an impact on the subject's Chinese literacy development and how this takes place.

Home literacy environment and identity

From the data, we found that the home literacy environment played a vital role in Adam's literacy identity and learning practice. Adam's family had only some Chinese books, and his parents' engagement in parent-child literacy activities in Chinese was limited. Adam's parents' expectation and affective factors in literacy also influenced his literacy identity. They viewed him as an American boy with Chinese heritage. So did Adam. As a result, Adam didn't form a strong identity for Chinese literacy learning.

Adam's home literacy resources for learning Chinese remained very limited. The lack of resources and literacy practice at home hindered Adam's progress in reading and writing. The empirical evidence from previous studies indicates that the quantity and quality of Chinese cultural and social resources available to CHLLs influence their CHL proficiency. Some studies (Xiao, 2008; Lao, 2004) found that having inadequate Chinese reading materials in Chinese immigrant homes impedes further development of children's CHL. Adam's literacy identity as a Chinese learner was weak in part because of his limited home literacy environment for Chinese learning.

Xia (2016) found that Chinese immigrant parents' language attitudes and ideologies are largely influenced by English-only ideology. This is also true in Adam's case. For his parents, the priority for learning English surpassed the importance of Chinese learning. Adam's parents invested more in English literacy activities and materials for children. Compared with his Chinese learning, Adam's English learning was much more frequent, and his identity as an English learner was strong and confident.

However, Adam's parents still encouraged him to keep his roots and heritage, especially the spoken language. Adam's parents spoke Chinese in everyday life. So, Adam was motivated to use and learn Chinese to some extent. This confirms what Xiao (2006) found in this study, which concludes that the majority of Chinese heritage learners claim "family background" as their primary motivation for studying Chinese.

It has been found that parent-child and grandparent-grandchild cohesion (Luo & Wiseman, 2000) contributes to children's CHL identity and retention. Adam was close to his parents and grandparents. His grandmother unconsciously reinforced Adams's identity as a learner of Mainland language and culture, which led to Adam's identity conflicts with the Chinese weekend school and eventually became one of the direct causes for him to withdraw from that school.

Adam's parents represent a special group of first-generation immigrants. Within the United States, many immigrants were viewed as individuals who moved from their home country to obtain economic improvement or release from political complications. Thus, these immigrants were believed simply to accept poor treatment and low status because they were supposedly still better off than they would have been in their homeland (Ogbu, 1991). However, this view has changed. The characteristics of ethnic and/or linguistic minorities today in the U.S. are much more complex and fluid. The traditional figure of the immigrant did not take into account the unique characteristics of the middle-class minorities (like Adam's parents) who moved to the U.S. mainly for academic advantages. Adam's parents belonged to a special group of people who enjoy two cultural identities brought by two languages and two cultures. For them, their previous home country and current residential country are not dichotomous entities, thus they developed multiple identities while flexibly shifting between the two languages/cultures on a continuous basis (Guerra, 1998; Patron, 2003). A typical example of such first-generation immigrants is the mother of Eileen Gu. Eileen is half-Chinese born and grew up in the United States. Yet she competed for China in the 2022 Winter Olympic Games and won two gold and one silver medals. Owing to her mother and maternal grandmother's influence and education, Eileen claimed to be both Chinese and American, as she told the reporters that "I'm Chinese when I'm in China, and American in the United States" (Har & DiLorenzo, 2022). This group of first-generation immigrants, like Eileen's mother and Adam's parents, were concerned about their children's education and helped their children's learning. However, because some parents' experiences of practicing the English language and/or other academic exercises in the United States tend to be based on their highly specified instrumental motivation, their approaches to education of their children tend to be goal-driven. For them, the goal of their children's education is to achieve success in the United States. English is essential for this goal, whereas Chinese is supplementary if there are any conflicts between the two languages. The parents' attitudes can greatly influence their children's learning in Chinese, as shown in Adam's case.

This study confirms that "literacy is social practice" (Barton & Hamilton, 1998). Adam's development of literacy is influenced by Adam's personal history and his family, and social contexts available for learning. This study also supports He's identity theory of CHL development (2006). Adam's Chinese literacy development takes place in a multifaceted world, where learners' personal and family history, social contexts, and learners' identity are intertwined.

Conclusion and implication

Adam's case illustrated this complexity of his identity formation. We found that the Chinese literacy resources in the community remained limited for heritage learners like Adam. Chinese weekend schools were a major channel for Adam to learn Chinese literacy skills. Home literacy environments also played a significant role in Adam's identity formation. The attitudes and approaches of Adam's parents and grandmother regarding learning Chinese all influenced his literacy development.

In summary, heritage learners are affiliated with their ethnolinguistic community (Fishman, 2001). Since these learners must learn the mainstream language and culture to survive and at the same time remain connected (whether willingly or unwillingly) in some degree to their heritage language, culture and community, these HL learners may have unique socio-psychological complexity in their identity formation, compared to non-heritage learners.

Adam's case shows again that Chinese literacy development takes time and commitment from both the community and the home. Community literacy practice and home environment are crucial to the children's language and literacy development. Together, the community and the home provide a site for the young learner to form and develop his identity by and through reading.

The findings suggest various theoretical and practical implications for the education of English language learners in and out of the United States. The theoretical implications are: 1) to examine CHL literacy development as a multidimensional configuration of intersecting tenets; 2) to recognize language minorities in the United States as a heterogeneous and multivoiced group of people; and 3) to appreciate and value parent-child research.

The practical implications are: 1) Chinese as a second literacy takes much more effort due to the sociocultural environment in the United States and 2) Home environment is crucial to the children's language and literacy development.

References

Anderson, J. (1995). Listening to parents' voices: Cross cultural perceptions of learning to read and to write. *Reading Horizons, 35*(5), 394–413.

Barton, D. (2006). *An introduction to the ecology of written language* (2nd ed.). Blackwell Publishing.

Barton, D., & Hamilton, M. (1998). *Local Literacies: Reading and writing in one community*. Routledge.

Barton, D., & Hamilton, M. (2000). Literacy practices. In D. Barton, M. Hamilton, & R. Ivanic (Eds.), *Situated literacies: Reading and writing in practice* (pp. 7–15). Routledge.

Carrington, V., & Luke, A. (1997). Literacy and Bourdieu's sociological theory: A Reframing. *Language and Education, 11*(2), 96–112.

Chinen, K., & Tucker, G. R. (2005). Heritage language development: Understanding the roles of ethnic identity and Saturday school participation. *Heritage Language Journal, 3*(1), 27–59.

Cope, B., & Kalantzis, M. (2009). "Multiliteracies:" New literacies, new learning. *Pedagogies: An International Journal, 4*(3), 164–195.

Creese, A., Bhatt, A., Bhojani, N., & Martin, P. (2006). Multicultural, heritage and learner identities in complementary schools. *Language and Education*, *20*(1), 23–43.

Ding, T. (2013). New type of learner emerging: Understanding learners of Chinese as a Heritage language. *Journal of Cambridge Studies*, *8*(2), 49–61.

Fishman, J. A. (2001). 300-plus years of heritage language education in the United States. In J. K. Peyton, D. A. Ranard, & S. McGinnis (Eds.), *Heritage languages in America: Preserving a national resource* (pp. 81–98). Center for Applied Linguistics & Delta Systems.

Francis, B., Archer, L., & Mau, A. (2008). *'British-Chinese pupils' identities, achievement and complementary schooling: Full research report ESRC End of Award Report, RES-000–23–1513'*. ESRC.

Gee, J. P. (1990). *Sociolinguistics and literacies: Ideology in discourse*. Falmer Press.

Gee, J. P. (1996). *Social linguistics and literacies: Ideology in discourses*. Taylor & Francis.

Gee, J. P. (2000). The new literacy studies: From 'socially situated' to the work of the social. In D. Barton, M. Hamilton, & R. Ivani (Eds.), *Situated literacies: Reading and writing in context* (pp. 180–196). Routledge.

Gee, J. P., Hull, G., & Lankshear, C. (1996). *The new work order: Behind the language of the new capitalism*. Westview Press.

Guerra, J. C. (1998). *Close to home*. Teachers College Press.

Hall, S. (1994). Cultural identity and diaspora. In P. Williams & L. Chrisman (Eds.), *Colonial discourse and postcolonial theory: A reader* (pp. 392–403). Columbia University Press.

Har, J., & DiLorenzo, S. (2022, February 15). Eileen Gu: Navigating two cultures, judged by both of them. *AP News*. https://apnews.com/article/winter-olympics-Eileen-Gu-navigating-two-cultures-7536da11aec15dfcd34a949e017a6328

He, A. W. (2004). Identity construction in Chinese heritage language classes. *Pragmatics*, *14*(2/3), 199–216.

He, A. W. (2006). Toward an identity theory of the development of Chinese as a Heritage language. *Heritage Language Journal*, *4*(1), 1–28.

Jo, H.-Y. (2001). Heritage" Language learning and ethnic identity: Korean Americans' struggles with language authorities. *Language, Culture and Curriculum*, *14*(1), 26–41.

Kim, E. J. (2004). Korean-English bilinguals and heritage language maintenance. In H.-Y. Kim (Ed.), *Korean language in America 9: Papers from the eighth annual conference and professional development workshop* (pp. 244–258). American Association of Teachers of Korean.

Kim, E. J. (2006). Heritage language maintenance by Korean-American college students. In K. Kondo-Brown (Ed.), *Heritage language development: Focus on East Asian immigrants*. John Benjamins Publishing Company.

Kim, H. H. (2002). The language backgrounds, motivations, and attitudes of heritage learners in KFL classes at University of Hawaii at Manoa. In J. J. Ree (Ed.), *Korean language in America 7: Papers from the seventh annual conference and professional development workshop* (pp. 205–222). American Association of Teachers of Korean.

Lankshear, C., & Knobel, M. (2003). *New literacies: Changing knowledge and classroom learning*. Open University Press.

Lao, C. (2004). Parents' attitudes toward Chinese—English bilingual education and Chinese-language use. *Bilingual Research Journal*, *28*(1), 99–122.

Lee, J. S. (2002). The Korean language in America: The role of cultural identity in Heritage language learning. *Language, Culture and Curriculum*, *15*(2), 117–133.

Li, W. (2006). Complementary schools, past, present and future. *Language and Education*, *20*(1), 76–83.

Lincoln, Y., & Guba, E. G. (1985). *Naturalistic inquiry*. Sage.
Lü, C., & Koda, K. (2011). Impact of home language and literacy support on English-Chinese biliteracy acquisition among Chinese Heritage language learners. *Heritage Language Journal*, *8*(2), 44–80.
Luke, A. (2004). On the material consequences of literacy. *Language and Education*, *18*(4), 331–335.
Luo, S. H., & Wiseman, R. L. (2000). Ethnic language maintenance among Chinese immigrant children in the United States. *International Journal of Intercultural Relations*, *24*(3), 307–324.
Muspratt, S., Luke, A., & Freebody, P. (Eds.). (1997). *Constructing critical literacies*. Hampton Press.
Ogbu, J. U. (1991). Understanding cultural diversity and learning. *Educational Researcher*, *21*(8), 5–14.
Patron, M. (2003). *I'm bien pocha: Transnational teachers of English in Mexico* (Doctoral dissertation). The University of Texas at Austin.
Patton, M. (1990). *Qualitative evaluation and research methods*. Sage.
Peirce, B. N. (1995). Social identity, investment, and language learning. *TESOL Quarterly*, *29*(1), 9–31.
Saracho, O. N. (2000). Literacy development in the family context. *Early Child Development and Care*, *163*(1), 107–114.
Stake, R. E. (1994). Case studies. In N. K. Denzin & Y. S. Lincoln (Eds.), *Handbook of qualitative research* (pp. 236–247). Sage.
Stake, R. E. (1995). *The art of case study research*. Sage.
Stake, R. E. (2005). Qualitative case studies. In N. K. Denzin & Y. S. Lincoln (Eds.), *The Sage handbook of qualitative research* (3rd ed., pp. 443–466). Sage.
Street, B. (Ed.). (1993). *Cross-cultural approaches to literacy*. Cambridge University Press.
Street, B. (2004). Futures of the ethnography of literacy? *Language and Education*, *18*(4), 326–330.
Street, B. (Ed.). (2005). *Literacies across educational contexts: Mediating learning and teaching*. Caslon.
Weeks, J. (1990). The value of difference. In J. Rutherford (Ed.), *Identity: Community, culture, difference* (pp. 88–100). Lawrence & Wishart.
Wenger, E. (1998). *Communities of practice: Learning, meaning, and identity*. Cambridge University Press.
Wong, K. F., & Xiao-Desai, Y. (2010). Diversity and difference: Identity issues of Chinese Heritage language learners from dialect backgrounds. *Heritage Language Journal*, *7*(2), 153–187.
Xia, Q. (2016). Heritage language maintenance and biliteracy development for immigrants' children: A study of Chinese immigrants' family language policy and biliteracy practices (Unpublished doctoral dissertation).
Xiao, Y. (2006). Heritage learners in the Chinese language classroom: Home background. *Heritage Language Journal*, *4*(1), 47–56.
Xiao, Y. (2008). Home literacy environment in Chinese as a Heritage language. In W. He & Y. Xiao (Eds.), *Chinese as a Heritage language: Fostering rooted world citizenry* (pp. 151–166). University of Hawai'i Press, National Foreign Language Resource Center.
Zhang, D., & Koda, K. (2011). Home literacy environment and word knowledge development: A study of young learners of Chinese as a Heritage language. *Bilingual Research Journal*, *34*(1), 4–18.

Part III
Reading instruction and assessment

10 Beyond the pages of a book

A Chinese language teacher's discursive behaviors of conducting guided book reading

Zheng Gu

Introduction

As one of the most important mediational tools, teachers' discursive behaviors, which refer to the moves and processes teachers use to construct meaning and scaffold teaching through discourses (Potter, 2013), play an essential role in language learning and literacy development. In foreign language classrooms, teachers use various discursive strategies (e.g., questions, comments, feedback) to scaffold students' improvement of language, literacy, and problem-solving skills. Classroom activities that involve various discursive strategies are widely conducted to model and monitor students' learning. Among these, one of the most common activities is guided book reading (Fisher et al., 2008).

Guided book reading contributes in various ways to literacy and language development (Dickinson & Snow, 1987; Dickinson & Tabors, 1991). From a sociocultural perspective (e.g., Barton & Hamilton, 2000; Rogoff, 2003), guided book reading creates a learning environment where teachers can scaffold and support students' conceptual understanding, language knowledge construction, and problem-solving skills. Much of the research on guided book reading has focused on the first language (L1) learning environment, including studies on vocabulary and reading development and quality of adults' instruction (Dickinson & Tabors, 1991; Dickinson & Smith, 1994; Gerde & Powell, 2009; Zucker et al., 2010). Less attention has been paid to second language (L2) classrooms, where students need to develop language proficiency and content knowledge at the same time. To address this gap, this study used a teacher in a Chinese immersion program as an example to explore her discursive behaviors when she conducted guided book reading across two book genres. In this case study, the Chinese teacher's discursive behavior was carefully observed and examined through the lens of sociocultural theory to highlight her pedagogical purpose of conducting guided book reading in different subject areas.

This study is meaningful in several ways. First, it can enhance teachers' awareness of guided reading and encourage them to use more efficient language strategies to support students' language, literacy, and content knowledge development. In addition, it can also provide information for teacher educators in understanding the complexity of teachers' use of discursive strategies and their complete

DOI: 10.4324/9781003029038-14

repertoire of practice. With a better understanding of how teachers use language strategies in L2 guided reading, teacher education programs or professional development training centers could create opportunities for foreign language teachers to engage in intentional guided practice in guided reading, such as asking questions and giving feedback to students.

Literature review

Sociocultural theory

Sociocultural theory (SCT) focuses on how interaction influences individual learning, as well as how beliefs and attitudes impact the enacting of instruction and learning. It has been used in different fields such as child development, cognitive psychology, and education. The current study draws on the perspectives of the inseparable relationship between content (mathematics) and language in SCT to analyze the participant's planning, practice, and decision-making.

SCT perspectives of content and language

Previous research drawing on SCT has argued for inseparable language and content (e.g., mathematics) (Vygotsky, 1978). Researchers challenged the views that separate language and content. They argued that content and language development are integrated and the learning of content knowledge is embedded in knowing and using the target language (e.g., Brown, 2002; Bao & Du, 2015; Martínez & Dominguez, 2018). For instance, Martínez and Dominguez (2018) claimed that students' experience of learning content knowledge in an English-Spanish immersion program is an inseparable activity where teachers focus on teaching language that can be used in content learning and content knowledge that provide contexts for language acquisition. For the current study, this notion of language and content as inseparable indicates that foreign language teachers undertake multiple tasks of supporting students' improvement of language proficiency, literacy skills, and content knowledge. Additionally, this perspective indicates teachers' problem-solving strategies through employing various discursive strategies, which refer to a set of intentional discourse moves and tactics that teachers planned and employed to achieve certain teaching goals (Wodak & Meyer, 2009).

To apply this notion of language and content entanglement, content-based foreign language instruction offers insights and strategies to help classroom teachers plan, teach, and assess students' learning in foreign language classrooms by conducting various activities (e.g., Tedick & Cammarata, 2012; Duff et al., 2013; Cenoz et al., 2014). One such activity is teacher-guided book reading.

Guided book reading

Guided book reading is one of the most typical approaches and popular reading strategies teachers use with small groups of students in the United States (Ford &

Opitz, 2008; Bus et al., 1995). Guided book reading can be traced back to the late 1980s (Pinnell & Fountas, 2010) and refers to the practice of adults reading a book aloud, asking questions, and making comments to emphasize critical knowledge of the book. It is identified as a significant "best practice" in literacy instruction because of its focus on promoting students' language and literacy development and providing scaffolding to students' varying learning needs (Iaquinta, 2006, p. 414). When conducting guided book reading, teachers employ various discursive strategies to prompt students' language output, literacy development, as well as knowledge construction through reading, thinking, and talking across a range of texts, such as literary fiction, or expository, non-fiction texts. Such activities are "geared toward creating richly textured opportunities for students' conceptual and linguistic development" (Goldenberg, 1992, p. 317).

Previous studies have identified the benefits of guided book reading from different aspects, including short-term benefits (e.g., Nyhout & O'Neill, 2014; Korat et al., 2013; Connor et al., 2011) and long-term benefits (e.g., Bus et al., 1995). Scholars found that guided book reading improves students' language and literacy abilities and enhances their positive attitudes toward reading.

In terms of short-term benefits, guided book reading influences learners' vocabulary and early literacy skills development (e.g., Elley, 1991; Doyle & Bramwell, 2006; Connor et al., 2011), such as generic language construction (e.g., Nyhout & O'Neill, 2014; Kim & Anderson, 2008) and phonological awareness improvement (e.g., Ukrainetz et al., 2000; Stadler & McEvoy, 2004; Korat et al., 2013). For example, Lever and Sénéchal (2011) examined the relationship between young learners' narrative construction, which refers to a learner's oral skills to produce a story, and guided picture book reading. The findings indicated a direct correlation between participants' narrative language output and shared book reading, especially reading chapter books. A significant increase of vocabulary acquisition was also found in this study.

From a long-term perspective, guided book reading can help students establish a positive attitude toward reading and increase their chances of success with reading in schools (Elley, 1991; Bus et al., 1995), regardless of language. For instance, closely examining 29 studies, Bus et al. (1995) found a strong relationship between guided book reading and learners' language and literacy development, as well as the overall success in establishing a reader's identity. Students were more confident that "I can understand the book," "I can read aloud," "I can recognize characters, or I know what I like to read," and so on after continuously reading books, especially narrative books, with parents or teachers.

In addition to recognizing the strength of guided book reading, scholars further explored the factors that influence the quality of conducting guided book reading, including teachers' questions and text genres. Previous studies examined the interaction between teachers and students, such as questions asked and scheduled by teachers (e.g., Ranker, 2009; Nyhout & O'Neill, 2014). For instance, Hindman et al. (2008) argued that parents and teachers prefer to ask meaning-related questions rather than decoding-related questions (e.g., questions about rhyming or alphabet). This strategy directly influenced children's initial levels of vocabulary skills. Blewitt et al. (2009) explored the question teachers ask when conducting guided book readings and found that students' comprehension skills of new words significantly increased after listening and answering teachers' questions, regardless of when and how, or in which part of the reading process those questions were asked.

Scholars also believe that book genres, such as fictional genres (e.g., narrative texts), non-fictional genres (e.g. expository texts) and media genres (e.g. webpages), are an essential factor that influences the quality of shared book reading (e.g., Ranker, 2009). For example, Anderson et al. (2012) found that parents engaged more in non-narrative text reading with their kids and asked a greater number of inferential questions to communicate with them. Price et al. (2012) argued that more discussion and questions occurred during the guided reading of informational books. Moreover, teachers ask more literal questions when reading informational books and mainly inferential questions when reading narrative books.

The current study

Previous studies have placed a great amount of attention on guided book reading for younger learners, especially for L1 learners. Even though guided book reading continuously attracted more attention from Chinese teachers in the United States, little research on this topic has been done in classrooms where Chinese is an additional language. Specifically, Chinese language teachers' discursive strategies of conducting guided book reading across genres are still unexamined. To address this gap, this study focused on one Chinese language teacher by closely observing and examining her discursive behaviors of conducting guided book reading of two book genres: informational and narrative. Two research questions drive the current study:

1. What are the discursive strategies that the teacher employed when conducting guided book reading in Chinese classes?
2. To what extent do guided book reading strategies differ across the two different genres in this Chinese language classroom?

Methods

Research method

Case study research is a widely-used method of conducting research in the field of language education and applied linguistics (e.g., Duff et al., 2013). This method can "exemplify larger processes or situations in a very accessible, . . . personal manner" (Duff et al., 2013, p. 96). The case study method was used in this study based on the nature of research questions, the number of the participants involved, and the research context available to the researcher. Because "the focus of the study is the knowledge, performance, or perspectives of a single individual, such as a language learner or teacher" (Duff et al., 2013, p. 1), one third-grade Chinese teacher was recruited as a focal participant to observe her pedagogical strategies of conducting guided book reading across the two book genres with the hope of providing a rich description and analysis of her teaching strategies. As such, case study is a suitable method when the researcher has "little control over the phenomenon and context" (Yin, 2014, p. 13) but is there to observe. Given the nature of the research questions posed here, and for the purpose of triangulating the data-collection process, as well as after reviewing "prior development of theoretical propositions to guide data collection and analysis" (Yin, 2002, pp. 13–14), the researcher designed this case study with other data-collection methods including interviews, materials collection, classroom observation, and after-class debriefing. These were selected and deployed to document the Chinese teacher's discursive behavior when she was reading books with different genres during the guided book reading time.

Sites and participants

The current study was conducted in an urban school in Michigan with approval from the school's principal. The involved school is an authorized International Baccalaureate (IB) world school providing the Primary Years Program (PYP) in Chinese and Spanish. The Chinese PYP provides a 50/50 Chinese immersion education where Chinese language is not only a target language to be learned but also a medium of instruction. To ensure sufficient Chinese language input, more than 90% of Chinese instruction is required in classrooms. Wang Laoshi (the first name is a pseudonym, and the surname, "Laoshi," means "teacher" in Chinese), a third-grade teacher, and her 25 students participated in this study. She is a native Chinese speaker with a certificate to teach K-12 Chinese in the U.S. with an endorsement in elementary education. She received a bachelor's degree in English from a Chinese university and a master's degree in teaching and curriculum from an American university.

Wang Laoshi had taught in the school district for about eight years and was responsible for teaching Chinese language and mathematics (and did so with more than 90% of the instruction in Chinese). The Chinese curriculum (Better Chinese) was assigned by the school district. However, Wang Laoshi also used authentic Chinese children's books, for example, short stories (e.g., 小鸟和大树 *The Bird and the Tree*) and science introductions (e.g., 美丽的宇宙 *The Beautiful Universe*) as supplementary materials, and did guided book reading with her students. Most of her students had been enrolled in the program since preschool and had been learning Chinese for more than four years. According to the last M-STEP report, 71% of the focal class were identified as "over average" in reading. Her principal identified her as a "very effective" teacher.

Materials

Two books about mathematics knowledge were used for the guided book reading activity when the current research started. Both books were read during the small group instruction time in math classes. One book was a narrative book called 《买卖国的乘法队长》 (*Captain Multiplication of The Country of Business*), which tells a story involving how to do multiplication. It has 19 pages, each of which consists of a huge picture and a paragraph in Chinese. Each paragraph consists of five or six sentences. Another book was an informational book named 《数学星球》 (*Math Planet*), which introduces 37 mathematics concepts. Each page of the book also has one huge picture and a one-sentence introduction. Wang Laoshi read two to five pages every time when teaching certain math concepts and read the four pages about multiplication of this book during the period of this research.

Data collection and analysis

Two categories of data, spoken data and observational data, were collected through classroom observations, video recordings, and after-observation interviews. Consent to participate was obtained through a form emailed to Wang Laoshi. The forms were distributed, signed, and collected before the classroom observation. According to Wang Laoshi's schedule, she conducted a guided book reading three times a week for about 25 minutes each. Thus, the author went to the school to observe her class for two weeks in November 2017, took notes during the class time, and video recorded the classes. Altogether, there were about three hours of class visits and video recordings of the teachers' instruction of guided book reading in Chinese. After the classroom observation, the author interviewed Wang Laoshi and asked questions on her practice, pedagogical purpose, and rationale for using guided book reading. The interview took 34 minutes.

The video recording of classroom observations and audio recordings of the interview were transcribed verbatim and subsequently analyzed through thematic analysis (Saldana, 2015), including in vivo coding and open coding, in which essential segments of the scripts about discursive strategies in guided book reading were thematically coded with keywords or short phrases based on the research questions. In vivo coding, which refers to a practice that draws on participants' words or phrases as the themes, was used to analyze the interview. Therefore, results of this study can be explained through the "participant language, perspectives, and world views" (Saldana, 2015, p. 91).

As a consideration for credibility (Lincoln & Guba, 1985), open coding, which refers to developing substantial codes describing, naming, or classifying the phenomenon under consideration, was adopted to analyze the observational data. In this study, open coding means a coding process in which essential segments of the scripts during the book reading process will be coded with keywords or short phrases based on the research questions (e.g., connection, prediction, etc.), such as the frequency of Wang Laoshi's discursive episodes.

These formats of coding can avoid the concern that researchers select "data that fit [their] existing theory, goals, or preconceptions, and the selection of data that 'stand out' to the researcher" (Maxwell, 2012, p. 147) and are primarily used to generalize "categories taken from participants' own words and concepts"

(Maxwell, 2012, p. 121). As a consideration for validity, the coding was also sent to the participating teacher to ensure the interpretation of her words was accurately represented in the coding decisions (Ezzy, 2002). In addition, the coding and analysis were not discussed among the researcher and her colleagues when it was being processed.

Findings

Discursive strategies of conducting guided book reading

The first research question sought to examine which discursive strategies Wang Laoshi used when conducting guided book reading across different genres. To address this question, during the classroom observation, the researcher recorded each short episode of Wang Laoshi's discursive moves, such as her questions, feedback, explanations, and comments.

From the overall results, the data indicate that Wang Laoshi used four strategies that have been identified in previous research on guided book reading in English (e.g., Leech & Rowe, 2014): Connection, Prediction Questions, Test Questions, and Explanations. In addition, there is one type of utterance in which the teacher asked a question and next explained explicitly the cultural difference between China and the United States. Given the nature of foreign language teaching, this type of utterance was categorized as Comparison in this study.

Table 10.1 Examples of Wang Laoshi's Discursive Behavior in Shared Book Reading

Discursive behavior	Informational book 《数学星球》 *Math Planet*	Narrative book 《买卖国的乘法队长》 *Captain Multiplication of the Business Country*
Connection	你什么时候用乘法？(When would you use multiplication?)	你平时去哪里买东西？ (Where do you do grocery shopping usually?)
Prediction question	你觉得这本书是讲什么的？(What do you think the book is about?)	你觉得国王能不能想到好办法？你觉得国王会想到什么好办法 (Do you think the king can have a good idea? What kind of good idea he would have?)
Test question	"总和"是什么意思？(What is the meaning of sum?)	他想干什么？(What does he want to do?)
Explanation	法则，就是方法 (Law is method)	把你们放在一起，你们就是一组 (When I put you guys together, you are one group.)
Comparison	美国人要背九九乘法表吗？(Do Americans memorize the multiplication table?)	在中国，4或者5都没关系，但是在美国，组要放在前面。 (In China, it doesn't matter you place 4 or 5 [at the beginning of an equation]. But in the United States, you always put groups in the front)

Table 10.1 provided examples of each discursive behavior when reading the two book genres.

When reading both books, Wang Laoshi employed various discursive moves during different instructional episodes to assess students' reading comprehension, negotiate meaning of vocabulary, and encourage their higher-order thinking. To better describe those moves, two episodes are analyzed here to showcase how Wang Laoshi used different discursive strategies to interact with students. The first one is an episode of reading the first page of the informational book 《乘法星球》 *Multiplication Planet*; the second one is a moment of reading the narrative book 《买卖国的乘法队长》 *Captain Multiplication of the Business Country*. In the following analyses, four annotation conventions were used: Stress, <slow down>, [-] silence, and (author translation).

Episode 1: Reading the informational book 《数学星球》 **Math Planet**

The purposes of reading this book were to introduce 1) the background information for students to understand the concept of multiplication, and 2) the culture of learning mathematics in China, at the beginning of a unit. For this purpose, Wang Laoshi read four pages of *Multiplication Planet* to explain the definition of multiplication and how Chinese students learn multiplication through memorizing the multiplication table.

Episode 1:

Line	Speaker	Spoken Utterances	Strategy
1	Wang Laoshi	你们猜猜，这本书是讲什么的？ (Can you guess what this book is about?)	Predict Question
2	Ss		-
3	Wang Laoshi	我们来看第一幅画 (Let's see the first picture.)	
4		"乘法是关于增加的一种**运算法则**" (Multiplication is an operations of addition)	
5		你觉得这是讲什么的？ (What is it about?)	Test Question
6	Yuesi	乘法 (Multiplication)	
7	Wang Laoshi	你怎么知道 (How do you know that?)	Test Question
8	Yuesi		-
9	Wang Laoshi	<乘法>是 blablabla，所以我们在说乘法. (Multiplication is blablabla, so we are talking about multiplication.)	Explanation

In this episode, Wang Laoshi started the guided book reading activity by asking a predicting question ("Can you guess what this book is about?"), and then asked a test question ("What is it about?") to assess students' reading comprehension. After emphasizing the key vocabulary "是", she explained the sentence structure ". . . is . . ." to confirm students' understanding.

Episode 2: Reading the narrative book 《买卖国的乘法队长》
Captain Multiplication of the Business Country

The purpose of reading this book was to wrap up the lesson by assessing students' understanding of solving word problems. According to Wang Laoshi, her expectation was that students could use daily Chinese to comprehend and solve multiplication problems. Therefore, she focused on highlighting, teaching, and assessing several key words.

Episode 2:

Line Speaker Spoken Utterances Strategy

Line	Speaker	Spoken Utterances	Strategy
1	Wang Laoshi	他<一共>买了多少把香蕉？ (How many bunches of bananas did he buy?)	Test Question
2	Mingming	五 (5)	
3	Wang Laoshi	一把香蕉有几根？ (How many bananas are in one bunch？)	Test Question
4	Sisi	四 (4)	
5	Wang Laoshi	所以接下来他要做什么？ (So, what will he do next?)	Prediction Question
6	Ss	乘法 (multiplication)	
7	Wang Laoshi	你怎么知道？ (How do you know that?)	Test Question
8	Sisi	一共。 (Altogether.)	
9	Wang Laoshi	<一共！所以?> (Altogether！So?)	
10	Ss	四乘五/五乘四/ 20 . . . (4 times 5, 5 times 4, 20. . . . . .)	
11	Wang Laoshi	五乘四. 知不知道为什么？ (5 times 4, do you know why?)	Test Question
12	Liang Xiao	五大 (5 is bigger.)	
13	Yuesi	组，组在前面 (group, group should go first.)	
14	Wang Laoshi	非常好！记住，在中国，四或者五都没关系， Great! Remember, in China, it doesn't matter if you place 4 or 5 [at the beginning of an equation].	Comparison
15		但是在美国，<组>要放在前面。 (But in the United States, groups should go first.)	

In this episode, Wang Laoshi intentionally assessed students' understanding of the content, drew students' attention to mathematics problems in daily life, and discussed methods of solving word problems in simple language. She first asked test questions (e.g., "How many bunches of bananas did he buy?") to check students' comprehension of the text. Then she posed prediction questions (e.g., "What will he do next?") to guide students to guess the King's solution. After that, she provided an explanation to help students understand the principle of writing multiplication equations in the U.S and made a comparison ("In the U.S., you always put groups in the front").

Frequency of various discursive behaviors in reading books with different genres

The second research question sought to compare the details of what discursive behaviors Wang Laoshi used when she was conducting guided book readings across two genres. To address this research question, the researcher calculated the quantity of each strategy Wang Laoshi used when she was reading the picture book and the chapter book. The results show that Wang Laoshi's pattern of discursive behavior is an uneven distribution of attention among language learning, literacy development, and problem solving. Table 10.2 summarizes the frequency of different discursive strategy episodes.

Based on Table 10.2, Wang Laoshi asked more questions and made more connections when reading the narrative book. When reading the informational book, Wang Laoshi provided a number of explanations to engage students in discussing the meaning of certain vocabulary. She asked test questions mainly to assess students' reading comprehension. When reading the narrative book, she also asked test questions most frequently. However, the majority of the test questions were not reading comprehension questions. Instead, Wang Laoshi used the test questions to assess students' problem-solving skills verbalized in Chinese. She also made a great number of connections in the attempt to relate the book content to students' real lives so that she could engage students in discussing their experiences of using multiplication in the target language. From this perspective, Wang Laoshi's use of discursive strategies in conducting guided book reading varied from (narrative) genre to (informational) genre. Each strategy served its own teaching purposes.

Table 10.2 Episodes of Discursive Behaviors When Reading Different Book Genres

Discursive Behavior	Informational Book	Narrative Book
Connection	2	19
Prediction Questions	1	8
Test Questions	9	27
Explanations	11	12
Comparison	2	1
Total	26	67

The teacher's rationale for employing discursive strategies in guided book reading

The researcher interviewed Wang Laoshi after her guided book reading activities. To answer the researcher's question, "Did you prepare these questions in advance?" Wang Laoshi gave a positive answer and showed the questions she wrote on a sticky note and taped on the book she used. To answer the researcher's follow-up question, Wang Laoshi explained why she purposefully selected particular discursive behavior to fulfill specific pedagogical needs and goals. For Wang Laoshi, the purpose of choosing discursive strategies to conduct discussions with students was to help them improve their language output, literacy skills, and problem-solving skills when reading a narrative book. She demonstrated:

> . . . 乘法队长这本书里有很多我们之前反复学过的词、句子啊，所以我可以有很多机会带他们复习、练习已经学过的词和语法。 . . . 这样就是看他们，就是每个语言点都掌握，是不是都掌握了，能不能读，用中文表达出来，比如，遇到这个情况，我们要用乘法，为什么用乘法呢，因为有组啊，还有组员，讲的是东西变多了。就是用日常的语言来讨论事情，*problem-solving*。 (*. . . There is a lot of language recycling in the book Multiplication Captain. Thus, I have many opportunities to guide students to review and practice vocabulary and grammar that we have learned . . . . So, you can tell whether they have mastered each grammar points, whether they can read those books, use Chinese to express [their ideas]. For example, why should we use multiplication here? Because we can see groups, group members, and addition. Just let them use daily life Chinese to discuss problem-solving.*)

Compared to narrative books, Wang Laoshi believed that the purpose of reading informational books was mainly to support students' literacy skills, especially the ability to write in different genres, such as writing expository texts. She said:

> 那个数学星球的话其实主要是讲概念，各种不同的概念，用的词也比较难（*Author*：正式？）对，比较正式，很多他们没学过，我要解释。而且你也看到，它是比较短的，内容也少，确实也就不怎么好谈，就主要看能不能把句子读出来，理解了，知道以后写这些介绍性的文章可以用这样的句式。 (*The book Math Planet is all about concepts, different concepts with hard vocabulary [Author: formal language?]. Yes, formal, I need to explain these words since they have not learned them yet. You can see, it [the informational book] is short with less content. Indeed, it is hard to conduct a discussion. My primary expectation is that they can read the sentences, understand them, and know that they can use these sentences structures later if they need to write expository articles.*)

Discussion

The first purpose of this case study was to find out the pattern of a Chinese teacher's discursive behavior when she was conducting guided book reading in a classroom with Chinese as an additional language. Another purpose was to find out if she differentiated the strategies when employing them to read books in different genres. From the data, several trends were identified. The following are the strategies used by the students.

1. Similar strategies for various pedagogical purposes

The hypothesis before conducting this study was that the teacher would display different discursive behaviors when reading the books in different genres, because Wang Laoshi expressed her different pedagogical purposes when selecting and reading the two books. Previous studies have reported the challenge foreign language teachers have faced—how to balance language and content teaching—in subject-matter immersive classrooms. Wang Laoshi explained that she focused on language teaching when reading the narrative book because the language in that story is simple and made of high-frequency words. Yet, she aimed to teach concepts of multiplication when reading the informational book. To achieve the different teaching goals, Wang Laoshi had to use distinct moves to deliver different content. Meanwhile, the findings also indicated that she used similar discursive strategies when reading both the informational book and the narrative book.

By asking questions and making comments, Wang Laoshi made connections between students' lives and the texts. Specifically, she asked questions regarding the content of the book, did picture walks with students to predict the content of the two books, and compared some different cultural phenomena between China and the United States. Such moves she made echo the previous research findings (e.g., Leech & Rowe, 2014) that teachers ask particular types of questions (e.g., predict, text, connection, explanation) to engage students in reading processes when conducting shared book reading. This suggests that there might be a single reading strategy repertoire for teachers across different book genres.

The interview results indicate that Wang Laoshi understood the different characteristics of these two genres and purposefully selected similar strategies to prepare the students to reach the designated learning goals. As such, the same repertoire of discursive strategies could be used to deal with different genres in L2 guided reading. Even though the pedagogical goals may not be the same due to the genre differences, instructors can still make use of the same or similar strategies to teach reading.

2. More interaction when reading the narrative book

Results of this study showed that the participating teacher, Wang Laoshi, employed more discursive strategies, such as asking more questions when reading the narrative book 买卖国的乘法队长 *Captain Multiplication of the Business Country*. This finding resonates with the previous studies on adults' reading engagement with young learners during guided reading (e.g., Trionfi & Reese, 2009; Price et al., 2012; Robertson & Reese, 2015). Similar to Trionfi and Reese's study (2009), the current study found that, when reading narrative books, both the teacher and students were more engaged, consequently producing more teacher-student interaction. Moreover, this finding showed how Wang Laoshi managed language and content teaching through similar discursive strategies when reading different book genres.

She paid more attention to students' language production when reading the narrative book, as evidenced by asking more questions and providing more explanations. As a result, the students had more opportunities to use the target language to communicate with her. On the other hand, when reading the informational book, Wang Laoshi did not verbally communicate with students as much. Instead, she observed students' body language, such as nodding their heads during reading, to check whether students could understand the concepts. These examples indicate that similar discursive strategies were employed to fulfill different pedagogical purposes across both genres. In sum, Wang Laoshi interacted with students differently while reading two different genres because she wanted to fulfill different pedagogical purposes. The focus of reading the informational book was for concept teaching. As a result, when she saw students' body language indicating they thought they understood the concepts, she no longer engaged in further interactions.

3. Interplay of language and content teaching in shared book reading

Previous studies on content-based instruction have argued that a tension exists between language and content teaching and unveiled teachers' struggles when dealing with such a tension (e.g., Barwell, 2005; Swain, 2011). These studies have also identified the needs of classroom teachers who are managing this tension. Based on the findings, this study suggests that a single repertoire of discursive strategies may exist for different genres to create "a continuum [of] teaching foci" (Martínez & Dominguez, 2018) that support students' language and content development simultaneously. This repertoire is consistent with the SCT conceptualization that language and content learning is integrated and inseparable (e.g., Cammarata & Tedick, 2012; Snow, 2005). This study elaborates on this conceptualization by showcasing a nuanced example of a teacher's decision-making to foreground different aspects—Chinese language or math concepts—during guided reading in Chinese across two genres.

When reading the informational book (*Math Planet*), the teacher's discursive strategies were focused on teaching word meanings, grammar patterns, and reading strategies. In other words, the purpose of the discursive strategies was to support students' language and literacy learning, especially to help students move from informal to formal expression in Chinese writing.

Unlike in reading the informational book, the discursive strategies in reading the narrative book (*Captain Multiplication of the Business Country*) focused on language learning, assessing students' reading skills, and teaching them how to solve real-life problems in Chinese. In classrooms with Chinese as an additional language, teachers can construct opportunities through various discursive strategies for students to produce meaningful output and negotiate meaning in the target language for proficiency development. At the same time, they could also be strategic with methods of questioning in the target language in order to scaffold students' understanding of content and problem-solving skills.

Conclusion

Though research indicated that teachers' discursive behavior during guided book reading activities could influence students' development of language, literacy, and reader identities, little research has been done to examine guided book reading in foreign language classrooms, especially in classrooms with Chinese as an additional language. This study attempted to provide some empirical evidence to this field by carefully examining one Chinese-as-a-second-language teacher's discursive strategies in guided reading across two book genres. In general, the data collected reveals the teacher's plan, practice, and pedagogical decision-making when she was conducting guided book reading across book genres. More specifically, the findings first echo the finding from previous research on teacher's questioning that, when conducting shared book reading, teachers usually ask various questions to guide learners' prediction of the content, test their comprehension, and make connections between the texts and their real life.

The results also suggest that Wang Laoshi used a similar discursive strategy repertoire when reading two book genres. However, the frequency of various strategies used by the teacher differed according to her pedagogical purposes, which included supporting students' vocabulary learning, reading comprehension, and problem-solving. When conducting guided book reading, teachers use similar discursive strategies to prepare pathways to support students' development of language proficiency level, literacy skills, and problem-solving knowledge. Along with that repertoire, the quantity of each discursive strategy differs to serve various pedagogical goals. For example, more test questions were asked when reading the narrative book to assess students' literacy skills. Therefore, this study argues that there is one single repertoire of discursive strategies across different book genres. However, which strategy should be used depends on the teachers' pedagogical purpose during the guided reading of different books.

Applications and limitations

In this discussion, the researcher indicated that teachers could strategically employ various discursive strategies from the same repertoire to achieve their pedagogical goals by conducting guided book reading across two different writing genres: narrative and expository. Such findings have implications on foreign language teacher education and professional development. One significant implication is that, through proper training, teachers can be equipped with a repertoire of different discursive strategies for guided book reading in L2. They can be trained in the specific procedures on how to conduct guided readings (Pinnell & Fountas, 2010).

Proper teacher training includes explicit instruction on how to design strategies such as asking questions to check reading comprehension. With such training, teachers could better support students' language and literacy learning, as well as problem-solving development.

Several aspects of this study might be considered limitations, and directions for future research are noted. First, Becker (2010) asserted that, the longer the observation, the richer the data about specific situations. This study might not be able to provide that much data, as this is a short-term study. The study only observed one class four times and involved one classroom and one teacher. Thus, the data might not be rich enough for generalization. Although the sample sizes were small, as a case study, this study can serve to encourage future researchers to expand the ways guided book reading could be better implemented in classrooms with Chinese as an additional language. Secondly, this case study reported only the observation of the students' language and literacy development, yet no assessment was used to check students' uptake. Thus, future studies might employ mixed methods to link teachers' discursive strategies in guided book reading activities and students' actual language proficiency and content knowledge development, which would be an important addition.

References

Anderson, A., Anderson, J., Lynch, J., Shapiro, J., & Eun Kim, J. (2012). Extra-textual talk in shared book reading: A focus on questioning. *Early Child Development and Care*, *182*(9), 1139–1154. https://doi.org/10.1080/03004430.2011.602189

Bao, R., & Du, X. (2015). Learners' L1 use in a task-based classroom: Learning Chinese as a foreign language from a sociocultural perspective. *Journal of Language Teaching and Research*, *6*(1), 12–20. http://dx.doi.org/10.17507/jltr.0601.02

Barton, D., & Hamilton, M. (2000). Literacy practices. In D. Barton, M. Hamilton, & R. Ivanic (Eds.), *Situated literacies: Reading and writing in practice* (pp. 7–15). Routledge.

Barwell, R. (2005). Integrating language and content: Issues from the mathematics classroom. *Linguistics and Education*, *16*(2), 205–218. https://doi.org/10.1016/j.linged.2006.01.002

Becker, C. A. (2010). *An analysis of the quality and quantity of parent/child reading utterances while reading different genres*. http://hdl.handle.net/1903/10279

Blewitt, P., Rump, K. M., Shealy, S. E., & Cook, S. A. (2009). Shared book reading: When and how questions affect young children's word learning. *Journal of Educational Psychology*, *101*(2), 294. https://doi.org/10.1037/a0013844

Brown, H. D. (2002). *Strategies for success: A practical guide to learning English*. Addison Wesley Longman, Inc., a Pearson Education Company, Order Processing Center, PO box 11071, Des Moines, IA 50336.

Bus, A. G., Van Ijzendoorn, M. H., & Pellegrini, A. D. (1995). Joint book reading makes for success in learning to read: A meta-analysis on intergenerational transmission of literacy. *Review of Educational Research*, *65*(1), 1–21. https://doi.org/10.3102/00346543065001001

Cammarata, L., & Tedick, D. J. (2012). Balancing content and language in instruction: The experience of immersion teachers. *The Modern Language Journal*, *96*(2), 251–269. https://doi.org/10.1111/j.1540-4781.2012.01330.x

Cenoz, J., Genesee, F., & Gorter, D. (2014). Critical analysis of CLIL: Taking stock and looking forward. *Applied Linguistics*, *35*(3), 243–262. https://doi.org/10.1093/applin/amt011

Connor, C. M., Morrison, F. J., Schatschneider, C., Toste, J. R., Lundblom, E., Crowe, E. C., & Fishman, B. (2011). Effective classroom instruction: Implications of child characteristics by reading instruction interactions on first graders' word reading achievement. *Journal of Research on Educational Effectiveness*, *4*(3), 173–207. https://doi.org/10.1080/19345747.2010.510179

Dickinson, D. K., & Smith, M. W. (1994). Long-term effects of preschool teachers' book readings on low-income children's vocabulary and story comprehension. *Reading Research Quarterly*, 105–122. https://doi.org/10.2307/747807

Dickinson, D. K., & Snow, C. E. (1987). Interrelationships among prereading and oral language skills in kindergartners from two social classes. *Early Childhood Research Quarterly*, *2*(1), 1–25. https://doi.org/10.1016/0885-2006(87)90010-X

Dickinson, D. K., & Tabors, P. O. (1991). Early literacy: Linkages between home, school and literacy achievement at age five. *Journal of Research in Childhood Education*, *6*(1), 30–46. https://doi.org/10.1080/02568549109594820

Doyle, B. G., & Bramwell, W. (2006). Promoting emergent literacy and social—emotional learning through dialogic reading. *The Reading Teacher*, *59*(6), 554–564. https://doi.org/101598/RT.59.6.5

Duff, P., Anderson, T., Ilnyckyj, R., VanGaya, E., Wang, R., & Yates, E. (2013). *Learning Chinese: Linguistic, sociocultural, and narrative perspectives* (Vol. 5). Walter de Gruyter.

Elley, W. B. (1991). Acquiring literacy in a second language: The effect of book-based programs. *Language Learning*, *41*(3), 375–411. https://doi.org/10.1111/j.1467-1770.1991.tb00611.x

Ezzy, D. (2002). *Qualitative analysis*. Routledge.

Fisher, D., Frey, N., & Lapp, D. (2008). Shared readings: Modeling comprehension, vocabulary, text structures, and text features for older readers. *The Reading Teacher*, *61*(7), 548–556. https://doi.org/10.1598/RT.61.7.4

Ford, M. P., & Opitz, M. F. (2008). A national survey of guided reading practices: What we can learn from primary teachers. *Literacy Research and Instruction*, *47*(4), 309–331. https://doi.org/10.1080/19388070802332895

Gerde, H. K., & Powell, D. R. (2009). Teacher education, book-reading practices, and children's language growth across one year of Head Start. *Early Education and Development*, *20*(2), 211–237. https://doi.org/10.1080/10409280802595417

Goldenberg, C. (1992). Instructional conversations: Promoting comprehension through discussion. *The Reading Teacher*, *46*(4), 316–326. www.jstor.org/stable/20201075

Hindman, A. H., Connor, C. M., Jewkes, A. M., & Morrison, F. J. (2008). Untangling the effects of shared book reading: Multiple factors and their associations with preschool literacy outcomes. *Early Childhood Research Quarterly*, *23*(3), 330–350. https://doi.org/10.1016/j.ecresq.2008.01.005

Iaquinta, A. (2006). Guided reading: A research-based response to the challenges of early reading instruction. *Early Childhood Education Journal*, *33*(6), 413–418. https://doi.org/10.1007/s10643-006-0074-2

Kim, J. E., & Anderson, J. (2008). Mother—child shared reading with print and digital texts. *Journal of Early Childhood Literacy*, *8*(2), 213–245. https://doi.org/10.1177/1468798408091855

Korat, O., Shamir, A., & Heibal, S. (2013). Expanding the boundaries of shared book reading: E-books and printed books in parent—child reading as support for children's Language. *First Language, 33*(5), 504–523. https://doi.org/10.1177/0142723713503148

Leech, K. A., & Rowe, M. L. (2014). A comparison of preschool children's discussions with parents during picture book and chapter book reading. *First Language, 34*(3), 205–226. https://doi.org/10.1177/0142723714534220

Lever, R., & Sénéchal, M. (2011). Discussing stories: On how a dialogic reading intervention improves kindergartners' oral narrative construction. *Journal of Experimental Child Psychology, 108*(1), 1–24. https://doi.org/10.1016/j.jecp.2010.07.002

Lincoln, Y. S., & Guba, E. G. (1985). *Naturalistic inquiry*. Sage.

Martínez, J. M., & Dominguez, H. (2018). Navigating mathematics and language tensions in language immersion classrooms. *Teaching and Teacher Education, 75*, 1–9. https://doi.org/10.1016/j.tate.2018.05.013

Maxwell, J. A. (2012). *Qualitative research design: An interactive approach* (Vol. 41). Sage Publications.

Nyhout, A., & O'Neill, D. K. (2014). Storybooks aren't just for fun: Narrative and non-narrative picture books foster equal amounts of generic language during mother-toddler book sharing. *Frontiers in Psychology, 5*. https://doi.org/10.3389/fpsyg.2014.00325

Pinnell, G. S., & Fountas, I. C. (2010). *Research base for guided reading as an instructional approach*. Scholastic: Guided Reading Research.

Potter, J. (2013). Discursive psychology and discourse analysis. In J. P. Gee & M. Handford (Eds.), *The Routledge handbook of discourse analysis*. Taylor and Francis.

Price, L. H., Bradley, B. A., & Smith, J. M. (2012). A comparison of preschool teachers' talk during storybook and information book read-alouds. *Early Childhood Research Quarterly, 27*(3), 426–440. https://doi.org/10.1016/j.ecresq.2012.02.003

Ranker, J. (2009). Learning nonfiction in an ESL class: The interaction of situated practice and teacher scaffolding in a genre study. *The Reading Teacher, 62*(7), 580–589. https:/.doi.org/10.1598/RT.62.7.4

Robertson, S. J. L., & Reese, E. (2015). The very hungry caterpillar turned into a butterfly: Children's and parents' enjoyment of different book genres. *Journal of Early Childhood Literacy, 17*(1), 3–25. https://doi.org/10.1177/1468798415598354

Rogoff, B. (2003). *The cultural nature of human development*. Oxford University Press.

Saldana, J. M. (2015). *The coding manual for qualitative researchers* (3rd ed.). Sage Publications.

Snow, M. A. (2005). A model of academic literacy for integrated language and content instruction. In *Handbook of research in second language teaching and learning* (pp. 717–736). Routledge.

Stadler, M. A., & McEvoy, M. A. (2004). The effect of text genre on parent use of joint book reading strategies to promote phonological awareness. *Early Childhood Research Quarterly, 18*(4), 502–512. https://doi.org/10.1016/j.ecresq.2003.09.008

Swain, M. (2011). Integrating language and content in immersion classrooms: Research perspectives. *Research and Practice in Immersion Education*. doi:10.3138/cmlr.52.4.529

Tedick, D. J., & Cammarata, L. (2012). Content and language integration in K—12 contexts: Student outcomes, teacher practices, and stakeholder perspectives. *Foreign Language Annals, 45*(s1), s28–s53. https://doi.org/10.1111/j.1944-9720.2012.01178.x

Trionfi, G., & Reese, E. (2009). A good story: Children with imaginary companions create richer narratives. *Child Development, 80*(4), 1301–1313. https://doi.org/10.1111/j.1467-8624.2009.01333.x

Ukrainetz, T. A., Cooney, M. H., Dyer, S. K., Kysar, A. J., & Harris, T. J. (2000). An investigation into teaching phonemic awareness through shared reading and writing. *Early Childhood Research Quarterly*, *15*(3), 331–355. https://doi.org/10.1016/S0885-2006(00)00070-3

Vygotsky, L. (1978). Interaction between learning and development. *Readings on the Development of Children*, *23*(3), 34–41.

Wodak, R., & Meyer, M. (2009). Critical discourse analysis: History, agenda, theory, and methodology. In R. Wodak, & M. Meyer (Eds.), *Methods for critical discourse analysis* (pp. 1, 33). Sage.

Yin, R. K. (2002). *Applications of case study research*. Stage Publications.

Yin, R. K. (2014). *Case study research design and methods* (5th ed.). Sage. doi:10.3138/cjpe.30.1.108

Zucker, T. A., Justice, L. M., Piasta, S. B., & Kaderavek, J. N. (2010). Preschool teachers' literal and inferential questions and children's responses during whole-class shared reading. *Early Childhood Research Quarterly*, *25*(1), 65–83. https://doi.org/10.1016/j.ecresq.2009.07.001

11 Teaching modern Chinese literature to second-language Chinese students through the use of drama

Ziv W.N. Kan and Elizabeth K. Y. Loh

Background

There is an increasing demand for Chinese as an additional language (CAL) instruction in Hong Kong due to the rapidly growing ethnic minority (EM) population in the past decade. After the handover in 1997, the Hong Kong Special Administrative Region (HKSAR) government introduced the "Biliteracy and Trilingualism" policy (Hong Kong SAR Government, 1999). Students have to obtain both English and Chinese qualifications for undergraduate admissions and job applications.

However, the Chinese language has long been considered a very difficult language to learn, particularly to L2 students with alphabetic language background (e.g., Leong et al., 2019; Loh & Tam, 2016; Shum et al., 2012). Chinese proficiency has become one of the factors hindering EM students' academic and career advancement. The HKSAR government spends about 300 million HK dollars per year to support their Chinese language learning, yet the students are still found to be left behind by their native Chinese-speaking peers in academic performance (Equal Opportunity Commission, 2020a, 2020b; Hong Kong Legislative Council, 2018). Hence, the number of EM students receiving tertiary education remains low (Equal Opportunity Commission, 2020a, 2020b).

Because of this, EM parents are increasingly sending their children to local schools for better social integration and advancement of proficiency in the Chinese language. The HKSAR government has also revised several policies, including the cancellation of the designated school policy in 2014, as well as increasing the number of local school places for EM students through the Secondary School Places Allocation (SSPA) System. As of the academic year 2019/2020, EM students have spread out to more than 200 primary schools and 200 secondary schools, as most of these schools admitted fewer than 10 EM students across different grade levels. How to improve the language proficiency of Hong Kong CAL students is a heated issue that has attracted much attention from the educational field as well as the public.

DOI: 10.4324/9781003029038-15

The teaching and learning of Chinese as an additional language in Hong Kong

Most of the local schools in HK offer a mainstream Chinese language curriculum focusing on native Chinese-speaking students. Although the Hong Kong Education Bureau (EDB) has provided teachers with guidelines on developing school-based Chinese language curricula (2008, 2019) for CAL students, teachers still find the task challenging due to the lack of suitable teaching materials and effective pedagogy that cater to their students' learning diversity (Equal Opportunity Commission, 2020a; Tsang et al., 2012; Tse et al., 2012). At the same time, CAL students also find it difficult to learn the language, since an understanding of the learning materials depends on the cultural contexts. Particularly, some students find learning CAL a laborious and painful experience (Loh et al., 2019), with reading as one of the most challenging tasks. Reading requires students to decode the texts, as well as to comprehend the cultural context of the learning materials. Struggling with their learning, many CAL students perform poorly. Their learning motivation is low, and they show little interest in classroom activities, or even give up their study (Loh & Tam, 2016; Loh, Tam et al., 2019; Tsang et al., 2012; Tse et al., 2012). Their low CAL proficiency makes it difficult to compete with their Chinese-speaking peers.

In light of this, EDB (2016) accepted some international examinations as alternate qualifications to replace the Chinese examination in the Hong Kong Diploma of Secondary Education Examination (HKDSE), so that CAL students could fulfill the minimum application requirements for university programs. Those international examination qualifications include the General Certificate of Secondary Education (GCSE), International General Certificate of Secondary Education (IGCSE), and General Certificate of Education (GCE).

Among all these international public examinations, the GCE A-Level has been drawing increasing attention as it is considered a more advanced and suitable curriculum for high-achieving CAL students. A new syllabus of GCE A-Level introduced in 2017 made reading literacy texts a compulsory unit for all candidates. This is in contrast to other curricula such as GCSE or IGCSE levels, where teaching literary texts to students is not a focus.

In the GCE A-Level syllabus, learners' literacy understanding and text comprehension are assessed through writing. They are allowed to choose one work among the selected three pieces of set literary texts or three films; then they analyze and compose a 225- to 300-word essay on their chosen text in a given timeframe to demonstrate their critical thinking and language accuracy. More specifically, in order to reach the highest band on the test, students should demonstrate the following qualities in the essay:

- Responses throughout that are relevant to the question;
- Points of view demonstrating their critical thinking on the question through coherent argumentation, with the appropriate evidence from the text;
- Arguments that lead to a valid conclusion.

(Edexcel, 2017, p. 16)

Text reading of literature works is not a new domain in GCE A-Level curriculum. It was previously offered as an optional module for students who wanted to produce a research-based essay on literary texts. *Old memories of Peking* (城南舊事), authored by Lin Hai-yin in 1957, was one of the several literary texts students could choose from in the former syllabus, and subsequently became the only constant option offered in both the old syllabus and the new syllabus introduced in 2017. Students were required to study two chapters of the book: "Hui-an Hostel" (惠安館) and "Papa's Flowers Have Fallen" (爸爸的花兒落了). This study focuses on the latter one.

The GCE A-Level Chinese language examination is designed to assess L2 students' mastery of Chinese literary reading. Students need to first comprehend the literary texts, and then write their personal opinions from an analytical perspective by drawing on evidence from the texts. There is an urgent need to enhance CAL students' Chinese language proficiency and cultural knowledge in order to pass this examination (Loh & Tam, 2016).

Previous studies indicated that applying drama conventions in L2 lessons have positive impacts on students' learning performance (e.g., Chang, 2012; Chang & Winston, 2012; Kilinc et al., 2017; Loh, Woo et al., 2019). By taking part in drama activities, L2 students can easily engage in literary reading, since it involves both cognitive and affective domains of learning. As proposed by the *Reader-response Theory* and *Situational Model*, drama conventions help the readers to visualize the episode depicted in the literature, elicit their emotional reaction, and facilitate their interpretation of the texts, all of which lead to a deeper understanding of the reading. This study therefore attempts to find out the impact of drama conventions on learning to read Chinese texts among CAL students.

Literature review

Cognition or affection? We take both

Research used to focus on cognitive aspects of learners until there was increasing evidence showing that affective factors, such as self-efficacy and learning motivation, could regulate the learners' interest in language learning, persistence, and learning behaviors (Hidi & Anderson, 1992). Successful L2 learning should take emotion as a core component of cognition. Therefore, the cognitive and affective processes in L2 learning are inextricably interconnected and should not be separated (Swain, 2013). Hidi (1990), using the learning of reading as an example, pointed out that reading comprehension takes place only when the readers enjoy and engage in reading, particularly when they find that the information being processed is interesting. They tend to show better concentration and longer persistence of reading time, and to acquire more knowledge when compared with those reading materials they find uninteresting.

However, L2 learners may not have the freedom to decide what to learn at school, as the curriculum is pre-set by the regional curriculum guide and the school (Loh, 2019). Hong Kong CAL students were found to be three years behind their native Chinese-speaking peers (Tse & Loh, 2014). It is because they are emotionally disengaged that they are cognitively having difficulty in learning to read in Chinese (Loh & Tam, 2016; Loh, Woo et al., 2019; Tsang et al., 2012; Tse et al., 2012). This situation has motivated educators and researchers to find suitable pedagogies to reboot students' learning interest and motivation. Furthermore, reading interests are personal. It is a challenge for teachers to cater to each student's learning needs. Thus, teachers need pedagogies that can strike a balance between the knowledge to be delivered and their students' interests, in order to develop students' autonomy and critical thinking (Dewey, 1902) and advance their L2 proficiency.

Drama in second language education

According to the input hypothesis (Krashen, 1985, 1989), when learners are exposed to language input that is comprehensible for them, acquisition can occur, and meaningful output can be produced (output hypothesis) (Krashen, 1981, 2003). It is more efficient and long-lasting when students are immersed in a natural learning environment with comprehensible input. Based on Krashen's hypotheses, Long (1985, 1996) further developed the interaction hypothesis. It states that learners can acquire a language through numerous language exchange activities in a natural language environment. Other scholars like Bernstein (see Stinson & Winston, 2014, p. 1) stressed the interaction of the readers and the reading materials in language acquisition; i.e., students should form bonds with cultural contexts of the texts and their own social experience (Vygotsky, 1978). If learners can be motivated and engaged in the reading process, language acquisition can take place more readily.

Drama conventions (also known as drama in education pedagogy) work well with the Second Language Acquisition (SLA) theories as language is the cornerstone of drama (O'Neil & Lamber, 1990, p. 4), and the reading context is an important drama element (O'Toole, 1992). Empirical studies using drama conventions in teaching English as L1 or L2 found that this pedagogy has a significantly positive impact on students' learning (e.g., Bolton, 1984; Heathcote, 1980; Needlands, 1992; O'Neill, 1983; Winston, 2012). It is also found to be effective in teaching Chinese and Chinese literature to native Chinese-speaking students from different age groups with various levels of language proficiency to acquire reading and writing skills.

The advantages of using drama conventions are obvious. As students have a general preference for participating in classroom drama activities because their emotions toward different characters are elicited easily, they are willing to study the texts repeatedly with great care, helping each other find the clues from the texts to infer characters' personalities and relationships. They also show a better understanding of how the cultural context affects the characters and even critique the characters' behaviors by producing meaningful written outputs (Liu, 2010; Ho, 2011; Loh, 2017; Loh, Woo et al., 2019). More importantly, participating in drama activities allows students to immerse in an authentic language environment. Thus, their learning efficiency and motivation increase significantly.

Teaching modern Chinese literature to second-language students 221

Situational Model Theory and drama conventions

The positive results on students' reading performance and learning behaviors when they are participating in drama activities (Ho, 2011; Loh, 2017; Loh, Woo et al., 2019) can be explained by the Situational Model Theory and Reader-response Theory. The Situational Model Theory suggests that good readers can construct their mental representations of what they are reading (Johnson-Laird, 1983; van Dijk & Kintsch, 1983) and build up a coherent situation model gradually through various dimensions being described in the narrative texts, including time and space, along with the characters' personalities, relationships, and tensions (Zwaan et al., 1995). This reading process will enhance their comprehension of the texts to a higher-level mental and cognitive processing (Bestgen & Dupont, 2003; Noordman & Vonk, 1998) through integrating the underlying semantic meaning structures (Kintsch, 1988).

The reading process of the Situational Model Theory is as follows: (1) activating the mental stimulation of the text's perceptual and motoric elements of scenario (de Koning & van der Schoot, 2013; Fischer & Zwaan, 2008; Glenberg, 2007; Yaxley & Zwaan, 2007) and establishing various multisensory situation blocks to derive meaning; (2) drawing upon prior knowledge and text clues to fill the information gaps by inference generation and integration to complete and make cohesive the descriptions of narrative situations (Cain & Oakhill, 2007; van den Broek & Espin, 2012); (3) updating the mental stimulation with the new information coming in while maintaining the overall coherence with existing information through the comprehension monitoring process (van der Schoot et al., 2012). The more the readers engage in the monitoring processes, the greater the chance they attain a deep understanding of the text with better memorization of the acquired knowledge (Wassenburg, 2016).

When this theory is applied in the teaching of reading, teachers need to guide their students to identify and retrieve key information from the texts, establish and update their perceptual stimulation and situation model with the new information, and construct their individual comprehension of the texts. Students can thus have a better understanding of the texts, particularly the situation of various characters (van Dijk & Kintsch, 1983), and gradually form their empathy with deep affection for the characters. Taking *reader's theater* as an example (one of the drama conventions requires students to read the text aloud with appropriate circumflex to express the emotions), the students will naturally construct their situation model in the reading process, imagine the described scenario, and construct various mental representations such as mental image, visual imagination, causality, and emotions (Bestgen & Dupont, 2003; Johnson-Laird, 1983; Noordman & Vonk, 1998; van Dijk & Kintsch, 1983; Law, 1997).

Reader-response Theory and drama conventions

Drama conventions also align with Reader-response Theory (Iser, 1978; Rosenblatt, 1968), which emphasizes combining the cognitive and affective elements of the text and giving them personal meaning. The theory hypothesizes that interaction and mutual relationship between reader and the text within a particular language context can lead to a deeper understanding of a literary work. Readers play multiple roles when responding to the text, whereas the developing process increases intellectual and emotional participation in the text and facilitates meaningful reading. This in turn provides readers with better comprehension and awareness of what they have read.

When this theory is applied in daily classroom teaching, teachers need to nourish their perspectives to deepen their interpretation, verify their opinions, provide students the opportunities to express their emotional reactions, and construct their responses for building a social relationship with the text (Mart, 2019; Spirovska, 2019). Drama conventions may help students to perform more adequate responses to the texts, actively engage in dialogues to pose literal and inferential questions, initiatively explore a range of possible meanings, foster cognitive development with more in-depth comprehension, appreciate the artistic value of literature (Berk & Winsler, 1995, p. 36; Loh, 2015), and promote the sublimation of moral value (Ho, 2011). Drama conventions can also help the students overcome learning difficulties, while unconsciously mastering the context and learning the language (Loh, Woo et al., 2019).

After the completion of the drama activities, students can have a thorough comprehension of the text. Students' emotional responses and new insights into the text will stimulate their writing motivation and generate writing ideas (Chang, 2012, pp. 10–11), which help to reduce their writing anxiety. Teachers can conclude and further comment on their performance, as well as to assign in-role writing tasks to further extend and consolidate their learning outcomes. For students with low L2 proficiency, drama activities allow them to present their ideas with their facial expressions and body gestures. They can then write down their thoughts and feelings and make it a complete article. Writing is no longer a chore (Loh, Woo et al., 2019).

In short, drama activities were found to help CAL students in the following ways. First, students were found to be more engaged in reading tasks and were able to overcome reading difficulties subconsciously. Second, the activities could also stimulate their imagination to build up their own perceptual situation model. They could "feel" and appreciate the texts when they understood the text both cognitively and emotionally. Third, students were more willing to use the target language for communication and emotional expression in drama activities. These previous findings suggest that drama activities can potentially foster a space and time for CAL students to learn in a desirable language environment.

The present study aims to further investigate a topic that has not been fully investigated before: how well drama conventions can help CAL learners to learn to read modern Chinese literature of the GCE A-Level examination. It is hypothesized that the students would have a better understanding of the literature and be able to critically reflect on their reading.

Research questions

This chapter aims to address the following research questions:

1. Does the application of drama conventions in class help draw more CAL students' attention to the details of the selected Chinese literature text?
2. Does the application of drama conventions in class promote CAL students' in-depth understanding of the selected Chinese literature texts?
3. Does the application of drama conventions in class enhance CAL students' critical thinking skills toward the learning of the selected Chinese literature texts?

Research methodology

Research participants

Background of the participating school

Research participants came from a secondary school in Hong Kong offering both CAL and mainstream Chinese language curricula. The school assigned the students to different classes based on their Chinese proficiency.

Students studying mainstream Chinese language curriculum would sit for the HKDSE in Grade 12 (N=20), while those studying CAL curriculum would sit for IGCSE in Grade 9 and then GCE examination in Grade 12 (N=8). The major challenge for the CAL students was the switch of instructional language and script from Cantonese and traditional Chinese characters used in their primary schooling to Mandarin and Simplified Chinese characters used in the secondary school where this case study was conducted. These CAL students felt confused and frustrated because their prior knowledge of Chinese language seemed unhelpful to their secondary education. The CAL students were observed to have low learning motivation, lack of self-confidence, and could not engage in CAL lessons. Their CAL proficiency was low, and learning Chinese became laborious and painful (please refer to Loh, Tam et al., 2019 for more details).

The eight participants in this study all received grade C or above in their IGCSE Chinese. They were able to read 500-word articles and write 300-word essays that covered material in the previous lessons. Except for three students who had studied under the mainstream curriculum till Grade 8 and Grade 10, most of the participants had no experience of learning Chinese literature throughout their CAL curriculum.

In order to teach the CAL students more effectively, the school assigned the CAL students to different classes based on their Chinese proficiency. Only eight students chose to sit for the GCE Chinese examination as one of their subject choices in the school. They were assigned to the same class. Since the setting and examination criteria are different between DSE and GCE, the comparison between these two groups would be hard to interpret. Therefore, it makes more sense to focus on the CAL students exclusively as a case study. Moreover, these CAL students voluntarily chose the GCE Chinese curriculum. An in-depth case study like this would reveal the motivation behind their choice.

The participants of this study include: (1) a class of CAL students, and (2) their Chinese language teacher, who is one of the researchers of this study.

CAL students

A class of eight secondary Grade 12 students who enrolled in a GCE Chinese language class in a secondary school in Hong Kong participated in this study. Their ethnicities included Indian, Pakistani, Malaysian, as well as Malaysian-Chinese. The participants were between 14 and 16 years old, with three boys and five girls (see Table 11.1 for the details of their background).

Six of them had studied CAL since primary school and they all passed IGCSE CAL examination with Grade C or above. Two participants studied mainstream Chinese language curriculum in their primary school years till Grade 11. These two students said that they had studied the chosen literature in Grade 8, but they said their teacher spent only two days teaching the text and they did not fully understand the plot of the text.

CAL teacher

The teacher had been teaching CAL for ten years at the participating school. He had a bachelor's degree in L1 Chinese language education, and a master's degree in teaching CAL. He was also studying for a doctoral degree specializing in effective CAL pedagogy for the teaching of Chinese grammar. He had no prior training on drama conventions in second language education before this study.

Table 11.1 Participants' Background Information

Participant	Ethnicity	Gender	Experience of learning CAL
A	Indian	M	Mainstream Chinese language curriculum until Grade 8
B	Pakistani	M	Mainstream Chinese language curriculum until Grade 10
C	Malaysian	F	CAL curriculum for 10 years
D	Malaysian Chinese	F	Mainstream Chinese language curriculum until Grade 10
E	Indian	F	CAL curriculum for 10 years
F	Pakistani	M	CAL curriculum for 10 years
G	Malaysian Chinese	F	CAL curriculum for 10 years
H	Indian	F	CAL curriculum for 10 years

Design: case study and action research

Single-case design was adopted in this study to investigate how well drama conventions can help to enhance CAL students' comprehension of reading modern Chinese literature and their critical reflection on what they have read within the real-life classroom context. A class of secondary school students with intermediate CAL proficiency were recruited. Multiple sources of research evidence were collected for an in-depth investigation of the hypotheses (Levy, 2008).

The present study also adopted action research to diagnose the problems of CAL teaching and learning in a mainstream secondary school in Hong Kong. The aim was to help educators develop practical solutions to address the issues quickly and efficiently. The researchers hope that the findings of the present study can create a simple, practical, repeatable process of teaching steps that lead to better learning outcomes for students, and that this process can be applied to daily CAL classroom teaching, particularly for less experienced CAL teachers.

Six cycles of the teaching intervention were conducted, and six drama conventions were examined. The whole intervention process lasted for two weeks, with 14 55-minute lessons. The teacher, who was also one of the researchers in this study, reflected on his own teaching performance after each cycle and revised the teaching designs of the following teaching cycles for better progress.

Research instruments

Teacher's teaching log

The teacher wrote teaching logs to reflect on the drama activities in the class. The logs were used to evaluate the effectiveness of the drama conventions, analyze students' learning behaviors in class, and examine the teacher's own professional development throughout the entire intervention process.

Semi-structured interview

The researchers conducted a semi-structured interview with each student after the completion of the action research. The student interviews included a set of questions about the impact of drama conventions on their comprehension of literary texts, as well as the impact on their learning motivation. To reduce the anxiety of the student and to collect more in-depth information, some warm-up questions were prepared for icebreaking. The researchers did not strictly follow a formal list of questions, but asked more open-ended queries, allowing for a discussion with the interviewee, rather than following a straightforward question-and-answer format.

The interview lasted for approximately 30 minutes. The CAL student with the greatest behavioral changes in the class was selected for a 30-minute interview. He was a 16-year-old Pakistani male student who had been living in Hong Kong since he was three years old. He had been following the mainstream Chinese language curriculum with his native Chinese-speaking peers since kindergarten till the age of 15. He received Grade C in IGCSE CAL examination before enrolling in this GCE class.

Students' assignments

Students' assignments (written works and in-role speeches) were collected by the researchers upon completion of the drama activities for in-depth text analysis. Their works were evaluated with reference to the GCE marking criteria to assess their critical thinking ability and how well they had met the examination standards in analyzing the text.

Lesson design

"Papa's Flowers Fell (爸爸的花兒落了)" is the final story of the *Memories of Peking: South Side Stories* (Lin, 2002 [1960]). It is about the author's life in Beijing in the 1950s and contains 3,447 words. The text was divided into six parts by the teacher based on the story scene-setting as well as its timeline, and was taught over two weeks. Each part covered a piece of the text, a short reading comprehension exercise, and one class drama activity.

Based on the content of this narrative text, six drama conventions were used and examined. They included:

(1) Thought tracking. Students assumed they were one of the assigned characters, stopping their action in one of the most important scenes, sharing thoughts and telling how they felt. The purpose was to lead the students to explore the characters and scenes of what they had read in greater depth, enabling them to better understand how the character is thinking or feeling at any given moment. If they said something different from what the text described, they needed to explain their thoughts. The explanation and discussion helped students to discover the many layers of meaning within a scene.
(2) Reader's theater. Students were required to read orally through parts in the text, mainly the selected dialogues. They needed to use the most appropriate tones to express the emotions of the characters in groups and took turns to reread the scripts several times. Through this activity, they subconsciously analyzed all the details of the text, making inferences about the relationships and the emotions of the characters. By reading aloud in class, the students also enhanced the fluency of their speaking and self-confidence.
(3) Still image. Students were required to produce still static images, like frozen pictures. Still image is an explorative strategy that helps students to gain a deeper understanding of the characters and to explore the selected scenes. The still images also show the relationships, interactions, and emotions among the characters.
(4) In-role speech. Students were asked to write a speech from a character's perspective and then deliver it to the whole class. This technique was used as

a reflective tool and performance-based assessment, guiding the students to make inferences about a character's motivation, opinions, and hidden feelings, or to predict what might happen next in a dramatic problem based on what they had read from the text.

(5) Role play. Students role-played the selected characters in a scenario described in the text. Through these activities, target functional language for effective communications as required by the GCE examination could be activated and practiced through their participation in an authentic language environment. Their communication skills and self confidence in using CAL could also be enhanced.

(6) In-role writing. Students were required to put themselves into the characters' shoes. Specifically, they needed to make effective use of the context to produce a diary of Ying Zi on what she saw and experienced after she arrived in a hospital and found her father had passed away.

The rationale for the selection of drama conventions is explained in Table 11.2:

Table 11.2 Summary of the Lesson Designs

Text	Summary of the Plot	Drama Convention(s)	Duration (55 mins./lesson)
"新建的大堂裏，坐滿了人" to "我真的被選中做這件事"	Ying Zi (英子) is in the graduation ceremony of her primary school. She receives the diploma as the representative of the whole year group and gives a vote of thanks. However, her father was unable to attend the ceremony due to his illness.	(1) Thought tracking: Students were required to imagine how they would feel if they were Ying Zi and her father was not able to attend her graduation ceremony. Teaching objectives: Empathize with the character Ying Zi to understand her feelings when she found her father was not able to attend her graduation ceremony.	1 lesson
"爸爸啞着嗓子" to "我何曾遲到過"	A day before the graduation ceremony, Ying Zi was visiting her father in the hospital. Ying Zi wanted her father to come but her father could not do so. Moreover, he decided not to disclose his health condition to Ying Zi.	(2) Reader's theater: Students were required to use the reader's theater strategy and to read aloud the conversation between Ying Zi and her father with suitable intonations. Teaching objectives: To understand the tension between Ying Zi and her father because her father was unable to attend the graduation ceremony.	1 lesson

(*Continued*)

Table 11.2 (Continued)

Text	Summary of the Plot	Drama Convention(s)	Duration (55 mins./lesson)
"當我在一年級的時候" to "送給親愛的韓老師，她教我跳舞"	A memory flashes back to the time when Ying Zi was still a Grade 1 student. She refused to get up to go to school. Her father forced her to go back to school by physically disciplining her.	(3) Still image: Students were divided into four groups. They were required to take four photos to recreate the scene of Ying Zi being disciplined by her father and combine them into a short comic story. Furthermore, they had to write captions for each picture to describe the scenarios. Students then presented their work in the class. The whole class read the work of each group and provided feedback for improvement. Teaching objectives: To help students understand the plot that Ying Zi got punished by her father through visualizing the scene.	3 lessons
"啊, 這樣的早晨" to "老師, 你要永遠拿我當孩子呀!"	During the graduation ceremony, Ying Zi had a flashback of memory on how her father watered the flowers with his children.	(4) In-role speech: Students were required to play the role of Ying Zi. They needed to write a speech for the graduation ceremony and then read aloud to the whole class. Teaching objectives: Empathize with Ying Zi; use the information collected from previous parts of the text to create an appropriate speech and deliver it as if they were Ying Zi.	2 lessons
"做大人，常常有人要我做大人" to "並且要他明天在花池裏也種滿蒲公英"	Another flashback of memory on how Ying Zi's father asked her to go to the bank alone to transfer money to an uncle in Japan. It was a challenging task in her life as she had to do this alone at a young age.	(5) Role play: Each student was required to assume a role: either Ying Zi or the bank teller, and role play the whole scenario in class. Teaching objectives: Empathize with the character of Ying Zi and understand how she felt after she completed the task assigned by her father.	1 lesson

Teaching modern Chinese literature to second-language students 229

Text	Summary of the Plot	Drama Convention(s)	Duration (55 mins./lesson)
"快回家去" to "我也不再是小孩子了"	Ying Zi returned home after her graduation ceremony. She received the news that her father had just passed away. She felt that she had grown up and had the responsibility to take care of the family.	(6) In-role writing: Students were required to see the world from Ying Zi's eyes. They needed to write a diary of what she saw and felt after she arrived at the hospital and witnessed her father dying. Teaching objectives: Students use the information in the previous parts of the text to make inferences and add reasonable imagination. Then they write a diary, pretending they were Ying Zi on the day her father passed away. This way, students would feel the character's emotion better.	2 lessons

Results and findings

The results found in this study provide positive answers to the three research questions we raised: 1) students paid more attention to the details of the text; 2) students had in-depth understanding of the literary text; and 3) students improved their critical thinking skills.

1) Students paid more attention to the details of the text

Drama convention

Throughout the intervention process, students showed greater awareness of the text's details, particularly while preparing for and after participating in various drama activities.

Drama activity 3's "still image" is an example. Students were grouped into four small groups and took four pictures to create a four-frame comic story illustrating how Ying Zi was disciplined by her father. The scenario is: Ying Zi's father ordered her to get up from the bed, but she refused to listen. He then dragged her out of the bed, took up the whip and beat her.

Although the four groups had created similar photos, they selected different perspectives to restate the scenario. The written descriptions of their photos (see Table 11.3), as well as the questions they raised in the peer evaluation activity, both showed they had dug deep into the details and clearly understood the plot, since the students could use the most important information to create comics.

Table 11.3 Summary of Students' Still Image Captions

Group	Students' Written Scripts			
	Picture 1	Picture 2	Picture 3	Picture 4
Group 1 (Student B and Student G) (See Appendix 11.1 for the comic)	Father asked Ying Zi to get up from the bed. Father said, "Get up!" (爸爸叫英子「快起!」爸爸:「起身!」)	Ying Zi did not get up. Her father asked, "Why don't you get up from the bed? Hurry up!" (英子沒有起床，爸爸就叫:「怎麼還不起來？快起!」)	Her father grabbed a whip and counted, "1, 2, 3!" (爸爸拿了雞毛撢子。爸爸:「一!二!三!」)	Ying Zi got beaten by her father and exclaimed, "It hurts!" (英子被爸爸打。英子:「很痛呀!」)
Group 2 (Student A and Student D) (See Appendix 11.2 for the comic)	Ying Zi said, "Father, it's late now." (「晚了!爸!」)	Father said, "You have to go to school even if it is late. How could you play hooky from school?" (「晚了也得去，怎麼可以逃學!」)	The whip flipped in the air. (藤鞭子在空中一掄。)	The whip made the cracked sounds and I was beaten!) (就發出咻咻的聲音，我挨打了!)
Group 3 (Student F and Student C) See Appendix 11.3 for the comic	Father said, "How could you still lay in bed? Get up! Get up!" (「怎麼還不起來？快起!快起!」)	Father was so fierce, he dragged me out of the bed. (爸爸氣極了，一把我從床上拖起來。)	The whip made the cracked sounds. (就發出咻咻的聲音。)	I was beaten! (我挨打了!)
Group 4 (Student E and Student H) See Appendix 11.4 for the comic	Father came to Ying Zi's bed and stared at her. (站在床前來瞪着英子。)	Father dragged Ying Zi out of the bed. (一把把英子從床上拖起來。)	Father looked around and grabbed a whip. (爸左看右看，結果從桌上抄起雞毛撢子倒轉來拿。)	He hit Ying Zi. She cried, "Ah!!!" (他打英子。英子:「啊!!!」)

Students put their still images on the whiteboard of the classroom, then were asked to look at the others' works closely and write down the questions about the contradictions between what was written in the text and what their peers captured in the still images on the whiteboard.

Some students raised questions that the images failed to capture some details in the text, like, "Why did not Ying Zi cry?" (為什麼英子沒有哭？) and, "Why Ying Zi was not lying down?" (為什麼英子沒有躺下？).

One of the students asked, "Why was the father hitting Ying Zi's head?" (為什麼爸爸打英子的頭？) She further explained that, according to the text, Ying Zi was checking on her wounds on her limbs. So, she thought her peers did not draw the still image accurately, because the father might have not hit Ying Zi's head.

2) Students had an in-depth understanding of the literary text

Critical and analytical response is one of the criteria being assessed when candidates produce a written work in the exam. In order to achieve this, the marking criteria suggests that students should demonstrate the following skills: (1) select relevant material, (2) present and justify points of view, (3) develop arguments, (4) draw conclusions based on understanding, and (5) evaluate issues, themes, and cultural and social contexts.

Students should have in-depth understanding of the texts in order to select relevant material, as well as to draw conclusions based on their understanding.

Findings from the drama convention

In this study, it was found that the students also showed a better understanding of the literary work after taking part in various drama activities. This was demonstrated in the "in-role speech" after they read Part 4 of the text. The activity required them to pretend they were Ying Zi, who wrote a vote of thanks speech and delivered it to their peers at the graduation ceremony. This vote of thanks was not provided by the text, so the students needed to write one on their own.

Four out of the eight students mentioned in their vote of thanks speeches that her father was not able to attend the graduation ceremony. The following were directly quoted from their written work:

STUDENT C: "I want to dedicate this time to my father, although he is not here today. I know he is proud of me." (我想把這個時間奉獻給我的爸爸，因為他今天不能來這裡。即使他不在這裡，我知道他為我感到驕傲。)

STUDENT D: "Last but not least, I would like to thank my father, although he could not be here today." (最後我想感謝今天不能夠在這裡的父親。)

STUDENT E: "The reason why I can stand here and share my feelings at this graduation ceremony is all because of my father. He is not here today, but I will still try my best." (今天我站在這裡分享是因為爸爸得鼓勵，雖然他今天不在這裡，但是我會努力。)

STUDENT G: "Finally, I would like to thank my father. Although he is not here today, without his support I would not be able come on stage to share with you." (最後，我就係要感謝我嘅爸爸，雖然佢今日唔喺度，但係如果無咗佢我唔會而家在台上同你哋分享。)

Although it was not specified in the text, the students were aware that Ying Zi's father was not able to attend her graduation ceremony due to his sickness (see the quotations of students' written scripts attached). From the last two excerpts, they showed that they still remembered that Ying Zi's father encouraged her to study hard so that she could represent her peers to deliver the speech in the graduation ceremony, which is mentioned in Part 1 of the text.

Neither Ying Zi nor any other character described what Ying Zi's father is like in the text. But two students were able to describe him as a strict father. This might be due to repeated, careful readings which enabled them to gather clues from the text, make an inference of his personality, and draw a conclusion that Zing Yi loves her father, even though he is strict.

STUDENT C: "Some people may say he is strict, but he helped me in my studies." (有些人可能會認為他是嚴格的，但是他幫助我學習。)

STUDENT G: "He is a strict father, but I still thank him and I love him." (佢雖然係一個嚴格嘅爸爸，但係我都好感謝同好愛佢。)

These two excerpts showed the students' in-depth understanding of the text. They tried to give their opinion that the father still cared about Ying Zi, even though he punished her for her misbehavior.

Something worth noting is Student B's in-role speech performance. He choked a bit emotionally before he started to deliver his speech. He explained to the researchers that Ying Zi must have been feeling sad when she became aware that her father was not able to attend the graduation ceremony due to his sickness,

Figure 11.1 Students analyzed and described details of the graduation ceremony upon completion of the in-role speech activity

Teaching modern Chinese literature to second-language students 233

although he really wanted to witness her growth and to celebrate her academic achievement. Ying Zi also tried her very best to perform well in her study. She made it finally and was selected to deliver the vote of thanks on behalf of all the graduates. Therefore, she must have been feeling sad at that moment. Student B's explanation of his in-role performance demonstrated his deep understanding of the plot, as evidenced by his ability to empathize with what Ying Zi had gone through with her father, described in different parts of the text, and further inferred what Ying Zi's feelings were in that particular moment.

The teacher also used the students' vote of thanks as a stimulus and asked them to write down (1) who attended the graduation ceremony, (2) what clothing they would put on during the ceremony, (3) what objects they would see in the ceremony, as well as (4) what possible feelings they would have in the ceremony. The goal of this activity was to help students put themselves in Ying Zi's shoes and understand her feelings more thoroughly.

Findings from the semi-structured interview

After the completion of the action research, the researcher invited Student B for the semi-structured interview. It was observed that the interviewee was motivated throughout the intervention, and he could recite the plot of the text with his peers in the class. Student B revealed that the drama activities helped him to better comprehend the story's details. Although he did learn the same text when he was studying mainstream Chinese language with his Chinese native speaking peers in Grade 8, he did not understand what it meant at that time. After participating in various drama activities, he understood more information, including the personality of Ying Zi's father and how he showed his love to Ying Zi. Student B could even "feel" how Ying Zi feels about her father. Moreover, he was able to act out Ying Zi's emotion when he conducted the "in-role speech" based on his interpretation of the story.

Based on the evidence presented here, the students not only showed their understanding of the plots of the story, but also empathized how Ying Zi feels. Thus, they were able to deliver the speeches with the acceptable emotions.

In the semi-structured interview, Student B told the researchers that still image helped him to better understand the text.

> "If you don't understand the story because your Chinese is not good enough, activity like still image might make you understand more."(如果你中文唔係幾好，故事唔明白，咁呢啲活動例如影相呀，咁可能會有啲⋯⋯明白囉。)

He also found that the drama conventions had helped him in his attempts to write in Chinese:

> "[W]hen you talk more, you would think more about what to write. Then when you write it, you would know what to write. It may still be difficult to understand, but at least you know what to write first." (因為你講多啲，你寫

嗰時都會諗吓你寫咩，跟住你寫出嚟，你就會知道你要寫咩，雖然都係寫唔明，但起碼都會知道你想寫咩先。）

From these excerpts, it shows that drama conventions helped students understand the text and further helped them in producing output.

Findings from the teaching log

The teaching log provided by the teacher also indicated that the students had come to an in-depth understanding of the text. In the log, the teacher revealed that teaching Chinese literary works to CAL students had never been his focus before, as it was not a core module in the past syllabus. Furthermore, teaching CAL students modern Chinese literature seemed like a mission impossible due to the students' low Chinese language proficiency, lack of learning motivation, and unfamiliarity with the cultural background of the selected text. He also admitted that the traditional pedagogy he had used was not effective in engaging his students in class activities, understanding the plot of the text, or feeling confident to sit for the GCE examination:

> This was not the first time I taught this literary text. Since it was not a compulsory module in the former GCE syllabus, I usually just skim through it and so-called let CAL students have a taste of modern Chinese literature. But as all students (who sit for the GCE examination) are required to remember the plot to show their comprehension of the text, and answer the questions to demonstrate their critical thinking skills in the examination, I don't think the traditional pedagogy will be as effective as before in the new syllabus. (這不是我第一次教授，往時也在課程中，因為不是指定篇章，我通常意思意思一下好讓第二語言學生覺得自己總算接觸過中國文學便算了。但改革後篇章成了指定讀物，學生得記住情節，考試時要回答問題，過往教學方法可能用不上。)

He then shared his self-reflection on using drama conventions to teach this literary text in the action research. The following is a summary of his observation on the students' learning performance:

> In these two weeks they showed that they really understand the context of the text, and they have developed "empathy" towards Ying Zi, the character. (這兩個星期他們真的理解了故事內容，也真的對英子這個角色有點感受。)

From the excerpt mentioned here, it shows that drama conventions in CAL lessons did bring an impact on both the teacher and the students. The students showed that they understood not only the story but also the characters.

3. Students improved critical thinking skills

The GCE examination defines critical thinking as a process that "usually involves general cognitive skills such as analyzing, synthesizing, and reasoning skills"

Findings from drama convention

As reported in the previous section, some of the questions raised by the students demonstrated a higher level of cognitive skills and better comprehension. Many students could analyze and synthesize the text, and then critique their peers' work based on the information they cognitively processed during and after reading. For example, one of the students criticized the work of Group C that "Ying Zi's portrait was wrong, she should not be holding her head but her limbs." According to the text, Ying Zi's father hit her limbs, not her head. It shows that students could remember all the details, analyze, and comment on their peers' work based on their understanding of the plots being described in the text.

The teacher pointed out that Student F struggled a lot in Chinese learning. He was ranked as the lowest in his CAL class and could not understand the literary text without help. However, he posted a question next to Picture 4 of Group D's work, asking, "Why didn't Ying Zi lie down?" (為什麼英子不要躺?) Although his question contained grammatical errors, he was able to point out a problem in the picture. He further clarified his question in English that he wanted to ask why the student portraying Ying Zi as kneeling on the floor rather than as lying in bed. He explained that according to the text, Ying Zi was lying in bed when her father dragged her out and disciplined her. In this sense, he pointed out that this still image was inaccurate and could not show what the text described.

Student G also posted a question to Picture 2 of Group B's work. She asked, "Why Ying Zi's mother was in the picture?" (為什麼媽媽在圖片裡) as the text did not mention her mother at all when Ying Zi was being punished by her father. So she pointed out that there was no need to have Ying Zi's mother in the still image pictures. Student G further commented on Picture 3 of Group C's work. She questioned, "Why was Father hitting Ying Zi's head?" (為什麼爸爸打英子的頭) and pointed out that the still image posture was incorrect. She further explained that according to the text, Ying Zi was in the car after being punished by her father. She rolled down her pants and tried to cover the wounds on her legs. Therefore, this implied that Ying Zi's father hit her on her legs and not on her head.

Participants also demonstrated their critical thinking skills in their in-role speech after reading Part 4 of the text.

STUDENT B: "I would like to say thank you to all of the teachers who put lots of effort on us in the past six years. Without your hard work, I would not be able to share my experience here." (我想同所有老師講多謝，因為你哋用咗六年去教我。如果你哋無擺啲心落去教我嘅話，咁我唔係，咁我而家就唔會喺度講緊開於我嘅經驗")

"I would also want to thank my parents. Although they are not here right now, I know they care about me deeply in their hearts." (我都想同我啲家長講多謝，雖然佢哋而家唔喺度，但係我知道佢哋心入面關於[關心]我嘅。)

The second part of the excerpt was based on the plot of Parts 2 and 3 of the text, which mentioned that Ying Zi picked some flowers on her way to the school for her teacher as she had taught Ying Zi how to dance (Part 2 of the text). Furthermore, after punishing Ying Zi, her father headed to the school and gave her a coat and some money (Part 3 of the text). Her father did not say anything to show his love for Ying Zi or apologize for punishing her physically, but showed his care and love through his actions. Students were able to synthesize all the details and infer how much Ying Zi's father loved his daughter.

STUDENT C: "My father helps me to be the best version of me. I thank him because he asked me to try my best. Some people may think he is strict to me, but he helped me in my studies." (我的爸爸幫助我成為我最佳的版本，我想感謝他因為囑咐我盡我所能，有些人可能會認為他是嚴格的，但是他幫助我學習。)

This excerpt refers to Ying Zi's father asking her to study hard (Part 1 of the text) so that she could be the student representative to receive the graduation certificates and deliver a vote of thanks in the graduation ceremony.

STUDENT G: "Finally, I would like to take this opportunity to thank my father. He is not here today. But I would not be able to deliver the vote of thanks right now without him. I have something special to share. He is a strict father, but I still thank him and love him." (最後，最後，我就係要感謝我嘅爸爸，雖然佢今日唔喺度，但係如果無咗佢我唔會而家在台上同你哋分享，我仲有啲特別嘅事情，佢雖然係一個嚴格嘅爸爸，但係我都好感謝同好愛佢。)

Student G was able to use the clues collected from Parts 1, 2, and 3 of the text to write her in-role speech. She was able to point out that Ying Zi's father could not attend the graduation ceremony. Furthermore, she could synthesize all the previous scenarios and correctly deduce the relationship between Ying Zi and her father, and then further correctly infer aspects of the father's personality. She could even delve into Ying Zi's emotional world, including her profound affection toward her father, and conclude that although her father was strict, she still loved him as he was a loving father, caring about her in his unique way.

These excerpts show that still image activity allowed the students to use the clues of the text, analyze the information in great detail, identify the discrepancies between their peers' work and what they had read, and ask the right questions. The students demonstrated a high level of critical thinking skills when participating in the drama activities.

Discussion, implications, and recommendations

Inspired by the Reader-response Theory and Situational Model Theory, this study aims to investigate whether and how well the application of drama conventions in daily classroom teaching promotes CAL students' in-depth understanding of modern Chinese literature and develops their critical thinking skills.

With reference to the evidence presented, drama conventions provided numerous comprehensible language exchange activities in the classroom for CAL students that enabled them to study Chinese literature in a more engaging way (Long, 1985, 1996). The drama conventions motivated the students to take part in various classroom activities and writing tasks, to concentrate on reading the text and to memorize the details they were originally not interested in. Drama helped them to interact with the reading materials, forming bonds with the unfamiliar cultural contexts of the text to gain a more in-depth understanding (Vygotsky, 1978). Using their performance in the "in-role speech" activity as an example, the students conveyed their points of view by taking Ying Zi or other characters' perspectives while integrating various dimensions being described in the texts (Zwaan et al., 1995). This demonstrated their understanding and interpretation of the cognitive and affective elements as proposed by the Reader-response Theory (Iser, 1978; Rosenblatt, 1968).

By participating in different drama activities, the students were able to come up with a coherent and cohesive description of narrative situations by integrating existing information (Cain & Oakhill, 2007; van den Broek & Espin, 2012). For example, they identified the discrepancies between their peers' "still-image" pictures and what they had read and thus demonstrated a deeper understanding of the text (deep-level processing) (Bestgen & Dupont, 2003; Noordman & Vonk, 1998).

Furthermore, various drama conventions helped the students to construct the underlying semantic meaning of the text (Kintsch, 1988), which was evidenced by drawing a correct inference of Ying Zi father's personality and the deep affection between the father and the daughter. Students' learning outcomes in different drama activities manifested the activation of their mental stimulation of the texts' perceptual and motoric elements of scenario (de Koning & van der Schoot, 2013; Fischer & Zwaan, 2008; Glenberg, 2007; Yaxley & Zwaan, 2007) during the learning process, and established their multisensory situation blocks to derive deeper meaning and individual interpretation as suggested by the Situation Model Theory. The students' in-role writings also demonstrated high-level critical thinking skills like synthesizing and inference. Therefore, classroom drama activities may help solve some of the reading problems CAL students are faced with, like the resistance to Chinese reading due to the decoding difficulties and the unfamiliar cultural contexts described in the texts, and also boost their learning motivation, which may potentially advance their Chinese language proficiency and relieve the tension between teachers and students.

The present study is subject to several limitations. It adopted the single case and action research designs and investigated the impact of drama conventions on one piece of narrative text with a small number of CAL students for a short period of two weeks. The findings cannot be generalized to other school contexts. Furthermore, only a few drama conventions have been investigated. Therefore, it is recommended that the scope of future study be extended to a larger group of

CAL students and their teachers in order to examine the impact of a wider range of drama pedagogies on diverse types of texts for a longer period of time.

Postscript

After the completion of this study, the teacher continued to use drama conventions to teach the first chapter, "Hui-an Hostel," of the book *Memories of Peking: South Side Stories* to the class. Since it was the last day before the Christmas break, the teacher brought snacks to celebrate Christmas as well as the new chapters of the literary text. The students were so excited by the new chapters that they ignored the snacks and forgot the Christmas party. They tried to read the story by themselves and find out what happened to Ying Zi. They competed with each other to complete the exercise worksheet before the lesson ended, eager to know the ending of the story.

References

Berk, L. E., & Winsler, A. (1995). *Scaffolding children's learning: Vygotsky and early childhood education*. National Association for Education.

Bestgen, Y., & Dupont, V. (2003). The construction of spatial situation models during reading. *Psychological Research, 67*(3), 209–218. https://doi.org/10.1007/s00426-002-0111-8

Bolton, G. M. (1984). *Drama as education: An argument for placing drama at the centre of the curriculum*. Addison-Wesley Longman.

Cain, K., & Oakhill, J. (2007). Reading comprehension difficulties: Correlates, causes, and consequences. In K. Cain & J. Oakhill (Eds.), *Children's comprehension problems in oral and written language: A cognitive perspective* (pp. 41–75). Guilford Press.

Chang, L. S. (2012). "Dramatic" language learning in the classroom. In J. Winston (Ed.), *Second language learning through drama: Practical techniques and applications*. Routledge.

Chang, L. S., & Winston, J. (2012). Using stories and drama to teach English as a foreign language at primary level. In J. Winston (Ed.), *Second language learning through drama: Practical techniques and applications* (pp. 15–30). Routledge.

de Koning, B. B., & van der Schoot, M. (2013). Becoming part of the story! Refueling the interest in visualization strategies for reading comprehension. *Educational Psychology Review, 25*(2), 261–287.

Dewey, J. (1902). *The child and the curriculum*. The University of Chicago Press.

Edexcel. (2017). *GCE A-Level Chinese specification*. Pearson.

Education Bureau. (2008). *Chinese language education key learning area: Supplementary guide to the Chinese language curriculum for non-Chinese speaking students*. www.edb.gov.hk/attachment/tc/curriculum-development/kla/chi-edu/sg%20to%20chi%20lang%20curr%20ncs%20proper%20eng%20upload.pdf

Education Bureau. (2016). *LCQ13: Chinese language education for non-Chinese speaking students*. www.info.gov.hk/gia/general/201611/30/P2016113000686.htm

Education Bureau. (2019). *Chinese language curriculum second language learning framework*. www.edb.gov.hk/attachment/tc/curriculum-development/kla/chi-edu/second-lang/NLF_brief_2019.pdf

Equal Opportunity Commission & The Centre for Youth Research and Practice Hong Kong Baptist University. (2020b). *A study on education and career pathways of ethnic minority youth in Hong Kong: Research report.* www.eoc.org.hk/EOC/upload/ResearchReport/20200619_em.pdf

Equal Opportunity Commission, Oxfam Hong Kong, Loh, K. Y. E., & Huang, O. Y. (2020a). *A study on the challenges faced by mainstream schools in educating ethnic minorities in Hong Kong.* Oxfam Hong Kong and The University of Hong Kong. www.eoc.org.hk/eoc/upload/ResearchReport/researchreport_20200115_e.pdf

Fischer, M. H., & Zwaan, R. A. (2008). Embodied language: A review of the role of the motor system in language comprehension. *Quarterly Journal of Experimental Psychology*, *61*(6), 825–850. https://doi.org/10.1080/17470210701623605

Glenberg, A. M. (2007). Language and action: Creating sensible combinations of ideas. In M. Gareth Gaskell (Ed.), *The Oxford handbook of psycholinguistics* (pp. 360–370). https://doi.org/10.1093/oxfordhb/9780198568971.013.0021

Heathcote, D. (1980). *Drama as a context for talking and writing.* National Association for the Teaching of English Papers in Education.

Hidi, S. (1990). Interest and its contribution as a mental resource for learning. *Review of Educational Research*, *60*(4), 549–571. https://doi.org/10.2307/1170506

Hidi, S., & Anderson, V. (1992). Situational interest and its impact on reading and expository writing. In K. A. Renninger, S. Hidi, A. Krapp & A. Renninger (Eds.), *The role of interest in reading and development* (pp. 215–238). Psychology Press. https://doi.org/10.4324/9781315807430

Ho, S. Y. (2011). *Classroom as a stage for life: Teaching literature through drama.* Hong Kong University Press.

Hong Kong Legislative Council. (2018). *Home affairs: The educational challenges faced by the east Asian ethnic minorities.* Hong Kong SAR Government. www.legco.gov.hk/research-publications/chinese/1819issh10-education-challenges-faced-by-south-asians-20181128-c.pdf

Hong Kong SAR Government. (1999). *The 1999 policy address: Quality people quality home, positioning Hong Kong for the 21st century.* www.policyaddress.gov.hk/pa99/english/highlight.htm

Iser, W. (1978). *The act of reading: A theory of aesthetic response.* Johns Hopkins University Press.

Johnson-Laird, P. N. (1983). *Mental models: Towards a cognitive science of language, inference, and consciousness.* Cambridge University Press.

Kilinc, S., Farrand, K., Chapman, K., Kelley, M., Millinger, J., & Adams, K. 2017). Expanding opportunities to learn to support inclusive education through drama-enhanced literacy practices. *British Journal of Special Education*, *44*(4), 431–447. https://doi.org/10.1111/1467-8578.12186

Kintsch, W. (1988). The role of knowledge in discourse comprehension: A construction-integration model. *Psychological Review*, *95*(2), 163–182. https://doi.org/10.1037/0033-295X.95.2.163

Krashen, S. D. (1981). *Second language acquisition and second language learning.* Pergamon.

Krashen, S. D. (1985). *The input hypothesis: Issues and implications.* Longman.

Krashen, S. D. (1989). We acquire vocabulary and spelling by reading: Additional evidence for the input hypothesis. *The Modern Language Journal*, *73*(4), 440–464. https://doi.org/10.1111/j.1540-4781.1989.tb05325.x

Krashen, S. D. (2003). *Explorations in language acquisition and use: The Taipei lectures.* Heinemann.

Law, D. Y. K. (1997). Pianzhang tuili yu Zhongwen yuwen nengli de guanxi: Xiaoliu xuesheng Zhongwen yuedu lijie gebie chayi fenxi [Relationship between Chinese language competence and inferential skills]. *Curriculum Forum, 6*(2), 106–117.

Leong, C. K., Shum, M. S., Tai, C. P., Ki, W. W., & Zhang, D. (2019). Differential contribution of psycholinguistic and cognitive skills to written composition in Chinese as a second language. *Reading and Writing: An Interdisciplinary Journal, 32*(2), 439–466. https://doi.org/10.1007/s11145-018-9873-2

Levy, J. S. (2008). Case studies: Types, designs, and logics of inference. *Conflict Management and Peace Science, 25*(1), 1–18. https://doi.org/10.1080/07388940701860318

Lin, H. Y. (2002 [1960]). *Memories of Peking: South side stories*. The Chinese University of Hong Kong Press.

Liu, P. L. (2010). Jiaru xiju yuansu: Jiaose banyan zai xiaoxue Zhongguo Yuwen ke de yingyong [Adding the element of the drama: The application of role-play in primary Chinese language classroom]. *Hong Kong Teachers' Centre Journal, 9*, 79–88.

Loh, E. K. Y. (2015). Using drama in education to enhance Chinese language proficiency of non-Chinese speaking secondary school students. *IB Journal of Teaching Practice, 13*(1), 1–17.

Loh, E. K. Y. (2017). Yuyong xiju jiaoxuefa he yuedu lilun, dui tisheng xiaosi xuesheng yuedu nengli de chengxiao yanjiu [Enhancing Primary 4 students' reading comprehension ability through drama in education and reading theories]. In Z. W. Liu (Ed.), *Understanding and dialogue: Education of literature and language in the globalization context* (pp. 249–259). Zhejiang University Press.

Loh, E. K. Y. (2019). What we know about expectancy-value theory, and how it helps to design a sustained motivating learning environment. *System, 86*, 102–119. https://doi.org/10.1016/j.system.2019.102119

Loh, E. K. Y., & Tam, L. C. W. (2016). Struggling to thrive: The impact of Chinese language assessments on social mobility of Hong Kong ethnic minority youth. *The Asia-Pacific Education Researcher, 25*(5–6), 763–770. https://doi.org/10.1007/s40299-016-0315-0

Loh, E. K. Y., Tam, L. C. W., & Lau, K. C. (2019). Moving between language frontiers: The challenges of the medium of instruction policy for Chinese as a second language. *Language Policy, 18*(1), 131–153. https://doi.org/10.1007/s10993-018-9465-7

Loh, E. K. Y., Woo, J. P. S., Ki, W. W., & Tang, F. K. L. (2019). Drama in education pedagogy assists students in learning Chinese as a second language: Theories and research. In E. K. Y. Loh, P. W. Y. Chou, M. S. K. Shum, & W. W. Ki (Eds.), *Chinese language education in the multilingual and multicultural contexts: Theories and practice* (pp. 87–102). Hong Kong University Press.

Long, M. H. (1985). Input and second language acquisition theory. In S. M. Gass & C. G. Madden (Eds.), *Input in second language acquisition* (pp. 377–393). Newbury House.

Long, M. H. (1996). The role of the linguistic environment in second language acquisition. In W. C. Ritchie & T. K. Bhatia (Eds.), *Handbook of second language acquisition* (pp. 413–468). Academic Press.

Mart, C. (2019). Reader-response theory and literature discussions: A springboard for exploring literary texts. *The New Educational Review, 56*(2), 78–87. https://doi.org/10.15804/tner.19.56.2.06

Needlands, J. (1992). *Learning through imagined experience: The role of drama in the national curriculum*. Hodder Education.

Noordman, L., & Vonk, W. (1998). Discourse comprehension. In A. D. Friederici (Ed.), *Language comprehension: A biological perspective* (pp. 229–262). Springer.

O'Neill, C. J. (1983). *Context or essence: The place of drama in the curriculum*. Routledge.

O'Neill, C. J., & Lambert, A. (1990). *Drama structures: A practical handbook for teachers*. Stanley Thornes.

O'Toole, J. (1992). *The process of drama: Negotiating art and meaning*. Routledge.

Rosenblatt, L. M. (1968). *Literature as exploration*. Heinemann.

Shum, M. S. K., Zhang, Y. H., Zhang, Q. Y., Ki, W. W., & Ng, S. L. (2012). Difficulties faced by ethnic minority students in Hong Kong. In L. Tsung, M. S. K. Shum, W. W. Ki, & Q. Zhang (Eds.), *Studies of teaching Chinese as a second language to ethnic minority students in Hong Kong: Theories, challenges, and practices* (pp. 53–76). Hong Kong University Press.

Spirovska, E. (2019). Reader-response theory and approach: Application, values and significance for students in literature courses. *SEEU Review*, *14*(1), 20–35. https://doi.org/10.2478/seeur-2019-0003

Stinson, M., & Winston, J. (2014). Drama education and second language learning: A growing field of practice and research. *Drama Education and Second Language Learning*, *16*(4), 479–488.

Swain, M. (2013). The inseparability of cognition and emotion in second language learning. *Language Teaching*, *46*(2), 1–13. https://doi.org/10.1017/s0261444811000486

Tsang, T. H., Shum, M. S. K., Ki, W. W., & Zhang, Q. (Eds.). (2012). *Studies of teaching Chinese as a second language to ethnic minority students in Hong Kong: Theories, challenges, and practices*. Hong Kong University Press.

Tse, S. K., Ki, W. W., & Shum, M. K. (Eds.). (2012). *Devising a Chinese-language curriculum for non-Chinese-speaking students in Hong Kong*. Hong Kong University Press.

Tse, S. K., & Loh, E. K. Y. (Eds.). (2014). *Effective teaching and learning of Chinese characters to non-Chinese speaking kindergarten students*. Beijing Normal University Press.

van den Broek, P., & Espin, C. A. (2012). Connecting cognitive theory and assessment: Measuring individual differences in reading comprehension. *School Psychology Review*, *41*(3), 315–325. https://doi.org/10.1080/02796015.2012.12087512

van der Schoot, M., Reijntjes, A., & van Lieshout, E. C. D. M. (2012). How do children deal with inconsistencies in text? An eye fixation and self-paced reading study in good and poor reading comprehenders. *Reading and Writing: An Interdisciplinary Journal*, *25*(7), 1665–1690. https://doi.org/10.1007/s11145-011-9337-4

van Dijk, T. A., & Kintsch, W. (1983). *Strategies of discourse comprehension*. Academic Press.

Vygotsky, L. (1978). *Mind in society: The development of higher psychological processes*. Harvard University Press.

Wassenburg, S. (2016). *Children's reading for meaning: A Situation Model perspective on deep text comprehension* (Unpublished doctoral dissertation). University of Amsterdam.

Winston, J. (2012). *Second language learning through drama: Practical techniques and applications*. Routledge.

Yaxley, R. H., & Zwaan, R. A. (2007). Simulating visibility during language comprehension. *Cognition*, *105*(1), 229–236. https://doi.org/10.1016/j.cognition.2006.09.003

Zwaan, R. A., Magliano, J. P., & Graesser, A. C. (1995). Dimensions of situation model construction in narrative comprehension. *Journal of Experimental Psychology: Learning, Memory, and Cognition*, *21*(2), 386–397. https://doi.org/10.1037//0278-7393.21.2.386

Appendix 11.1

Based on the reading text, students took four pictures and put them together to create a comic. Group A students added speech balloons in the comic.

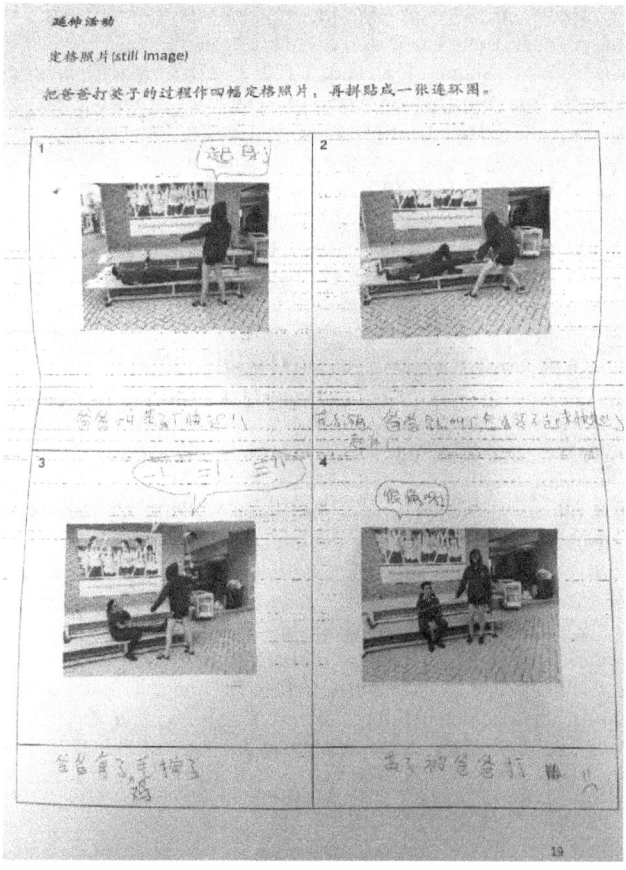

Figure 11.2 Pictures of Group A's still images

Appendix 11.2

Based on the reading text, students took four pictures and put them together to create a comic. Group B students took the lines from the text as their captions in the comic.

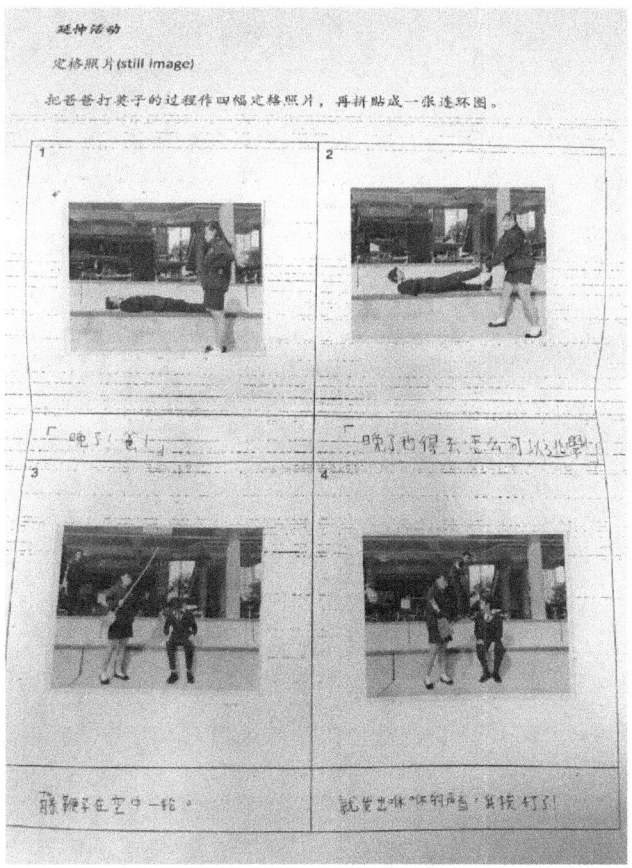

Figure 11.3 Pictures of Group B's still images

Appendix 11.3

Based on the reading text, students took four pictures and put them together to create a comic. Group C students took the lines from the text as their captions in the comic.

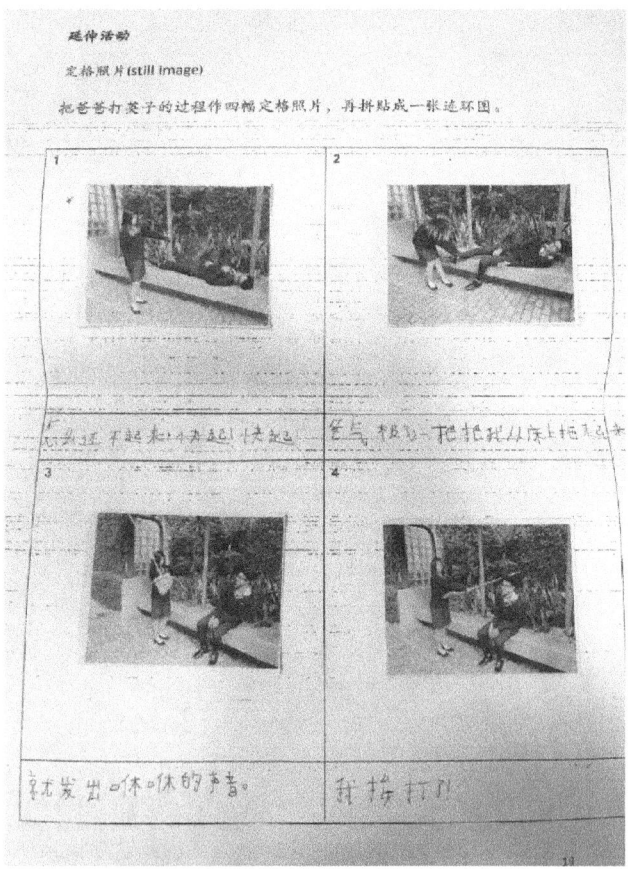

Figure 11.4 Pictures of Group C's still images

Appendix 11.4

Based on the reading text, students took four pictures and put them together to create a comic. Group D students described their pictures in their own words.

Critical thinking is the intellectually disciplined process of actively and skillfully conceptualizing, applying, analyzing, synthesizing, and/or evaluating information gathered from, or generated by, observation, experience, reflection, reasoning, or communication, as a guide to belief and action.

Figure 11.5 Pictures of Group D's still images

12 Reading assessment in Chinese as a foreign language

Keiko Koda and Xiaomeng Li

As a process of text-meaning construction, reading entails several distinct operations necessary for identifying printed words, integrating their meanings, and connecting them with the stored knowledge of the reader. These operations rely heavily on linguistic knowledge and the ability to use that knowledge to generate, integrate, and reflect on text information. Linguistic knowledge and reading ability thus are functionally interdependent, as they mutually enhance text-meaning construction. The major objective of this chapter is to explore a principled approach to reading assessment that aims to foster the concurrent development of reading ability and linguistic knowledge by exploiting their reciprocity. To that end, we first describe the major operations of reading and how distinct facets of linguistic knowledge support each operation. We then discuss the potential of the proposed approach for promoting high levels of reading proficiency with still-developing linguistic knowledge in a foreign language.

Reading as a complex construct

For assessments to serve as tools for enhancing learning, the focal construct must be identified. As noted earlier, reading entails three major operations, each requiring a distinct set of subskills. These operations include *text-meaning building*, *personal-meaning construction*, and *knowledge refinement*. Based on the descriptions of reading subskills in Koda (2016) and colleagues (Koda & Ke, 2018), this section explains how these operations contribute to meaning generations both at the local and global text levels.

Text-meaning building refers to the operation through which local text meanings are constructed based on the linguistic information encoded in the visual form of words. To succeed in this operation, the learner must acquire a set of subskills that is necessary for analyzing sequences of graphic symbols to identify which words they represent and those for retrieving their meanings from memory. In addition, it is equally critical for the learner to develop the ability to incorporate the information of a word into the emerging meaning of the local text in which it appears. As such, the text-meaning operation entails the following subskills:

- Segmenting the graphic form of a word into its phonological and morphological constituents
- Identifying the word

DOI: 10.4324/9781003029038-16

- Retrieving its meaning
- Integrating word meanings into the emerging interpretation of a local text segment (e.g., sentence and adjacent sentences)
- Inferring the meaning of an unfamiliar word based on word form analysis, local text meanings, and prior knowledge
- Integrating local text segments into a coherent text meaning

The second operation, *personal-meaning construction*, is important for achieving a deeper text understanding. To do so, language-based text meanings must be personalized both at the local and global levels. At the local level, the learner must draw upon prior knowledge to infer the implied meaning of explicitly stated text segments. S/he also needs to fill conceptual gaps between statements to infer the meaning of unstated information. At the global level, personalization is needed for the learner to make out how language-based text meanings fit with her/his real-life experiences. Through this process, locally and globally assembled text meanings are connected to personal experiences of the learner stored in memory. As such, *personal-meaning construction* necessitates the following skills:

- Comparing text information with the learner's real-life experiences
- Comparing text information with what the learner knows about the topic
- Comparing the view presented or implied in the text with the learner's own view on the topic

The third operation, *knowledge refinement*, involves the incorporation of personalized text meanings into the learner's existing knowledge bases. Given that new insight is generated when text information induces a change in a relationship, or a set of relationships, among existing concepts (Britton, 1994), it seems reasonable to assume that knowledge acquisition is dependent on, and at the same time restricted to, what the learner knows. Under this assumption, additional subskills are proposed as the requisite constituents of the *knowledge refinement* operation:

- Reflecting on how text information relates to what the learner already knows about the topic
- Being aware of a change, however subtle it might be, in the learner's knowledge of the topic

Of the three operations, text-meaning building most heavily relies on knowledge of the language. In developing reading assessment for language learners, it is important to understand how a specific facet of linguistic knowledge is involved in a distinct text-meaning building operation.

Roles of linguistic knowledge in text-meaning building

Word form analysis

In word form analysis, the learner segments the graphic form of a word into its phonological and morphological constituents. The operation allows the learner to discriminate a particular sequence of graphic symbols representing a real word from that consisting of random symbols. As such, it heavily relies on knowledge of permissible symbol sequences in a particular language. For example, Seidenberg and McClelland (1989) define orthographic knowledge in English as "an elaborate matrix of correlations among letter patterns, phonemes, syllables, and morphemes" (p. 525). The inter-letter associations for a particular word evolve gradually through cumulative experience of connecting a word's forms and its meaning across textual contexts. The more frequently a particular pattern is experienced, the stronger the associations that hold it together. In essence, automated word recognition occurs as a result of durable representations of a particular word in memory (e.g., Adams, 1994; Ehri, 1994, 1998, 2014). Once formed, "orthographic knowledge becomes a powerful mnemonic device that bond the spellings, pronunciations, and meanings of specific words in memory" (Ehri, 2014, p. 5).

Thus, efficient word form analysis affords effortless access to word meanings stored in memory. The unit of word segmentation shifts over time from smaller phonological segments (e.g., phonemes and onset/rime distinctions), to larger morphological, or even lexical, information (e.g., prefixes and suffixes). Thus, word recognition efficiency depends on knowledge of the language (vocabulary and grammar, in particular) and exposure to its printed form. The skilled reader can not only recognize a familiar word instantly but is also adept at analyzing the graphic form of an unfamiliar word, such as letters and letter clusters, to infer its pronunciation and meaning (e.g., Ehri, 1998, 2014; Hogaboam & Perfetti, 1978; Shankweiler & Liberman, 1972; Share, 2008).

Phonological processing entails accessing, storing, and manipulating phonological information of a printed word (Torgesen & Burgess, 1998). Studies involving native speaking students consistently document that poor readers are handicapped in a variety of phonological tasks. Their deficiencies tend to be "longitudinally predictive, and relatively unaffected by non-phonological factors—such as general intelligence, semantic, or visual processing" (Share & Stanovich, 1995, p. 9). Thus, efficiency in phonological decoding is causally related to word reading, learning, and comprehension.

Because morphemes are the smallest functioning unit in the composition of words, knowledge of morphemes is reciprocally related to print information processing at all levels (Ehri, 2014; Frost, 2012; Nunes & Bryant, 2006). Because writing systems graphically encode phonological and morphological information, the degree to which knowledge of morphemes is necessitated in the initial stages of reading acquisition varies across languages. For example, the English writing system is morphophonemic. Although its orthographic conventions are bound by phonemic constraints, its strong tendency to preserve morphological information allows both phonemic and morphemic constituents to explain its orthographic conventions. For example, distinct orthographic patterns, such as "threw" and "through," encode two unrelated morphemes even though they share the same pronunciation. Conversely, shared morphemes are spelled identically despite their distinct pronunciations, as in "anxious/anxiety" and "electric/electricity," or the past tense marker "-ed" (e.g., /-d/ in "moved", /-t/ in "talked", /-id/ in "visited").

As such, morphological knowledge plays an increasingly critical role in later grades, wherein the learner is expected to use reading ability as a tool for learning new words and contents. According to Nagy and Anderson (1984), children encounter roughly 2,000 new words every year in printed school materials, roughly 60% of which are structurally transparent multi-morphemic words, such as "fire-fight-er" and "un-lady-like." This implies that the meaning of at least half the new words could be inferred by analyzing a word's morphological structure.

In sum, the importance of word form analysis should be understood as a process of identifying a word by converting sequences of graphic symbols into phonological and morphological information. The process is vital for linking word forms with word meanings, and then with real-life experiences of the learner.

Word meaning retrieval

The ability to retrieve word meanings interacts directly and reciprocally with every one of the other operations in reading comprehension. As noted earlier, word meaning retrieval depends on accurate and speedy word form analysis. At the same time, the ability is constrained by local text meanings for deriving the context-appropriate meaning of individual words. Knowledge of word meanings connects the graphic form of words in a text with learners' knowledge stored in long-term memory. Such mediation is necessary because stored knowledge of word forms has an arbitrary relation to meaning representations (Schreuder & Flores d'Arcais, 1992). The knowledge thus connects the definitional meaning of printed words with real-life experiences of learners as it represents "information about the things to which words refer—be they related to the external world or internal states of the mind" (p. 422).

The visual form of a word often represents different meanings (e.g., "river bank" and "money bank") and different senses of a meaning (e.g., "house" evoking images of a shack vs. a mansion). Knowledge of word meanings must include the ability to select the sense that best fits the emerging interpretation of the textual context in which the word appears. The selection of the context-appropriate sense is constrained by local text meanings and real-life experiences, and at the same time, constrains subsequent text meaning construction. Anderson and Nagy (1991) underscore the importance of flexibility in word sense selection during reading by stating that "really knowing a word . . . always means being able to apply it flexibly but accurately in a range of new contexts and situations" (p. 721). The centrality of word sense selection clearly attests to the fact that knowledge of word meanings is continuously augmented and refined through reading, as is that of word forms.

Text-meaning construction

Sentence-level meaning construction entails the incremental integration of individual word meanings in such a way that an integrated "chunk" reflects the overall meaning of larger linguistic units, such as phrases and clauses. The integration process, often referred to as "syntactic parsing," involves two major operations: phrase construction through word meaning integration and case assignments to the constructed phrases.

To build coherent text representations, locally constructed text meanings must be integrated across sentences and paragraphs. A text's surface structure offers a variety of reliable clues signaling coherence relations among text elements. Significant elements often are placed in prominent text locations to highlight their relative weights (Goldman & Rakestraw, 2000). Linguistic devices are also used to achieve text coherence, such as connectives and co-references. Studies have demonstrated that knowledge of coherence devices differs considerably among native English-speaking children (e.g., Garner et al., 1986); that explicit training on coherence awareness tends to improve text comprehension and memory (e.g., Pearson & Fielding, 1991); that explicit demonstrations of text organization generally improve text comprehension (e.g., Baumann & Bergeron, 1993; Buss et al., 1985); and that efforts to increase the structural salience of a text generally facilitate comprehension (e.g., Anderson & Davison, 1988; Beck & Dole, 1992). These findings suggest that while knowledge of discourse structure and devices of signaling text coherence are important for global text-meaning building, its acquisition occurs only through substantial reading experience, and formal training can expedite the process by directing attention to specific text features.

In sum, linguistic knowledge serves as building blocks with which meanings are constructed at all text levels. Local text meanings are then linked to stored knowledge of the learner. Linguistic knowledge thus plays a critical role as a pivot that mediates between sequences of graphic symbols on the page and personal experiences of the learner. Reading provides the learner opportunities to use linguistic knowledge for generating, analyzing, and reflecting on content information, and in so doing, allows her/him to expand her/his knowledge of the language.

Reading ability in a foreign language

Over the past three decades, FL reading studies have examined the relative contributions of L2 linguistic knowledge (as the major force of text-meaning construction) and L1 reading ability (as a proxy of the learner's personal knowledge) to L2 text comprehension. As shown here, their findings have demonstrated that of the two, L2 linguistic knowledge is by far the stronger predictor of L2 reading ability.

In an initial study, for example, Lee and Schallert (1997) tested the threshold hypothesis by comparing the proportions of the variance in L2 reading accounted for by L1 reading ability and L2 language proficiency among 809 high school students learning English as an FL in Korea. Their analyses showed that L2 linguistic knowledge accounted for nearly twice as much variance in L2 reading ($r^2 = .56$) as did L1 reading ($r^2 = .30$). The study also revealed that reading scores in the two languages were more closely related among higher-proficiency learners than their lower-proficiency counterparts. The researchers concluded that L2 linguistic knowledge is a stronger predictor of L2 text comprehension than L1 reading ability, and that sufficient linguistic knowledge is necessary for the L2 learner to draw on her L1 reading ability.

Using 246 EFL college students in China, Jiang (2011) also investigated the relative contributions of L1 reading and L2 linguistic knowledge to L2 text comprehension. Her results corroborate those from the Lee and Schallert study described earlier. L2 linguistic knowledge accounted for 35% of the variance in one L2 reading test and 27% in another measure, while L1 reading explained only about 6% of the variance in both measures.

A study involving 325 college students studying English in Japan (Yamashita & Shiotsu, 2017) yielded an even more dramatic contrast in the contributions of L2 linguistic knowledge and L1 reading ability. They reported that virtually all the variance (94%) in L2 reading scores was accounted for by L2 linguistic knowledge, which, in the study, was treated as a latent variable comprised of grammar, vocabulary, and listening comprehension. Their follow-up analysis with higher-proficiency participants showed that their L1 reading ability made a small, but statistically significant, contribution to L2 text comprehension, over and above L2 linguistic knowledge.

These results clearly demonstrate that L2 linguistic knowledge is by far a stronger predictor of L2 reading performance than L1 reading ability. Interestingly, Yamashita and Shiotsu's follow-up analysis suggests that L1 reading ability may interact with L2 proficiency, and thus, provides support for the notion of linguistic threshold hypothesis (Cummins, 1979) positing that sufficient L2 knowledge is necessary for L1 reading ability to contribute to L2 reading. Caution must be exercised, however, in interpreting the findings. Considering that the tasks used for estimating L2 reading were adopted from a standardized language proficiency test, it is possible that the task properties of the L2 reading and L2 linguistic knowledge measures could have been more similar than those of the L1 reading ability test. Should this be the case, the contribution of L1 reading ability may have been grossly underestimated. As described earlier, linguistic knowledge plays a central role, but in itself is insufficient for the acquisition of broad-based reading ability that is necessary for personalizing text information for deeper levels of comprehension.

A small but growing body of research has begun to address cross-linguistic text-reader interaction during L2 reading. As a case in point, Horiba and Fukaya (2015) investigated how L1 topic-related knowledge and L2 proficiency affects L2 text comprehension and incidental vocabulary learning. Their participants were two groups of college students (nursing majors and non-nursing majors) in Japan ($N = 145$). By comparing text comprehension and incidental vocabulary learning between the groups, the researchers found that L2 linguistic knowledge and L1 background knowledge (topic familiarity) contributed to text comprehension differently. While L2 knowledge facilitated global text understanding, background knowledge enhanced the retention of detailed, topic-relevant information. Using covariance analyses, the researchers found the facilitative effect of L1 knowledge was observable only when L2 linguistic knowledge was controlled. These results imply that L2 linguistic knowledge, or a lack thereof, restricts the incorporation of L1 resources during L2 reading.

Similarly, Ke and Koda (2017) tested the hypothesis that L2 linguistic knowledge mediates the learner's access to L1 resources during L2 reading. They compared the relative contributions of L1 and L2 morphological awareness (MA) to L2 word meaning inference among college students ($N = 50$) learning Chinese as a foreign language in the United States. They found that L1 and L2 MA are closely related between two languages, but L1 MA does not support L2 word meaning inference. L2 MA contributes to L2 word meaning inference, but only indirectly, via L2 linguistic knowledge.

The emerging picture from these studies captures the complexities arising from the involvement of L1 reading ability and the constraints posed by L2 linguistic knowledge on the learner's utilization of L1 resources. Clearly, the contributions of L2 linguistic knowledge and L1 reading ability are neither as distinct nor independent as had been assumed in earlier studies. A clear implication is that FL reading instruction and assessment must go beyond language-focused exercises and activities. To achieve higher levels of reading proficiency, the learner needs to acquire the skills to use linguistic knowledge for constructing and personalizing text meanings, as well as those to use reading ability to expand and elaborate on her/his L2 linguistic knowledge. However, these skills are rarely incorporated in FL reading assessment.

Language-focused approaches to reading assessment

Traditionally, reading assessment in a foreign language has centered on probing the learner's knowledge of grammar and vocabulary. It remains uncertain as to how such language-focused approaches could fulfill the potential of reading assessment for promoting L2 linguistic knowledge through their functional reciprocity. This section discusses projected implications of language-focused approaches for maximizing the potential of classroom assessment for promoting the simultaneous development of reading ability and language learning through the exploitation of their developmental reciprocity.

According to a brief survey of Chinese textbooks used in U.S. colleges, reading is generally viewed as a facet of language proficiency (Koda & Ke, 2018). Under the language-focused view, reading exercises even in second- and third-year courses are embedded in language instruction with the primary focus being placed on the enhancement of grammar and vocabulary knowledge. Although the view may look sensible, from the *reading as language* perspective, it could yield two potentially undesirable consequences. First, under this view, reading instruction does not provide any authentic purposes of reading, other than answering comprehension questions. Because such practice does not explicitly ask the learner to connect text information with her/his personal experiences, it rarely provides the learner with opportunities and motivation to internalize text information. A predictable consequence would be that FL instruction under this view offers the learner little incentive to draw on her/his cognitive and conceptual resources.

The language-focused view moreover may provide a basis for forming a simplistic assumption that once the learner acquires sufficient linguistic knowledge, s/he becomes able to "read" linguistically appropriate texts for learning in the target language. In fact, widely used proficiency guidelines describe reading competence as a gradual increase in the ability to understand written texts that demand progressively more sophisticated knowledge of the language and text types (American Council on the Teaching of Foreign Languages, 2012; Council of Europe, 2001). As shown earlier, linguistic knowledge is critical, but insufficient for *text-meaning building*, let alone *personal-meaning construction* and *knowledge refinement*. Neither consequence seems conducive to enhancing the learner's engagement in the purposeful use of language for meaning construction and knowledge generation during reading.

Reading assessment as a tool for promoting language learning

This section describes an approach to developing a system of classroom reading assessment that is designed to promote the concurrent development of reading ability and linguistic knowledge in a foreign language based on *Reading to learn in a foreign language* (Koda & Yamashita, 2018). The approach is construct driven, in that assessment tasks are designed directly from the construct definitions described earlier. Intended uses of the assessment include (a) monitoring the learner's progress in developing reading ability and knowledge of the language, (b) promoting the learner's skills to monitor her/his progress in reading ability and language development, and (c) providing the learner opportunities to reflect on her/his progress. To actualize these uses, the system assessment should be fully integrated in the curriculum both at the course and program levels and administered multiple times for both formative and summative purposes.

In formative assessment, the learner is given opportunities to practice the focal subskills in a particular course through various forms of instructional tasks, such as in-class activities and homework assignments. The instructor's in-class observations of the learner's engagement and participation in those tasks constitute a primary source of making formative decisions about ongoing learning, or a lack thereof, on a day-by-day basis. Formative assessment by the student should also be included as a part of learning activities. It would be useful to provide explicit training on metacognitive skills and strategies for tracking progress, reflecting on learning outcomes, and adjusting learning strategies.

Summative assessment can easily be incorporated in the assessment system. Summative information is useful if it allows the instructor to gauge the relative attainment in the focal subskills as specified in the learning objectives and construct definitions. Assessment outcomes can be used to (a) determine the appropriateness of the program's outcome expectations, (b) evaluate the effectiveness of instructional approaches, and (c) promote the student's awareness of the learning objectives.

For assessment outcomes to be informative for making instructional decisions, all forms of assessment must be aligned with the learning objectives of the course and the program. It is also important to ensure that all forms of assessment are consistent with the descriptions of the focal reading subskills. In this regard, the development of assessment tasks can be conceptualized as a process of eliciting the mental activities that are presumed to occur during reading as defined. In theory, construct-referenced tasks should allow one to convert elicited behaviors into numerical indices of the focal subskills. This in turn makes it possible for the instructor of the course and other instructors of the program to track changes in a particular set of reading subskills both diachronically within the learner and synchronically across multiple learner groups in different instructional levels.

Assessment practices in Chinese as a foreign language

To examine how the conceptualization of reading ability is reflected in instruction, we examined and compared several features of five widely used Chinese textbooks used in the beginning- and the advanced-level foreign language classrooms. The two beginning-level textbooks are *Chinese Link* (referred to as CL; Wu et al., 2011) and *The Routledge Course in Modern Mandarin Chinese* (referred to as RMC; Ross et al., 2010). The three advanced-level textbooks are *The Routledge Advanced Chinese Multimedia Course: Crossing Cultural Boundaries* (referred to as CCB; Lee et al., 2014), *Reading into a New China: Integrated Skills for Advanced Chinese* (referred to as RNC; Li & Liu, 2010), and *A Changing China: Advanced Chinese* (referred to as ACC; Wu & Yu, 2014). The features we compared include the learning objectives and expected outcomes, the knowledge and skills assumed to underlie each level of reading ability, passage types, post-reading exercises, comprehension questions, and other instructional activities.

What is of interest is whether the conceptualization of reading ability is aligned with current theories of reading, whether the assessment of reading ability is aligned with the reading conceptualization, and how these alignments differ between the elementary and the advanced levels of textbooks. We begin with how reading is conceptualized, taught, and assessed in these textbooks, and then present an analysis of the alignment between research evidence and real-life practices in these widely used textbooks.

How reading is conceptualized

As shown in Table 12.1, the two elementary-level textbooks clearly indicate that they focus on promoting linguistic knowledge as the core constituent of reading ability, though none of the textbooks explicitly provide their conceptualization of reading. Both textbooks list linguistic knowledge, especially lexical and syntactic knowledge, as the primary learning objectives. The input passages in the two textbooks also appear with the pinyin notation, the vocabulary list, and the grammatical instructions that help the students to understand the literal meaning of the texts. The reading exercises are designed to capture the student's linguistic knowledge through translation, sentence completion, and vocabulary exercises. Thus, the two elementary-level textbooks imply reading as a medium that facilitates the students' development of lexical and syntactic knowledge. In other words, students *read to learn* vocabulary and grammar.

Reading assessment in Chinese as a foreign language 255

Table 12.1 Features of Five Widely Used Chinese Textbooks

	RMC (elementary)	CL (elementary)	CCB (advanced)	RNC (advanced)	ACC (advanced)
Authors & publication years	Ross et al. (2010)	Wu et al. (2011)	Lee et al. (2014)	Li and Liu (2010)	Wu and Yu (2014)
Learning objectives (L: linguistic knowledge; C: Cultural competence; CO: Communication competence)	1. To develop all the basic spoken and written language skills (L). 2. To guide the students to make cross-cultural comparisons between China and the U.S. (C). 3. To learn culturally appropriate communicative skills in genre-specific situations (CO).	1. To develop basic communicative competence in four skills of listening, speaking, reading, and writing (L and CO). 2. To gain an understanding of Chinese culture and exercise the ability to compare aspects of different cultures (C).	1. To develop the advanced-level language proficiency in four skills (L). 2. To develop critical thinking on Chinese and culture as well as cross-cultural awareness (C). 3. To develop the oral communicative skills that are appropriate the cultural literacy in the spoken idiom (CO).	1. To develop all language skills with special focus on reading and reading skills (L). 2. To understand Chinese society at the 21st Century (C). 3. To promote the development of written communication skills and begin to learn formal written Chinese (CO).	1. To develop language skills in all four skills to the advanced level (L). 2. To reflect and compare cross-linguistic differences on contemporary and ancient China (C). 3. To develop the culturally and linguistically appropriate spoken and written communicative competence (CO).
Knowledge underpinned	No prior background in Chinese study	No presumed knowledge	The advanced-low or advanced-mid levels of competence (6th or 8th semester for students who have not studied abroad, earlier for students who have).	A high intermediate or beginning advanced level of proficiency; Or 3rd-year Chinese language courses; Or heritage students at the intermediate level.	5 to 6 semesters of Chinese learning

(Continued)

Table 12.1 (Continued)

	RMC (elementary)	CL (elementary)	CCB (advanced)	RNC (advanced)	ACC (advanced)
Passage types	Dialogue in pinyin (and gradually replaced by characters)	Dialogues on daily life and study	Either written from scratch or paraphrased from a Chinese original to introduce interesting and accurate information about contemporary China.	Modified written materials to suit the literacy level and linguistic needs of 3rd-year students (not purely authentic materials); Narrative, expository and news	Narrative, expository, and media literacy in the style of newspapers, magazines, and internet articles.
Conceptualization of reading ability	Reading for information	Not provided	Not provided	Both top-down and bottom-up processes are important; Asking students to use their prior knowledge to understand the text and relate it to their own worldview and opinion; close attention to detailed information and deeper meaning by decoding.	Not provided
Comprehension questions	No comprehension questions for main text	No comprehension questions for main text	Yes-or-no questions; short-answer questions	Yes-or-no questions; short-answer and open questions	Yes-or-no questions; open-ended questions
Pre-reading activities	Communicative goals and grammatical structures; introductory passages in English and visual stimuli	Learning objectives; discussion questions; vocabulary list; grammar and sentence patterns exercises	Learning objectives; watching the short films on the same topic; exploring the topic online; introductory reading; discussion questions; vocabulary list	English overview; discussion questions; visual stimuli; vocabulary list and exercise	Learning objectives; vocabulary list, grammar; visual stimuli; preview questions (yes-or-no questions, multiple-choice questions, cloze test)

Reading assessment in Chinese as a foreign language 257

Post-reading activities	Communicative activities (oral speaking, conversation, and role play); vocabulary and character exercises; grammatical exercises and sentence pyramids; pronunciation and pinyin exercise; notes on language use	Listening, character, and grammar exercises; supplementary reading (yes-or-no questions); communicative activities (role play, conversation); composition; cultural notes (with discussion questions)	Vocabulary and expression exercises; translation; sentence writing and completion; translation; radical and character exercises; communicative activities (role play; interview; group discussion; debate); composition; cultural notes and annotations in English; supplementary reading (vocabulary; yes-or-no questions; multiple-choice questions)	Skill-focused activities; vocabulary exercises; sentence pattern and grammar exercises; pinyin exercise; cloze test; translation; supplementary reading (open-ended and short-answer questions; yes-or-no questions; multiple-choice questions); oral speaking; discussion questions; composition	Cultural notes; grammar exercise; vocabulary exercises; supplementary reading (yes-or-no questions, cloze test, character, and grammar exercises; multiple-choice questions); translation; communicative activities (role play, debate; group discussion); composition

The advanced-level textbooks focus on passage understanding rather than linguistic foundation building. RNC contends that both bottom-up and top-down processes are critical for tackling the complexity of reading. This conceptualization reflects the editors' view of reading as an interactive process that requires integration of text information and personal knowledge of the reader (Stanovich, 1984). CCB and ACC do not state their definition of reading. However, both textbooks (as well as RNC) underscore the importance of Chinese cultural awareness and cross-cultural comparison, both of which are assumed to be achieved through the text-reader interaction. Therefore, the advanced-level textbooks incorporate the central tenet of current reading theories. However, in the three textbooks, passage understanding is assessed mainly through accuracy of literal text meanings. This shows the authors' firm, yet implicit, assumption that comprehension is a product of linguistic information integration and manipulation.

How reading is taught and assessed

Reading is taught and assessed through various activities and exercises at the pre-reading, core-reading, and post-reading stages. Although the textbooks for the two proficiency levels are similar in their structure, they differ in terms of the scope, content depth, topical complexity, and focal skills to be practiced.

As the table shows, each unit of the two elementary-level textbooks consists of a dialogue, along with grammar and vocabulary exercises. The unit themes in the two textbooks are relevant to the student's life in everyday situations. The pre-reading activities include discussion questions that help the student to activate personal experiences (CL) or a brief description in English that introduces the situation in which the dialogue occurs (RMC). The textbooks provide somewhat limited background information of the passage contents, apparently because they focus on linguistic foundation building, including grammar, vocabulary, and basic communicative expressions.

The textbooks at the two levels also differ in comprehension questions, post-reading activities, and supplementary reading materials. Instead of comprehension questions, the beginning-level textbooks do not have comprehension questions following the main text. A variety of exercises designed to foster pinyin and character knowledge, grammatical knowledge, and communicative competence suggests the central role of reading as a tool to promote the students' linguistic and communicative competence. Rather than assessments that support the students' reflection and expansion on the personal knowledge system, assessments at this level are designed as a tool to reinforce the learners' command of linguistic knowledge, character handwriting, and basic communicative competence. To foster the students' understanding of the Chinese culture, however, the two textbooks design a separate section, namely culture notes, to introduce Chinese culture and society generally. CL also lists several discussion questions encouraging students to make cross-cultural comparisons, though the information in the cultural parts is limited. Therefore, in the beginning-level texts, reading is mainly used to foster linguistic and communicative competence.

In the three advanced-level textbooks, reading plays a more central role. All of them include a sequence of pre-reading activities that prepares the student both linguistically and substantively. For example, a list of new words appears before the input passage in each unit, to help students study the passage by themselves. In addition, the textbooks provide relevant background information to promote a deeper understanding of the topic in each unit. For instance, CCB encourages the students to look for relevant information online. RNC starts with a brief overview in English.

Post-reading activities jointly contribute with the pre-reading activities to the students' personal meaning construction and knowledge refinement. For instance, the supplementary reading materials complement the thematic content of the main text from different perspectives. The discussion questions and the writing exercises are geared toward critical thinking and cross-cultural comparison between the students' personal experience and cultural identity with Chinese culture. However, despite the content-rich information provided in the text, the comprehension questions following the main texts (as well as supplementary reading materials) are still limited to yes-or-no questions, multiple-choice questions, and short-answer questions that examine the students' grasp of the text gist and detailed information. A significant number of the exercises, like vocabulary exercises, sentence completion, and translation, are designed to improve linguistic knowledge and handwriting skills.

To sum up, advanced-level textbooks are built around reading. Linguistic and cultural competence are achieved through a variety of pre- and post-reading activities. The activities that set up the students' background knowledge indicate the editors' acknowledgement of reading as a product of the reader-text interaction, though the comprehension questions are still limited to the detection of the basic text information. The comparison between the reading activities and exercises between the elementary and the advanced level reflects the different philosophies of "reading as linguistic knowledge" vs. "reading as the text-reader interaction."

Analysis

The collective research evidence indicates three scientific perceptions of reading: 1) reading is a multifaceted construct that entails multiple sets of interconnected yet distinct processes (Carr & Levy, 1990); 2) reading to learn entails the text-reader interaction, through which the readers can construct personal meaning and refine knowledge systems; 3) L2 reading is both a linguistic problem and a reading problem. However, L2 linguistic knowledge is the deciding factor, especially for beginning learners, and its level determines the accessibility of L1 reading skills (Clarke, 1988; Cummins, 1979; Lee & Schallert, 1997).

The conceptualization of reading in the textbooks both aligns with and deviates from these research findings. While the beginning-level textbooks do not clearly distinguish reading ability and linguistic knowledge, RNC explicitly conceptualizes reading as an interaction of the bottom-up and top-down processes. Other advanced-level textbooks are also designed to provide relevant background information to activate the student's personal experiences by using multimedia materials and discussion questions. These features show the prominence of top-down processes in the structure design of the textbooks.

The definition of reading in the advanced-level textbooks also implies the influences of the componential view of reading. Although none of the textbooks pinpoints all the components of reading, the advanced-level textbooks commonly incorporate vocabulary, grammar, background information, strategy instruction, and language-use exercises. For instance, RNC has a separate section for the exercises of reading skill. The reading skills taught throughout the textbook include the skills of guessing word meanings from context, understanding written structures, identifying text organization, making text-based inferences, and distinguishing facts from speculations. These separate sections suggest that the authors conceptualize reading as a constellation of mutually enhancing yet independent component skills, each necessitating a distinct facet of linguistic knowledge.

It is noteworthy that reading skills are not even mentioned in the beginning-level textbooks. But in the advanced-level textbooks, reading skills are introduced by component, and are explicitly taught and practiced as a component. The difference is clearly due to the sole emphasis on linguistic knowledge building at the beginning level.

Interestingly, the language-focused orientation continues to dominate instruction exercises and assessment activities, even in the advanced-level textbooks. It appears to be critical for language programs to consciously identify with their stakeholders a particular time(s) in the curriculum to start shifting the instructional foci from building the linguistic foundations to promoting purposeful uses of language for thinking, analyzing, reflecting on, and communicating content information.

Additionally, what is also of interest is whether the reading assessment reflects the empirical evidence from current reading research and the reading conceptualization presented, though implicitly, in the textbooks. As the table shows, the post-reading exercises in the beginning-level textbooks comprise mainly two types of exercises. The first type includes sentence completion and vocabulary exercise. The other type uses yes-or-no and short-answer questions to detect the students' grasp of the main idea and detailed information of the input passage. These activities suggest that linguistic knowledge and reading ability are not clearly distinguished and their relationship is not well recognized.

The exercises used in the advanced-level textbooks include grammar and vocabulary practices, translation, comprehension questions, communicative activities, and supplementary reading materials. There is a striking similarity in these tasks between the textbooks for beginning- and advanced-level learners. This seems to suggest that Chinese as a foreign language instruction by and large fosters language-focused, rather than language and content dual-focused approaches. Two implications arise. First, the conceptualization of reading ability has emerged in the heavily linguistically driven contexts. As a consequence, reading assessment is designed to probe a product only from one (of the three) reading operations, namely text-meaning construction. To cultivate higher levels of proficiency among adult language learners, it might be useful to explore legitimate ways of enhancing linguistic growth through purposeful uses of language for generating meanings at deeper levels of reading, like personal-meaning construction and reflection.

Summary and conclusion

In this chapter, we attempted to conceptualize reading ability as a complex construct that entails text-meaning building, personal-meaning construction, and knowledge refinement. Our analyses of beginning- and advanced-level textbooks have revealed that the beginning-level textbooks strongly emphasize reading as linguistic knowledge, while the foci of the advanced-level textbooks uniformly shift toward a balanced weight placed on linguistic knowledge enhancement and deeper cultural understanding. They also explicitly acknowledge the centrality of the reader's involvement in text meaning generation by incorporating a variety of tasks that are designed to activate the student's background information, personal experiences, and critical thinking. Such a shift is consistent with findings from reading development research. Beyond that, however, the potential of reading ability for linguistic knowledge enhancement remains largely unexplored. Sufficiently developed reading ability allows the reader to use linguistic knowledge as a tool for generating local text meanings, discovering an additional sense of a known word, and inferring the meaning of an unfamiliar word. It is through this functional reciprocity that the exponential growth of vocabulary knowledge is attained. Clearly, reading assessment greatly benefits from the incorporation of the notion of the reciprocity between reading ability and linguistic knowledge, in general, and the reverse contributions of reading ability to language development, in particular.

References

Adams, M. J. (1994). *Beginning to read: Thinking and learning about print*. The MIT Press.
American Council on the Teaching of Foreign Languages. (2012). *Proficiency guidelines: Reading*. American Council on the Teaching of Foreign Languages.
Anderson, R. C., & Davison, A. (1988). *Conceptual and empirical bases of readability formulas*. Center for the Study of Reading.
Anderson, R. C., & Nagy, W. E. (1991). Word meaning. In R. Barr, M. L. Kamil, P. Mosenthal, & P. D. Pearson (Eds.), *Handbook of reading research* (Vol. II, pp. 512–538). Longman.
Baumann, J. F., & Bergeron, B. S. (1993). Story map instruction using children's literature: Effects on first graders' comprehension of central narrative elements. *Journal of Reading Behavior, 25*(4), 407–437.
Beck, I. L., & Dole, J. A. (1992). Reading and thinking with history and science text. In C. Collins & J. Mangieri (Eds.), *Teaching thinking: An agenda for the twenty-first century* (1st ed., pp. 1–22). Routledge.
Britton, B. (1994). Understanding expository text: Building mental structures to induce insights. In M. A. Gernsbacher (Ed.), *Handbook of psycholinguistics* (pp. 641–674). Academic Press.

Buss, R. R., Ratliff, J. L., & Irion, J. C. (1985). Effects of instruction on the use of story structure in comprehension of narrative discourse. In J. A. Niles & R. B. Lalik (Eds.), *Issues in literacy: A research perspective* (Vol. 34, pp. 55–58). National Reading Conference.

Carr, T. H., & Levy, B. A. E. (1990). *Reading and its development: Component skills approaches*. Academic Press.

Clarke, M. A. (1988). The short circuit hypothesis of ESL reading—or when language competence interferes with reading performance. In P. L. Carrell, J. Devine, & D. E. Eskey (Eds.), *Interactive approaches to second language reading* (pp. 114–124). Cambridge University Press.

Council of Europe. (2001). *Common European framework of reference for languages: Learning, teaching, assessment*. Cambridge University Press.

Cummins, J. (1979). Cognitive/academic language proficiency, linguistic interdependence, the optimum age question and some other matters. Working Papers on Bilingualism, No. 19.

Ehri, L. C. (1994). Development of the ability to read words: Update. In R. Ruddell, M. Ruddell, & H. Singer (Eds.), *Theoretical models and processes of reading* (4th ed., pp. 323–358). Erlbaum.

Ehri, L. C. (1998). Grapheme-phoneme knowledge is essential to learning to read words in English. In J. L. Metsala & L. C. Ehri (Eds.), *Word recognition in beginning literacy*. (pp. 3–40). Erlbaum.

Ehri, L. C. (2014). Orthographic mapping in the acquisition of sight word reading, spelling memory, and vocabulary learning. *Scientific Studies of Reading*, *18*(1), 5–21.

Frost, R. (2012). Towards a universal model of reading. *Behavioral and Brain Sciences*, *35*(5), 263–279.

Garner, R., Alexander, P., Slater, W., Hare, V. C., Smith, T., & Reis, R. (1986). Children's knowledge of structural properties of expository text. *Journal of Educational Psychology*, *78*(6), 411–416.

Goldman, S. R., & Rakestraw, J. A., Jr. (2000). Structural aspects of constructing meaning from text. In M. L. Kamil, P. B. Mosenthal, P. D. Pearson, & R. Barr (Eds.), *Handbook of reading research* (Vol. 3, pp. 311–335). Lawrence Erlbaum Associates.

Hogaboam, T. W., & Perfetti, C. A. (1978). Reading skill and the role of verbal experience in decoding. *Journal of Educational Psychology*, *70*(5), 717–729.

Horiba, Y., & Fukaya, K. (2015). Reading and learning from L2 text: Effects of reading goal, topic familiarity, and language proficiency. *Reading in a Foreign Language*, *27*(1), 22–46.

Jiang, X. (2011). The role of first language literacy and second language proficiency in second language reading comprehension. *Reading Matrix*, *11*(2), 177–190.

Ke, S. E., & Koda, K. (2017). Contributions of morphological awareness to adult L2 Chinese word meaning inferencing. *The Modern Language Journal*, *101*(4), 742–755.

Koda, K. (2016). Development of word recognition in a second language. In X. Chen, V. Dronjic, & R. Helms-Park (Eds.), *Reading in a second language: Cognitive and psycholinguistic issues* (pp. 70–98). Routledge.

Koda, K., & Ke, S. E. (2018). Advanced reading proficiency in collegiate foreign language learners. In P. A. Malovrh & A. G. Benati (Eds.), *The handbook of advanced proficiency in second language acquisition* (pp. 483–504). Wiley.

Koda, K., & Yamashita, J. (Eds.). (2018). *Reading to learn in a foreign language: An integrated approach to foreign language instruction and assessment*. Routledge.

Lee, J.-W., & Schallert, D. L. (1997). The relative contribution of L2 language proficiency and L1 reading ability to L2 reading performance: A test of the threshold hypothesis in an EFL context. *TESOL Quarterly*, *31*(4), 713–739.

Lee, K. C., Liang, H., Jiao, L., & Wheatley, J. (2014). *The Routledge advanced Chinese multimedia course: Crossing cultural boundaries* (2nd ed.). Routledge.

Li, D., & Liu, K. (2010). *Reading into a new China: Integrated skills for advanced Chinese*. Cheng & Tsui Company.

Nagy, W. E., & Anderson, R. C. (1984). How many words are there in printed school English? *Reading Research Quarterly, 19*(3), 304–330.

Nunes, T., & Bryant, P. (2006). *Improving literacy by teaching morphemes*. Routledge.

Pearson, P. D., & Fielding, L. (1991). Comprehension instruction. In R. Barr, M. L. Kamil, P. Mosenthal, & P. D. Pearson (Eds.), *Handbook of reading research* (Vol. II, pp. 815–860). Lawrence Erlbaum Associates.

Ross, C., He., B., Chen, P., & Yeh, M. (2010). *The Routledge course in modern Mandarin Chinese: Textbook level 1, Simplified characters*. Routledge.

Schreuder, R., & Flores d'Arcais, G. B. (1992). Psycholinguistic issues in the lexical representation of meaning. In W. Marslen-Wilson (Ed.), *Lexical representation and process* (pp. 409–436). MIT Press.

Seidenberg, M. S., & McClelland, J. L. (1989). A distributed, developmental model of word recognition and naming. *Psychological Review, 96*(4), 523–568.

Shankweiler, D., & Liberman, I. Y. (1972). Misreading: A search for causes. In J. F. Kavanagh & I. G. Mattingly (Eds.), *Language by ear and by eye: The relationship between speech and reading* (pp. 293–317). The MIT Press.

Share, D. L. (2008). On the Anglocentricities of current reading research and practice: The perils of overreliance on an "outlier" orthography. *Psychological Bulletin, 134*(4), 584–615.

Share, D. L., & Stanovich, K. E. (1995). Cognitive processes in early reading development: Accommodating individual differences into a model of acquisition. In J. S. Carlson (Ed.), *Issues in education: Contributions from psychology* (Vol. 1, pp. 1–57). JAI.

Stanovich, K. E. (1984). The interactive-compensatory model of reading: A confluence of developmental, experimental, and educational psychology. *Remedial and Special Education, 5*(3), 11–19.

Torgesen, J. K., & Burgess, S. R. (1998). Consistency of reading-related phonological processes throughout early childhood: Evidence from longitudinal-correlational and instructional studies. In J. L. Metsala & L. C. Ehri (Eds.), *Word recognition in beginning literacy* (pp. 161–188). Erlbaum.

Wu, S., & Yu, Y. (2014). *A changing China (Advanced Chinese)*. Carnegie Mellon University Press.

Wu, S., Yu, Y., Zhang, Y., & Tian, W. (2011). *Chinese link: Beginning Chinese* (2nd ed.). Pearson.

Yamashita, J., & Shiotsu, T. (2017). Comprehension and knowledge components that predict L2 reading: A latent-trait approach. *Applied Linguistics, 38*(1), 43–67.

13 Validation of a Chinese online placement test

Liu Li

Introduction

With the development of Chinese programs at K-12 levels in the United States, an increasing number of incoming college students have had some previous Chinese learning experience. To accurately assess their language proficiency and correctly place them into the appropriate proficiency level at college has become a challenge for college faculty who teach Chinese. Adding to the complexity of the challenge is the presence of heritage language learners of Chinese. These students have unbalanced language abilities—many of them are superb in listening comprehension, and some of them are good at speaking as well, but most of them are poor at reading or writing and have to start from the very beginning of the course sequence in order to be literate in Chinese. In many U.S. colleges and universities, there are not enough heritage language learners to offer a separate track of classes for them. So blended classes with both non-native speakers and heritage learners are more common. In such universities, a placement test with listening comprehension will skew the interpretation of the overall test results, as many heritage learners may score very high in the listening comprehension section, which may lead to their being placed to a proficiency level higher than their actual literacy ability.

To deal with this problem, this study employed the method of action research to combine teaching and research together. First, the researcher, as one of the faculty members teaching Chinese at the university level, worked with colleagues to design an online placement test focusing more on literacy abilities. Then, this study validated the online placement test at a university in the midwestern United States. The purpose of the placement test was that students, despite their various language backgrounds, would be placed in appropriate classes based on their Chinese literacy proficiency. The Chinese program in this study offered language courses at three levels (beginning, intermediate, and advanced). Incoming students with previous learning experience needed to take a placement test to decide which level of the course was most suitable for their current level of Chinese literacy ability. The web-based placement test was designed to achieve the goal of placing incoming students into one of the three proficiency levels before the classes started. With a high enough score, students could be placed out of the

DOI: 10.4324/9781003029038-17

lower-division courses, making them eligible for enrollment in other upper-division courses, which focus on topics related to culture, linguistics, and literature. The cutoff score for the web-based test was determined by the performance criteria and levels established using the previous paper-based test that students took on campus.

Prior to the development of the online placement test, a paper-based version of the placement test was used to place students into courses of the Chinese language program. The decision to move to an online format was first initiated by the university administrators, who determined that incoming students' orientation campus visits could be used more effectively if all university placement tests were taken online prior to the campus visit. This necessitated the creation of an online exam. The movement to an online format afforded the opportunity to address certain limitations of the paper-based test. First, it could make quick placement decisions and promptly inform students, teachers, and administrators of the results. Second, it has been found that a web-based language test could provide greater, more authentic breadth of content and permit diverse, multimodal test inputs (Shin, 2012). This chapter reports the process for developing and validating a Chinese placement test.

The first part of this chapter introduces the background information of the study. The second part explains how to design the placement test to include different test tasks. Altogether, 125 items were created and refined. In the third part, the test response data was analyzed. Both quantitative and qualitative evidence were used to support test inferences. Quantitatively, the response data was first analyzed to test its reliability and validity. Qualitative evidence (interviews and questionnaires) was collected for the evaluation of the test. After discussing the findings, this chapter concludes with suggestions for future research.

Literature review

Action research

Action research is a systematic process of examining the evidence. According to Burns (2009), action research is the combination and interaction of two modes of activity—action and research. The action is located within certain social contexts, like classrooms and schools. Typically, the components of "action" involve developments and interventions into the process to bring about improvement and change. The components of "research" involve systematic observation and analysis of the developments and changes in order to identify the underlying rationale for the action and to make further changes as required based on findings and outcomes. The main purpose of doing action research is to bridge the gap between the ideal (the most effective ways of doing things) and the real (the actual ways of doing things) in a certain social situation (Burns, 2009).

The results of action research are practical and relevant. They can inform theory. Action research is different from other forms of research as there is less concern for the universality of findings. Instead, more value is placed on the relevance of the findings to the researcher and the local collaborators. Action research is often conducted by teachers who also play the role of the researchers. While they are exploring the theoretical significance of their research, they are equally interested in finding ways to improve the specific educational situation for their students. Statistics may be collected, but they are not the only focus of the research.

Action research was used in the current study for two reasons. First, instead of conducting an experiment, this study was designed to solve a specific, real-world problem. This constitutes the component of "action." Second, the researcher in this study was interested in providing a model to bridge the gap between academic research findings and practical applications. This constitutes the component of "research."

Test validity and validation approaches

Although validity theories have changed over time, validity is still a central concept in testing and has remained the main purpose in all language assessment investigations (Chapelle, 2012; Fulcher & Davidson, 2007; Weir, 2005). Test validity refers to the degree to which the test actually measures what it claims to measure (Fulcher & Davidson, 2007). It is the extent to which inferences and conclusions made on the basis of test scores are appropriate and meaningful. The term "validation" refers to the process through which evidence is gathered to make validity arguments. Validation involves an evaluation of the plausibility and appropriateness of proposed interpretations and uses of test scores.

The test validation process is informative for assessment development and refinement (Kane, 1992, 2012). Validation involves many distinct research procedures. Kane (2012) suggested that the best way to substantiate the proposed claim is to be specific about all the pieces of evidence that can be presented.

Language testing has undergone a similar trend, like the developments of testing and assessment in general education. In the beginning of the 20th century, language testing used the traditional types of validity (Lado, 1961; Henning, 1987). At that time, validity was traditionally examined through Messick's validity framework (Messick, 1989). In this framework, Messick argued that different aspects of validity, including content, concurrent, construct, and consequential validity, should be viewed as a unitary concept that integrates both evidential and consequential basis for validation. At the beginning of the 1990s, Bachman (1990) adopted the unitary concept of validity to guide the collection of multiple sources of evidence to support the interpretations and uses made of test scores. Later, Bachman (2004) further developed the model and created the evidence-centered test design approach to emphasize the importance of basing test design, test development, test scoring, and test use on sound evidentiary reasoning.

More recently, a model developed by Kane (1992, 2012) has increasingly gained popularity. The model, called the argument-based approach, was meant to guide assessment researchers to justify the proposed interpretations and uses of test scores. Kane created this model to collect and interpret validity evidence.

The argument-based approach requires building a conceptual framework to investigate empirical evidence and draw inferences based on the evidence. The argument-based approach consists of three main stages: a clear claim, an interpretive argument, and a validity argument, which work together to achieve the validation of score interpretations and uses. During the validation process, several factors are normally examined. The first one is called the Discrimination Index (DI), which is a basic measure of the validity of an item. It is a measure of an item's ability to discriminate between those who scored high on the total test and those who scored low. One of the major concerns about a test was whether it could differentiate between low- and high-proficiency students, and this depends upon the selection of test items. The more discriminating the items in a test are, the more reliable the test is. The value of the range of DI is from 1 to -1. If an item has a "0" value of DI, it shows that the item cannot discriminate between low- and high-proficiency students. A value of 0.4 for DI is considered good. This approach has been used as one of the standard frameworks for conceptualizing validity in language testing (McNamara, 2006). Another factor to take into consideration during the validation process is Facility Value (FV), which is the difficulty of a test item; that is, the percentage of the students who give the right answer. The usual aim of the test designer is to achieve middling facility indices ranging from about 40–60% required of FV for a test item ranges from 0.33 to 0.67. A value below 0.33 reveals the item is difficult, whereas a value above 0.67 shows that the item is easy.

The argument-based approach has been used as one of the standard frameworks for conceptualizing validity in language testing (McNamara, 2006). The co-existence of multiple approaches to validation in language testing means that it is up to individual researchers and educators to select the workable model for themselves based on their own needs and specific educational situations.

In the present study, we adopted Kane's argument-based approach. Based on this approach, assessment evidence from various sources in our study was integrated into a coherent validity discussion and conclusion. The reason for this is that none of the evidence is sufficient by itself as evidence of validity. Validity is an integrative evaluative argument (Messick, 1989). The test is considered valid if it does what it is supposed to test. This means, our test would be said to be valid if it had measured accurately what it was supposed to measure.

Reliability

If a test is not reliable, it is also not valid. Test validity also requires test reliability. Determined by the consistency of its scores, test reliability refers to the degree to which a test is consistent and stable in measuring what it is intended to measure (Hughes, 2003). That is, a test is reliable if it is consistent within itself and across time.

There are several types of reliability estimates: 1) Test-retest reliability, which indicates the repeatability of test scores with the passage of time. This estimate also reflects the stability of the characteristic or construct being measured by the test. 2) Alternate or parallel form reliability, which indicates how consistent test scores are likely to be if a person takes two or more forms of a test. 3) Inter-rater reliability, which indicates how consistent test scores are likely to be if the test is scored by two or more raters. Inter-rater reliability coefficients are typically lower than other types of reliability estimates. However, it is possible to obtain higher levels of inter-rater reliability if raters are appropriately trained. 4) Internal consistency reliability, which indicates the extent to which items on a test measure the same thing. A high internal consistency reliability coefficient for a test indicates that the items on the test are very similar to each other in content. Cronbach's alpha (Cronbach, 1951) is a measure of internal consistency; that is, how closely related a set of items are as a group.

The current study employed two of these methods to examine the reliability of the test. We could not determine the test-retest reliability of our test, as it was conducted just once as the trial. However, Cronbach's alpha was used to measure the reliability of our test. The reliability of a test can be indicated by the reliability coefficient. It is denoted by the letter "r," and is expressed as a number ranging between 0 and 1.00, with r = 0 indicating no reliability, and r = 1.00 indicating perfect reliability.

Language placement test and its validation

Previous research on placement testing for languages other than English has grown remarkably over the past several decades (e.g., Bernhardt et al., 2004; Eda et al., 2008). Issues of reliability and validity have drawn considerable attention in the empirical literature. In many studies on language placement tests (e.g.: Wall et al., 1994; Fulcher, 1997), several approaches to assessing reliability (e.g., correlation coefficients, inter- and intra-rater reliability, Rasch data modeling, etc.) and validity (e.g., analyses of cut scores, principal component analysis, concurrent validity, content validity, and feedback from students and instructors) were employed. These studies demonstrate the range of approaches that are appropriate for the development and assessment of language placement tests. In fact, these approaches have been widely adopted in more recent studies, which have served to strengthen methods of language placement testing development and evaluation (e.g., Bernhardt et al., 2004; Eda et al., 2008; Pardo-Ballester, 2010; Shin, 2008).

Several studies have investigated the practicality and efficiency of online language placement testing in a university-level foreign language program. For example, Bernhardt et al. (2004) examined the process of using the internet to deliver language placement tests to incoming and transfer students at Stanford University, showing that web-based placement testing could be conducted in a reliable and valid manner. Furthermore, their findings revealed that online testing was particularly beneficial for testing administrators and instructors because they could make more effective decisions when they had more time to contemplate a student's performance. For students, it was convenient to take the exam at a time and place of their choosing, which could save them an additional trip to campus.

Most previous studies on language placement tests were about a language other than Chinese. The current study examined a Chinese placement to fill in the void. The analysis of a Chinese placement test in this chapter could improve and expand research such as Bernhardt et al. (2004) by gathering and presenting additional evidence in support of test validity. The findings could also provide urgently needed information on the test validation procedures that are based on a logical framework of argumentation and supporting evidence to address the appropriateness of both score interpretations and uses (Carr, 2011).

Research questions

As discussed before, few studies examining the validity and use of placement tests have offered models of validation geared toward Chinese language programs. The present study investigated the validity and reliability of an online Chinese placement test to illustrate how to examine issues of validity and reliability for Chinese language programs. Specifically, Kane's argument-based approach was adopted to design and validate the placement test.

The purpose of the study was twofold. First, the study was undertaken to develop a placement test appropriate for the Chinese program in a university in the Midwest. The second purpose was to validate and evaluate the newly developed placement test. That is, the primary focus of the study was to examine the procedures followed in the development of the placement test and find justification for using its scores for placement decisions. Although different types of evidence were required for each aspect, evidence from multiple sources would be subsequently integrated into a coherent validity discussion and conclusion.

The study was designed to answer the following research questions:

1. How valid is the test? More specifically, is there any evidence related to the following types of validity?
   a. Content validity— Do the items in the placement test represent what the students have learned?
   b. Criterion-related validity—Do students' performances in the placement test match other measures of their abilities?
2. How reliable is the test? More specifically:
   a. What is the inter-rater reliability of the test?
   b. What is the internal consistency reliability of the test?
3. What is the result of the test takers' evaluation of the test?

In the section that follows, specific data collection and data analysis methods will be presented.

Methodology

As the purpose of the study was twofold—to develop and to validate a new online placement test for the Chinese program of a U.S. university—the study had two steps. First, the researcher investigated the procedures for developing a good placement that could serve as an accurate placement measurement device on students' literacy development. Then, the emphasis was placed on gathering evidence to support the validity of the newly developed placement test.

Test development

Designed for incoming college students who had studied Chinese before, the test was delivered via the internet. Specifically, incoming students took the test on their own (at home using their computers) before arriving at the institution for their first academic semester of study. The online test was not adaptive, meaning that subsequent items were not presented to the students from a bank of items depending on their response to the previous item. To facilitate comprehension of the demands of the assessment, all instructions were provided in English. Students were permitted to take the test one time only, after which their responses were recorded and scored electronically.

The placement test consisted of three sections: vocabulary, grammar, and reading comprehension. Three proficiency levels needed to be separated: Beginning, Intermediate, and Advanced. Altogether there were 50 items of vocabulary questions (25 points in total), 40 items of grammar questions (40 points in total), and 35 items of reading comprehension from five passages (35 points in total). Altogether, there were 100 points. The cut-off points were: <34 points for the Beginning Level; 34–66 points for the Intermediate Level; >67 for the Advanced Level. The total time for the test was 60 minutes. The Intermediate Level was about the equivalent of the ACTFL Intermediate Low, and the Advanced Level was about the equivalent of the ACTFL Intermediate High.

The vocabulary section was designed to measure the ability to understand common words. The examinees were presented with an underlined word in a sentence. Then, the examinees identified from among the alternatives in English the one that best matched the meaning of the underline Chinese word.

The grammar section was designed to measure the students' grammatical abilities through completing Chinese sentences. There was a blank in each sentence. The students needed to complete the sentence by choosing the correct answer from the four alternatives.

Reading comprehension was designed to measure the ability to derive meaning from written Chinese texts. The participants were presented brief passages followed by several questions regarding facts contained in the passage and interpretation of the information. The passages contained in the test were designed to be representative of the types and different levels of reading proficiency. Allowing different topics to be covered reduces the potential bias from a restricted range of topic areas. The test chose texts from general readings rather than specialized textbooks. The texts were relatively non-technical and able to be understood by a general audience. Each chosen text was of an appropriate level of difficulty. The information required to solve the task was stated in or could be implied from the text.

To write the reading comprehension question items, the test designers sampled different sentences, texts, and topics. In reading comprehension, both global and local questions were designed to ask test takers to synthesize information or draw conclusions at a subtle level. Questions that asked for a superficial understanding of clearly stated information were avoided. Important information in the text was the focus, rather than the trivial information.

The test adopted a multiple-choice format, which is one of the most widely used of the objective test formats. There were four alternatives for each question. Cohen et al. (1996) recommended the use of four alternatives, because it decreases the percentage of getting an item right by chance to 25%. Although multiple-choice format may have some limitations, such as the difficulty to construct the items and the facilitation of cheating and guessing (Hughes, 2003), it has the ability to assess higher mental skills such as analysis, application, inference, and evaluation (Green, 2012). Technically, the quality of the multiple-choice items can be monitored through the statistical analyses of the items (Haladyna & Rodriguez, 2013). Using item analysis enables test constructors to determine the difficulty and discriminatory power of the multiple-choice items. It also directs the attention of the test constructors to potentially problematic items. More importantly, the multiple-choice format can be easily and objectively scored. For these reasons, multiple choice has become the most suitable format for placement tests.

The test designers made a commitment that the test would relate to and represent the content of the Chinese curricula in use in the Chinese program at the university. They conducted individual content analysis of all the test items. They also identified the specific knowledge and skills needed to get each item right, specified the testing points of each distractor (i.e., the wrong answer choice alternative), and recorded their judgments.

Test validation

The newly developed online placement test needed validating before it could be officially launched and used on the university website. Trial testing items were operationalized to gain their psychometrical properties and carry out the validity study. In this section, trial test demographic information is presented first, followed by information on how results from the trial tests and the follow-up survey through a questionnaire and semi-structured interviews helped further refine the construct validity. Specific data collection and data analysis methods will be presented in the section of the validation process.

Participants

The participants of this trial test comprised 56 college students. These students were from classes at three different proficiency levels: 23 students were in Chinese 101, 20 were in Chinese 201 and 13 were in Chinese 301. They took the test online within the week after their midterm examination.

Students' responses to each item of the placement test were scored electronically. The maximum possible score was 100. No partial credit was given in the scoring of students' responses to each test item. Students' test scores were computed as the sum of all correct responses to each item of the test.

Instruments

QUANTITATIVE MEASUREMENTS

Two analyses of validity were conducted. The first examined test content in relation to curriculum content; the second examined the nature of placement decisions generated by the scores of the new online placement test. Regarding the assessment of content validity, the test designers manually examined the content of the textbooks for each course students could be placed into. The assigned textbooks for each course that were examined were *Integrated Chinese Book 1, 2, & 3*. Regarding the second method of test score validation, the scores of the new online placement test were compared with students' midterm exam scores. Both scores were examined by means of correlation analysis (Pearson r). The test constructors also measured the discrimination power and difficulty level of the test items through calculating their discrimination index and facility value.

Cronbach's alpha was examined as the statistical measure of internal consistency (Cronbach, 1951) for the test scores of the 56 test takers. Reliability coefficients were also examined to identify items that may have influenced the internal consistency of the test to a greater degree. Specifically, Cronbach's alpha for each item of the test was examined if it was to be removed from the test.

QUALITATIVE MEASUREMENTS

The instruments were intended to measure a variety of issues regarding test takers' perceptions: overall experience, issues related to the computer delivery system, clarity of instructions, and difficulty level of tasks. Using the approach of action research, this study asked students to evaluate the test by means of a survey questionnaire. The aim of the survey was to understand test takers' feelings about their experiences of taking the placement test and to gain feedback to inform further test item development. The design of the survey primarily took the format of five Likert-scales (strongly agree, agree, no opinion, disagree, and strongly disagree), rather than asking questions. Details of the items on the survey were:

1. The test was easy to navigate.
2. It was difficult to know when to start/stop the test.
3. The format of the test (multiple-choice questions) is acceptable.
4. The reading section was easy.
5. The vocabulary section was easy.
6. The grammar section was easy.
7. The test is fair, and reflects my Chinese proficiency level appropriately.

Semi-structured interviews were conducted after the survey. The main interview prompts and the number of comments were:

1. Overall, how did you find the experience? (Structure, layout, difficulty, timings, etc.)
2. Did you encounter any significant problems?
3. Do you think the test gives a good measure of your Chinese skills?
4. Which item type did you find most challenging?
5. Please provide general comments on Reading Questions.
6. Please provide general comments on Vocabulary Questions.
7. Please provide general comments on Grammar Questions.

Results

Validity

Validity coefficient

For construct validation, a correlation study was carried out between the subjects' scores on the placement test and their midterm examination scores. The results are shown in Table 13.1:

Table 13.1 Pearson Product-moment Correlations Between Scores on the Placement Test and Scores on the Midterm Exams

	Grammar	Reading comprehension	Vocabulary	Total
Placement test	0.72**	0.78**	0.66**	0.71**

* Significant at .005
** Significant at .01

The correlation coefficients reveal that there was a moderate relationship between the placement test and students' midterm examination scores ($r = 0.71$). The coefficients also demonstrate that the placement test had the stronger relationship with the grammar and reading comprehension sections in the students' midterm examinations. The finding is expected because to some extent, there was a relationship between the scores obtained on the placement test and these two sections in the midterm examinations.

We also conducted the correlation analysis between the placement test scores and the listening section of the midterm examinations, which turned out to be low ($r = 0.33$). This finding is an important piece of evidence of construct validity because it supports our assumption that reading and listening measure different skills and may not be expected to be related to one another, especially if heritage students are involved.

274   Liu Li

Table 13.2 Discrimination Index of 8 Randomly Selected Items

Item #	Item1	Item6	Item21	Item35	Item50	Item66	Item79	Item97
DI	0.62	0.64	0.47	0.43	0.52	0.48	0.39	0.34

Table 13.3 Facility Value of Some Items

Item #	Item 13	Item 27	Item 44	Item 55	Item 77	Item 91	Item 103	Item 117
FV	0.675	0.7	0.25	0.325	0.325	0.325	0.25	0.275

Item discrimination

The discrimination power of each item is indicated by its Discrimination Index (DI). In our test, we calculated the value of DI for about eight items randomly selected from the test. The values are shown in Table 13.2.

These values show that these items in the test are discriminating well. However, items with DI below 0.4 need to be modified and improved.

Item difficulty

The difficulty of an item is its Facility Value (FV). The FV of every test item was calculated. Some items having the value of FV below 0.33 and above 0.67 are shown in Table 13.3.

These statistics provided information about the effectiveness of the placement test. Since the FV indices provided information on the difficulty level of individual items, they informed the test designers about the power of individual items to distinguish proficient students from the less proficient ones.

About 20% of the items in the test are in the extreme range of difficulty (i.e., they have IF values higher than 80%). The majority of the items were in a median level of difficulty (i.e., they have IF values within the range of 20%-80%). About 20% of the items are considered easy (i.e., they have IF values lower than 20%). The FV indices of the items indicate that the items could discriminate the high-scoring students from the low-scoring ones fairly. The majority of the items had satisfactory FV values ranging from 0.24 to 0.78. Such a distribution was expected, as the aim of the placement test was to separate students into different proficiency levels.

Reliability

The inter-rater reliability

To evaluate the content relevance, content representativeness, and technical quality of the test, Messick (1994) acknowledged the importance of expert judgment. In order to mitigate against parochial topics and items, all items written were peer reviewed by three instructors from two other universities. These two other universities used the same textbooks and had similar proficiency levels for their beginning, intermediate, and advanced classes. Peer reviewers were instructed to focus their review on questions related to authenticity and sensitivity. The relevant parts of their checklists include:

1) Does the length of each item match its specification?
2) Does the linguistic complexity of each item match its specification?
3) Does the genre of stimulus match its specification?
4) Does the rhetorical structure of each item match its specification?
5) Is each item appropriate in terms of academic topic?
6) Can test takers get each item correct from world or background knowledge alone?
7) Does the item introduce any requirement with respect to subject matter content knowledge?
8) Is the test level appropriate for the content of each item?
9) Are the level of knowledge and skills of each item appropriate for its difficulty level?

Three types of status were given to the peer reviewed items: "accept," reject," and "discuss/pending." If no issue was identified by the peer reviewers, the item was accorded the status of "accept." All three reviewers obtained an average acceptance rate of 91.3%.

Internal consistency reliability

The students' performance on the placement was scored. A standardized item analysis was conducted on the score obtained. The analysis provided the researcher with descriptive statistics and item statistics. The descriptive statistics are shown in Table 13.4, which presents the descriptive statistics for the placement test.

As shown in Table 13.4, the reliability of the placement test was high (.89), indicating the test is fairly reliable. The mean of the placement test is 45.7, reflecting that the placement test was not too easy for the students. The finding was expected because many students who took the placement test were from lower-level classes.

Table 13.4 Descriptive Statistics for the Placement Test

Descriptive statistics	Index
Number of participants	56
Number of items	125
Maximum score	100
Mean	45.7
Standard deviation	15.20
Standard error of measurement in raw score	4.98
Kuder-Richardson Formula 20 reliability	.89

The value of Cronbach's alpha for our test was 0.843, which proved the reliability of the test. However, this high value of reliability of the test is due to the objective nature of the test. As indicated in our validation framework, there may have been items that greatly influenced estimates of reliability. To address this rebuttal, the test designers examined reliability coefficients to identify those items that may have had a greater influence on the overall internal consistency of the test relative to other test items. With regard to this measure, we found that no single item greatly influenced estimates of the test's internal consistency. Specifically, hypothetically removing any item of the test did not result in change of the test's overall reliability by more than .002. This finding suggests that the test was internally consistent.

Examining the findings for reliability by test section, in contrast, it was revealed that the vocabulary section (k = 50) was very reliable, α = .89. The other sections were not found to be as internally consistent as the vocabulary section, possibly due to the lower number of test items in the Grammar Section and Reading Comprehension Section: for Grammar Section, α = .81 (K=40), for Reading Comprehension Section, α = .76 (k = 35).

Qualitative evidence: evaluation from test takers

The best approach to check test usefulness is to let the test users evaluate it. Thus, this section describes their evaluation. The 56 students completed a short questionnaire after the trial test. Qualitative data obtained through this posttest survey showed that a large proportion of students found that it was a fair test of their literacy ability, which was a positive comment about the content validity of the test. In response to the question about test format, students found that the multiple-choice questions were acceptable. However, some of them complained that it was time-consuming to read four options in the Reading Comprehension Section, as the options were long sentences. The students also found the texts in Reading Comprehension interesting, but had some difficulty in reading Text 4 and Text 5. It may be because Text 4 and Text 5 were longer and more difficult than the previous ones.

Follow-up semi-structured interviews were conducted with 15 randomly-chosen students covering their concerns about the test in terms of layout, structure, difficulty level, item type, and content. These interviews provided supplementary data to the faculty on test takers' perceptions and helped highlight areas for further improvement.

Overall, the students reported positive experiences of taking the test. They considered the layout, structure, item types, and content generally acceptable. They all reported that they liked the web-based version, as it is more convenient and flexible.

The main problems or challenges the students encountered, which could possibly undermine the argument of establishing construct validity, were:

1. Some test takers felt that the test was difficult because it included three different sections. The difficulty level of the reading texts could be higher than that

of other Chinese tests of a similar nature. As a result, some items took them longer to understand.
2. Some test takers who had problems completing the test asked for more time.
3. Even though they thought the test instructions and test structure were clear overall, students still felt that the standard directions for certain item types could be made more understandable.

Discussion

This chapter has presented the work that supports the validity claims of a Chinese online placement test. It represents an attempt to collect in one document the wide range of work, both qualitative and analytical, that has contributed and continues to contribute to the development of high-quality test items.

In response to the first research question, the researchers found that the online placement test was valid in terms of content and the placement decisions being made based on test scores. Most of the items being examined had appropriate discrimination power and difficulty levels suitable for a placement test. Nevertheless, there were areas in which the test validity could be strengthened. For example, test content could be modified to reflect the range of cultural topics observed in the course materials and syllabi of the target enrollment classes.

To address the second research question of the study, the designers found that the online placement test was reliable, as demonstrated by means of statistical estimates of internal consistency using the Cronbach's alpha and examination of reliability coefficients.

As for the third research question, the data from the students' survey and the interviews also indicated that a majority of the students had positive comments on the layout, format, and difficulty level of the test. The qualitative data supported that validity of the test from a different angle. The students also provided some feedback on how to improve the test for a better experience. The results indicated the validity of the placement test.

As discussed before, the researchers adopted the argument-based approach to design and validate the placement test following the three main stages: making a clear claim, setting an interpretive argument, and planning a validity argument, which work together to achieve the validation of score interpretations and uses. During the validation process, several indexes were used to examine and interpret the scores. The process suggests that the argument-based approach could also be used to guide the design and validation of tests assessing Chinese proficiency.

In general, the insights drawn from these methods for test validation can be used to inform other test constructors of how to prepare their Chinese language placement test. This information may be particularly helpful for large Chinese programs in which administrators or coordinators need to make prompt decisions about course placement of incoming students. This chapter illustrated how to outline, substantiate, and provide evidence for the reliability, validity, and use of a placement test. Specifically, using this study as an example, Chinese programs should set clear goals at the beginning stage. With the goals in mind, the test constructors could work on the designing specifics of the test, including content, types, items, and format, etc. After the design has been completed, the trial test is needed to demonstrate that the test consistently produces similar results, which can be shown by examining simple statistical measures, such as Cronbach's alpha. Once the test has been determined to be valid, it must be demonstrated that, as a measure, it is reliable for its intended uses. Validity and reliability can be determined in a number of ways. Utilizing several methods, the designers can successfully examine the validity and reliability of their online placement test with both qualitative and quantitative data.

Conclusion and implications

Every year, Chinese language instructors and language program administrators face the task of developing, administering, and assessing online placement tests for the purpose of enrolling incoming and transfer students into courses that are suitable for their proficiency levels. In response to the need for a concise, accessible example of test validation from which Chinese programs can benefit, this chapter reports the findings of a study using action research that used the argument-based approach (Kane, 2012) to develop and then examine the reliability and validity of an online Chinese placement test.

This chapter first reported on the measures taken to design and validate validity and reliability of the online Chinese placement test. The results demonstrate that the item types, online presentation modes, content, task types, required competencies, and response format have enabled the construction of the assessment, resulting in a coherent model of test takers' Chinese literacy skills. Furthermore, a global perspective and standard has been developed from the design and validation processes involved in item writing and item peer review, and a mixed-method approach for item sensitivity review has provided a systematic method of scrutinizing items for validity and reliability. Data from the validity process both underpins and permits the comprehensive analysis presented in this chapter. Concurrent validity has been established from the beginning of the test development process by analyzing the coefficient results and by comparing results from another test of a similar nature.

This study will have multiple implications. Regarding the production of knowledge, the researchers hope to contribute to the literature on Chinese language test validation in other universities. This is an under-researched area in the world, where the level of Chinese language testing is trying to keep up with the increasing need of Chinese language learning. This study will be helpful to those who would like to learn more about the way institutions select their students and the quality of their Chinese placement tests. Also, the conceptual framework and the methodology used in the study are applicable to other validation projects where similar assumptions are made by test users. The work done to date on validating the Chinese placement test continues to be scrutinized to add further weight to the validity proposition.

Another point of discussion here is the pedagogical impact of designing and implementing an online test. Perhaps the most notable impact in the departmental context of the present study is the ability to keep test and course content more closely matched over time. The online test offers the flexibility to update test content as minor adjustments to curriculum are made. Additionally, in a society that has been witness to an ever-increasing use of computer-based and online technologies, especially during the Covid pandemic period, using a web-based test has the potential to deliver input and content in a manner that not only is familiar to language learners, but also mirrors the use of technology that learners are exposed to in the classroom. For instance, within the institutional context of the present study, instructors are increasingly moving to a web-based format for the design and delivery of course examinations. This pedagogical practice is one that has likely been influenced by current education context and has proven to be an accessible and flexible means for test delivery.

References

Bachman, L. F. (1990). *Fundamental considerations in language testing*. Oxford University Press.

Bachman, L. F. (2004). *Statistical analysis for language assessment*. Cambridge University Press.

Bernhardt, E. B., Rivera, R. J., & Kamil, M. L. (2004). The practicality and efficiency of web-based placement testing for college-level language programs. *Foreign Language Annals*, *37*(3), 356–365.

Burns, A. (2009). Action research in second language teacher education. In A. Burns & J. C. Richards (Eds.), *The Cambridge guide to second language teacher education* (pp. 289–297). Cambridge University Press.

Carr, N. T. (2011). *Designing and analyzing language tests*. Oxford University Press.

Chapelle, C. A. (2012). Validity argument for language assessment: The framework is simple . . . . *Language Testing*, *29*(1), 19–27.

Cohen, R., Rothman, A. I., Bilan, S., & Ross, J. (1996). Analysis of the psychometric properties of eight administrations of an objective structured clinical examination used to assess international medical graduates. *Academic Medicine*, *71*(Suppl 1), 22–24.

Cronbach, L. J. (1951). Coefficient alpha and the internal structure of tests. *Psychometrika*, *16*(3), 297–334.

Eda, S., Itomitsu, M., & Noda, M. (2008). The Japanese skills test as an on-demand placement test: Validity comparisons and reliability. *Foreign Language Annals*, *41*(2), 218–236.

Fulcher, G. (1997). An English language placement test: Issues in reliability and validity. *Language Testing*, *14*(2), 113–138.

Fulcher, G., & Davidson, F. (2007). *Language testing and assessment: An advanced resource book*. Routledge.

Green, A. (2012). Placement testing. In C. Coombe, B. O'Sullivan, P. Davidson, & S. Stoynoff (Eds.), *The Cambridge guide to language assessment* (pp. 164–170). Cambridge University Press.

Haladyna, T. M., & Rodriguez, M. C. (2013). *Developing and validating test items*. Routledge.

Henning, G. (1987). *A guide to language testing: Development, evaluation, research*. Newberry House Publishers.

Hughes, A. (2003). *Testing for language teachers* (2nd ed.). Cambridge University Press.

Kane, M. T. (1992). An argument-based approach to validity. *Psychological Bulletin, 112*, 527–535.

Kane, M. T. (2012). Validating score interpretations and uses. *Language Testing, 29*(1), 3–17.

Lado, R. (1961). *Language testing: The construction and use of foreign language tests: A teacher's book*. Longman.

McNamara, T. (2006). Validity in language testing: The challenge of Sam Messick's legacy. *Language Assessment Quarterly, 3*(1), 31–51.

Messick, S. (1989). Validity. In R. L. Linn (Ed.), *Educational measurement* (3rd ed., pp. 13–103). American Council on Education and Macmillan Publishing Company.

Messick, S. (1994, October 25–26). *Alternative modes of assessment, uniform standards of validity. Research report*. Presented at a Conference on Evaluating Alternatives to Traditional Testing for Selection sponsored by Bowling Green State University.

Pardo-Ballester, C. (2010). The validity argument of a web-based Spanish listening exam: Test usefulness evaluation. *Language Assessment Quarterly, 7*, 137–159.

Shin, S.-Y. (2008). Examining the construct validity of a web-based academic listening test: An investigation of the effects of constructed response formats in a listening test. *The Spaan Fellowship Working Papers in Second or Foreign Language, 6*, 95–129.

Shin, S.-Y. (2012). Web-based language testing. In C. Coombe, B. O'Sullivan, P. Davidson, & S. Stoynoff (Eds.), *The Cambridge guide to language assessment* (pp. 274–279). Cambridge University Press.

Wall, D., Clapham, C., & Alderson, J. C. (1994). Evaluating a placement test. *Language Testing, 11*(3), 321–344.

Weir, D. (2005). *Spanish grammar: A quick reference* (2nd ed.). Pearson Education.

Index

Note: Page locators in **bold** indicate a table. Page locators in *italics* indicate a figure

accuracy: behavioral 35; language 218, 258; reading 13; stroke order 2, 13, 18–20, 24; writing 3, 66, 71, 76–77
acquisition: character 2, 44; literacy 46–47, 179, 183; stroke-order 15, 20
alphabetic: language 56, 63, 103, 217; letters 43, 45, 56; writing system 13, 46
analysis of variance (ANOVA) 18, 122, 143
Anderson, Ann 202
Anderson, Jim 185
Anderson, Richard C. 113, 249
Appendix 80, 84, 242
authentic language environment 220, 227

Bachman, Lyle F. 266
Baldauf, Richard B. Jr. 62
basic: accuracy 150; characters 23, 44, 62, 70, 91, 115, 168, 179; communication 258; strokes 13
Bear, Donald R. 20
Becker, Cynthia A. 213
behavioral: accuracy 32, 35; changes 225; testing 35, 38
Bell, Jill Sinclair 62
Bernhardt, Elizabeth B. 157, 162, 268–269
bilingual: dual coding theory 29; learners 29, 125, 183 (*see also* CFL learners; L2 learners); reading/readers 4, 93–94, 125; study, 92participants 50, 54
Blewitt, Pamela (*et al* 2009) 202
Bruton, Anthony (*et al* 2011) 128
Burns, Anne 265
Burt, Jennifer S. 13
Bus, Adriana G. (*et al* 1995) 201

Cantonese-Speaking Heritage Language Learners (Can-HLLs) 95–96
Cao, Fan (*et al* 2017) 32, 35, 38
Carruthers, Jean J. 13
Causes of Comprehension Breakdown and Their Frequencies **163–164**
Chan, Shui-duen 159
Chang, Li Yun (*et al* 2015) 32, 35, 38
character: acquisition 2, 44, 65; misconception 14, 44; production 14, 50–51, **52–53**, 58; reading 14, 45, 56, 58, 149; recognition skills 50–51, **52**, 55–57, 89 (*see also* character recognition [CR]); single component 17; three-character recognition 4, 30, 64, 96; typing vs handwriting 43
character recognition (CR): subskills 91–94, 100, 105
character stings 28, 30
character writing: efficiency 24, 61, 64, 66, 71, 75–78; process 14, 23, 47; stroke distance 22; stroke order, effects of 13–15
Chen, Chen (*et al* 2014) 33–35
Chen, Hongjun 138, 149
Chen, Ouhao 29
Chen, Xi (*et al* 2009) 113
Cheng, Yahua (*et al* 2016) 94
Cheung, Him (*et al* 2007) 92–93
Chinen, Kiyomi 190–191
Chinese: language instructors 14, 21, 23, 95, 278; reading, as challenging 45, 57, 156, 218; textbooks **255–257**; writing system 13, 21–24, 30, 46, 111, 156, 174
Chinese American 6, 179
Chinese as a foreign language (CFL) 3, 32, 43, 48, 61, 246, 252, 260
Chinese as a heritage language (CHL) 4, 111, 160, 179; *see also* heritage language (HL)

Chinese as a second language (CSL) 14, 32, 96, 111, 175
Chinese as additional language (CAL): learning/learners 1, 3, 5, 8, 222; reading strategies 157–159, 161, 164; students 217–219, 223, 234, 237
Chinese Foreign Language Learners (CFLLs) 95–96
Chinese language proficiency 234, 237
Chinese as additional language (CAL): reading skills 3, 8–9, 45, 125, 137, 211, 259–260
Chuang, Hui-Ya 34
Chung, Kevin K. H. 34, 37
coding *see* word coding
cognition 7, 28, 31, 219
Cognitive Load Theory (CLT) 28–30, 32, 38, 40
Cohen, R. (*et al* 1996) 271
comprehension breakdown 5, 156, 160, 162–163, 174
computers 43, 45, 47, 50, 188, 270
cross-lagged panel (CLP) 5, 133, 141, *142*, 144, **145**
cross-language transfer 114, 127
curriculum, mainstream Chinese 218, 223, **224**

Dang, Y. 15
data collection 185, 203–204, 269, 271
deep comprehension 4, 97, 103–104
deep reading comprehension 89, 94, 100
DeFrancis, John 62
Dew, J. E. 62
Ding, Ting 182
Discrimination Index (DI) 267, 272, **274**
Dominguez, Higinio 200
Dong, Yang (*et al* 2020) 103
drama performance 6
Dual Coding Theory (DCT) 28–30, 32, 35, 38, 40
dual-coded word learning 28, 36, 39
DVC triangle (golden triangle of reading skill) 133, 137, 148, 150–151

East, Martin 63
Education Bureau (EDB) 218
electronic devices: impact of using 45–46; orthographies 44; pinyin-based learning 43
English: as first language 43, 50, 56, 157; language skills 185, 193–194; translation 28, 34, 37–39, 50, 165

ethnicity 190, **224**
event related potentials (ERPs) 32, 35, 39–40
Everson, Michael E. 147
eye tracking 9, 39–40

Facility Value (FV) 267, **274**
Fidell, Linda 99
first language (L1) 29, 43, 45, 128, 157, 199
foreign language (FL) 150, 250, 252; *see also* Chinese as a foreign language
Fukaya, Atsushi 251
functional magnetic resonance imaging (fMRI) 32

General Certificate of Education (GCE) 218–222
General Certificate of Secondary Education (GCSE) 218
Giovanni, Flores B. d'Arcais 14
Grabe, William 90, 158
grammar knowledge 164, **165**, 166, **171**, 173, 175
Guder, Andreas 62
guided book reading 199–200, 202–203, 209, 212

Hall, Stuart 181
hand-writing skills 22–23, 259
handwriting *versus* typing 3, 49–50, **51**–**54**, 54–58
Hanzi test: coding and scoring 71; measures fluency and accuracy 70; responses and results 71–72, **73**, 74–75
He, Agnes Weiyun 182–183, 193
He, Xuchong 39
heritage language (HL) learners 111, 115–116, 122, 125–128, 179, 264
Hidi, Suzanne 219
hierarchical regression 100–101, 103
Hindman, Annemarie H. (*et al* 2008) 201
Holmes, Virginia M. 13
Hong Kong Diploma of Secondary Education Examination (HKDSE) 218, 223
Hongyan, Wang 33, 36
Hooper, Simon 30, 34, 38
Horiba, Yukie 251
Hsiao, Hsien-Sheng (*et al* 2015) 64
Hsiung, Hsiang-Yu (*et al* 2017) 16, 22, 64
Huang, Sha 158

identity: ethnic 182, 190–191; literacy 1, 6, 179, 187, 189, 192; reader's 201
International General Certificate of Secondary Education (IGCSE) 218, 223–224, 226
intervention studies 175

Jared, Debra (*et al* 2013) 29
Jen, Theresa 47
Jiang, Xiangying 251
Jin, Hong Gang 33–34, 64
Jo, Hye-Young 190

Kalyuga, Slava 29–30, 37
Kane, Michael 266
Kang, Hana 15, 25n2, 47
Ke, Sihui 159, 252
Kim, Hi-Sun Helen 190
knowledge refinement 246–247, 253, 259, 261
Koda, Keiko 114–115, 125, 181, 246, 252
Kong Special Administrative Region (HKSAR) 217
Ku, Heng-Yu 34
Ku, Yu-Min 113
Kuo, Li Jen 113
Kuo, Mei Liang Amy 30, 34, 38

L2 learners: English speaking 93, 95, 104–105, 134, 137, 250; reading comprehension subskills 87, 116, 124
lagged effects 5, 142
Lambert, Wallace 29
language knowledge 174, 199
language stimuli 28
language teacher's discursive behavior 199, 212
Laoshi, Wang (participant) 203–210
learner autonomy 3, 74–75, 220
learning environment 181, 184, 199, 220
Lee-Thompson, Li-Chun 157–158
Lee, Chee Ha 30, 37, 39
Lee, Jeong-Wong 250–251
Lever, rosemary 201
lexical competence 4, 132
Li, Chi-Keung (*et al* 2007) 14
Li, Duanduan **255**
Li, Wei 14
Lien, Y. J. 65
Lin, Chin Hsi 65
Linda (participant): comprehension scores 163; non-heritage learner 160; reading difficulties 164, **165**, 165–167; top-down strategy 168–169
literacy: development 2–3, 22, 45–46, 113, 179, 183–184, 186, 190, 192; identity 179, 187, 189, 192; variables 5
literature: reading 148; review 43, 61, 89, 156, 180, 200, 219, 265; search 31
Liu, I. 63
Liu, Irene **255**
Lo (*et al* 2015) 14
logographic 30, 44–45
Long, Michael H. 220
Lü, Chan (*et al* 2015) *114*, *181*
Lu, Ming-Tsan Pierre (*et al* 2013) 35
Lyu, Boning (*et al* 2021) 48

Mandarin: dialect 96, 115, 182, 190; speaking 95, 160; writing system 30–31
Mandarin-Speaking Heritage Language Learners (Man-HLLs) 95
Martínez, José Manuel 200
McClelland, James L. 248
McNeil, Levi 157
mental imagery 28
Messick, Samuel 266, 274
Modern Chinese Frequency Dictionary 141
morphemes 91, 112, 114, 136, 248
morphological awareness (MA): character knowledge and reading comprehension 126–127; development of 111–112, 114–115, 122; reading subskill 105, 112, 116; tasks 117, 120; test scores *121*, **126**; underdeveloped 4, 112 115
morphological skill (MS) 4, 92–93
morphosyllabic language 13, 135

Nagy, William E. 249
Nation, Paul 65
neurolinguistic data 32, 35–36

Okada, Aya 66
online placement test: conclusions 278; difficulty 274; methodology 269; reliability 275; test development and validation 270–272; validation 7, 264, 268; validity coefficient 273, 276
orthographic knowledge 13, 20, 23–24, 33, 91, 248
orthographic system 21–23, 43–44
orthographies 44, 46, 92, 103

ortho-phonetic skill (PS) 4
ortho-semantic (radical) skill (RS) 4, 93, 96–97, 99–100, 104

Padilla, Amado M. 39
paired t-test results 3, 47
Paivio, Allan 29
Pappas, G. S. 77
participants: proficiency level 15, **54**; results summary **18**, 19
Pasquarella, Adrian (*et al* 2011) 114
Pellicer-Sanchez, Ana 128
Perfetti, Charles A. 32, 132–134
personal-meaning construction 246–247, 253, 261
phonetic: component 91, 97–98; radical 44, 117, 135; strategies 136, 147
phonological processing 248
pinyin (Romanized script of Chinese characters based on their Mandarin pronunciations): presentations 30, 37–38, 43, 45, 56, 58; typing with 2, 45, 53, 55–56, 58
Pittsburgh Chinese School 116
Price, Lisa Hammitt (*et al* 2012) 202
proficiency: language 2, 14, 16, 18, 24, 65, 111, 120, 126
prompts 28, 39, 273

Qian, Kan (*et al* 2018) 62
qualitative/quantitative research 5, 47, 156, 160, 175, 184, 272, 276

radical skills (RS) 4, 93
reader: identity 187, 201; Response Theory 219, 221, 236
reader's theatre 7, 221, 226, **227**
reading: accuracy 13; assessment 246, 252–253, 260; comprehension **125–126**, *133*, 276; *see also* L2 learners
Reading into a New China (RNC) 254, 258–259
reading strategies 156, 174; *see also* Chinese as additional language (CAL)
recall protocols 5, 162, 175
Reese, Elaine 210
research questions (RQs): best practices, use of 31; ethnicity/identity 190, 192; guided book reading 205, 208; heritage learners 115; implications 39; learner proficiency 18, *19*, 20–21; online placement testing 277; reading comprehension 100; systemic increments of morphological awareness 122
Roberts, Leah 104

Samuels, Jay J. 20
Saracho, Olivia N. 185, 189
Sawyer, J. 77
Schallert, Diane Lemonnier 250–251
Schmitt, Norbert 128
Second Language Acquisition (SLA) 32, 40, 182, 220
second language learners 14, 114–115; *see also* L2 learners
Secondary School Places Allocation (SSPA) System 217
Seidenberg, Mark S. 248
Sénéchal, Monique 201
Sham, Diana Po Lan 33, 37
Shen, Helen H. 20, 30, 36–38, 115
Shiotsu, Toshihiko 251
Shu, Hua 113
Silver, S. 77
Singapore 5, 95, 132, 139, 150
Singaporean Chinese Mother-Tongue Language Learners (Singaporean CMTLLs) 95–96
single-coded word learning 28, 34, 36, 39
Situational Model Theory 221, 236
smartphones 43, 45, 65
social-economic status (SES) 188
sociocultural factors 150, 179–180, 182–183
sociocultural theoretical perspective (SCT) 6, 200, 211
spaces 15, 30, 36–37
standard deviations (SDs) 18, 99, 120, *121*, 123, *124*, **125**
State Language Commission of China 13
strategy use 5, 156, 159, 165, 173, 175
stroke order: accuracy 9, 13–16, 18, *19*, 20, 24; composite 13, 17; horizontal 13, 37–39; learner development *19*; vertical 13, 37–39
stroke-by-stroke writing 21–23, 41, 43, 47, 55, 65, 76
stroke-order accuracy task 16
stroke-sequence 15, 47
student: high-proficiency 267; performance 31
study participants: awareness tasks 117; background 116, **117**; character knowledge 119; reading comprehension 119; results

120, *121*, 122, **123**, *124*, **125–126**; task administration and rating 120
Su, Yi Fen 20
Sweller, John (*et al* 2019) 29
syntactic analysis 174–175
syntax knowledge 5

Tabachnick, Barbara 99
tablets (device) 43, 45, 50, 65
Taft, Marcus (*et al* 1997) 22
Taiwanese 160, 172, 188
Tamaoka, Katsuo 14
Tan, Li Hai (*et al* 2013) 45, 55–56
Tan, Li Hai (*et al* 2013) 45, 55–56
Tate, Helene 13
Teaching modern Chinese literature 217
Teresa (participant): comprehension scores 163–164, 173; heritage learner 160, 172; reading performance 169–170, **171**
test validation: approaches 266; conclusion/implications 278; Descriptive Statistics for the Placement Test **275**; difficulty level 274; language placement 268; methodology 269–270; participants/test takers 271–272, 276; reliability 267, 274–275; reliability questions 269; test development 270–271; testing batteries and procedures 50; validity coefficient 266, 273–274
text-meaning: building 246–247, 250, 253, 261; construction 7, 249–250, 260
theoretical frameworks 32, 267
think-aloud task 175
timed dictation (TD): as an activity 65, **67**, *69–70*; effects of 3, 61; measures accuracy and fluency 70 (*see also* Hansi test); performance report 76–77; training website 67
Tong, Xuili 92, 104
trends 32, 158, 210
Trionfi, Gabriel 210
Tsai, Chen-hui (*et al* 2012) 35
Tucker, G. Richard 190–191

United States: bilingual literacy development 46, 49; reading comprehension skills 95, 111, 115

validity *see* test validation
vocabulary knowledge 132

Wang, Danping 63
Wang, Ling 34
Wang, Yanlin 34
Wenger, Étienne 182
Wong, Ka F. 182, 190–191
Wong, Yu Ka 137–139, 147
word: activation 13; characteristics 38, 40; decoding 5, 132, 139–140, **141**, **143**, **145**; form analysis 247–249; meaning 37, 103–104, 158, 167, 249, 252; segmentation 136, 147, 174, 248
word learning: single-character 33, 36, 38–39; single/dual coded 36–39; two character 30, 33, 36, 38–39
writing systems 13, 44, 46, 112, 248

Xia, Qiong 192
Xiao-Desai, Yang 182, 190–191
Xu, Ping 47
Xu, Xiaoqiu 39
Xu, Yi (*et al* 2013) 35, 64

Yamada, Hiroyuki 14
Yamashita, Junko 251
Yan, Cathy Ming Wai (*et al* 2012) 66
Yeung, Pui-sze 136
Yim-ng, Y. Y. (*et al* 2000) 14

Zhang, Dongbo 94, 114, 181
Zhang, Haiwei 104
Zhang, Haomin 94, 114, 125
Zhang, Jie (*et al* 2014) 94
Zhang, T. R. 63
Zhang, Yanhui 128
Zhao, Shouhui 62
Zhu, Yu (*et al* 2016) 33, 36, 48

For Product Safety Concerns and Information please contact our EU representative GPSR@taylorandfrancis.com
Taylor & Francis Verlag GmbH, Kaufingerstraße 24, 80331 München, Germany

www.ingramcontent.com/pod-product-compliance
Lightning Source LLC
Chambersburg PA
CBHW061345300426
44116CB00011B/1997